Second Edition

Youth Basketball Drills

Burrall Paye
Patrick Paye

Human Kinetics

Library of Congress Cataloging-in-Publication Data

Paye, Burrall, 1938-
Youth basketball drills / Burrall Paye, Patrick Paye. -- 2nd ed.
p. cm.
1. Youth league basketball--Coaching. I. Paye, Patrick, 1965- II. Title.
GV886.3.P39 2013
796.323'077--dc23
2012015054

ISBN-10: 1-4504-3219-0 (print)
ISBN-13: 978-1-4504-3219-1 (print)

Acquisitions Editor: Justin Klug
Managing Editor: Amy Stahl
Assistant Editors: Rachel Brito and Anne Rumery
Copyeditor: John Wentworth
Graphic Designer: Fred Starbird
Cover Designer: Keith Blomberg
Photographer (cover): © Human Kinetics
Photo Production Manager: Jason Allen
Art Manager: Kelly Hendren
Associate Art Manager: Alan L. Wilborn
Illustrations: © Human Kinetics
Printer: United Graphics

Human Kinetics books are available at special discounts for bulk purchase. Special editions or book excerpts can also be created to specification. For details, contact the Special Sales Manager at Human Kinetics.

Printed in the United States of America 10 9 8 7 6 5 4 3 2 1

The paper in this book is certified under a sustainable forestry program.

Human Kinetics
Website: www.HumanKinetics.com

United States: Human Kinetics
P.O. Box 5076
Champaign, IL 61825-5076
800-747-4457
e-mail: humank@hkusa.com

Canada: Human Kinetics
475 Devonshire Road Unit 100
Windsor, ON N8Y 2L5
800-465-7301 (in Canada only)
e-mail: info@hkcanada.com

Europe: Human Kinetics
107 Bradford Road
Stanningley
Leeds LS28 6AT, United Kingdom
+44 (0) 113 255 5665
e-mail: hk@hkeurope.com

Australia: Human Kinetics
57A Price Avenue
Lower Mitcham, South Australia 5062
08 8372 0999
e-mail: info@hkaustralia.com

New Zealand: Human Kinetics
P.O. Box 80
Torrens Park, South Australia 5062
0800 222 062
e-mail: info@hknewzealand.com

E5784

Second Edition

Youth Basketball Drills

Contents

Part I
OFFENSIVE
Skills and Drills

Part II
DEFENSIVE
Skills and Drills

Drill Finder

Drill no.	Drill title	Time (min)	Team	Individual	Beginner	Intermediate	Advanced	Page no.
1	Running Outside the Lines	3	X	X	X	X	X	4
2	Mirror Slap	2	X		X	X	X	6
3	Dribbling Off the Wall	1		X	X	X	X	8
4	Lane Slide	1	X	X	X	X	X	10
5	Quick Hands	2	X	X	X	X	X	12
6	Quick Foot Movement	2	X	X	X	X	X	14
7	Agility Tip Drill	1	X	X		X	X	16
8	Basic Layup	3	X		X	X	X	18
9	Triple-Threat Position	2	X	X	X	X	X	20
10	Post Position	5	X	X	X	X	X	22
11	Rocker Step	5		X	X			24
12	In-and-Out Move	5		X	X			26
13	Crossover Move	5		X	X			28
14	Spin (Reverse) Move	5		X	X			30
15	Half-Spin Move	5		X	X			32
16	Combination Dribbling Moves	3		X			X	34
17	Paye Drill	10	X	X	X	X	X	35
18	Fingertip Drill	30 sec		X	X	X		45
19	Standing Figure 8	2	X	X	X	X		46
20	Figure 8 Dribble	2	X	X	X	X	X	48
21	Side-to-Side Dribble	2	X	X	X	X	X	50
22	Spider Dribble	30 sec	X	X	X			51
23	Speed Dribble	1	X	X	X		X	52
24	Control Dribble	1	X	X	X		X	54
25	Change of Pace	1	X	X	X		X	56

Drill no.	Drill title	Time (min)	Team	Individual	Beginner	Intermediate	Advanced	Page no.
26	Hesitation Dribble	1	X	X		X	X	58
27	Retreating Dribble	1	X	X		X	X	60
28	In-and-Out Dribble Maneuver	1	X	X		X	X	62
29	Crossover Dribble Maneuver	1	X	X		X	X	64
30	Spin (Reverse) Dribble Maneuver	1	X	X		X	X	66
31	Half-Spin Dribble Maneuver	1	X	X		X	X	68
32	Fun Cone Dribbling Drill	2	X	X	X	X		70
33	Dribble Tag	1	X	X	X	X		71
34	Team Dribble Tag	1	X	X	X			72
35	Front Pivot	2	X	X	X	X		76
36	Reverse Pivot	2	X	X	X	X		78
37	Jump Stop	1	X	X	X	X	X	80
38	Stride Stop (One-Two)	1	X	X	X	X	X	82
39	One-on-Two Pivoting	1 ½	X	X	X	X		84
40	Dribble, Stop, Pivot	1	X	X	X	X		86
41	Dribble, Stop, Pivot, Pass, Cut	3	X			X	X	87
42	Dribble, Stop, Jump Shot	5	X	X	X	X	X	88
43	Four-Corner Stopping, Pivoting	3	X			X	X	90
44	Two-Line Standing Still Drill	3	X		X	X	X	94
45	Two-Line Moving Drill	3	X		X	X	X	96
46	Two-Line Full-Court Passing	2	X			X		97

(continued)

Drill Finder *(continued)*

Drill no.	Drill title	Time (min)	Team	Individual	Beginner	Intermediate	Advanced	Page no.
47	Two-on-One Passing Drill	1 ½	X			X		98
48	Pepper Passing	2	X		X		X	99
49	Three-on-Three Trapping and Passing	3	X			X	X	100
50	Passing, Dribbling, Trapping	10	X				X	102
51	Four-Corner Passing	3	X		X	X	X	104
52	Touch Passing and Layup	3	X			X		105
53	V-Cut	3	X	X	X	X	X	108
54	Middle Cut	3	X	X	X	X	X	110
55	Backdoor Cut	3	X	X	X	X	X	112
56	Flash Pivot Cutting	3	X	X	X	X		114
57	Flash Pivot, Triple Threat, and Offensive Moves	10	X	X	X	X	X	116
58	Two-Player Cutting	3	X		X			118
59	Three-Player Cutting	9	X		X			120
60	Defeat Help and Recover	7	X		X	X	X	122
61	Full-Court Cutting	2	X		X	X		124
62	Two-on-Two Pass, Dribble, and Cut	3	X		X			129
63	Two-on-Two Recognition	6	X			X	X	132
64	Three-on-Three Passing, Cutting, and Spacing	4	X			X		134
65	Three-on-Three Passing, Cutting, Dribbling, Spacing	6	X			X		136
66	Three-on-Three Pass, Cut, and Recognition	6	X			X	X	138
67	Pass, Cut, and Rebound	4	X			X	X	140
68	Outlet Pass, Cutting, Shooting	6	X		X	X	X	142

Drill no.	Drill title	Time (min)	Team	Individual	Beginner	Intermediate	Advanced	Page no.
69	Full-Court Passing, Cutting	6	X		X	X		144
70	Individual Combo	4	X	X	X	X	X	146
71	Pass and Screen Away	10	X	X	X	X	X	151
72	Pass and Screen on Ball	6	X	X		X		154
73	Three-Player Screening Drill	4	X		X			155
74	Three-on-Three Pass, Screen, and Recognition	4	X			X	X	156
75	Three-Player Continuous Screening	8	X				X	158
76	Tip Ball Off the Wall and Pivot	1		X	X		X	164
77	Bull in the Ring	4	X	X	X	X	X	165
78	Jab Step and Roll	2	X	X		X	X	168
79	One-on-One Blockouts	1	X	X	X			170
80	Superman	1		X	X	X		172
81	Count-Slide-Pivot-Savvy	4	X	X	X	X	X	173
82	Two-on-Two Rebounding	4	X			X	X	176
83	Post Moves: Passing-Shooting-Rebounding	4	X			X	X	178
84	Wave Good-Bye	1	X	X	X			182
85	Flip-Ball Drill	1	X	X	X			183
86	Lift, Extend, Flip	1	X	X	X	X		184
87	Lying-Down Flip-Ball Drill	1	X	X	X	X		186
88	Flip the Ball Off the Wall	1		X	X	X		187
89	Around the World	10	X	X	X	X	X	190
90	No Rim	10	X	X	X		X	192
91	21	6	X		X			194
92	NBA Shooting Drill	2		X	X			195
93	Mikan Drill for Baby Hook	1		X	X	X		196

(continued)

Drill Finder *(continued)*

Drill no.	Drill title	Time (min)	Team	Individual	Beginner	Intermediate	Advanced	Page no.
94	Rebound-Pass-Shoot	4	X		X	X		198
95	Quick Shooting Drill for Two Players	2	X		X			200
96	Post-Up Mechanics	5	X	X			X	202
97	Slide-Step Dribble	1	X	X	X		X	204
98	Fronting	2	X	X		X		205
99	Two-Step Drill	5	X	X		X		206
100	Roll Step	5	X	X			X	208
101	Three-Quarter Drill	5	X	X		X		210
102	High Low Post Passing	6	X			X	X	211
103	Post Screening	10	X			X	X	212
104	One-on-One Lane Drill	4		X	X			216
105	One-on-One Relief Drill	4		X	X			217
106	One-on-One Team Drill	2		X	X			218
107	One on One on One on One	4	X		X			219
108	One-on-One Full-Court Game	5	X	X	X			220
109	Recovery Drill	6	X	X	X			221
110	One on One on One	3	X			X		222
111	Approach and Close Out	6	X	X	X			224
112	Basic Three-Step Read	2	X	X	X	X	X	225
113	Penetration Drill	6	X			X		228
114	Drop-Step Baseline/ Middle	5		X	X	X		232
115	Post Spin and Half-Spin	6		X		X		236
116	Post Up-and-Under	5		X		X	X	239
117	Pump Fake	2	X	X		X		242
118	Bull-in-the-Ring Post Drill	8	X	X	X	X	X	244
119	Three-Player Continuous Low Post	4	X	X		X		246
120	Post to Post	4	X			X		248

(continued)

Drill Finder *(continued)*

Drill no.	Drill title	Time (min)	Team	Individual	Beginner	Intermediate	Advanced	Page no.
147	Deny the Wing	4	X		X	X		308
148	Deny the Flash Pivot	4	X		X	X		309
149	Dribble Closeout	1	X	X	X	X	X	310
150	Skip Pass and Closeout	6	X			X		312
151	Eight-Point Drill	10	X	X			X	314
152	One-on-One Multiple Skills Drill	6	X	X		X		316
153	Shell Drill	10	X				X	320
154	Five on Five	---	X		X			322
155	Run and Jump	10	X	X		X		324
156	Run and Trap	7	X	X		X		326
157	Trap the Dribble	5	X	X	X			328
158	Trap the Pass	7	X	X	X			330
159	Channeling	4		X		X	X	332
160	Zigzag With a Trapper	2		X	X	X	X	334

Skill Finder

Skills are listed under two sections: Offensive Skills and Defensive Skills.

Skills are then listed under the category in which they belong. For example, Perimeter Moves as Dribbling is a category. The crossover move is listed as a skill under this category. The number of the drill in which the crossover move is found is given in parentheses. So if you see (13, 29) in the Skill Finder, you go to drills 13 and 29 to learn the details of teaching the crossover move.

The Skill Finder is very easy to use. Another example: Let's say you have recognized the need to teach your players how to front at the low post. You know fronting is a defensive skill, so you look under Defensive Skills in the Skill Finder and find the category Defending the Low Post. Fronting is a skill listed under this category. The drill referenced is 98. Go to drill 98, and you are ready to teach your players how to front at the low post.

<table>
<tr><th colspan="2">OFFENSIVE SKILLS</th></tr>
<tr><td>Perimeter Moves Before Dribble
• Triple-Threat (9)
• Rocker Step (11)
  • Jab Step (11)
  • Jab-Step Pullback (11)
  • Jab-Step Crossover (11)
  • Jab-Step Direct Drive (11)</td><td>Perimeter Moves as Dribbling
• In-and-Out (12, 28)
• Crossover (13, 29)
• Spin (14, 30)
• Half-Spin (15, 31)</td></tr>
<tr><td>Pivots
• Front Pivot (35)
• Reverse Pivot (36)</td><td>Stops
• Jump Stop (37)
• Stride Stop (38)</td></tr>
<tr><td>Dribbling
• Speed (23)
• Control (24)
• Change of Pace (25)
• Hesitation (26)
• Retreat (27)
• Out-of-Traps (157-158)</td><td>Passing
• Receiving (44)
• Bounce (44)
• Chest (44)
• Overhead (44)
• Baseball (44)
• One-Handed Chest Pass (44)
• One-Handed Bounce Pass (44)
• Skip (44)
• Fake Pass (47)
• Passing Off Dribble (113)
• Out of Traps (157-158)</td></tr>
</table>

(continued)

Cuts	Screening

• V-Cut (53)
• Middle Cut (54)
• Backdoor Cut (55)
• Flash Pivot Cut (56)
	• Screen Away (71)
	  ◦ Pass and Screen Away (71)
	  ◦ Screen Away and Roll (71)
	  ◦ Screen Away and Fade (71)
	• Screen on Ball (72)
	  ◦ Screen and Roll (72)
	  ◦ Screen and Fade (72)
	• Down Screen (75)
	• Back Screen (75)
	• Screen the Screener (75)
	• Pass and Blast (122)

Offensive Rebounding	**Shooting**
• Jab Step and Roll (78) • Jab Step and Go (78) • Body Positioning (79) • Approaching the Rebound (79) • Swim Technique (81) • Primary Rebounding Area (81) • Secondary Rebounding Area (81) • Blast Out (82)	• Basic Layup (8) • Jump Shots (84-88) • Baby Hook (93) • Power Layup (114) • Step-Back Jump Shot (116)
DEFENSIVE SKILLS	
Defensive Stances Before Fake or Dribble	**Defensive Steps Before Dribble**
• Front Foot to Pivot Foot (129) • Front Foot to Free Foot (130) • Parallel (130)	• Advance Step (137) • Retreat Step (137) • Swing Step (137) • Overplay Step (138)
Defensive Steps While Dribbling	**Individual Trapping**
• Defensive Fakes (33) • Slide Step (46, 137) • Overplay (138)	• How To Trap (50) • Safety Pass Interception (156) • All-Out Pass Interception (156) • Trapping With Dribble Alive (157-158)
Defensive Steps Before Player Receives Pass	**Defensive Rebounding**
• Fence Slide (128) • Interception Stance (131) • Close-the-Gap Stance (132) • Deny the Wing (147)	• Slide and Boxout (79) • Immediate Boxout (79)

Introduction

In this book, basketball coaches will find all they need for developing outstanding players—which translates into win after win on the court. While winning results from player development, a coach's greatest pleasure comes from seeing his protégés' dribbling improve, moves unfold, stances and slides emerge, passing skills evolve, and shooting talents develop. There is no fulfillment like it. For new coaches, the book includes an appendix on how to run a practice and create a practice schedule. Absolutely no prior coaching experience is required.

Young players ages 6 to 14, male or female, who want to become super basketball players will also find the tools they need in this book. Many of the drills can be practiced alone. For improvement to begin, all a young player needs is a basketball, a hoop, and this book.

Parents want their children to learn fundamentals correctly. By working closely with their youngsters in developing athletic skills, parents and children form solid bonds much like those that develop among teammates of ball clubs.

Each drill, when practiced correctly and diligently, leads to acquiring an advanced basketball basic skill. After muscle memory takes hold, the skill becomes as automatic for the young player as riding a bicycle—the player's muscles never forget it. The key is to execute each fundamental correctly from the get-go so it does not have to be relearned later.

How This Book Will Help You

This book offers unlimited opportunities to perfect the skills of basketball. Each drill is presented in a format intended to teach a specific technique until it is learned. Most drills begin with an individual basic fundamental. Many drill sections then follow with an intermediate and an advanced skill-development drill. These drills are progressive, aimed at developing skill levels from the biddy league through the collegiate level.

It is very important that players execute fundamentals exactly as instructed in the drills. Once the skill is learned correctly, players can quicken the execution. The quick, explosive first steps are all important in basketball. Players should not execute with speed, but they should execute *quickly* and *explosively.* Speed—both in trying to rush the learning process and in trying to rush the execution of the skill—is often a deterrent to learning. Basketball moves should be made quicker and quicker until they are explosively quick, but they should not be hurried.

For example, in the section on shooting, readers will find that the beginning drill shows simply how to position the ball properly in the hand. Next comes learning how to flip the ball. Then proper lifting and extending the arm is instructed. This is followed by a drill to keep the elbow in (a crooked elbow is the worst fault in all of basketball and almost uncorrectable once muscles have remembered it incorrectly). After that, players develop a follow-through with a simple "waving goodbye" drill. Put all of this together, and the result is picture-perfect technique on the shot. All that remains is to practice getting shots off more quickly without rushing.

Coaches will find that each drill in the book teaches another phase of basketball. The progressiveness of each drill's mechanical movement allows you to teach even the youngest members of your squad the basics—and to teach them correctly. Learning skills correctly is absolutely crucial to proper development. The authors of this book are high school basketball coaches. Together we have seen hundreds of potentially good athletes be forced to step aside as they tried to advance to higher levels of competition because their muscles had memorized incorrect techniques, such as the crooked elbow in shooting. They simply could not shoot well enough to succeed on a competitive team—all because they learned the fundamental incorrectly in the beginning. The problem is common enough that it bears repeating: *Skills must be learned and practiced correctly from the very start* or else you will pay the price down the road.

Coaches will also find as they teach these drills that players are not only learning basic fundamentals of basketball but also understanding a *system of play.* Your squad will become proficient at moving with the basketball, cutting without the basketball, and understanding the strategies of the game. At the end of the drilling, you will find your team can execute the motion offense, the most widely used offensive system on high school and college teams. Your team members will also know how to play man-to-man defense.

You do not have to know basketball to teach these skills to your players. All the little details (teaching points) are presented with each drill. Each drill is also broken down to beginner, intermediate, and advanced levels.

Every drill in the book refers the user to related drills. This allows coaches to continue teaching the same skill while adding the next step in development, keeping practice sessions from becoming stale. Young players want to learn, but they also want to stay active. You can teach the same skill using a variety of drills, thus keeping things fresh and fun for your young learners.

About the Drills

This book is made up of 160 drills. Each drill starts with the simplest and goes to the more complex. Each is clearly marked by number and by name. Each indicates whether it is for individuals, teams, or both.

Every drill starts with a section called Skill Focus. You will know immediately whether you want to work on this drill today or leave it for another day, because each fundamental to be drilled is listed. Numbers in parentheses show which drills contain an explanation of how to teach that basic skill.

At the top of each drill we indicate how much time it takes to execute the drill with 10 players and 2 coaches. Should your squad consist of more players or fewer coaches, you may need to adjust the timing. The time needed to run a drill is also listed in the Drill Finder, which can be used as a reference tool when you are creating your practice schedule.

Next we give procedures that instruct how to run the drill. You simply follow the numbered guidelines step by step. Progressions are offered in nearly all drills. The progression sequence is always clearly marked for beginner, intermediate, and advanced skills. Coaches at the youngest levels of play may initially choose to use only the beginner drills, and then progress to the intermediate level as the skills of your players improve. Coaches of older, more developed players can use all the drills; you will make choices based on the particular needs of your squad.

Variations, or options, of the drill are presented under the procedures for each skill level. This allows you to choose a slightly different setup to accomplish the same fundamental.

The teaching points included in each drill provide the details you need to know to best teach the drill, including what to watch for as your players run the drill. The teaching points are presented in a form that requires no previous knowledge of the techniques of basketball.

For every drill we list all related drills, which allows you to build a practice plan of perfect order. The second skill to be learned is derived from the first, and so on. You can use one drill to teach mechanics and then use a related drill to provide the enjoyment that makes learning the mechanics more fun. You can change your drills and still teach the same fundamentals. Just go to a related drill.

Finally, nearly every drill is accompanied by an illustration to give you a visual of how the drill looks in action. We want to make the drills simple to run. We have learned that simplicity is key to teaching and learning any skill.

By using the drills in this book, by teaching the fundamentals correctly, your practices will become more intense, competitive, and fun. Concentration will reach a zenith. Your players will enjoy practice sessions as much as real games. Your practices will also be more difficult, more intense than most games. Once you have completed all the drills, your squad will have fine-tuned the motion offense and man-to-man defense. Players will be executing team concepts using accurate and errorless techniques, fundamentals, foot movement, strategy, and methodology.

Additions to the Second Edition

We have added 50 new drills to this edition. All additions follow the same three central themes of the book: individual player improvement, developing the motion offense, and developing the man-to-man defense. All the drills are progressive; all stress fundamentals.

One new drill is the Paye Drill (drill 17), which covers the art of playing one on one from the reception of the pass to the taking of the shot, both offensively and defensively. Your players will easily see and understand the details of the one-on-one offensive and defensive struggles. Specific principles of attack are presented, such as *always attack the front foot of the defender,* to take best advantage of the defender's stance, step, or movement.

Once your players can read their defenders and know how to attack them, they will have learned *savvy*, an element as valuable as it is rare. At this point your players will be *basketball players* in the fullest meaning of the phrase.

Two new beginning stances are provided in this edition: the front-foot-to-free-foot stance and the parallel stance (drill 130). All the advantages and disadvantages of these stances are explained in detail.

Help-side defense receives extensive coverage in this edition, with new drills on closing the gap (drill 132), jumping to the ball (drill 146), ball-you-man tactics (drill 133), flat triangle tactics (drill 133), rotation (drill 143), helping the helper (drill 135), and closeouts (drills 149 and 150). To defeat your man-to-man defense, opponents will have to beat their defender, get by the closest helper, and then face the rotation—a daunting task just to get a shot off.

In other new drills your help-side defenders will learn to help and recover (drill 142), to hedge and recover (drill 142), and to draw the charge (drill 141) without risking injury. The entire help-side package is covered in this edition (drills 131-135, 143, 146, and 148).

Four new individual low-post moves (drills 114-116) are also included. Your players will learn how to read defenders and take advantage of their positioning and their mistakes; they will learn how to *always* choose the single best move to meet each situation at the low post. Other new drills cover moves at the end of the dribble, making both perimeter players and post players more effective near the basket (drills 96, 116, and 117).

Rebounding techniques and fundamentals also receive extensive treatment in this edition, including finding the primary and secondary rebounding areas. Players must learn to move to where the ball will go; otherwise they have no chance for the rebound. Once at the exact best spot to rebound, players require a solid rebound technique to beat opponents to the ball. This technique is completely covered in drills 78 through 82, all focusing on the rebound. Experienced coaches know that strong rebounding is every bit as important to success as accurate shooting ability. Teams that get the second, third, and fourth shots per possession almost always win the game.

By adding one new rule on offense—*two players and the ball must not come together at the same spot on the court*—you can easily slow down your motion offense late in games when your team has the lead. This new rule helps prevent defenses from double-teaming the ball while your team is stalling. This means you need not teach a stalling game separate from your motion offense (see drill 75).

Another new drill shows a continuous motion offense from the two-three set with emphasis on low-post play; this drill is especially effective if you have a very tall player you want near the basket at all times (drill 75).

When behind late in a game, your team needs to force turnovers. When an opponent is playing at an unbelievable level, you need to disrupt their execution and take them out of their rhythm. For these situations, we have added new tactics for the run and jump and the run and trap as well as for trapping the first pass and trapping the dribbler crossing midcourt (drills 155-158). Other drills have been added to teach defenders how to channel a dribbler to the spot they want the dribbler to go (drills 159-160). In this way your defenders can dictate the offense of your opponents.

Coaches who have used the book have helped us supplement and expand many of the teaching details and fundamentals for the drills from the first edition. The new information makes the drills even easier and more beneficial to run.

Finally, this edition contains a great new reference guide that we think coaches will get excited about. A Skill Finder including all of the basketball skills covered in the drills is presented on pages xiii-xv. Each major skill category in basketball is listed in the Skill Finder. Any skill you want to work on can be easily referenced by simply looking up numbers and flipping a few pages. We provide complete and clear instructions for using the Skill Finder on page xiii.

Now let's go drill.

Key to Diagrams

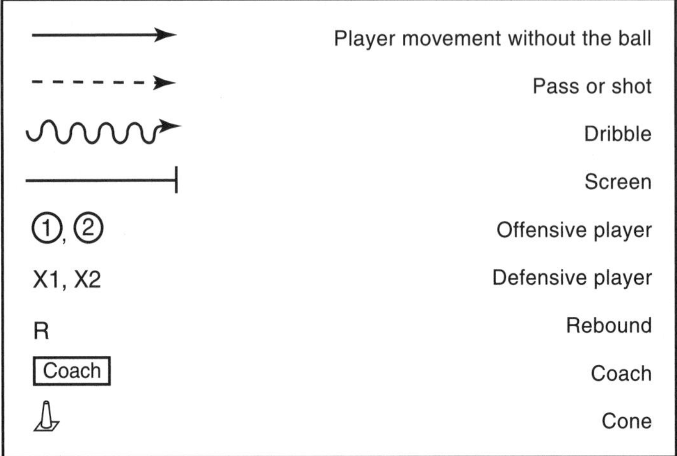

PART I

OFFENSIVE Skills and Drills

CHAPTER 1

Balance, Quickness, and Agility

Proper balance allows for explosive, quick movement, which is the top priority for a great one-on-one player.

There are two types of proper balance. The first type is needed when running full court, when speed is more important than control. Players should have an erect stance, head directly over torso, a slightly forward lean, a slight bend at the knees, and a long stride. They should land on their toes with each step.

Second, *control balance* requires a shorter step and more bend at the knees (no more than a 135-degree angle). Again, the head should be directly over the torso, and the torso should be bent slightly, back straight, not humped; toes should "grab" at the floor, and the foot should land heel to toe.

Proper balance promotes quickness, which requires playing on the toes until ready to stop. Players should then land heels first and come up on their toes. Concentration and intensity facilitate quickness.

Agility is control of the body; your players will need to put their bodies in all sorts of contortions as they climb the ladder of competition, and they must be able to do so under control.

Balance, quickness, and agility are developed in the seven drills presented in this chapter. Drill 1 requires not only quick movement but also basketball knowledge. As players become more skillful and knowledgeable, add other steps to the drill

Drill 2 compels players to react quickly and explosively, which is indispensable in one-on-one play. Drill 3 develops maximum agility. In drill 4 players practice "grabbing" the floor with their toes. Drill 5 develops quick hands, and drill 6 develops quick feet. Drill 7 requires a combination of balance, quickness, and agility and demands intense concentration.

1

RUNNING OUTSIDE THE LINES

Individual or team • 3 minutes

SKILL FOCUS Quickness, balance, and agility, conditioning, quick foot movement (6), triple-threat position (9), in and out (12, 28), crossover (13, 29), spin (14, 30), half-spin (15, 31), front pivot (35), reverse pivot (36), jump stop (37), stride stop (38), slide step (46, 137), V-cut (53), fence slide (128), advance step (137), retreat step (137), swing step (137)

1. Line players up in a straight line at one baseline.
2. Have all players face to the right.
3. On the command "jog," all players begin jogging around the out-of-bounds lines.
4. Have players react to the following verbal commands according to skill level.

Beginner

1. "Jump stop"—Players stop, using a jump stop. "Go"—Players begin jogging again. This continues around the court.
2. "Stride stop"—Players stop, using stride stop. "Go"—Players begin jogging again.
3. "Step in"—Players continue jogging but step once into the court, then back on the line. "Step out"—Players continue jogging but step once out of bounds, then back on the line.
4. "In and out"—Players execute the in-and-out offensive move, then resume jogging.

Intermediate

1. "Front pivot"—Players use a jump stop (or stride stop) and execute a front pivot. Players continue jogging but in the opposite direction.
2. "Reverse pivot"—Players use a jump stop (or stride stop) and execute a reverse pivot. Players continue jogging but in the opposite direction.
3. "Jab step"—Players execute a hard jab step with either foot, then continue jogging.
4. "Crossover step"—Players execute a crossover step with either foot, then continue jogging.
5. "Spin step"—Players execute a spin step with either foot as the pivot foot, then continue jogging.
6. "Half-spin step"—Players execute a half-spin step with either foot as the pivot foot, then continue jogging.

Advanced

1. "Sprint"—Players sprint for five steps, then resume jogging.
2. "V-cut"—Players V-cut, then resume jogging.

3. “Break down”—Players break down into proper defensive stance and remain there; they begin jogging again on “jog.”
4. “Pat the floor”—Players break down into defensive stance and pat the floor with their toes as quickly as they can, then resume jogging.
5. “Triple threat”—Players jump stop or stride stop and get into the offensive triple-threat position, then resume jogging.
6. “Fence slide”—Players use the defensive fence slide for five steps, then resume jogging.
7. “Advance step”—Players execute a jump stop, then one defensive advance step, then resume jogging.
8. “Retreat step”—Players execute a jump stop, then one defensive retreat step, then resume jogging.
9. “Swing step”—Players execute a jump stop, then one defensive swing step, then resume jogging.

➜ Options (all skill levels)

1. Instead of just jogging, players flip a basketball from hand to hand.
2. Instead of just jogging, players dribble a basketball.

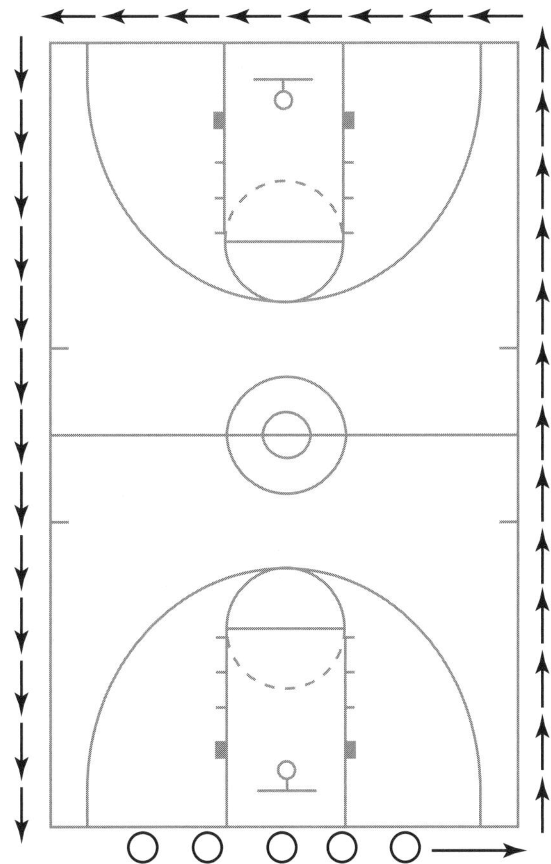

Related Drills *2, 9, 12-15, 25-31, 35, 36, 53, 56, 57, 62, 78, 104-126, 128, 137*

MIRROR SLAP

Team • 2 minutes

➲ **SKILL FOCUS** Quickness, stances (4-9), steps (12-15, 28-31, 129-132, 137), defensive fakes (33), pivots (35-36), step-through (39)

Beginner

1. One player lines up facing another; one is player A, and the other is player B. Have all your players do this in sets of two all over the court.
2. Player A executes a movement; player B tries to mirror the movement.
3. Instruct players to touch their head with their right hand, then with their left hand, and then with both hands; next, they touch their knee with their right hand, and then with their left hand; finally, players run in place, then pat the floor rapidly with both feet.
4. Player A leads; player B mirrors for 30 seconds or 1 minute. Then player B leads, and player A mirrors.
5. In player A, look for precision in performing the techniques; observe how quickly player B reacts.

Intermediate

1. In addition to the quick touches listed for the beginners, intermediate players should show the fakes: jab step, rocker step, in and out, spin, half-spin, front pivot, and reverse pivot.
2. After the players have learned the rebounding techniques in chapter 9, player A can use the jab step, the jab step and roll, and the jab step and go. Player B reacts with the same movement.
3. Player A can use the reverse pivot or the front pivot. Player B reacts with the same movement.

Advanced

1. Advanced players should add defensive stances, fakes, and footwork, including the interception stance, front foot to pivot foot stance, front foot to free foot stance, advance step, retreat step, swing step, slide step, and fence slide, as well as the triple-threat position and the V-cut.
2. Also have advanced players add the in-and-out defensive fake. To execute, players step in with the front foot and strike the front hand forward quickly (like the strike of a snake), then step back quickly. This move attempts to get the attacker to change direction or hesitate with the dribble.
3. Give both players a basketball.

Related Drills *1, 9, 12-15, 25-31, 35-36, 53, 56-57, 62, 78, 104-131, 137-153*

3

DRIBBLING OFF THE WALL

Individual • 1 minute

➲ SKILL FOCUS Ballhandling, agility, hand quickness, ball control, balance, conditioning

Beginner

1. Each player needs a basketball.
2. Players stand facing a wall and dribble the ball off the wall with the right hand.
3. They begin dribbling around head high (elbow at 90 degrees) and then extend to dribbling with elbow flexed at 135 degrees; then they go to full extension of the elbow.
4. Players repeat steps 2 and 3 using the left hand.

Intermediate

1. Dribbling off the wall as in the beginner drill, players use only the index finger of the right hand to dribble the basketball.
2. They then use only the middle finger, then only the ring finger, then only the little finger.
3. Players repeat steps 1 and 2 using the left hand.

Advanced

1. Players repeat steps 2, 3, and 4 of the beginner phase but now while running the length of the wall.
2. Players repeat steps 1, 2, and 3 of the intermediate phase but now while running the length of the wall.

➜ TEACHING POINTS

1. Players dribble using only the upper finger pads (see figure). The pads may be used to dribble, shoot, or pass the basketball; they should *not* use the palms to dribble, shoot, or pass.
2. During the dribble, players' wrists should follow an up-and-down motion, as if waving good-bye. Watch for whether a wrinkle is created behind the wrist and then released with each stroke of the ball.
3. Once players start dribbling the ball off the wall, they keep the ball at that level throughout that phase of the drill.
4. Remind players not to look at the ball; they should look straight ahead.

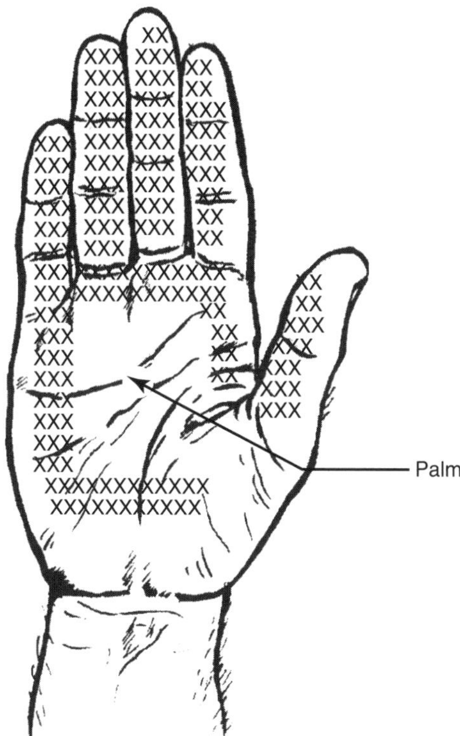

The hand pads. The ball can rest on parts of the hand marked with X only.

Related Drills *18-31, 34-35, 40-41, 76, 84, 97, 104-127*

4

LANE SLIDE

Individual or team • 1 minute per group

SKILL FOCUS Agility, quickness, conditioning, balance, defensive stances (129-131, 137), slide step (46, 137), change of direction, change of pace, defensive footwork (129-131, 137-144)

Beginner

1. Line players up at a foul lane, as shown in the figure. Use only three players at a time. Each player is about 3 feet (1 m) behind the player in front, and all players are facing out of bounds. Start players in the middle or on one of the lane lines.
2. Players slide from side to side using the defensive slide step; they touch the foul-lane line with the outside foot before sliding back in the other direction.
3. Count the number of touches per 30 seconds. (Each group initially goes 30 seconds. Later in the season you may extend time to 60 seconds.) Each player should get more touches each day this drill is done. The objective is to get quicker slides, and thus more touches.

Intermediate

As the group slides, each player executes an in-and-out defensive fake with each step taken.

Advanced

1. Change the sliding distance—allow players to slide only two steps in either direction from the middle.
2. Change the sliding distance—allow players to slide only one step in either direction from the middle.

Option (all skill levels) Have two players face each other. The first player slides in either direction (player's choice), while the second mirrors the first player's movements.

➔ TEACHING POINTS

1. Players must execute the slide step perfectly. They must not cross their legs.
2. They begin with a long step in the direction of the first movement; they then bring the trail foot up to the first foot, almost touching but never crossing.
3. They stay low for better body balance. Lower legs should be perpendicular to the floor, with upper legs forming a 135-degree angle with the lower legs. The torso is straight, perpendicular to the floor. Hands are both out, palms pointing upward. Players must not allow their arms to drop.
4. Toes should grab at the floor, and feet should rise only minimally from the floor to promote foot quickness.

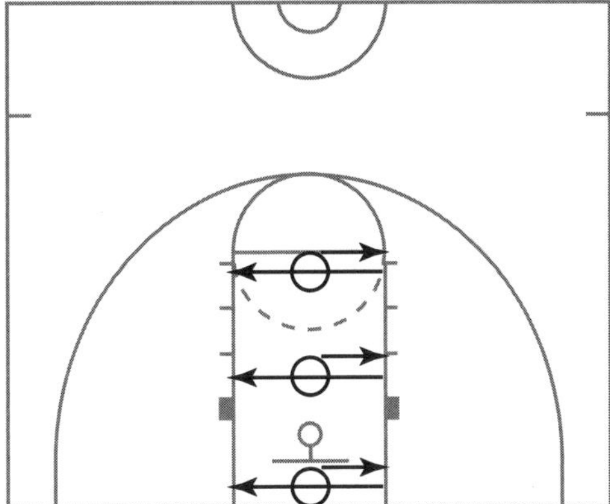

Related Drills *107-109, 137-153*

5

QUICK HANDS

Individual or team • 2 minutes

SKILL FOCUS Quickness, stances (4-9), rocker step (11), in and out (12, 28), crossover (13, 29), spin (14, 30), half-spin (15, 31), front pivot (35), reverse pivot (36), steps (12-15, 28-31, 129-132, 137), defensive fakes (129), advance step (137), retreat step (137), swing step (137)

Beginner

1. Line players up as shown in the figure.
2. Each player has a basketball.
3. Player 1 steps out directly in front of the coach. Player 1 hands the basketball to the coach to begin the drill.
4. Player 1 begins in the defensive stance the coach requests.
5. On signal from a coach, player 1 begins to move feet in rapid-fire motion. Player 1 wants this motion to be a tapping on the floor by the toes.
6. Player 1 begins with hands in proper defensive position. Tell the player to constantly be jabbing hands forward and pulling them back "like the strikes of a snake." The player can alternate hands striking, first right hand and then left hand.
7. After 5 seconds of player 1 displaying proper defensive stance and footwork, the coach dribbles one dribble, alternating speed of the dribble until player 1 has deflected the ball.
8. After deflecting the dribble, player 1 retrieves the basketball and moves to the end of the opposite line (if a team drill). Player 2 then steps out in front of the coach.

Intermediate

1. Instead of deflecting the basketball, player 1 tries to catch the basketball.
2. When catching a ball cleanly, player 1 pivots, faces the basket, executes a rocker step or another perimeter move, and then uses a dribbling move to drive to the basket.

Advanced

1. Instead of player 1 moving out in front of the coach, both players 1 and 2 move out in front of the coach. Both players get in defensive positioning, facing each other, using rapid-fire foot movement and defensive jabs at each other. This continues for 5 seconds. The coach then dribbles one dribble, alternating between hard and quick and slow and low.
2. Players 1 and 2 battle to try to deflect the dribble. They race to recover a slapped basketball. Whichever player recovers the ball is on offense, and the other is on defense in a one-on-one game to the basket.
3. Players go to the opposite end of the line from which they began. Players 3 and 4 then step out in front of the coach, and the drill continues.

➜ Options (all skill levels)

1. Divide teams into perimeter versus post, one-guards versus two-guards, or similar. Play a game to 10 with each basket counting 2 points and each offensive rebound 1 point. This is a highly competitive and fun drill and a great way to end a practice session.
2. Instead of dribbling, lay the ball on the floor for players to retrieve.
3. Instead of dribbling or laying the ball on the floor, toss the ball directly in front of you for players to retrieve.

➜ TEACHING POINTS

1. Players use proper defensive stances, slides, and quick hands.
2. Players make fundamentally sound offensive moves.
3. Players learn to read the defense and use the proper attacking move.

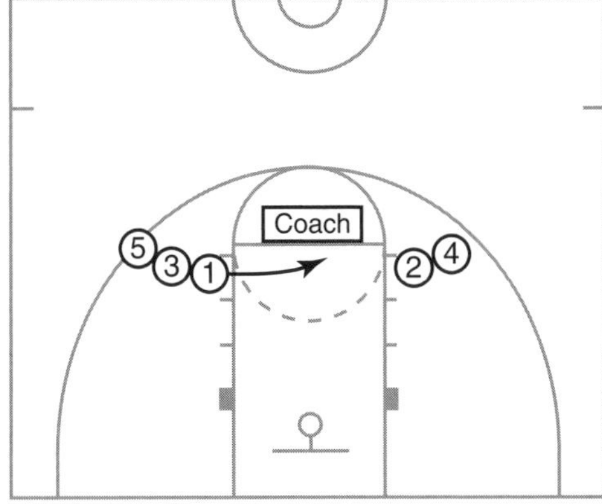

Related Drills *8, 9, 11-17, 26-31, 35-36, 84-95, 104-113, 122-127, 128-135, 137-144, 152-154*

6

QUICK FOOT MOVEMENT

Individual or team • 2 minutes

SKILL FOCUS Quickness, balance, agility, conditioning, pivoting (35-36)

Beginner

1. Three players place their feet on A and B in their area while facing the coach (see figure); they place right feet on A, left feet on B, as shown. If you wish, use only one player at a time.
2. Players jump in with right feet touching C, then out with right feet hitting D and left feet hitting E. They immediately make a 180-degree turn, putting left feet on D and right feet on E. They put right feet on C, and then jump out with left feet hitting A and right feet hitting B. They then execute another 180-degree turn. The drill continues for 25 seconds.
3. Beginners should never learn more than one of the possible foot movements. The one just described is the most simple.

Intermediate

1. Intermediate players can put their left foot on C in the initial jump, and the same drill continues.
2. Intermediate players can jump with both feet on C on the initial jump, and the same drill continues.

Advanced

Advanced players begin with left foot on A and right foot on B. The player's back is now to the coach. The player jumps into the C block backward, landing on both feet, on the right foot, or on the left foot (whichever you wish). The player jumps out with the left foot on D and the right foot on E. The player executes a 180-degree turn and is now facing the coach. The drill continues.

Option (all skill levels) Have players do a front or reverse pivot instead of a jumping 180-degree turn.

➲ TEACHING POINTS

1. Quickness is the important test on defense. You don't want your athletes to raise their feet off the floor. Neither do you want them to drag their feet on the floor—the friction between the shoe and floor slows them down. Nor do you want them to hop. You want them to glide quickly, lifting their feet ever so slightly. Players want the sensation of toes "grabbing" the floor as they slide through the drill.
2. Develop players psychologically—tell them to think *quickness, quickness, quickness.*
3. Run the drill for 25 seconds, recording the number of full revolutions each player manages. As players get quicker, their number of full revolutions should increase.

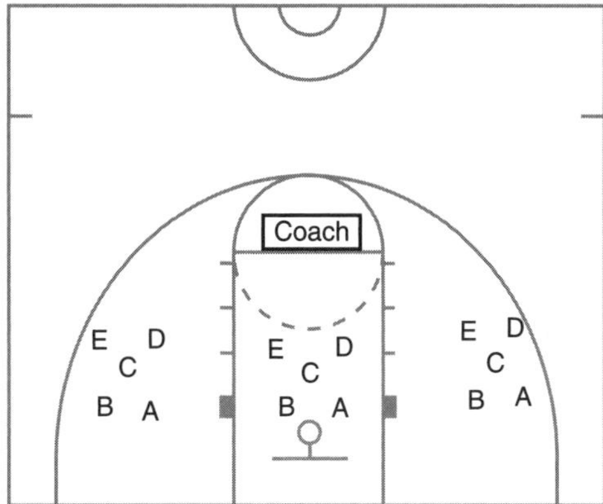

Related Drills *2, 4, 35, 36*

7

AGILITY TIP DRILL

Individual or team • 1 minute

SKILL FOCUS Quickness, balance, agility, conditioning, slide step (46, 137), fence slide (128), advance step (137), retreat step (137), swing step (137)

Intermediate

1. Line players up facing a wall, about a foot (.3 m) from the wall.
2. Players jump as high as they can and touch the wall with both hands.
3. On the way down, players do a 90-degree turn to the right. The right shoulder should now be facing the wall.
4. Players immediately jump back up and touch the wall with the right hand. On the way down, they execute another 90-degree turn. They should now be facing the wall.
5. Players immediately jump back up and touch the wall with both hands. On the way down, they execute another 90-degree turn. The left shoulder should be facing the wall.
6. Players immediately jump back up and touch the wall with the left hand. On the way down, they execute another 90-degree turn. They should now be facing the wall.
7. The drill continues for 30 seconds at the beginning of the season. By mid-season, players should be in condition to jump for 45 seconds. By the end of the season, they should be able to go a full minute.

Advanced

Players execute as described, but each time they land they do an advance step, a retreat step, a swing step, a slide step, or a fence slide before jumping again.

Options

1. Give each player a tennis ball. The player must touch the tennis ball off the wall.
2. Use a softball instead of a tennis ball to better develop strength in their grips.

TEACHING POINTS

Make sure players continue the jump the entire 30 seconds. You are trying to build constant effort on the boards and to develop well-conditioned legs.

Related Drills *3, 6, 46, 137*

CHAPTER 2

Stance and Footwork

Knowledge is the greatest aid in any sport. Practicing movements incorrectly limits improvement and diminishes the level of performance, whereas practicing correctly accelerates growth and raises the ceiling of your players' potential.

Proper stance and footwork are primary building blocks for developing highly skilled basketball players. Without these two skills, development of more advanced skills tends to be slower and more difficult, and peak performance might never be achieved.

In drill 8 we teach the first stance and footwork your players need—positioning for laying the ball in the basket properly, from both the left and right sides of the court.

If players want to be the next Michael Jordan, with abilities to create fantastic one-on-one moves, they must first learn the triple-threat position, presented in drill 9.

If players want to play like Tim Duncan, they must know how to properly position in the post, which is covered in drill 10.

Proper positioning, though vital, is only the beginning. Players must be able to move in ways to defeat their defenders. You want them to be able to coax defenders into making mistakes. When a defender makes a wrong movement, proper footwork allows the offensive player to exploit that mistake and explosively blast by the defender for a score.

Developing proper footwork is best divided into two phases: before putting the ball on the floor, and after starting the dribble. Drill 11 drills the rocker step for use before the dribble. Drill 12 is the first dribbling maneuver, the in-and-out move. Drill 13 adds the crossover, a countermove to the in-and-out move. Both are executed facing the opponent.

Drill 14 adds a spin move to your players' growing repertoire. Drill 15 works a countermove to the spin: the half-spin. Both of these moves are performed by turning the back on the defender. Drill 16 puts everything together, allowing players to create combinations that best suit the situation.

Drill 17 adds a defender. This drill is a savvy drill in which players execute the moves they have learned while gaining knowledge on which move to use when and why.

8

BASIC LAYUP

Team • 3 minutes

SKILL FOCUS Basic layup shot, balance, conditioning, catching the ball (44), bounce pass (44), chest pass (44)

Beginner

1. Line players up as shown in figure 1. Begin with shots from the right side of the basket. After 90 seconds, change to shooting from the left side.
2. Begin with a bounce pass to the receiver.
3. Player 2 passes to player 1, who shoots the layup. Then 2 goes to end of line 1, and 1 goes to end of line 2. Player 4 rebounds the ball. As 4 rebounds the shot (missed or made), 3 runs toward the basket. Then 4 passes to 3, who shoots. Both 3 and 4 go to ends of opposite lines. Repeat the sequence until each player masters the skill of shooting a layup.

Intermediate

The same as the beginner drill, but a coach stands beside the shooter and gently pushes the shooter as the shot is taken.

Advanced

Same as the intermediate drill, but allow passers to throw chest passes instead of bounce passes.

Options (all skill levels)

1. *Three-Line Layup Drill* (figure 2): Player 1 passes to 2, who passes to 3 at the free-throw line. Player 1 cuts behind 2, and 3 passes to 1 for the layup. Then 2 cuts behind 3 and races to get the rebound. Next, 1 goes behind 3's line and 2 goes behind 1's line, while 3 goes behind 2's line.
2. Run the layup drills without letting the ball touch the floor to keep players hustling to their positions.
3. Let the receiver catch the pass and then toss the ball from hand to hand before shooting the layup.
4. Let the receiver catch the pass away from the basket and then dribble-drive to the basket.

TEACHING POINTS

1. The layup should be shot from a high jump, not a broad jump. The shooter goes straight up with a slight lean forward, jumping off the opposite leg (i.e., righties jump off the left leg). The shooting hand is always on the out-of-bounds side. The hand should be behind the ball, palm pointing upward. As the ball is released, the wrist flips slightly, placing the ball in the small square above the rim. The ball should not go any higher after hitting the square.

2. To execute the bounce pass, players hold the ball in both hands with elbows flexed (one hand on each side of the ball). They step forward as they deliver the pass. As they pass the ball, they flip their wrist so thumbs finish pointing down. Palms begin pointed inward and end pointed outward. Elbows should fully extend. Players try to land the ball on the floor so that after the bounce the ball reaches the receiver near or slightly above the beltline. The receiver watches the ball into the hands and then goes up immediately for the shot. The passer should be in a sitting position when releasing the ball. From this low torso position, the passer is ready to make a quick cut.
3. The chest pass is delivered similar to the bounce pass. Hands are outside the ball (on both sides) with thumbs pointing up and palms in. The passer steps forward while passing and snaps the wrists, ending with thumbs pointing down and palms pointing out. The pass is delivered near the chest of the receiver, who watches the ball all the way into the hands.

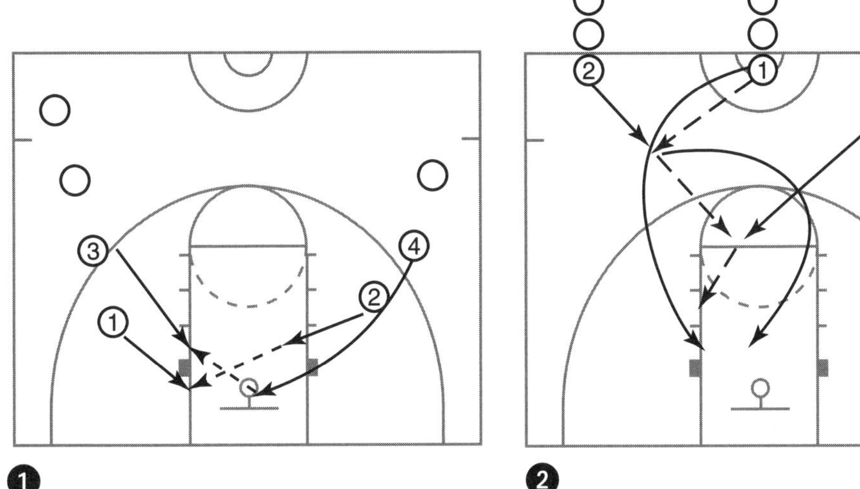

Related Drills 41-74

9

TRIPLE-THREAT POSITION

Individual or team • 2 minutes

SKILL FOCUS Perimeter positioning with the ball, pivoting (35-36), peripheral vision, offensive moves (11-15), balance, agility, quickness, foot movement (11), V-cut (53)

Beginner

1. Players line up as shown in the figure.
2. A player V-cuts; a coach passes the ball to the player.
3. The player reverse pivots and puts the ball in triple-threat position.
4. The player passes the ball back to the coach and goes to the end of the line.

Intermediate

After pivoting into triple-threat position, the player does a jab-step fake, a crossover fake, or a rocker-step fake (coach's choice).

Advanced

1. After executing one of the fakes (intermediate), the player begins a dribble-drive to the basket for a layup, or stops short with a jump stop and takes a jump shot.
2. Instead of driving all the way to the basket, the player stops with a jump stop and does a fake at the end of the dribble (e.g., a spin move, half-spin move, or up-and-under move) to get the jump shot off.
3. Instead of driving all the way to the basket, the player does a dribbling move (such as an in-and-out move, spin move, or half-spin move) after two dribbles before driving for the layup.
4. To practice alone, the player can pass the ball a few feet (1-2 m) away with backspin. The player then goes to catch the ball, reverse pivots, and completes the drill as described.

➲ **TEACHING POINTS** To get into triple-threat position, players crouch with a slight bend at the knees and the trunk. They bring the ball up under the chin, with one hand on each side of the ball. The ball can be slightly to the side of the torso opposite the pivot foot. From this position, players can pass the ball, begin a dribble, or shoot the ball (hence the name triple threat).

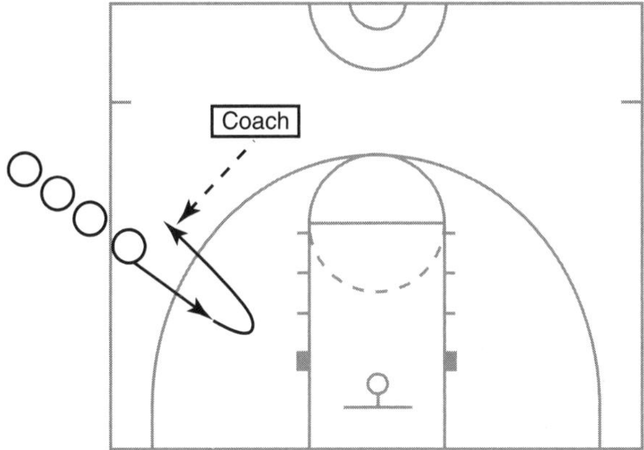

Related Drills *36, 37, 40-41, 53, 56-57, 104-126*

10

POST POSITION

Individual or team • 5 minutes

SKILL FOCUS Layup (8); reverse pivot (36); post moves (96-103), post position, drop step (96-103), spin (115), half-spin (115), up and under (116), pump fake (117)

Beginner

1. Players line up as shown in the figure.
2. As a player cuts across the lane, a coach tells the player where the (imaginary) defender is.
3. The player reacts by getting position on the would-be defender.
4. The coach passes the ball to the player, who executes a drop step for a layup.
5. The player goes to the end of the line after rebounding the layup and passing to the coach.

Intermediate

1. Instead of the player doing a drop step for a layup, the coach tells the player which post move to use (spin move, half-spin move, or face-up moves).
2. Instead of shooting a layup, the player shoots the power layup or the baby hook (based on which move is chosen and which side of the floor the player is on).

Advanced

1. Add a passive defender; now the player must read the defender and set up in proper position. The player must also decide which move to use to take advantage of that position.
2. While the player is in post position, a coach can race a few steps up or down the sideline, calling out a new defensive position, requiring the post player to establish a different post position.

➲ TEACHING POINTS

1. Players position at the big block. If a defender is above, the player nudges the defender a step or so up the lane (using body strength, not pushing with arms or hands). If the defender is below, the player pushes the defender one step toward the baseline. If the defender is fronting, the player takes one step toward the coach to create a greater passing area for the lob pass.
2. Players bend the "on" arm at the elbow to form a 90-degree angle, then place the forearm against the defender's lower torso or waist to hold the position.
3. They use the "off" arm as a signal to the passer. Again, they form a 90-degree angle, but now with forearm perpendicular to the floor. They spread the off hand as a target for the pass.
4. Players turn their bodies by ensuring the foot on the side of the defender is beyond the front foot of the defender, who is in a three-quarter denial position. This allows the quick drop step to the basket for the layup.

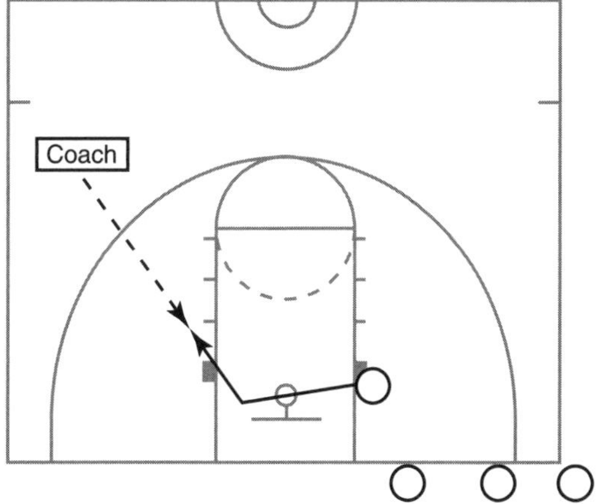

Related Drills *96-103*

11

ROCKER STEP

Individual • 5 minutes to teach; 1 minute to review

SKILL FOCUS Triple-threat position (9), jab step, jab-step pullback, jab-step direct drive, jab-step crossover, rocker step

Beginner

1. The first time through the drill, the teaching part, a player will be at the free-throw line with a coach. The coach acts as a defender and explains why a move is made and when to make it, and judges the player's quickness. When making a move, the player must give the defender time to react to that move before beginning another stage.
2. The first of the four stages of the rocker step is the jab step (figure 1).
3. After learning how and when to use the jab step, the player learns how and when to execute the jab-step pullback (figure 2).
4. Next the player learns how and when to do the jab-step direct drive (figure 3).
5. The last stage of the rocker step is the jab-step crossover (figure 4).
6. After teaching the rocker step, a coach lines players up and calls out the stage of the rocker step to execute, and then checks for proper execution. After each call, the coach reviews when each portion is to be used.

TEACHING POINTS

1. The jab step is the key; drill this step until players have perfected it. The step should be a short, hard-thrust step, no more than 18 inches (.45 m), if that. Players should land on the toes of the nonpivot foot, making a screeching sound as they touch the floor. (For this drill, let's say the left foot is the pivot foot, and the right foot is the nonpivot foot.) Explain that a player must check the defense while executing the jab step. From triple-threat position, players lower the ball slightly and lean forward slightly, creating the impression they intend to drive with the basketball.
2. Stage 2 is the jab-step pullback. Because the player landed on the toes of the right foot, the player is ready to move quickly with that foot. If the defender gives ground on the probing jab step, the attacker pulls back quickly to release a jump shot. This pullback should be not quite 18 inches (.45 m). The free right foot must be in front of the left foot for perfect shooting balance. However, the player can use the pullback to get the defender in motion for an ensuing drive, especially if the player has hit a few jumpers. The player can get the defender rocking with good jab-step pullback mechanics.
3. Stage 3: From the pullback or the jab step, the attacker checks the defender's front foot to see how far away it is. If the defender keeps the front foot near the original probing jab step, or if the defender races forward with the front foot to stop the jab-step pullback, the attacker picks up the right foot and puts it at least beside the defender's front foot (farther, if possible). The attacker pushes the ball out of the hand to the right of the body, and then

brings the left foot forward in an explosive manner, several feet (or over a meter) in front of the right foot, and then drives directly to the basket for the jab-step direct drive.

4. Stage 4: If the defender brings the right foot forward to challenge the jab-step pullback or the original jab step, then the attacker uses a jab-step crossover. To execute this successfully, the attacker places the right foot beside the defender's right foot (or farther, if possible). From this position, the player releases the ball out of the right hand to the left side of the body before picking up the left foot. The player then explodes by the defender in a direct line to the basket.
5. To get the best and easiest shot, your players must know the *when* as well as the *how*.

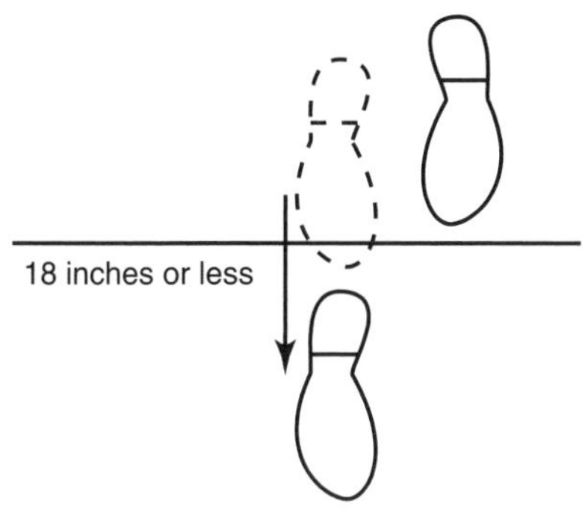

❶ Jab step.

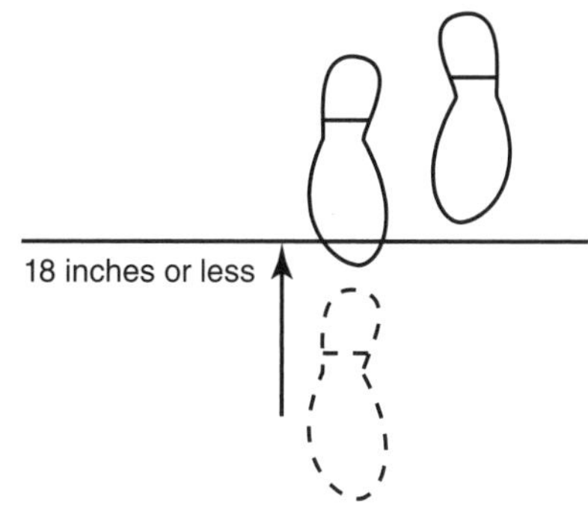

❷ Jab-step pullback.

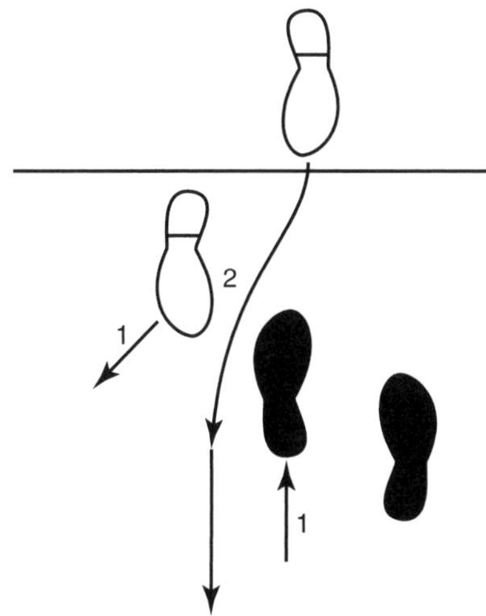

❸ Jab-step direct drive. As the defender is stepping forward (1), the attacker steps forward with the right foot (1) and then brings the left foot forward quickly (2).

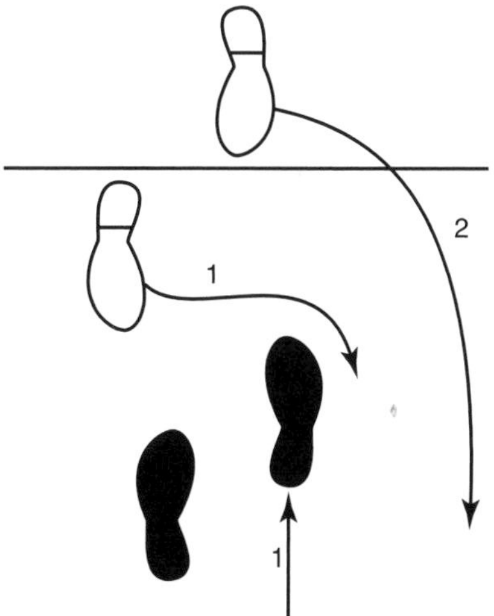

❹ Jab-step crossover. As the defender steps forward with the right foot (1), the attacker crosses over with the right foot (1) and then brings the left foot quickly forward (2).

Related Drills *9, 16, 53-54, 71*

12

IN-AND-OUT MOVE

Individual • 5 minutes to teach; 1 minute to drill

SKILL FOCUS In-and-out move (28)

Beginner

1. When teaching, use only one coach and one player. When drilling, line up as shown in figure 1.
2. Mark a 2-foot-by-2-foot (.6 m by .6 m) square using tape near a line (such as the free-throw line).
3. The dribbler starts about 10 feet (3 m) away and dribbles toward the coach. Start with a control dribble; allow the speed dribble on the next drilling.
4. At the square, the dribbler executes an in-and-out move. The coach moves in the direction of the step-in fake to teach the dribbler the *when* while teaching the *how*.
5. This move is the complement of the crossover.

TEACHING POINTS

1. Dribblers use the in-and-out move when a defender plays them straight up. They can also use the move to get the defender moving away from the intended move, or when the dribbler's fakes get the defender to put a foot forward on the same side as the dribble.
2. When dribblers step in, they fake in with the head and shoulders, bringing the ball in as they step in. To execute this without losing control of the ball, they cup their hand at the side of the ball, knowing they intend to place the hand on the other side of the ball as soon as it bounces back up. For example, if stepping in with the left foot, the right hand is the dribbling hand. The dribbler cups the dribbling hand from the right side of the ball and swings it through moderately low before taking the same hand and quickly pulling the ball back to the right. The dribbler may actually switch hands while dribbling in if the defender is far enough away to disallow a swipe at the dribble to deflect it.
3. While stepping in and faking with the ball and the head and shoulders, dribblers plant the left foot (using the toes) and swing the right foot forward with a long, hard step (figure 2). They get the right foot at least forward of the defender's left foot. If the fake is good enough, the defender will have stepped to the right, allowing a straight lane to drive to the basket.
4. Dribblers use this move when the defender plays them straight up (not an overplay).
5. After learning to use their dominant hand as their dribbling hand, players move to using their weaker hand.

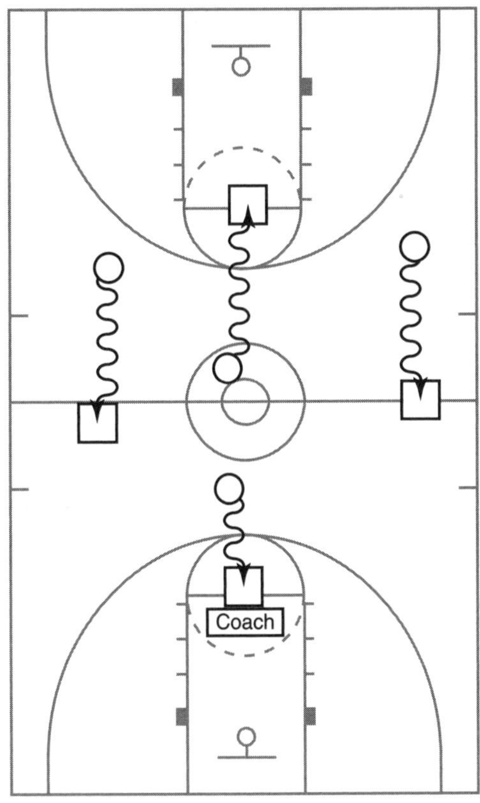

❶

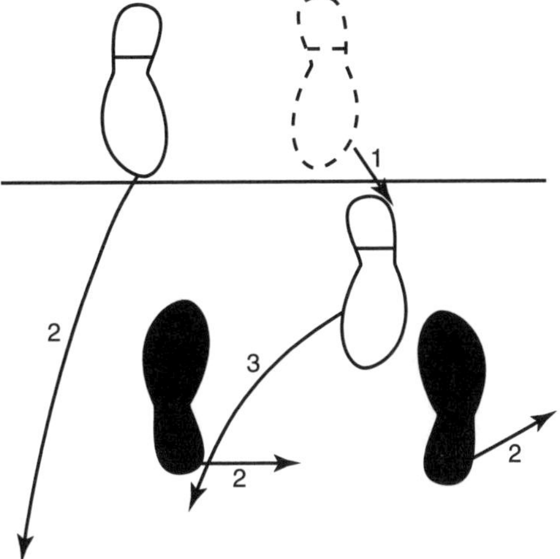

❷ The in-and-out move. The dribbler steps to the left (1). As the defender reacts by stepping to the right (2), the dribbler takes a step with the right foot (2) and then swings the left foot quickly beside the defender's left foot (3).

Related Drill 28

13

CROSSOVER MOVE

Individual • 5 minutes to teach; 1 minute to review

SKILL FOCUS Crossover move (29)

Beginner

1. When teaching, use only one coach and one player. When drilling, line up as shown in figure 1.
2. Mark a 2-foot by 2-foot (.6 m by .6 m) square using tape near a line (such as the free-throw line).
3. The dribbler starts about 10 feet (3 m) away and dribbles toward the coach. Start with a control dribble; allow the speed dribble on the next drilling.
4. At the square, the dribbler executes a crossover move. The coach moves in the direction of the step-out fake to teach the dribbler the *when* while teaching the *how*.
5. This move is the complement of the in-and-out move.

TEACHING POINTS

1. Dribblers use this move when the defender is overplaying them or playing them straight up. They may also use the move when they can get the defender to put a foot forward (opposite the side of the dribble).
2. Let's say the defender is overplaying the dribbler's right side (figure 2). The dribbler steps outside the defender with the right foot, faking with the head and shoulders. The dribbler may even dribble the ball slightly outside if adept enough. To execute this dribble, the right hand stays almost on top of the ball but slightly to the left top. The dribbler pushes the ball slightly right before bringing it back left.
3. Bringing the ball back to the left, the dribbler lowers the ball to a point no higher than the middle of the lower leg and pushes the ball through with great speed. At this moment the ball is exposed, and the defender can deflect it.
4. When stepping to the right and dribbling slightly to the right, the dribbler's right foot should be forward of the defender's left foot. Then when the ball is brought through to the left, the right foot follows. The right foot should be placed beside the defender's right foot.
5. The dribbler's left foot is now brought forward violently and as far forward as possible while maintaining good balance. The dribbler explodes in a straight line toward the basket.
6. After learning to use their dominant hand as their dribbling hand, players move to using their weaker hand.

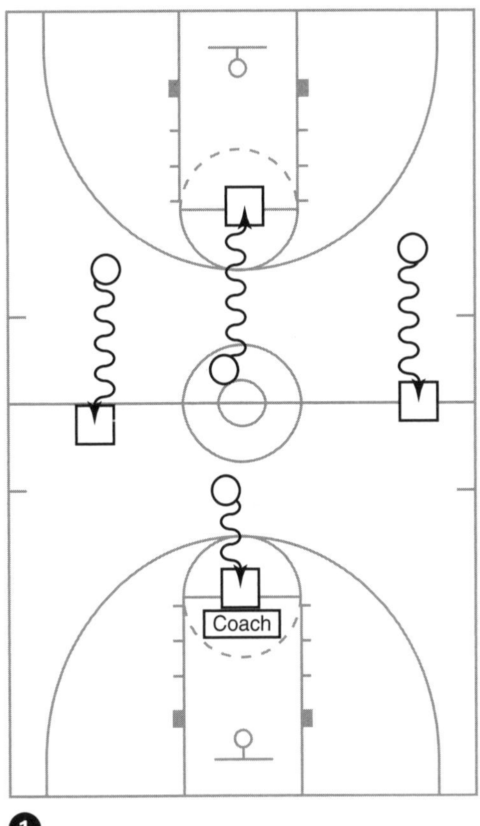

❶

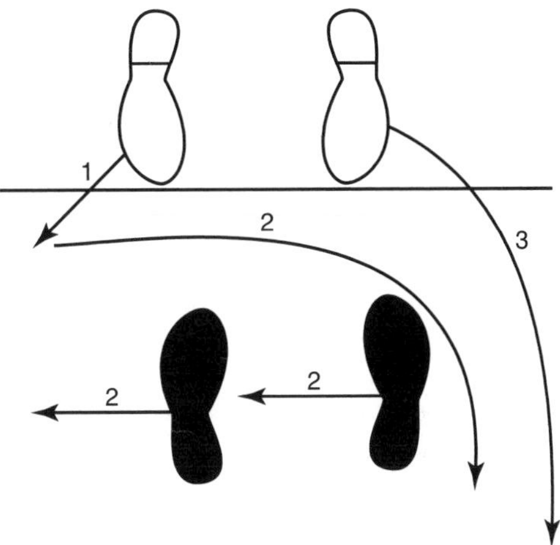

❷ The crossover move. The dribbler stops to the right (1). As the defender reacts by stepping to the left (2), the dribbler picks up the right foot and crosses over, placing the right foot beside the defender's right foot (2). The dribbler then steps forward quickly with the left foot (3).

Related Drill 29

14

SPIN (REVERSE) MOVE

Individual • 5 minutes to teach; 1 minute to review

SKILL FOCUS Spin (reverse) move (30)

Beginner

1. When teaching, use only one coach and one player. When drilling, line up as shown in figure 1.
2. Mark a 2-foot by 2-foot (.6 m by .6 m) square using tape near a line (such as the free-throw line).
3. The player starts about 10 feet (3 m) away and dribbles toward the coach. Start with a control dribble; allow the speed dribble on the next drilling.
4. At the square, the dribbler performs a spin move. The coach moves in the direction of the step-out fake to teach the dribbler the *when* while teaching the *how*. Or the coach may begin in an overplay position.
5. This move is the counter to the half-spin move.

TEACHING POINTS

1. If dribbling right-handed, the dribbler fake-steps to the right. The dribbler may also use head and shoulder fakes in that direction. If overplayed to the right, the dribbler won't need to fake to get the defender moving in that direction (figure 2).
2. The dribbler places the left foot aligned to the middle of the defender. This can be a jab step with the left foot.
3. The dribbler reverse pivots, executing a 360-degree turn, putting the back to the defender, using the left foot as the pivot foot.
4. The dribbler cups the ball with the right hand and pulls it all the way around during the pivot. The dribbler does not change hands until the pivot is complete. The dribbler positions the right foot at least even with, and preferably beyond, the defender's right foot.
5. The dribbler swings the right foot all the way around and well in front of the defender, and then explodes to the basket in a straight-line dribble.
6. After learning to use their dominant hand as their dribbling hand, players move to using their weaker hand.

❶

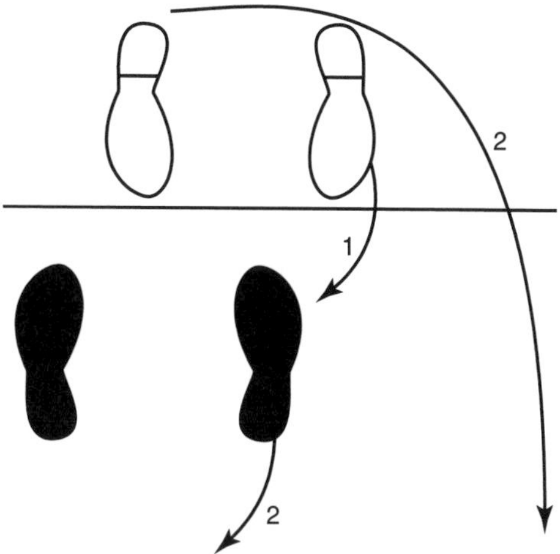

❷ The spin move. The dribbler jab-steps the left foot (1). As the defender retreat-steps (2) the dribbler executes a 360-degree pivot.

Related Drill *30*

15

HALF-SPIN MOVE

Individual • 5 minutes to teach; 1 minute to review

SKILL FOCUS Half-spin move (31)

Beginner

1. When teaching, use only one coach and one player. When drilling, line players up as shown in figure 1.
2. Mark a 2-foot by 2-foot (.6 m by .6 m) square using tape near a line (such as the free-throw line).
3. The dribbler starts about 10 feet (3 m) away and dribbles toward the coach. Start with a control dribble; allow the speed dribble on the next drilling.
4. At the square, the dribbler executes a half-spin move. The coach moves in the direction of the step-out fake to teach the dribbler the *when* while teaching the *how*. Or the coach may begin in an overplay position.
5. This move is the counter to the spin move.

TEACHING POINTS

1. The dribbler gets the defender to overplay by faking with the right foot to the defender's left foot and by using head and shoulder fakes. Once the defender is in an overplay, the dribbler positions the left foot in the middle of the defender (see figure 2).
2. The dribbler wants the defender to expect a spin move, so the dribbler swings the right foot so the body is sideways to the defender's body.
3. The dribbler begins a spin but goes only about 90 degrees. As the dribbler is executing the half-spin, the defender is shifting to the right. The dribbler immediately explodes with the right foot back in the direction started from. When swinging the right foot back to the right, the dribbler wants to get the right foot outside the defender's left foot.
4. The dribbler then brings the left foot around the defender's left foot and explodes in a straight line toward the basket.
5. After learning to use their dominant hand as the dribbling hand, players move to using their weaker hand.

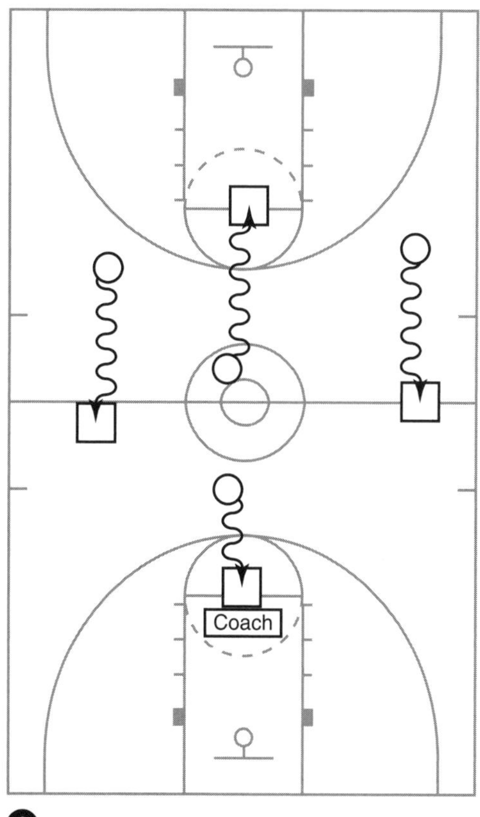

1

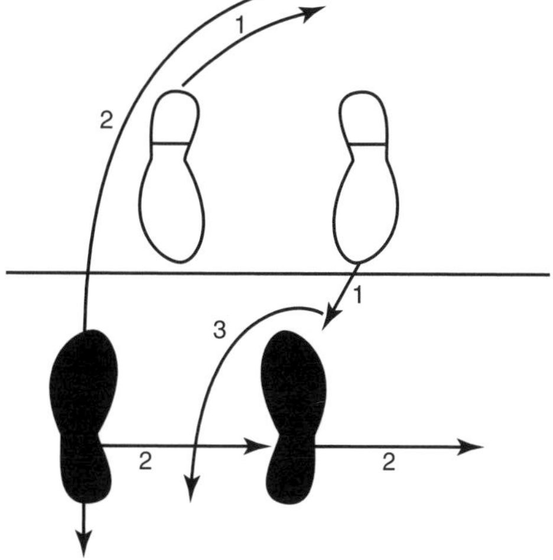

2 The half-spin move. The dribbler begins what looks like a spin move (1). As the defender reacts to the right (2), the dribbler quickly brings the right foot back at least to a position parallel to the defender's left foot. The dribbler then brings the left foot to a position beside the defender's left foot (3).

Related Drill *31*

16

COMBINATION DRIBBLING MOVES

Individual • 3 minutes

SKILL FOCUS Triple-threat (9) rocker step (11), in-and-out move (12, 28), crossover move (13, 29), spin move (14, 30), half-spin move (15, 31), V-cut (53)

Advanced

1. Players line up as shown in the figure. Using tape, make a 2-foot by 2-foot (.6 m by .6 m) box on the floor, as shown.
2. A player V-cuts to receive the ball from a coach.
3. The player receives the ball and assumes the triple-threat position.
4. The player performs the part of the rocker step the coach designates. (The coach explains when that portion of the rocker step would be used.)
5. The player then begins to dribble under control to the right, moving to the box, and then executes the dribbling move designated by the coach.
6. The figure shows the drill going baseline on the left side of the court. The next day move the box to the middle of the court, and the player will drive left and execute the move. The next two days after that, move the drill to the right side of the court.

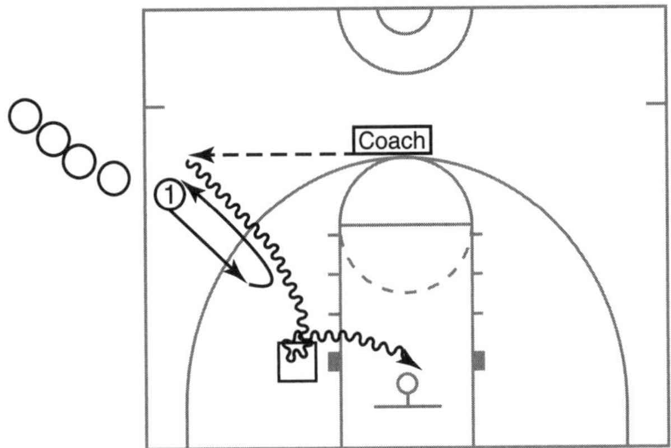

Related Drills *9, 11-15, 22-25, 28-31, 49, 53*

PAYE DRILL

17

Individual or team • 10 minutes

➲ **SKILLS FOCUS** Jab step (11), jab-step pullback (11), jab-step crossover (11), jab-step direct drive (11), in and out (12, 28), crossover (13, 29), spin (14, 30), half-spin (15, 31), defensive fakes (33), pump fake series (96, 116-117), front foot to pivot foot (129), front foot to free foot (130), advance step (137), retreat step (137), swing step (137), slide step (137), overplay (138)

In the Paye drill, the offensive player learns to read the defender and make the appropriate move to dominate the defender. The defender uses tactics and techniques to control and dominate the attacker.

1. The Paye drill is divided into three parts. Part I works on beginner and intermediate progressions before the dribble. This part includes two sections: the triple threat (before any movement) and the rocker step (foot movement). The offensive techniques are presented in drills 9 and 11. The defensive maneuvers are presented in drills 129 through 130 and 137.
2. Part II works on advanced progressions during the dribble. The offensive moves are the in-and-out and its counter, the crossover, and the spin and its counter, the half-spin. The offensive techniques are presented in drills 12 through 15 and 28 through 31. The defensive maneuvers are presented in drills 137 and 138.
3. Part III works on advanced progressions after the dribble. The offensive techniques are the pump fake, the pump-fake crossover, and the pump-fake up-and-under. Both the offensive techniques and the defensive maneuvers are presented in drills 96, 116, and 117. The step-back move is also presented in drill 116.

Part I: Before the Dribble

Beginner and Intermediate

Beginner

1. Line a player up in front of a coach as shown in figure 1. The player should be within shooting range. If you want the drill to be a team drill, put a defensive player on an offensive player at each bucket in the gym.
2. Following are the first three defensive maneuvers the attacker must read:
   a. *Stance* is either front foot to pivot foot, front foot to free foot, or parallel (even).
   b. *Coverage*, the second read, must be either tight or loose. Tight coverage means the defender is within one-half step of the attacker. Loose coverage means the defender is more than one-half step from the attacker.
   c. *Overplay* is the third read. The defender can overplay to the right of the attacker (called overplay right) or to the left of the attacker (called overplay left) or play straight up (no overplay).

(continued)

3. The attacker begins in a triple-threat stance in which any of the four fakes of the rocker step can be executed.
4. Drill on each phase for a series of 10 seconds each before progressing to the next phase. In the first three series of 10 seconds, emphasize stance (a, b, and c). In the next series of 10 seconds, emphasize coverage (d). In the last series of 10 seconds, emphasize the overplay (e).
    a. Begin with front foot to pivot foot stance for 10 seconds.
    b. Then go with front foot to free foot stance for 10 seconds.
    c. Then go with parallel stance for 10 seconds.
    d. Then emphasize coverage for 10 seconds: go tight first, then loose.
    e. Then emphasize overplay for 10 seconds per stance, using each stance in an overplay left and then an overplay right.
    f. Attackers should use the principles of attacking presented in sections 3 and 4 under the following Intermediate section. Beginners should use only the principles applicable to the rocker step. Intermediates may use all the principles except those that deal with after-the-dribble techniques. Advanced players use all the principles.
5. The coach next begins any combination of the stance, coverage, and overplay. For example, the coach begins in front foot to free foot stance, tight coverage, with no overplay.
6. The attacker reads the coach's defensive mode and calls out the read exactly. The attacker then tells the coach what move would best counter this defensive mode.

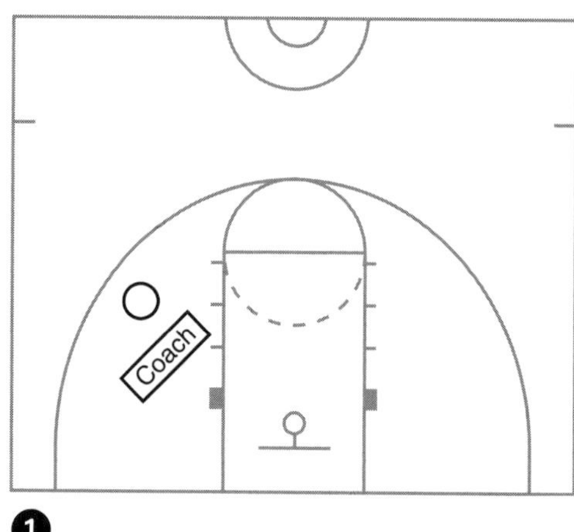

Intermediate

1. Instead of the attacker telling the coach what move would best counter the coach's defensive mode, the attacker actually executes the move that counters the mode.
2. Now we enter the second phase of the drills: The rocker step (offensive) and the advance, retreat, and swing step (defensive). This phase deals with the one-on-one first step (or fake) battle that ensues:
    a. If the coach begins in front-foot-to-pivot-foot stance, tight coverage, no overplay, for example, the attacker would execute a crossover step. The coach would react with a swing step to counter this offensive move. The attacker can now drive or pull back.
    b. If the coach begins in front foot to free foot, tight, no overplay, for example, the attacker would use a direct drive with the free foot. Again the coach would have to use a swing step to counter this.
    c. This mental combat between the attacker and the coach continues for 10 seconds. Then another series begins.
3. The attacker always responds to gain an advantage. That advantage comes from these attacking principles:
    a. Always shoot against loose coverage. Always attack with a direct drive step or a crossover step against tight coverage.
    b. Always attack toward the overplay. For example, if the defender overplays the attacker's left side by a half-step (called overplay left), the defender is trying to force the attacker to begin a move to the right. The attacker does not go for it. The first step should be to the *left* with a crossover step (if the left foot is the pivot foot).
    c. Always get the defender in motion, either with a direct jab step or a jab-step crossover, if the defender is playing straight and tight.
    d. Always attack front foot to pivot foot or front foot to free foot by going after the front foot.
    e. Jab-step direct drive and jab-step crossover are counter moves to each other. Where one will go to the right, the other will go to the left.
4. Players should use the following attacking principles when faced with the advance step, retreat step, or swing step.
    a. If the defender comes after you with an *advance step,* attack it with either the direct drive step or the crossover step. Treat the advance step as though the defender is in a front-foot-to-pivot-foot or front-foot-to-free-foot stance.
    b. If the defender uses a *retreat step,* pull back and shoot or start dribbling with the intention of using the crossover dribble-drive or the spin dribble-drive at the first opportunity. This will really create separation.
    c. If the defender uses a *swing step,* pull back and shoot or start dribbling with the intention of using the crossover dribble-drive or the spin dribble-drive at the first opportunity. Again, this will create significant separation.

(continued)

Part II: During the Dribble

Advanced

1. Instead of using just the rocker step and the initial defensive coverage, players can advance to the dribbling series.
2. To combat the dribbling offensive series, the defender must either use slide steps and stay equal to the attacker's dribbling advances or hustle into an overplay to cut off the attacker's opportunity to continue the dribble.
   a. If the defender uses slide steps and stays even with an attacker's advance, the attacker can execute a step-back move for a jump shot. This will create separation.
   b. If the defender hustles into an overplay, the attacker wants to use either a crossover dribble-drive or a spin dribble-drive. Remind your players not to confuse the initial step before the dribble with the dribble series. Before the dribble, the attacker wants to attack the overplay; during the dribble, the attacker wants to attack *away from* the overplay. To continue dribbling into an overplay usually results in a charging foul.
   c. To drill on making this decision off the dribble, place an offensive player in the right corner with a defender in a front-foot-to-free-foot overplay to the attacker's right (figure 2). The attacker would attack the front foot of the defender and dribble-drive toward the forward foot (to the attacker's right). The defender would use a swing step and try to either keep up with the attacker or jump into an overplay. A coach can designate an area for the moment of decision (let's say the free-throw circle inside the lane). At this moment the attacker must check the defender and make a decision. If played straight up, the attacker jump-stops and shoots a step-back jump shot (drill 116; figure 3). If the defender jumps into an overplay, the attacker spin dribbles for a layup (drills 14 and 30; figure 4) or crossover dribbles for the layup (drills 13 and 29).

➜ Options (Advanced)

1. You can always put a defender on the attacker. Now the defender and the attacker play the Paye drill.
2. If your gym has six goals, divide your squad into five sets of two and put two players at each basket. Observe from midcourt. Players explain their moves and reactions to each other.
3. As players advance in this drill, instead of telling each other their moves and their reactions, they can name other options they could have used and explain why these options would have worked.
4. Do not try to run all the parts of this drill in one setting. Break the drill down into at least three settings: before the dribble, during the dribble, and after the dribble. Run the drill for several days. Then let them go at it.

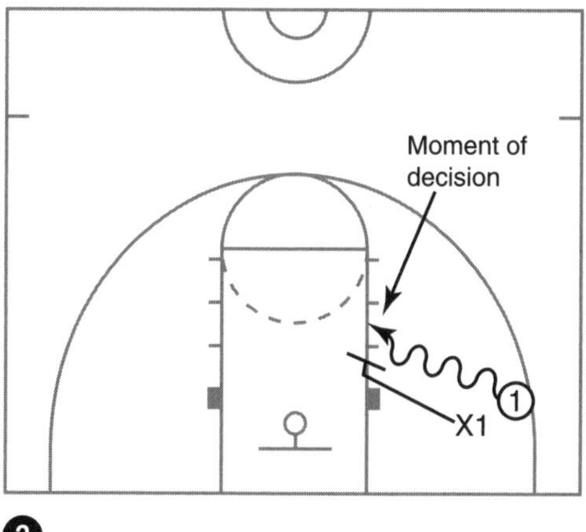

2

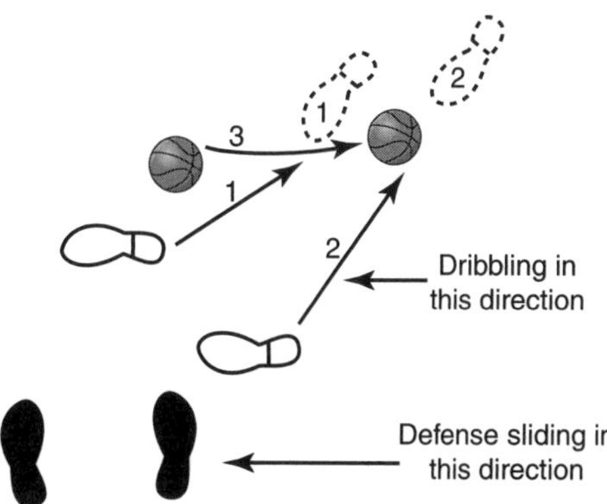

3 Step 1: Attacker steps back with right foot; Step 2: Attacker brings left foot back into a heel-toe relationship (fundamental shooting stance); Step 3: Meanwhile, attacker picks ball up with both hands and brings ball into shooting pocket.

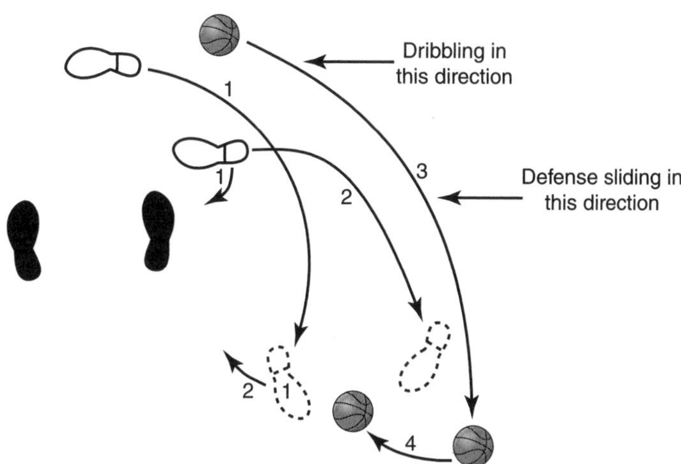

4 Step 1: Attacker stops on left foot and swings right foot 180 degrees or so. The left foot swings slightly. Attacker keeps ball in right hand for protection; Step 2: Attacker swings left foot another 180 degrees or so. Attacker is now facing the basket with right heel and left toe in the heel-toe relationship; Step 3: Attacker cups right hand on side of ball and pulls it the 360 degrees turn, protecting the ball with body. Step 4: Attacker brings the ball into the shooting pocket.

(continued)

Part III: After the Dribble

Advanced

After the dribble involves the pump fake series. You need not teach this series as part of the Paye drill until you have taught your low-post moves. The offensive and defensive techniques and maneuvers are taught in drills 96, 116, and 117. For the purpose of the Paye drill, you should not allow the attacker to shoot after the dribble unless the attacker has created separation. If there is no separation created, the attacker must pass the ball at the end of the dribble. Once the pump fake series is learned, the attacker may try to create a shot after completing the dribble.

At the end of the dribble, the attacker executes a jump stop. This gives the attacker a choice of pivot feet and a choice of two moves:

1. The defender is in an overplay. The attacker can execute a step-back jump shot (figure 3). The attacker steps back with the outside foot (step 1 in the figure) and then brings the inside foot back to a heel-toe position (step 2). The attacker squares up shoulders to the basket and leaps into the air for a jump shot. The step-back move should have created the required separation for the shot.
2. The defender is in an overplay. The attacker plants the toes of the inside foot and swings the outside foot into a spin move (step 1 in figure 4). The attacker immediately spins to a position of facing the basket (step 2 in figure 4). The attacker ends in heel-toe position and then leaps into the air for a jump shot.
3. Instead of using either of these options, the attacker may land on both feet, pump-fake, and use the reaction of the defender to execute the moves presented in drills 96 and 116-117.

TEACHING POINTS

1. You want to make sure your offensive players recognize what they see in the defense—and that they know how to attack what they see. Constantly correct your attackers if they see something that is not there.
2. Ensure that your defenders know all the stances, steps, and slides that will help them control the assignment. This also must constantly be corrected.
3. The purpose on offense is to get an uncontested shot; this means creating separation to get the shot off without a hand in the face.
4. The purpose on defense is to force attackers to a spot in which they cannot get an uncontested shot off (cannot create separation). Remember that the winner of nearly every game is the team that takes the most quality shots. A quality shot is one that is on balance, within the shooter's range, and taken after separation has been created.

5. *Before the dribble:* Defenders begin in either front-foot-to-pivot-foot stance, front-foot-to-free-foot stance, or parallel stance. See drills 129 and 130. Attackers begin in triple-threat position, intending to use the facets of the rocker step. See drills 9 and 11.
6. *Before the dribble:* Attackers execute a jab step, jab-step pullback, jab-step direct drive, or jab-step crossover with their free foot. See drill 11. Defenders react with either a retreat step or a swing step. If the attacker uses a jab-step pullback, the defender reacts with an advance step. See drill 137. The attacker is trying to compel the defender into a mistake or into an overplay.
7. *Before the dribble* and *during the dribble:* Defenders can begin in an overplay of the attacker, either to the right or to the left side of the attacker. The defender can still begin in either the front-foot-to-pivot-foot stance, the front-foot-to-free-foot stance, or the parallel stance. See drill 138. The attacker responds with a direct drive to the basket, a crossover drive to the basket, or the in and out, the spin, or the half-spin. See drills 12, 13, 14, 15, 28, 29, 30, 31.
8. The defender begins in either a tight coverage or a loose coverage. The loose coverage invites the jump shot. The attacker must take it. The tight coverage compels the attacker to make a movement with the free foot.
9. When the attacker has created separation from the defender, the attacker shoots. To create separation, the attacker must execute fakes and moves that force the defender at least a step away from the attacker.

Related Drills *9, 11-15, 28-31, 33, 37-38, 84-88, 116-118, 129-130, 137-138*

CHAPTER

3

Ballhandling

To become offensive dynamos, your players must be able to handle the basketball. You want to *drill, drill, drill* your players until the ball becomes an extension of their hands—both hands. Only then can they perform one-on-one offensive moves with explosive quickness.

The 17 drills in this chapter develop the velocity your players require while allowing you to work on the one-on-one offensive moves so essential to player success.

Once the ball becomes an extension of the hand, offensive players brim over with confidence. They feel they can complete any pass, drive by any defender, and move the ball at will. This poise carries over to other parts of their game. They need this disposition to become explosive in their dribbling fakes. Jason Kidd has this type of attitude and aptitude. To watch Kidd dribble and complete passes to teammates in unbelievable situations is a wondrous part of the game within the game. Developing this skill required hours upon hours of practice.

Drill 18 works on using the hand and the fingertips to handle the ball. Young players must learn the part of the hand that must never be used to handle the ball. In fact, this area must never be used to perform *any* fundamental in basketball.

Drills 19 and 20 help players begin to envision the basketball as an extension of the hand. The options to these drills add running, angle movement, and explosiveness. Drill 21 aids in developing the dribbling mechanics of the in-and-out move.

Drill 22 teaches players to dribble and move without looking at the basketball, a much-needed skill in the flowing movement of one-on-one play. Drill 23 gets the body accustomed to full-court, fast-paced action. Drill 24 shows the contrast of playing half-court basketball.

Drills 25, 26, and 27 add dribbling moves to four basic ballhandling techniques: the in-and-out move, the crossover tactic, the spin maneuver, and the halfspin. Players also need a change of pace (drill 25), a hesitation (drill 26), and a retreating dribble (drill 27) in their repertoire. These are new moves that players can also use when executing the basic four.

Drills 28, 29, 30, and 31 are dribbling drills that increase player ability to perform the basic four perimeter dribbling moves. One of the options is to use two balls, which helps improve the basic perimeter move as well as ballhandling.

Drills 23 through 31 all include two-ball dribbling variation drills. The better your players get, the harder they should work on the two-ball dribbling drills.

The last three drills are fun and competitive. Players use one ball or two and work on whichever technique they most need to improve.

FINGERTIP DRILL

Individual • 30 seconds

SKILL FOCUS Develop touch with a basketball

Beginner

1. Players pass the basketball from hand to hand in front of the body.
2. Players move the basketball from a low position to well over their heads as they tip the ball from hand to hand.

Intermediate

Players dribble the basketball in front of the body using only the fingertips. They first use the index finger, then the middle finger, then the ring finger, then the little finger. They practice on both the left and right hands.

TEACHING POINTS

1. Be sure players flip their wrists as they perform this drill. Check the back of players' wrists to see if a wrinkle forms with each flip.
2. Players should use only the fingertips of each hand.

Related Drills *3, 19-34, 40-41, 76, 84, 97, 104-126*

19

STANDING FIGURE 8

Individual or team • 2 minutes

SKILL FOCUS Develop touch with a basketball

Beginner

1. Players pass the ball from the right to the left hand and back as they circle the basketball around the right leg.
2. Players repeat step 1, circling the basketball around the left leg.
3. If drilling as a team, players should be about 15 feet (4.5 m) apart.

Options

1. Players line up as shown in the figure. Give a basketball to each player in the first line.
2. The first line walks down the court and back using the figure 8 movement of the basketball.
3. The first line passes to the second line and goes to the back of the line.
4. The second line does steps 2 and 3.

Intermediate

1. Players begin with the ball held in the right hand in front of the right leg.
2. They take the ball between their spread legs and pick it up behind the left leg with the left hand.
3. They bring the ball back around the front of the left leg with the left hand and through their spread legs to behind the right leg, where it is picked up with the right hand.
4. They bring the ball from behind the right leg to the front of the right leg with the right hand. Continue this pattern of figure 8 movement for 5 to 15 seconds, then reverse the ball movement.

Options

1. The first line races down the floor and back using the figure 8 movement of the basketball.
2. Players jump-stop 10 feet (3 m) from the second line and execute a pass (coach's call) to the second line.
3. The second line does steps 1 and 2.
4. Divide your squad into teams and turn the drill into a dribbling race. Race guards against post players, or first team against second team.

➜ TEACHING POINTS

1. Watch for players handling the ball low by bending at the knees and the trunk.
2. Players should use the pads of the hands, not the palms (see figure in drill 3). They can achieve the proper technique by spreading their hands until they hurt, and then relaxing them. This forms a perfect cup.

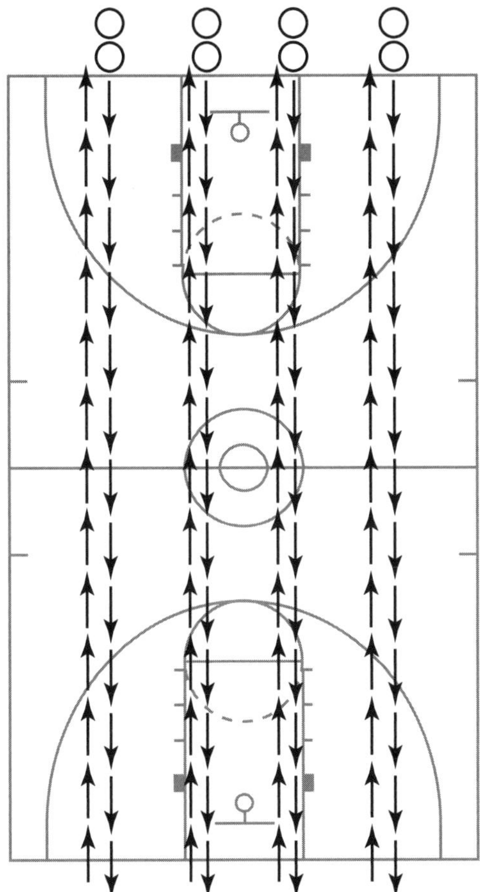

Related Drills *3, 18-34, 40-41, 76, 84, 97, 104-108, 122-126*

20

FIGURE 8 DRIBBLE

Individual or team • 2 minutes

SKILL FOCUS Develop touch with a basketball

Beginner

1. Players dribble a basketball very low (no higher than middle of lower legs) around the right leg using only the right hand. They use only their fingertips.
2. Players repeat 1, dribbling around the left leg with only the left hand.
3. If drilling as a team, players should be about 15 feet (4.5 m) apart.

Intermediate

Players begin dribbling in front of the right leg with the right hand, then dribble through the legs, picking the ball up with the left hand behind the left leg. They then dribble the ball in front of the left leg and back through the legs to behind the right leg, where the right hand picks up the dribble. From there, they dribble in front of the right leg and through the legs to behind the left leg, where the left hand picks it up. Players continue in this figure 8 pattern for 5 to 15 seconds, then reverse for another 5 to 15 seconds.

Options

1. Players spread around the half-court and begin by dribbling figure 8 in position.
2. Players dance while dribbling, moving the left foot forward when taking the ball through the legs from the right hand, then moving the right foot forward when taking the ball through the legs from the left hand. This dancing motion continues throughout the drill.

Advanced

1. Players race down the floor while dribbling figure 8. This race should begin as a walk until coordination is achieved. Then players race as fast as they can while maintaining control of the basketball (see the figure).
2. Divide your squad into teams and turn the drill into a dribbling race. Race guards against post players, or first team against second team.

➔ TEACHING POINTS

1. Players should use only the first pads on the fingers when dribbling.
2. They should keep the ball low and dribble rapidly.
3. Remind them not to watch the dribble.

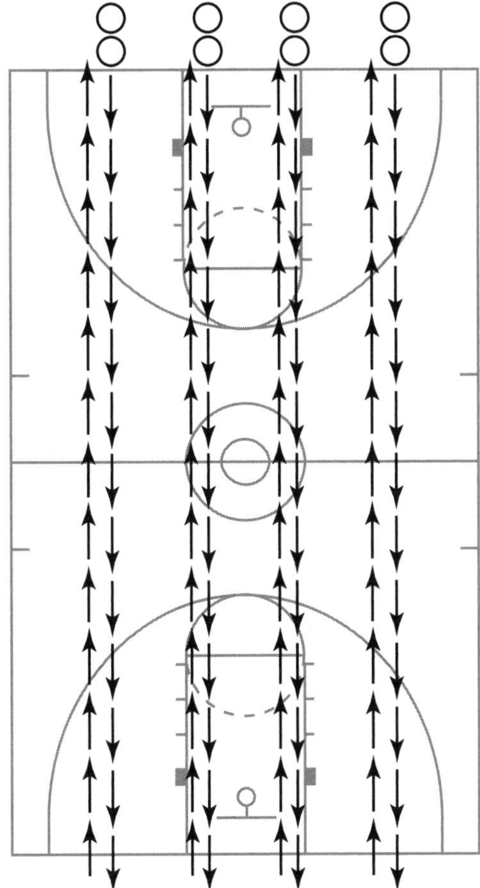

Related Drills *3, 18-34, 40-41, 76, 84, 97, 104-126*

21

SIDE-TO-SIDE DRIBBLE

Individual or team • 2 minutes

SKILL FOCUS Develop touch with a basketball

Beginner

1. If drilling as a team, players should be about 15 feet (4.5 m) apart.
2. Players dribble in front of the body from hand to hand without watching the dribble.
3. Players dribble behind the body from hand to hand without watching the dribble.

Intermediate

1. Players line up as in drill 20.
2. They walk down the floor dribbling the ball from side to side in front of the body.
3. They walk down the floor dribbling the ball from side to side behind the body.

Advanced

1. Players line up as in drill 20. The first line races down the floor in proper dribbling position, dribbling the basketball from side to side. On the first trip down the floor and back, the dribble should be about waist high (speed-dribbling position). On the second trip down the floor and back, the dribble should be low and quick (control-dribbling position).
2. Divide your squad into teams and turn the drill into a dribbling race. Race guards against post players, or first team against second team.

TEACHING POINTS

1. Players should dribble using only the first pads of the fingers.
2. The ball can be kept low and dribbled rapidly, as in a control dribble, or dribbled high as in a speed dribble.
3. Feet should be spread at least shoulder-width apart. Tell players to squat if this allows for a more rapid dribble.
4. Remind players not to watch the dribble.

Related Drills *3, 18-22, 24-34, 40-41, 76, 84, 97, 104-126*

SPIDER DRIBBLE

Individual or team • 30 seconds

SKILL FOCUS Develop touch with a basketball, hand–eye coordination, hand quickness (5)

Beginner

1. Players line up about 15 feet (4.5 m) apart, each player with a basketball.
2. In a semi-crouched position, they drop the ball directly below their crouch.
3. They begin with the right hand in front of the right knee, and the left hand behind the left knee.
4. They tap one dribble with the right hand and quickly move the right hand behind the right knee. Meanwhile, they bring the left hand in front of the left knee and tap the ball with the left hand. They move the left hand back behind the left knee. The right hand, which was behind the right knee, then taps the ball and begins to quickly move to the front of the right knee. Players continue this rapid hand movement for the length of the drill. With each movement of either hand from front to back, the ball is slightly tapped. This tapping should keep the dribble alive.

Option Instead of dropping the ball and keeping the dribble alive, players hold the ball with the right hand in front of the body and the left hand behind the body. The ball should be directly beneath the crouch. Players release the ball and move the right hand behind the body and the left hand in front of the body. They catch the ball without allowing it to bounce. They may toss the ball slightly in the air to make a better catch. Players continue this rapid hand movement throughout the drill.

TEACHING POINTS

1. Remind players to dribble using only the first pads on the fingers.
2. Players should keep the ball low and dribble rapidly.
3. Feet should be spread at least shoulder-width apart. Tell players to squat if this allows for a more rapid dribble.
4. They should not watch the dribble.
5. When drilling the option, players should be looking directly ahead.

Related Drills *3, 18-22, 24-34, 40-41, 76, 84, 97, 104-126*

23

SPEED DRIBBLE

Individual or team • 1 minute

SKILL FOCUS Touch with a basketball, speed-dribbling position (23), conditioning, front pivot (35), reverse pivot (36), jump stop (37), chest pass (44), bounce pass (44)

Beginner

1. Players line up as shown in the figure.
2. In speed-dribbling position, they dribble the length of the court as quickly as possible.
3. They reverse (or front) pivot at the far end of the court before returning with a speed dribble. They dribble down the floor with the right hand, then back with the left hand.
4. Players jump-stop about 15 feet (4.5 m) from the teammate next in line and pass to the teammate with a chest (or bounce) pass.
5. All players repeat the same sequence.

Options

1. Divide your squad into teams and turn the drill into a dribbling race. Race guards against post players, or first team against second team.
2. Tell players to take two trips down the floor and back, dribbling with the right hand on the first trip down and back, and with the left hand on the second trip.

Advanced

1. Players hold one ball in each hand. A variation is to alternate the dribbles while driving down the floor—bounce the left-hand ball while holding the right-hand ball, then bounce the right-hand ball when the other ball bounces back up to the left hand.
2. The other two-ball variation is for players to bounce both balls at the same height. Watch for each ball touching the left and right hand at the same time and bouncing at the same time.

➔ TEACHING POINTS

1. Proper speed-dribbling position requires being slightly flexed at the knee and the torso.
2. The ball should be bounced from 2 to 3 feet (.6-.9 m) in front of the right knee. The carom of the ball on each dribble should reach waist height.
3. Players should push the dribble out in front, keeping the ball away from their foot and knee to avoid turnovers.
4. Eyes should be straight ahead and not looking at the basketball.
5. Players should dribble with the first pads of the fingers.

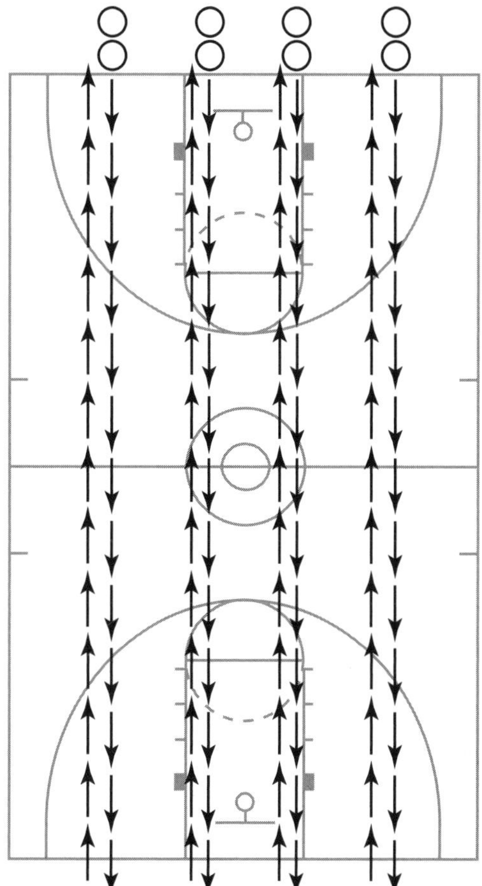

Related Drills *3, 18-22, 24-34, 40-41, 76, 84, 104-126*

24

CONTROL DRIBBLE

Individual or team • 1 minute

SKILL FOCUS Touch with a basketball, control-dribbling position, front pivot (35), reverse pivot (36), jump stop (37), chest pass (44), bounce pass (44), conditioning

Beginner

1. Players line up as shown in the figure.
2. They dribble the length of the court in the control-dribbling position, zigzagging a step or so off a straight line down the floor. They dribble down the floor with the right hand, and then back with the left hand.
3. Players reverse (or front) pivot at the far end of the court before returning with a control dribble, again zigzagging one step off a straight line down the floor.
4. Players jump-stop about 15 feet (4.5 m) from the teammate next in line and pass to the teammate with a chest (or bounce) pass.
5. All players repeat the sequence.

Options

1. Divide your squad into teams and turn the drill into a dribbling race. Race guards against post players, or first team against second team.
2. Players take two trips down the floor and back, dribbling with the right hand on the first trip down and back, and with the left hand on the second trip.

Advanced

1. Players hold one ball in each hand. They alternate dribbles while driving down the floor, first bouncing the left-hand ball while holding the right-hand ball, then bouncing the right-hand ball when the other ball bounces back up to the left hand.
2. Players hold one ball in each hand and bounce both at the same height. Each ball should touch the left and right hand at the same time and bounce at the same time.

TEACHING POINTS

1. Proper control-dribbling position requires players to be significantly flexed at the knee and torso. Speed is not the issue but rather quickness and protection of the ball. The off arm should be bent 90 degrees at the elbow and parallel to the floor.
2. The ball should be 2 to 3 feet (.6-.9 m) away from but beside the knee. As if playing against an opponent, players should keep the body between the ball and the defender.

3. Players should keep the ball to the side and under control, away from the foot and knee to avoid turnovers.
4. Eyes should be straight ahead, not looking at the basketball.
5. Players should dribble with the first pads of the fingers.

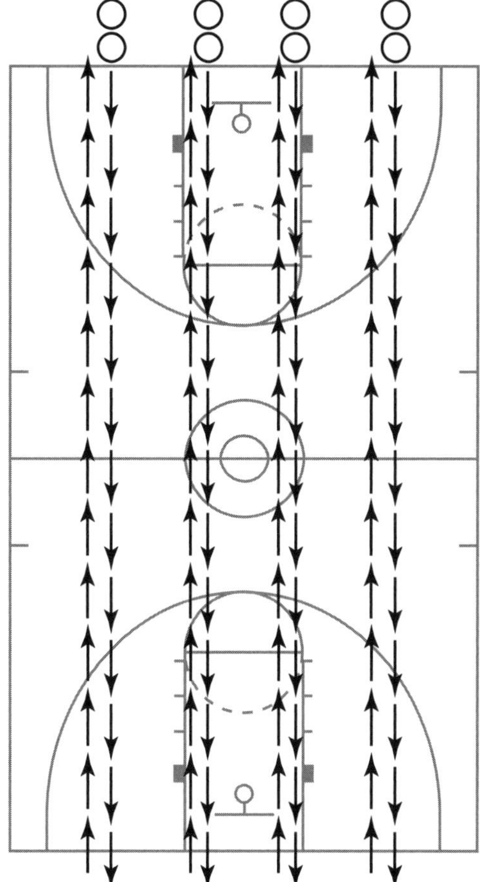

Related Drills *3, 18-22, 25-34, 40-41, 76, 84, 97, 104-126*

25

CHANGE OF PACE

Individual or team • 1 minute

SKILL FOCUS Develop touch with a basketball, change-of-pace dribbling move, conditioning, front pivot (35), reverse pivot (36), jump stop (37), chest pass (44), bounce pass (44)

Beginner

1. Players line up as shown in the figure.
2. They walk down the court with a fast dribble, then slow the dribble down, then go fast, and then slow down. You might even tell them to add a few medium-speed dribbles to change the pace. Players dribble down the floor with the right hand, and then back with the left hand.
3. Players reverse (or front) pivot at the far end of the court before returning, using a change of pace with every second or third dribble.
4. Players jump-stop about 15 feet (4.5 m) from the teammate next in line and pass to the teammate with a chest (or bounce) pass.
5. All players repeat the sequence.

Options

1. Divide your squad into teams and turn the drill into a dribbling race. Race guards against post players, or first team against second team.
2. Have players take two trips down the floor and back, dribbling with the right hand on the first trip down and back, and with the left hand on the second trip.

Advanced

1. Players hold one ball in each hand. They alternate dribbles while driving down the floor—bounce the left-hand ball while holding the right-hand ball, then bounce the right-hand ball when the other ball bounces back up to the left hand.
2. Players hold one ball in each hand and bounce both at the same height. Each ball touches the left and right hand at the same time and bounces at the same time.

TEACHING POINTS

1. Protection of the ball is a premium, but faking to get away from a defender is also a consideration. Thus players should assume a control-dribble body position—unless they are trying to clear the backcourt, in which case they should assume the speed-dribbling body position.
2. The ball should be 2 to 3 feet (.6-.9 m) away from but beside the knee. As if playing against an opponent, players keep the body between the ball and the defender.

3. Watch for players keeping the ball to their sides and under control, away from the foot and knee to avoid turnovers.
4. Eyes should be straight ahead, not looking at the basketball.
5. Players should train their feet to move quickly, stop on a dime, then move moderately quickly, then very quickly, and so on. This is called change of pace.
6. Players dribble with the first pads of the fingers.

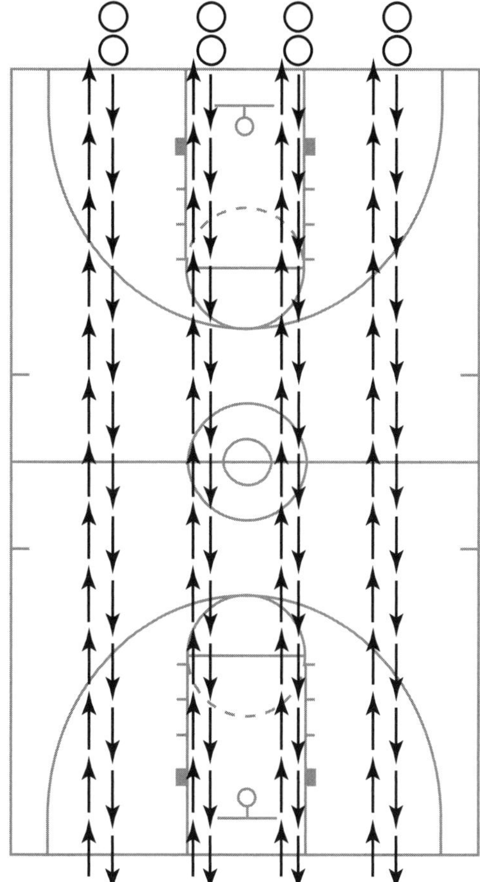

Related Drills *3, 18-22, 24, 26-34, 40-41, 76, 84, 97, 104-126*

26

HESITATION DRIBBLE

Individual or team • 1 minute

SKILL FOCUS Develop touch with a basketball, hesitation dribbling move, front pivot (35), reverse pivot (36), jump stop (37), chest pass (44), bounce pass (44), conditioning

Intermediate

1. Players line up as shown in the figure.
2. They dribble slowly down the floor a few dribbles, then stop, and then explode with a quick, hard dribble. This is the hesitation move. After exploding hard, the player stops, and then explodes again. Players throw the head and shoulders back when coming to a stop before exploding again. This technique freezes the defender before the next explosive dribble.
3. Players reverse (or front) pivot at the far end of the court, and then return to the other side of the court, using a hesitation move with every third or fourth dribble. They dribble down the floor with the right hand, and then back with the left hand.
4. Players jump-stop about 15 feet (4.5 m) from the teammate next in line and pass to the teammate with a chest (or bounce) pass.
5. All players repeat the sequence.

Options

1. Divide your squad into teams and turn the drill into a dribbling race. Race guards against post players, or first team against second team.
2. Players take two trips down the floor and back, dribbling with the right hand on the first trip down and back, and with the left hand on the second trip.

Advanced

1. Players hold one ball in each hand. They alternate dribbles while driving down the floor, bouncing the left-hand ball while holding the right-hand ball, then bouncing the right-hand ball when the other ball bounces back up to the left hand.
2. Players hold one ball in each hand and bounce both at the same height. Each ball touches the left and right hand at the same time and bounces at the same time.

TEACHING POINTS

1. Protection of the ball is a premium, but faking to get away from a defender is also a consideration. Thus players should assume the control-dribble body position—unless they are trying to clear the backcourt, in which case they assume the speed-dribbling position.

2. The ball should be 2 to 3 feet (.6-.9 m) away from but beside the knee. As if playing against an opponent, players keep the body between the ball and the defender.
3. Tell players to keep the ball to the side and under control, away from the foot and knee to avoid turnovers.
4. Eyes should be straight ahead, not looking at the basketball.
5. Train your players to move their feet quickly, stop on a dime, and then explode by the defender.
6. Players dribble with the first pads of the fingers.

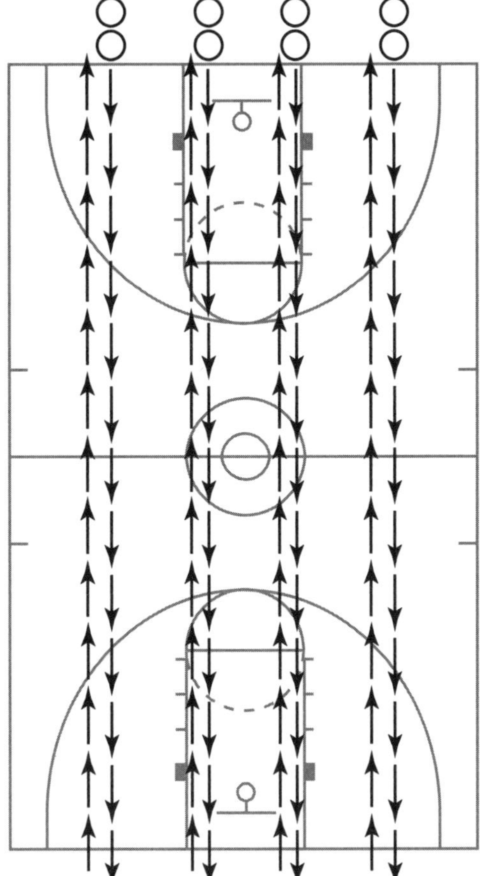

Related Drills *3, 18-22, 24-25, 27-34, 40-41, 76, 84, 97, 104-126*

27

RETREATING DRIBBLE

Individual or team • 1 minute

SKILL FOCUS Develop touch with a basketball, retreat-dribble move, front pivot (35), reverse pivot (36), jump stop (37), chest pass (44), bounce pass (44), slide-step dribble (97), conditioning

Intermediate

1. Players line up as shown in the figure.
2. They dribble slowly, then stop, and then dribble backward a few steps before circling a step or two and going down the floor at another angle. Too often, players pick up the basketball after dribbling into double teams or traps. The retreat-dribble move can prevent this. Instead of picking up the basketball, the player backtracks a few steps and then speeds off in another direction, hoping to leave the trapping defenders behind.
3. Players dribble 15 feet (4.5 m) or so, retreat, then go up the floor at a 45-degree angle, retreat again, then go in the opposite direction at a 45-degree angle, dribbling with the opposite hand, until they reach the far end of the court. They begin dribbling down the floor with the right hand, and then back with the left hand.
4. Players reverse (or front) pivot at the far end of the court before returning, using a retreat dribble with every third or fourth dribble.
5. Players jump-stop about 15 feet (4.5 m) from the teammate next in line and pass to the teammate with a chest (or bounce) pass.
6. All players repeat the sequence.

Option Divide your squad into teams and turn the drill into a dribbling race. Race guards against post players, or first team against second team.

Advanced

1. Players hold one ball in each hand, alternating dribbles while driving down the floor; they bounce the left-hand ball while holding the right-hand ball, and then bounce the right-hand ball when the other ball bounces back up to the left hand.
2. Players hold one ball in each hand and bounce both at the same height. Each ball touches the left and right hand at the same time and bounces at the same time.

TEACHING POINTS

1. Protection of the ball is a premium, but players must understand how to use the retreat dribble or they will constantly be dribbling into trouble.
2. The ball should be 2 to 3 feet (.6-.9 m) away from but beside the knee. As if playing against an opponent, players keep the body between the ball and the defender.

3. Tell players to keep the ball to the side and under control, away from the foot and knee to avoid turnovers.
4. When retreating, players use a slide-step dribble, keeping eyes down the floor. After a few retreat-slide steps, they come out of the control stance and move to a speed stance to explode away from defenders. When using the slide step backward, players should never turn their back on defenders. They should try to time the explosive forward move with the moment defenders rise up out of their low, trapping stance. Dribblers may also use head and shoulder fakes to make defenders think they are going to split them or go in the opposite direction.
5. Eyes should be straight ahead, not looking at the basketball.
6. Train your players to move their feet quickly, stop on a dime, and then explode by the defender.
7. Players dribble with the first pads of the fingers.

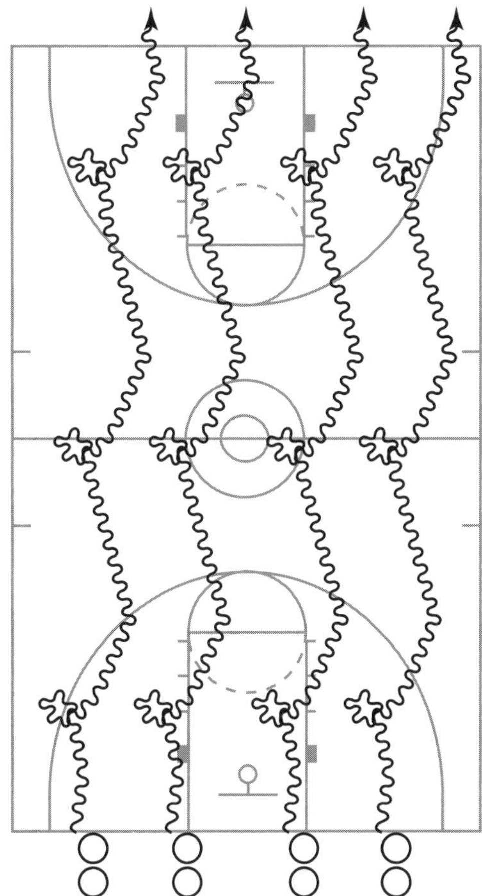

Related Drills *3, 18-22, 24-26, 28-34, 40-41, 76, 84, 97, 104-126*

28

IN-AND-OUT DRIBBLE MANEUVER

Individual or team • 1 minute

SKILL FOCUS Develop touch with a basketball, in-and-out dribbling move (one of the four basic perimeter dribbling moves—12), conditioning, front pivot (35), reverse pivot (36), jump stop (37), chest pass (44), bounce pass (44), slide-step dribble (97)

Intermediate

1. Players line up as shown in the figure.
2. As shown, use tape to mark boxes 2 feet by 2 feet (.6 by .6 m) at the mid-court line and about 20 feet (6 m) from each baseline.
3. Players dribble down the court, stopping at the boxes and performing the in-and-out basic dribbling fake.
4. Players reverse (or front) pivot at the far end of the court before returning, using the in-and-out dribbling fake at each box.
5. Players jump-stop about 10 feet (3 m) from the teammate next in line and pass to the teammate with a chest (or bounce) pass.
6. All players repeat the sequence.
7. Players dribble down the floor using the right hand, and dribble back with the right hand. This helps them learn the move going into the center of the court as well as out to the sideline. They should go down and back right-handed, and then down and back left-handed, before passing the ball to a teammate.

Option Divide your squad into teams and turn the drill into a dribbling race. Race guards against post players, or first team against second team.

Advanced

1. Players hold one ball in each hand, alternating dribbles while driving down the floor; they bounce the left-hand ball while holding the right-hand ball, and then bounce the right-hand ball when the other ball bounces back up to the left hand.
2. Players hold one ball in each hand and bounce both at the same height. Each ball touches the left and right hand at the same time and bounces at the same time.

TEACHING POINTS

1. Protection of the ball is a premium, but players must understand how to use the in-and-out move.
2. The ball should be 2 to 3 feet (.6-.9 m) away from but beside the knee. Players keep the body between the ball and the defender. They use the slide-step dribble, or they partially face the defender, using excessive head and shoulder fakes. No matter what, defenders must be kept on their heels.

3. Tell players to keep the ball to the side and under control, away from the foot and knee to avoid turnovers. Instead of keeping the ball on the side, they may fake a crossover dribble, using only one hand. To do this, they bring the dribble in front of the body with hand on top of the ball, dribbling with a semi-high bounce. When the ball is out in front of the body, pull it back to its original spot by cupping the side of the ball.
4. When performing the in-and-out dribbling move, the player must keep eyes on the downcourt area and avoid looking at the ball or the move. After the step in (using head and shoulder fakes as well), the player wants to explode on the step out. The step out should be in an almost straight line down the floor, which should allow the player to leave the defender behind. The player continues down the floor with a hard speed dribble for a step or two. This simulates blowing by the defender. Before going into the second box, the player returns to a control-dribbling stance.
5. Train your players to move their feet quickly, stop on a dime, and then explode by the defender.
6. Players dribble with the first pads of the fingers.

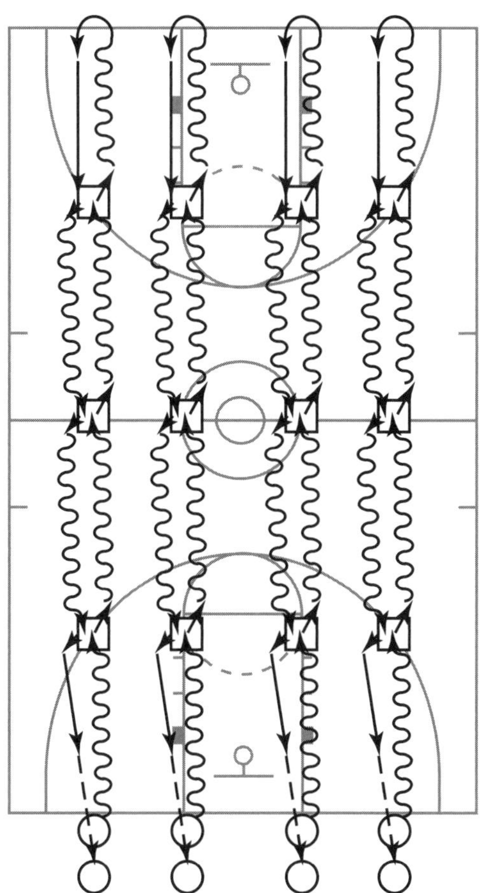

Related Drills *3, 12, 18-22, 24-27, 29-34, 40-41, 76, 84, 97, 104-126*

29

CROSSOVER DRIBBLE MANEUVER

Individual or team • 1 minute

SKILL FOCUS Develop touch with a basketball, crossover dribbling move (one of the four basic perimeter dribbling moves: 13), conditioning, front pivot (35), reverse pivot (36), jump stop (37), chest pass (44), bounce pass (44), slide-step dribble (97)

Intermediate

1. Players line up as shown in the figure.
2. As shown, use tape to mark boxes 2 feet by 2 feet (.6 by .6 m) at the mid-court line and about 20 feet (6 m) from each baseline.
3. Players dribble down the court, stopping at the boxes and performing the crossover basic fake.
4. Players reverse (or front) pivot at the far end of the court before returning, using the crossover basic dribbling move at each box.
5. Players jump-stop about 10 feet (3 m) from the teammate next in line and pass to the teammate with a chest (or bounce) pass.
6. All players repeat the sequence.
7. Players dribble down the floor using the right hand, and dribble back with the right hand. This helps them learn the move going into the center of the court as well as out to the sideline. They go down and back right-handed, then down and back left-handed, before passing the ball to a teammate.

Option Divide your squad into teams and turn the drill into a dribbling race. Race guards against post players, or first team against second team.

Advanced

1. Players hold one ball in each hand, alternating dribbles while driving down the floor; they bounce the left-hand ball while holding the right-hand ball, and then bounce the right-hand ball when the other ball bounces back up to the left hand.
2. Players hold one ball in each hand and bounce both at the same height. Each ball touches the left and right hand at the same time and bounces at the same time.

TEACHING POINTS

1. Protection of the ball is a premium, but players must be able to execute the crossover move.
2. Players keep the ball 2 to 3 feet (.6-.9 m) away from and in front of the knee, using excessive head and shoulder fakes. Or they protect the ball with the body, using slide steps. No matter what, defenders must be kept on their heels.

3. Tell players to keep the ball to the side and under control, away from the foot and knee to avoid turnovers. As they cross the ball over in front of the body, the ball is in its least protected position. So they should keep their dribble low (no higher than the middle of the lower legs) and quick. Once the ball has crossed over to the opposite hand (left), they bring the right foot forward and beside the defender's right foot. They then speed dribble, straight or even veering to the right, and explode to the basket.
4. When executing the move, the dribbler keeps eyes on the downcourt area and does not look at the ball or the move. After completing the crossover (using head and shoulder fakes as well), the dribbler explodes when touching the ball with the left hand. The dribbler's right side should be close to the ball to protect it. The explosion should be in an almost straight line down the floor, allowing the dribbler to leave the defender behind. The dribbler continues down the floor with a hard speed dribble for a step or two. Before entering the second box, the dribbler returns to control dribbling.
5. Train your players to move their feet quickly, stop on a dime, and then explode by their defender.
6. Always dribble with the first pads of the fingers.

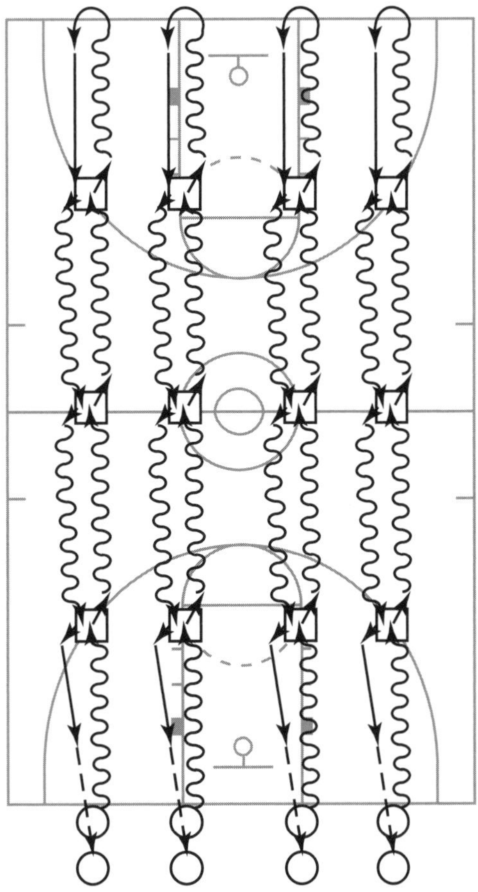

Related Drills *3, 13, 18-22, 24-28, 30-34, 40-41, 76, 84, 97, 104-126*

30

SPIN (REVERSE) DRIBBLE MANEUVER

Individual or team • 1 minute

SKILL FOCUS Develop touch with a basketball, spin (reverse) dribbling move (one of the four basic perimeter dribbling moves: 14), front pivot (35), reverse pivot (36), jump stop (37), chest pass (44), bounce pass (44), slide-step dribble (97), conditioning

Intermediate

1. Players line up as shown in the figure.
2. Use tape to mark 2-feet-by-2-feet (.6 by .6 m) boxes at the midcourt line and about 20 feet (6 m) from each baseline.
3. Players dribble down the court, stopping at the boxes and executing the spin (reverse) fake.
4. Players reverse (or front) pivot at the far end of the court before returning, using the spin (reverse) dribbling move at each box.
5. Players jump-stop about 10 feet (3 m) from the teammate next in line and pass to the teammate with a chest (or bounce) pass.
6. All players repeat the sequence.
7. Players dribble down the floor using the right hand, and dribble back with the right hand. This helps them learn the move going into the center of the court as well as out to the sideline. They go down and back right-handed, and then down and back left-handed, before passing the ball to a teammate.

Option Divide your squad into teams and turn the drill into a dribbling race. Race guards against post players, or first team against second team.

Advanced

1. Players hold a ball in each hand. They alternate dribbles while driving down the floor: they bounce the left-hand ball while holding the right-hand ball; then they bounce the right-hand ball when the other ball bounces back up to the left hand.
2. Players hold one ball in each hand and bounce both at the same height. Each ball touches the left and right hand at the same time and bounces at the same time.

TEACHING POINTS

1. Protection of the ball is a premium, but all players must be able to execute the spin (reverse) move.
2. Players should keep the ball 2 to 3 feet (.6-.9 m) away from and in front of the knee, using excessive head and shoulder fakes. Or they can protect the ball with the body, using slide steps. No matter what, defenders must be kept on their heels.

3. Tell players to keep the ball to the side and under control, away from the foot and knee to avoid turnovers. As they spin, they control the ball with the right hand until the spin is complete. Then they switch the ball to the left hand. If they switch too soon, they leave the ball out where a defender can step through and steal it.
4. As the move is executed, eyes stay on the downcourt area, not on the ball or the move. After spinning, the player explodes when ball touches the left hand. The right side should be close to the ball, protecting it. This explosion should be in an almost straight line down the floor, allowing the player to leave the defender behind. The dribbler continues down the floor with a hard speed dribble for a step or two. Before entering the second box, the dribbler returns to a control dribble.
5. Train your players to move their feet quickly, stop abruptly, and then explode by their defender.
6. Always dribble with the first pads of the fingers.

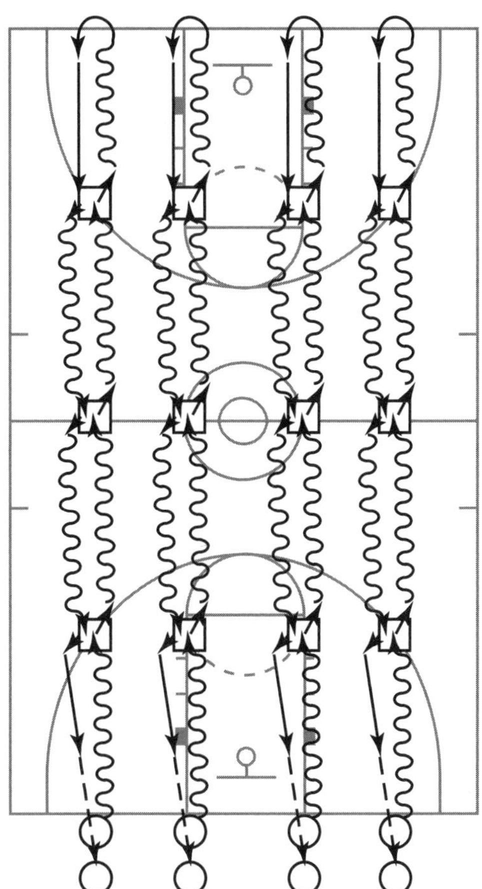

Related Drills *3, 14, 18-22, 24-29, 31-34, 40-41, 76, 84, 97, 104-126*

31

HALF-SPIN DRIBBLE MANEUVER

Individual or team • 1 minute

SKILL FOCUS Develop touch with a basketball, half-spin dribbling move (one of the four basic perimeter dribbling moves: 15), front pivot (35), reverse pivot (36), jump stop (37), chest pass (44), bounce pass (44), slide-step dribble (97), conditioning

Intermediate

1. Players line up as shown in the figure.
2. Use tape to mark 2-feet-by-2-feet (.6 by .6 m) boxes at the midcourt line and about 20 feet (6 m) from each baseline.
3. Players dribble down the court, stopping at the boxes and executing the half-spin fake.
4. Players reverse (or front) pivot at the far end of the court before returning, using the half-spin dribbling move at each box.
5. Players jump-stop about 10 feet (3 m) from the teammate next in line and pass to the teammate with a chest (or bounce) pass.
6. All players repeat the sequence.
7. Players dribble down the floor using the right hand, and dribble back with the right hand. This helps them learn the move going into the center of the court as well as out to the sideline. They go down and back right-handed, then down and back left-handed, before passing the ball to a teammate.

Option Divide your squad into teams and turn the drill into a dribbling race. Race guards against post players, or first team against second team.

Advanced

1. Players hold one ball in each hand, alternating dribbles while driving down the floor. They bounce the left-hand ball while holding the right-hand ball, then bounce the right-hand ball when the other ball bounces back up to their left hand.
2. Players hold one ball in each hand and bounce both at the same height. Each ball touches the left and right hand at the same time and bounces at the same time.

TEACHING POINTS

1. Protection of the ball is a premium, but all players must learn to use the half-spin move.
2. Players keep the ball 2 to 3 feet (.6-.9 m) away from and in front of the knee, using excessive head and shoulder fakes. Or they may protect the ball with the body, using slide steps. No matter what, defenders must be kept on their heels.

3. Tell players to keep the ball to the side and under control, away from the foot and knee to avoid turnovers. As they spin, they should control the ball with the right hand until the half-spin is complete by leaving the right hand cupped over the top of the ball. Just as they plant the right foot and raise the left foot, they move their hand beside the ball instead of on top of it. They then push the dribble back in the same direction they came from.
4. As players execute the move, they keep their eyes downcourt, not on the ball or the move. After the half-spin (using head and shoulder fakes as well), they explode back in their original direction. Their left side should be close to the ball, protecting it. The explosive move should be in an almost straight line down the floor, leaving the defender behind. They continue down the floor with a hard speed dribble for a step or two before entering the second box and returning to a control dribble.
5. Train players to move their feet quickly, stop abruptly, and then explode by the defender.
6. Always dribble with the first pads of the fingers.

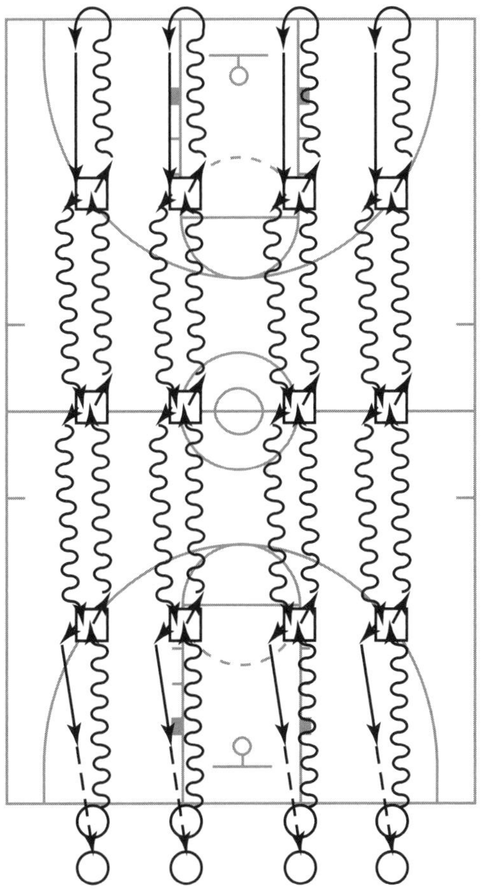

Related Drills *3, 15, 18-22, 24-30, 32-34, 40-41, 76, 84, 97, 104-126*

32

FUN CONE DRIBBLING DRILL

Individual or team • 2 minutes

SKILL FOCUS Develop touch with a basketball, in-and-out move (12, 28), crossover move (13, 29), spin (reverse) move (14, 30), half-spin move (15, 31), speed dribble (23), control dribble (24), hesitation dribble (26), retreating dribble (27), conditioning, body balance, agility, change of pace (25)

Beginner

1. Place cones around the court in a haphazard arrangement (see figure).
2. Using one ball, players dribble down the court following the cones.
3. Call out different moves for players to do at each cone, or have them use the same move throughout the cone maze.
4. A second player may begin dribbling when the first player passes the first cone.
5. Instead of using a move to go around a cone, you can have players circle the cone before moving to the next cone. This is especially fun when dividing the squad and making a race out of it.

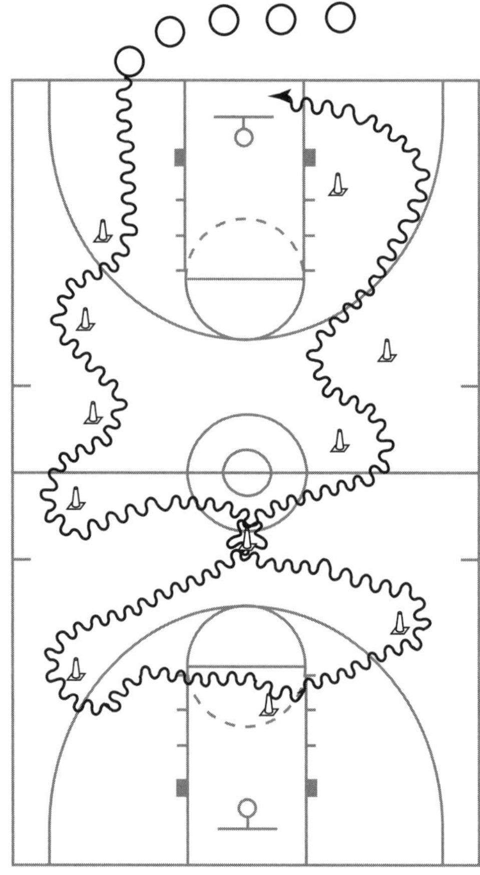

Intermediate

Let players use two balls instead of one.

Options (all skill levels)

1. Divide players into post players against guards, create two equal cone mazes, and have a race.
2. Divide players into first team against second team, create two equal cone mazes, and have a race.

Related Drills *3, 11-15, 18-31, 33-34, 40-41, 76, 84, 97, 104-126*

DRIBBLE TAG

Individual or team • 1 minute

SKILL FOCUS Develop touch with a basketball, quick hands (5), quick feet (6), aggressive nature, defensive in-and-out fakes (33)

Beginner

1. Players line up as shown in the figure, with two players in each circle. Other teammates wait their turns outside the circle.
2. Each player has a basketball. Players try to slap the other's basketball out of the circle. Any fake may be used, including forsaking the ball to slap away the opponent's ball.
3. When one player wins, two more players enter the circle.

Intermediate

1. Both players use two basketballs and must keep both alive. Both balls must be slapped out of the circle before a player is declared a winner. If a player has one of the balls slapped away, the player continues with the remaining one ball until it too is slapped away.
2. King of the Circle: Only one player moves into the circle to play the winner of the previous round. In this variation it is best to put post players on one circle and guards on another circle.

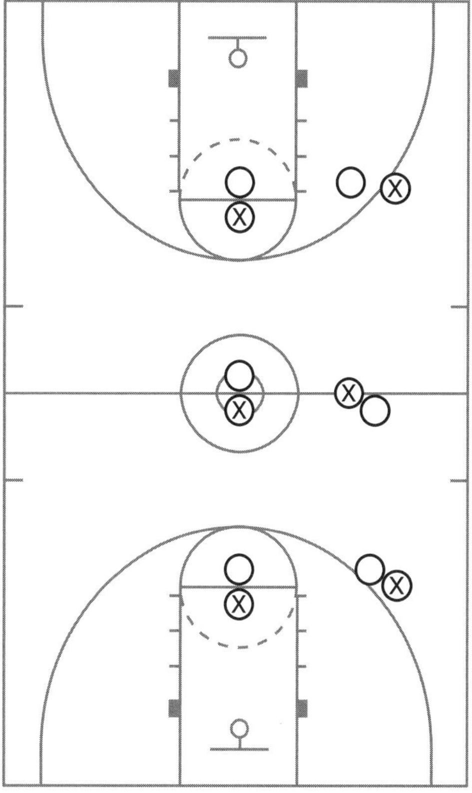

TEACHING POINTS

1. Remind players to keep all eyes up.
2. Players should dribble with the front joints of the dribbling hand.
3. Players use in-and-out defensive fakes to strike at their opponent's ball. They should try to time their opponent's dribble. When the ball leaves the opponent's hand, they dart in and strike at the ball, then quickly pull back to original position. Tell players to imagine they are striking like snakes.

Related Drills *3, 11-15, 18-32, 34, 40-41, 76, 84, 97, 104-126, 137*

34

TEAM DRIBBLE TAG

Individual or team • 1 minute

SKILL FOCUS Develop touch with a basketball, quick footwork while handling a basketball, quick hands (5), peripheral vision, agility, conditioning, balance

Beginner

1. Line players up with instructions to stay within a predetermined space. In the figure that space is bordered by the half-court line, sidelines, and baseline.
2. All players begin dribbling one basketball.
3. Designate one player as It. This player must tag another player, who then becomes It.

Options

1. The player who is It dribbles only one basketball, but the other players must dribble two. When the player who is It tags another player, that player gives up one of his two basketballs to the tagging player, and becomes the It player.
2. The It player dribbles only one basketball, but the other players must dribble two. When It tags a player, that player is out of the game and goes to the other end of the court to practice shooting.
3. Divide your squad into two teams. (All players dribble either one basketball or two.) Those on team A try to tag all members of team B. Teammates may double team to get the tag. When all members of team B have been tagged, the game is half over. The coach times how long it takes to get all members of team B tagged. Now team B tries to tag all members of team A. The team that tags out the opposite team in the least amount of time wins.
4. The It player dribbles two basketballs, and all other players dribble only one basketball.

➲ TEACHING POINTS

1. Remind players to keep eyes up when dribbling.
2. Players should dribble using only the first joints of the fingers.
3. All players must remain in a control-dribbling stance or a speed-dribbling stance, but not both.

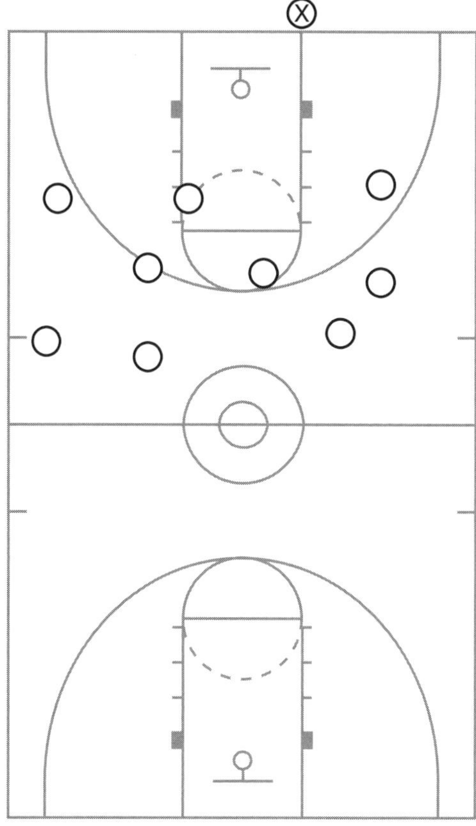

Related Drills *3, 11-15, 18-33, 40-41, 76, 84, 97, 104-126*

CHAPTER

4

Stopping and Pivoting

Pivoting is a basic skill all basketball players must have. Your players use pivots to escape defenders, pass to teammates, and execute spin moves and half-spins. Players also pivot in order to screen or block an opponent off the offensive board.

The ability to stop abruptly, under control, is also a must for a great one-on-one player. At the end of a dribble, a shot is often the best option, but players can't free themselves for a shot if they don't know how to stop on a dime and jump straight up into the air. There are also times when players receive a pass and want to have two pivot feet. Whether they can execute their stop abruptly often determines their effectiveness in such situations.

Front pivots and reverse pivots are the two types of pivots used in basketball. Front pivoting (drill 35) keeps players closer to the basket, and reverse pivoting (drill 36) allows players to watch their assignments longer and better protect the ball.

Jump stopping (drill 37) gives players two pivot feet when they need them. Stride stopping (drill 38) enables players to dribble quickly, stop abruptly, and jump shoot all in one motion, making it difficult for defenders to prevent the shot.

Protection of the basketball from double-teaming is covered in drill 39. In drill 40 players begin the multiple applications of fundamentals they have learned, requiring them to dribble, stop, and pivot all in the same possession. Drill 41 carries this multiple strategy one step further, adding passing to dribbling, stopping, and pivoting.

Drill 42 adds shooting to dribbling, stopping, and pivoting. Drill 43 presents individual offensive moves and cutting maneuvers.

35

FRONT PIVOT

Individual or team • 2 minutes

SKILL FOCUS Triple-threat position (9), in and out (12, 28), crossover (13, 29), spin (14, 30), half-spin (15, 31), speed dribble (23), control dribble (24), front pivot, jump stop (37), stride stop (38), chest pass (44), bounce pass (44), overhead pass (44), balance, quickness, agility

Beginner

1. Players line up as shown in figure 1.
2. The first player in line dribbles (control or speed dribbling) to the endline, executes a jump stop (or stride stop) and front pivot, and then passes to the second player in line. The pass may be a chest pass, bounce pass, or overhead pass.
3. All players repeat the sequence.

Intermediate

Each player executes a controlled dribble anywhere on the court. When the coach says "front pivot," each player jump-stops and executes the front pivot. On "go," players start dribbling again. Or players may execute dribbling moves, such as the spin dribble, while waiting for the command to front pivot.

TEACHING POINTS

1. See figure 2 for the steps involved in front pivoting.
2. To begin the front pivot, players come to a stop and establish their left foot as their pivot foot.
3. At the end of the stop, just before pivoting, they bring the ball to position just under their chin, holding the ball with both hands (with finger pads, not palms). This is the triple-threat position (chapter 2, drill 9).

4. Players pick up their right foot and pivot 180 degrees by bringing their right foot between themselves and their defender.
5. The front pivot has several advantages: It lets players stay closer to the basket at the end of a scoring fake. It allows defensive rebounders to watch their assignment longer (to be used against a quicker opponent, or if players are on the perimeter trying to block out). It also gives players a longer time to view the defensive tactics of their defenders.

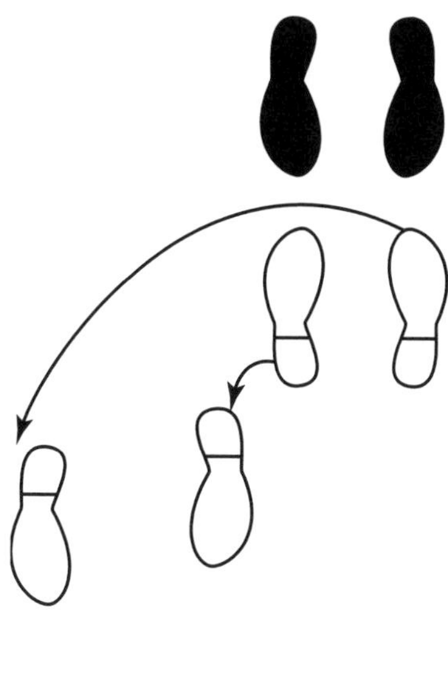

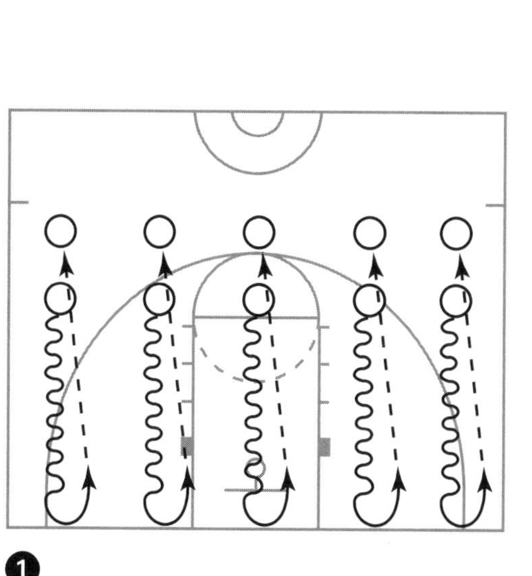

❶

❷ The front pivot.

Related Drills *1, 9-10, 23-34, 37-41, 52, 73, 78, 96, 103, 105-127*

36

REVERSE PIVOT

Individual or team • 2 minutes

SKILL FOCUS Triple-threat position (9), in and out (12, 28), crossover (13, 29), spin (14, 30), half-spin (15, 31), speed dribble (23), control dribble (24), reverse pivot, jump stop (37), stride stop (38), chest pass (44), bounce pass (44), overhead pass (44), balance, quickness, agility

Beginner

1. Players line up as shown in figure 1.
2. The first player in line dribbles (control or speed dribble) to the endline, jump-stops (or stride-stops), and then reverse pivots before passing to the second player in line. The pass may be a chest pass, bounce pass, or overhead pass.
3. All players repeat the sequence.

Intermediate

Each player executes a controlled dribble anywhere on the court. When the coach says "reverse pivot," each player jump-stops and executes the reverse pivot. On "go," players start dribbling again. Or players may execute dribbling moves, such as the spin dribble, while waiting for the command to reverse pivot.

TEACHING POINTS

1. See figure 2 for the steps involved in reverse pivoting.
2. To begin the reverse pivot, players come to a stop and establish their left foot as their pivot foot.
3. At the end of the stop, just before the pivot, they bring the ball to position just under the chin and hold it there with both hands (no palms). This is the triple-threat stance.
4. Players pick up the right foot and pivot 180 degrees by swinging the right foot away from the defender.

5. The reverse pivot has several advantages: It allows players to move away from the basket at the end of a scoring fake. It allows a defensive rebounder to watch the flight of the ball longer (used against a slower opponent, or when near the basket trying to block out). It gives a longer time to view the cuts and moves of teammates. It is necessary for the screen and roll (because a front pivot allows defenders to get back to position to stop the screen and roll).
6. Ordinarily, the reverse pivot moves players farther away from their defender.

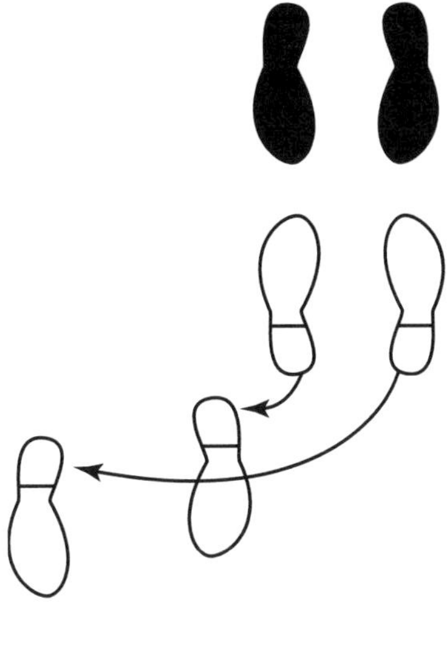

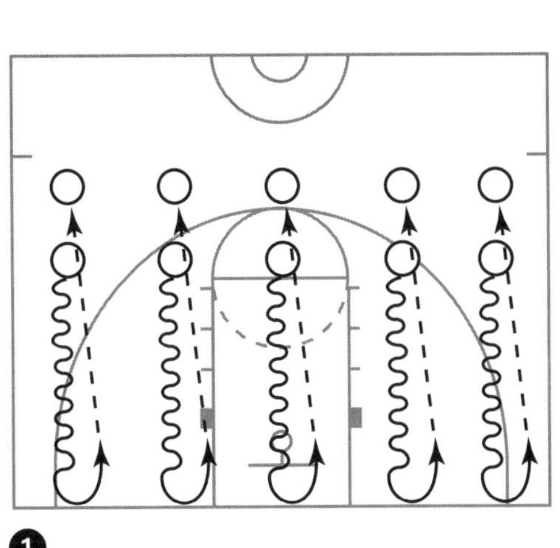

❶

❷ The reverse pivot.

Related Drills *1, 9-10, 23-34, 37-41, 52, 73, 78, 96, 103, 105-127*

37

JUMP STOP

Individual or team • 1 minute

SKILL FOCUS Agility, balance, conditioning, dribbling moves (in and out, crossover, spin, half-spin: 12-15, 28-31), front pivot (35), reverse pivot (36), jump stop

Beginner

1. Players line up on the baseline as shown in the figure.
2. They begin running downcourt at half-speed.
3. When a coach says "jump stop," players execute the jump stop.
4. On "go," players sprint again. A coach may give these commands at different locations on the court from day to day.
5. The coach gets in front of players and backpedals before turning and sprinting a step toward the racing team. Because much of basketball relates to players seeing and reacting, the coach here gives a visual command for the jump stop instead of a voice command.

Option If players have trouble jump-stopping, have them sprint toward the coach and jump-stop. The coach carefully observes their technique and corrects it.

Intermediate

Give each player a ball and tell the player which dribbling move to execute. At the end of the dribbling move, the player jump-stops. Lines on the court can serve as points at which the player executes the move followed by the jump stop. The player then dribbles to the next line to execute the move followed by a jump stop.

Advanced

1. As in the intermediate procedure, players execute a designated dribbling move and then a jump stop. But now players also pivot. They then dribble back to start position and execute a dribbling move, a jump stop, and a pivot (reverse or front). Players repeat the sequence, each time moving farther down the floor; first they do a move at the free-throw line extended, then at the half-court line, then at the far free-throw line extended, and finally at the far endline.
2. Same as 1, but players alternate dribbling moves between in and out, crossover, spin, and half-spin. They also alternate front and reverse pivots.

➲ TEACHING POINTS

1. The greater the speed before the jump stop is attempted, the lower the body's center of gravity must be. To lower the center of gravity, players lower their buttocks as though beginning to sit in a chair.
2. Players leap off both feet and land on both feet. This leap should not be a high jump but rather as low to the floor as possible. The buttocks may even touch the backs of the legs as the landing is completed.
3. The back should be straight, maybe bent slightly forward. The torso should be bent at the waist. The greater the speed, the more the bend.
4. Knees should be bent between 90 and 180 degrees.
5. When the stop is completed, players may move either foot to establish the pivot foot.
6. The jump stop is advantageous because it gives players two pivot feet—they can pivot in any direction without traveling.

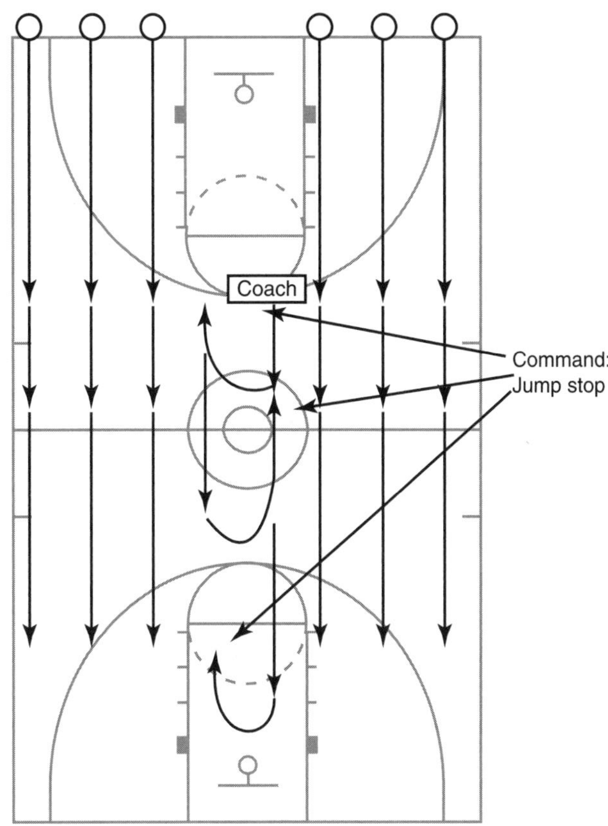

Related Drills *1, 9-10, 23-34, 52, 71, 91, 96, 104-126*

38

STRIDE STOP (ONE-TWO)

Individual or team • 1 minute

SKILL FOCUS Agility, balance, conditioning, dribbling moves (in and out, crossover, spin, half-spin: 12-15, 28-31), front pivot (35), reverse pivot (36), stride stop

Beginner

1. Players line up on the baseline as shown in the figure.
2. They run downcourt at half-speed.
3. When a coach says "stride stop," players execute the stride stop.
4. On "go," players sprint again. The coach may give these commands at different locations on the court from day to day.
5. The coach gets in front of players and backpedals before turning and sprinting a step toward the racing team. Because much of basketball involves players' ability to see and react, the coach here gives a visual command for the stride stop instead of a voice command.

Option If players have trouble stride stopping, have them sprint toward the coach and stride stop. The coach observes their technique and corrects it.

Intermediate

Give each player a ball and tell players which dribbling move to execute. At the end of the dribbling move, the player stride-stops. Lines on the court serve as points at which the player executes the move, followed by the stride stop. The player then dribbles to the next line to execute the move and the stop.

Advanced

1. As in the intermediate procedure, players execute a designated dribbling move and then a stride stop. But now the player also pivots. The player then dribbles back to start position while executing a dribbling move, a stride stop, and a pivot (reverse or front). The player repeats the sequence, each time moving farther down the floor; first the player does a move at the free-throw line extended, then at the half-court line, then at the far free-throw line extended, and then at the far endline.
2. Same as in 1, but players alternate dribbling moves using the in and out, crossover, spin, and half-spin. They also alternate front and reverse pivots.

TEACHING POINTS

1. The greater the speed before the stride stop is attempted, the lower the body's center of gravity must be. To lower the center of gravity, players lower their buttocks as though beginning to sit in a chair. However, if players are stride-stopping to prepare for a jump shot, they may begin to slow down slightly before the stride stop. Players will know this spot, but defenders will not.

2. Players sprint to the spot where they know they will use the stride stop. Then they place their left foot down, heel to toe. They swing the right foot forward and land on the toe. The left foot is the pivot foot. The player has stopped in a one-two step fashion.
3. The back should be straight, maybe bent slightly forward. The torso should be bent at the waist. The greater the speed, the more the bend.
4. The knees should be bent at least 90 degrees but never more than 150 degrees. The player should now be on the toes of both feet, ready to spring into the air for a jump shot.
5. When the stop is completed, the player must not move the left foot.
6. The stride stop allows shooters a quicker shot. Shooters use this stop to shoot a jump shot under pressure from a defender.

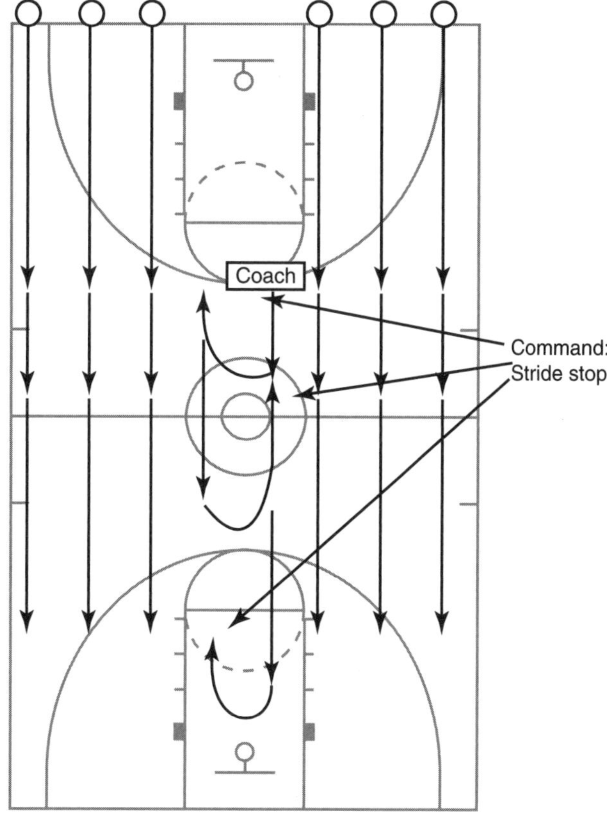

Related Drills *1, 9-10, 23-32, 36-37, 41, 52, 64, 91, 96, 104-126*

39

ONE-ON-TWO PIVOTING

Individual or team • 90 seconds

➲ **SKILL FOCUS** Defensive hand fakes (33), front pivot (35), reverse pivot (36), jump stop (37), stride stop (38), step-through move, double teaming defensively (50), balance

Beginner

1. Players line up as shown in the figure. Divide the team into squads of three, each with one ball.
2. The two players on defense are trying to steal the ball. These two defenders may move from side to side in any manner. Their mission is to at least deflect the basketball.
3. The offensive player tries to pivot away from the two defenders, constantly using the low swing-through of the ball to keep the defenders from deflecting the basketball. Warning: Players must keep their pivot foot on the floor—don't let them travel! They should make use of pivots to keep their bodies between their defenders and the basketball.
4. After 30 seconds, one of the defenders becomes the offensive player, and the offensive player becomes a defender. After 30 seconds more, the defender who has not been on offense becomes the new offensive player.

Intermediate

The offensive player may use the step-through move and dribble the ball twice before reestablishing a pivot foot (or pivot feet) by use of the jump stop or stride stop.

➲ TEACHING POINTS

1. To execute the step-through move, the attacker needs to fake in one direction and then come back to split the two defenders.
2. After splitting the two defenders, the attacker swings the ball through, no higher than the middle of the lower leg. The swing should be hard and quick.
3. If the player allows the dribble after the split, it should begin with a toss of the ball out a few feet (1-1.5 m). Now the dribbler runs to catch up with the basketball and begins to dribble. The ball must be out of the dribbler's hands before the dribbler picks up the pivot foot—otherwise, it's a walk. The tossing of the basketball prevents the defenders from flicking the ball from behind.

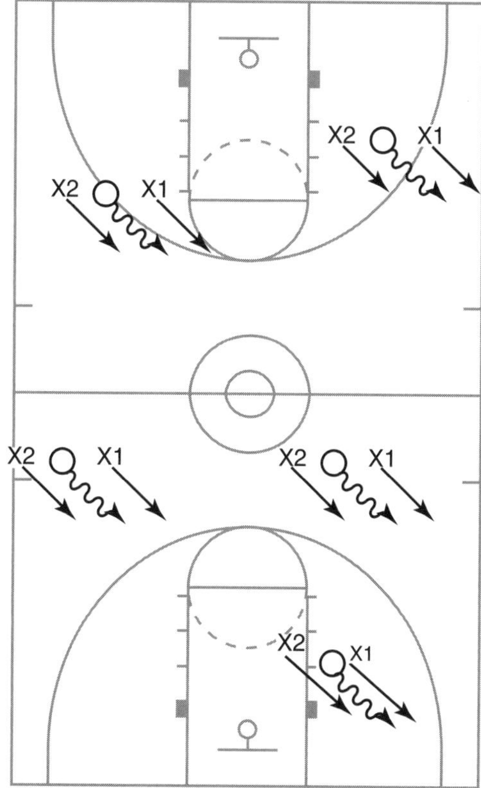

Related Drills *35-38, 40-41, 52, 76*

40

DRIBBLE, STOP, PIVOT

Individual or team • 1 minute

➲ SKILL FOCUS Speed dribble (23), control dribble (24), front pivot (35), reverse pivot (36), jump stop (37), stride stop (38), balance, conditioning

Beginner

1. Players line up at different spots on the floor as shown in the figure.
2. On a coach's signal, players begin to dribble. They may dribble in any direction, but they should use the speed or the control dribble as determined by the coach.
3. The players stop (jump stop or stride stop) after three dribbles.
4. After the stop, players pivot (front or reverse, as designated by the coach).
5. The coach checks whether all three techniques are correctly executed.

Intermediate

In a nonstop, 1-minute drill, players dribble, stop, and pivot. They then pause a few seconds. Next, players begin to dribble in the direction they face, then stop, then pivot.

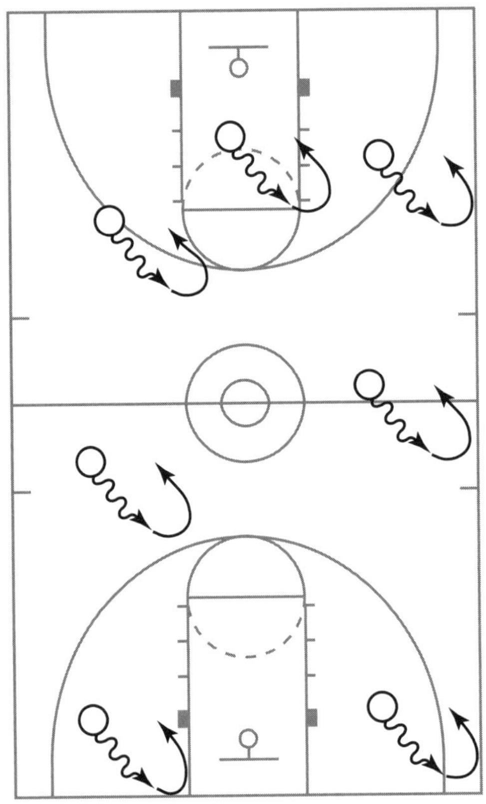

Related Drills *24-25, 35-39, 41, 52, 76*

DRIBBLE, STOP, PIVOT, PASS, CUT

Team • 3 minutes

➲ SKILL FOCUS Triple threat (9), speed dribble (23), control dribble (24), front pivot (35), reverse pivot (36), jump stop (37), stride stop (38), chest pass (44), bounce pass (44), overhead pass (44), V-cut (53), conditioning

Intermediate

1. Players line up in pairs of two, spaced all over the court. (For clarity, only one pair is shown in the figure.)
2. Player 1 dribbles, using the speed or the control dribble (coach's choice). After three to five dribbles, 1 stops (jump stop or stride stop: coach's choice).
3. After stopping, 1 pivots (front pivot or reverse pivot: coach's choice).
4. After pivoting, 1 passes to 2. The pass may be chest, bounce, or overhead, whichever is appropriate (if 2 is far away from 1, 1 executes a overhead pass. If 2 is near 1, 1 can use the bounce pass or the chest pass).
5. Meanwhile, player 2 has V-cut. Player 2 is yelling to 1 so that 1 knows where 2 is. Player 2 can V-cut anywhere.
6. Watch the execution of the dribble, the stop, the pivot, and the pass of 1, as well as 2's V-cut. All corrections should be made immediately.

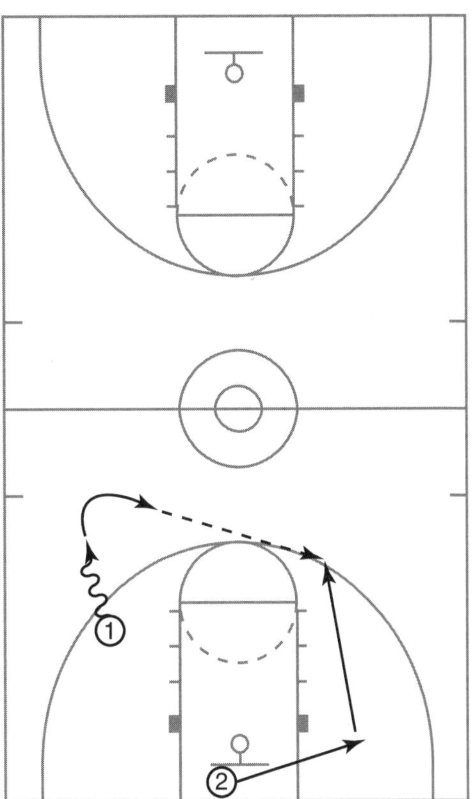

Advanced

For a continuous drill, require player 2 to receive the pass, get in triple-threat position, then begin to dribble in any direction. Player 2 now dribbles, stops, pivots, and passes while 1 is running a V-cut.

Related Drills *9, 23-24, 35-39, 44, 52-53, 76*

42

DRIBBLE, STOP, JUMP SHOT

Individual or team • 5 minutes

➲ **SKILL FOCUS** Triple threat (9), rocker step (11), in and out (12, 28), crossover (13, 29), spin (14), half-spin (15, 31), Paye drill (17), control dribble (24), hesitation dribble (26), jump stop (37), stride stop (38), pump fake (96), pump fake crossover (96), pump fake up and under (116), fakes at the end of dribble (116-117)

Beginner

1. Line players up as shown in the figure. Each player has a basketball.
2. Player 1 dribble-drives to a predetermined spot on the floor and either jump-stops or stride-stops and shoots a jump shot.
3. Player 1 rebounds the shot and dribbles back to the end of the line.
4. Five different spots on the floor can be chosen for the next series of shots. A coach can choose the area of the spots as well as the number of spots. Or one spot can be used for the entire 5 minutes.

Intermediate

1. A rocker step move is executed at the beginning of the drill. Players may shoot after the rocker step (coach's call) or proceed to step 2.
2. After the rocker step, a dribbling move is executed before the stop-and-shoot action (see figure).
3. A dribbling move can be made on the way back to the end of the line after the rebound.

Advanced

1. Split the squad in teams of two. A defender can be placed on the attacker. This requires the attacker to read the defense and use savvy (see the Paye drill, chapter 2, drill 17).
2. The defender and the attacker exchange places after the shot.

➜ **Option (all skill levels)** If your gym has six goals, divide the squad into groups of two at each basket. Coaches observe from midcourt.

Related Drills *9, 11-15, 17, 24, 26, 28-29, 31, 37-38, 84-88, 96, 104-112, 116-117*

43

FOUR-CORNER STOPPING, PIVOTING

Team • 3 minutes

SKILL FOCUS Conditioning, rocker step (11), in and out (12, 28), crossover (13, 29), spin (14, 30), half-spin (15, 31), Paye drill (17), ball control (24), hesitation dribble (26), front pivot (35), reverse pivot (36), jump stop (37), stride stop (38), catching the ball (44), bounce pass (44), chest pass (44), overhead pass (44), one-handed bounce pass (44), one-handed chest pass (44), fake passing (47), V-cut (53)

Intermediate

1. Line players up as shown in the figure. All four players on the court have a basketball.
2. All four players dribble to the middle simultaneously.
3. When players reach the middle, they jump-stop (or stride-stop) and then pivot, using either a front pivot or a reverse pivot.
4. The players who begin the drill out of bounds V-cut. These four players must time their cuts to correspond with the pivot of the players in the middle of the court.
5. The players in the middle of the court pass the ball to their V-cutting teammate. The passers use a bounce pass, chest pass, or overhead pass.
6. Rotation: 1 goes to 6; 2 goes to 7; 3 goes to 8, and 4 goes to 5. The drill continues for 3 minutes.

Advanced

1. As players drive to midcourt they execute a dribbling move—in and out, crossover, spin, half-spin, or hesitation.
2. They may use one of the rocker steps (jab step, jab-step direct drive, jab-step crossover, jab-step pullback) before they begin their dribble to midcourt.

Options (All skill levels)

1. Have your players call out how they are being defended and what move they will use to defeat the defense (both before the dribble and during the dribble).
2. You can break the drill down to focus on weak areas.

➲ TEACHING POINTS

1. Make sure all players execute each part of the drill using proper fundamentals. Players tend to take short cuts if you allow it.
2. You might prefer to break the drill down into two or three parts, such as drilling only the dribble, stop, and pass, with no cuts or offensive moves. Focus on your players' weak spots.

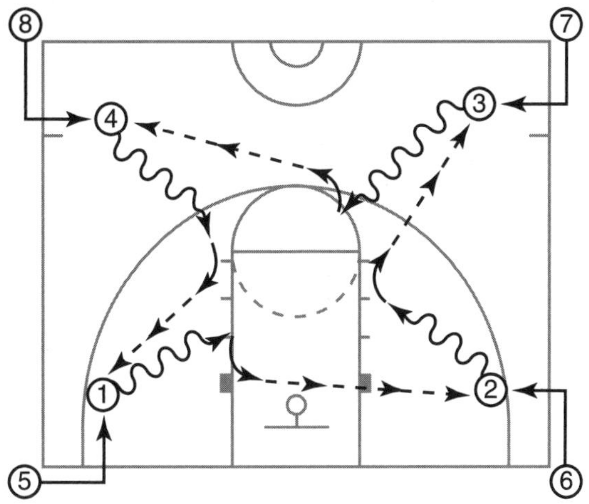

Related Drills *11-15, 17, 24, 26, 28-31, 35-38, 40-41, 44, 47, 53*

CHAPTER 5

Passing

"The most important fundamental is that of passing the ball," wrote Coach Adolph Rupp in 1948. All Rupp did that year was win the NCAA championship . . . and then he took his University of Kentucky team as *the* United States Olympic team and won the gold medal.

Today passing has become almost a lost art, yet it remains the most important basketball fundamental. Coaches love great passers because they glue a team together. And when great passers are also fantastic one-on-one players, a team develops to championship caliber on the shoulders of one individual. Allen Iverson was a prime example of a great one-on-one player who was so adept at passing that he brought every team he played on up to championship level. Great assist man John Stockton of the Utah Jazz made a hall of fame career out of being super skilled at executing passes and raising the level of play of all who played with him.

There are three basic passes: the bounce pass, chest pass, and overhead pass. Each can be developed by drills. But other complementary rudiments must also be promoted: the knack of seeing the whole court at all times, the ability to barely touch the reception before zipping off another pass, the skill to hit the correct teammate at exactly the right time. These are but a few of the fundamentals that go along with passing.

Use drill 44 to cultivate the fundamentals of the pass, as well as the *art* of passing—looking in one direction and passing another, or faking a pass in one direction before tossing it another. Drill 45 introduces passing on the move, and drill 46 takes this to full-court level.

Drill 47 pits a defender against the newly learned techniques and tactics. Drill 48 compels players to barely receive a pass before passing the ball off again. Drill 49 interjects trapping, in which players must use footwork and pass fakes to get a pass between two defenders and over or around a third defender.

Drill 50 works multiple skills, including passing, dribbling, and trapping. Drills 51 and 52 combine everything your players have learned into movement drills. Progress continues step by step.

44

TWO-LINE STANDING STILL DRILL

Team • 3 minutes

SKILL FOCUS Chest pass, bounce pass, overhead pass, baseball pass, pass receiving

Beginner

1. Players line up as shown in the figure, about 15 feet (4.5 m) apart. Each two-player line has a ball.
2. Players throw chest passes to each other, then bounce passes, then overhead passes.

Intermediate

Players throw one-handed chest passes to each other, then one-handed bounce passes.

Advanced

Players throw overhead outlet passes to each other, then baseball passes. Spread the squads of two 30 feet (9 m) apart for this drill.

Options (all skill levels)

1. Players fake a pass before delivering a pass (e.g., fake a chest pass, then throw a bounce pass).
2. Players step around an invisible defender to make the pass; they step left one time, and step right the next.

TEACHING POINTS

Chest Pass Players cup hands on both sides of the basketball, using the pads (not palms). Thumbs point upward; palms face the ball. The ball is held at chest level. Players step forward and pass the ball toward a receiver's chest, flipping both wrists. Thumbs finish pointing downward, and palms face outward. The receiver steps toward the pass to receive it, watching the ball all the way into the hands.

Bounce Pass Players follow instructions for the chest pass, but instead of aiming at the receiver's chest, they aim the ball at a point on the floor between themselves and their receiver. From this bounce spot, the ball should hit the receiver between the beltline and the chest.

Overhead Pass Players hold the ball slightly overhead with elbows flexed, forearms perpendicular to the floor, and upper arms parallel to the floor. They hold the ball with both hands cupped, one on each side but slightly behind the ball. Both thumbs are well behind the ball. The ball is not thrown but rather flipped with a slight wrist action. Arms move forward as the pass is delivered. Thumbs finish pointing toward the receiver, and palms are pointing outward.

➜ **One-Handed Chest Pass** Players place one hand on the side of the ball and the other behind the ball with a loose grip, using the pads of the fingers. With elbows flexed, they push the ball with the hand behind the ball. They then follow through so both arms finish fully extended.

➜ **One-Handed Bounce Pass** The one-handed bounce pass should be delivered exactly as the one-handed chest pass. Players pick a point on the floor so that the carom reaches the receiver somewhere between the belt and the chest.

➜ **Overhead Outlet Pass** The differences between the overhead (flip) pass described earlier and the overhead outlet pass are few. First, players hold the ball completely overhead with almost no flex in the elbow. Second, they bring the ball back toward the head as they prepare to deliver it. Third, they make the pass strong by bringing arms violently forward during the throw. Distance determines how violently they need to throw. Players flip their wrists as they complete the throw.

➜ **Baseball Pass** Passers turn sideways to their receiver. Keeping both hands on the ball, the passer pulls the ball back beside the ear. If throwing with the right hand, the passer keeps the left hand below the ball and the right hand behind the ball. The left hand keeps the ball balanced while the right hand provides the thrust. As the pass is delivered, the left hand drops and the ball is thrown like a baseball. The throwing hand comes straight forward. Passers should not put a twist on their throwing hand because that makes for a curveball. They follow through by stepping forward with the left foot as the ball is released.

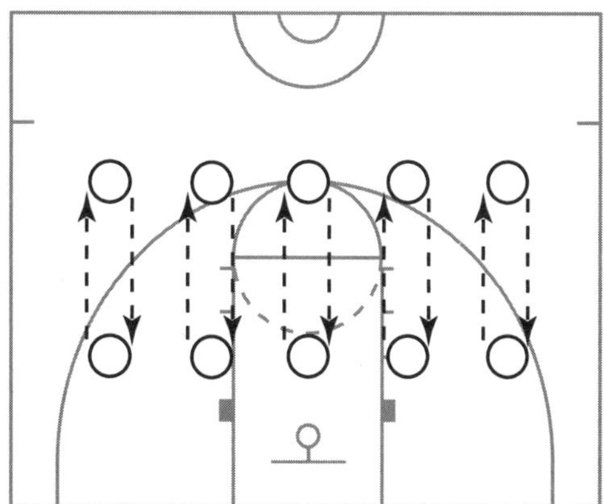

Related Drills *41, 45-52, 62-72, 74*

45

TWO-LINE MOVING DRILL

Team • 3 minutes

➲ SKILL FOCUS Chest pass (44), bounce pass (44), overhead pass (44), overhead outlet pass (44), one-handed chest pass (44), one-handed bounce pass (44), baseball pass (44), pass receiving (44)

Beginner

1. Divide team into two squads. Place one squad above the free-throw line and the other squad about 15 feet (4.5 m) away at a diagonal, as shown in the figure.
2. The squad at the top begins with a basketball. The first player in line passes to the first player in the other line. The first passer moves to the end of the lower line.
3. The lower-line player who received the pass from the upper-line player passes to the second player in the upper line. This lower-line passer then moves to the end of the upper line. The drill continues until stopped by a coach.
4. Tell players to execute chest passes for 1 minute, then bounce passes for 1 minute, and then overhead (flip) passes for 1 minute.

Intermediate

Same as the beginner drill, but add the one-handed chest pass for 1 minute and the one-handed bounce pass for 1 minute.

Advanced

Same as the intermediate drill, but add the overhead outlet pass for 1 minute and the baseball pass for 1 minute.

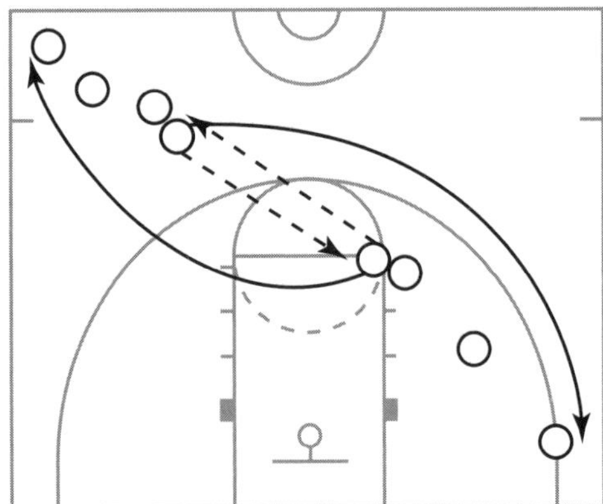

Related Drills *41, 44, 46-52, 62-72, 74*

TWO-LINE FULL-COURT PASSING

46

Team • 2 minutes

SKILL FOCUS Chest pass (44), bounce pass (44), overhead pass (44), overhead outlet pass (44), one-handed chest pass (44), one-handed bounce pass (44), baseball pass (44), pass receiving (44), slide step while running

Intermediate

1. Players line up as shown in the figure.
2. The first player in each line moves down the floor using slide steps. As they move down the floor, the two players from each line pass to each other, executing passes designated by a coach. When they get to the other end of the court, they wait until all players are there. Then players repeat the drill, slide-stepping and passing back up the floor.
3. The coach designates which pass to execute each trip up or down the floor. Players receive the pass and immediately pass back to their teammate without traveling.

TEACHING POINTS

1. See drill 44 for techniques of each pass. Make sure all passes are thrown without traveling. Check player execution of the slide step for correct technique.
2. In a slide step, the player (if going left) takes a long step with the left foot, then brings the right foot up to and almost touching the left foot. The player then again extends the left foot away from the right foot, and this movement continues without the feet ever crossing.

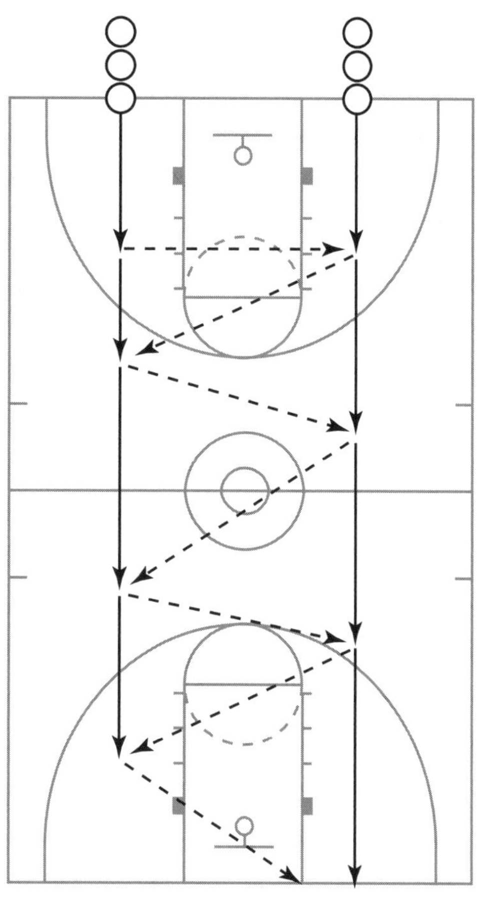

Related Drills *41, 44, 47-52, 62-72, 74*

47

TWO-ON-ONE PASSING DRILL

Team • 90 seconds

SKILL FOCUS Chest pass (44), bounce pass (44), overhead pass (44), overhead outlet pass (44), one-handed chest pass (44), one-handed bounce pass (44), baseball pass (44), pass receiving (44), fake passing, quickness, defensive footwork (129-131, 137)

Intermediate

1. Players line up as shown in the figure.
2. Two offensive players, 1 and 2, try to pass a ball using passing fakes and the pass designated by the coach without allowing X1, the defender, a deflection or an interception. Player 1 passes to 2, then 2 passes back to 1, and so on.
3. After 30 seconds, X1 and 1 trade places. After another 30 seconds, 2 becomes the defender.

Option When the defender deflects or intercepts a pass, the defender takes the place of the passer, and the passer becomes the new defender.

TEACHING POINTS

1. Techniques of the passes are discussed in drill 44.
2. To fake a pass, players fully extend the arms as though they are actually making that pass. They then pull the ball back and make the pass in another direction. They may also use eye fakes—looking in a direction they don't intend to pass and then quickly passing in another direction. When faking a pass, they must use two hands. When using the one-handed bounce pass or chest pass, they keep the guide hand on the ball to maintain control of the ball while faking.

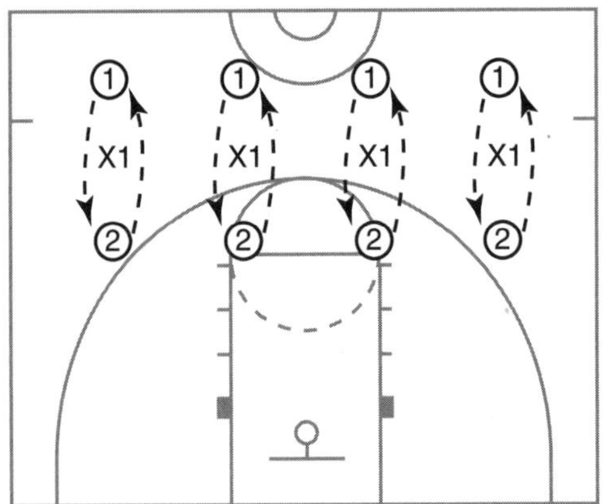

Related Drills *41, 44, 46, 48-52, 62-72, 74*

PEPPER PASSING

48

Team • 2 minutes

SKILL FOCUS Chest pass (44), bounce pass (44), overhead pass (44), slide step (46), quickness, agility, hand–eye coordination

Beginner

1. Divide players into two groups at opposite ends of the court. Player 1 has a ball and faces the other players in the group, as shown in the figure.
2. Player 1 passes to the first player in line (player 2). Player 2 passes back to 1 as 1 slides down the line, using slide steps; then 1 passes to 3, and 3 passes back to 1; 1 passes to 4, and 4 passes back to 1; 1 passes to 5, and 5 passes back to 1. Player 1 then begins sliding back in the other direction, passing back to 4 and repeating the sequence.
3. Player 1 goes down the line and back twice before getting back in line beside player 5. Players, 3, 4, 5, and 1 take a step to their left. Player 2 steps out front and executes the same passes and slides that 1 executed. The drill continues until all players have been out front.

Advanced

1. Tell players to use the bounce pass instead of the chest pass.
2. Add the overhead pass.

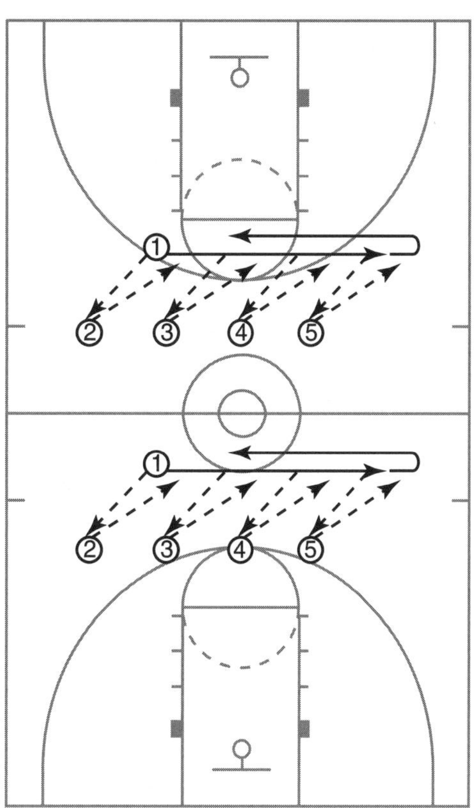

Option (advanced) Use two balls instead of one. Players 1 and 2 both begin with a ball. When 1 passes to 3, 2 passes to 1. When 1 passes to 4, 1 receives a pass from 3. As 1 passes to 5, 4 passes to 1. This continues down and back, down and back, and then 2 steps out front; the drill continues until all players have gone down and back twice.

Related Drills *27, 41, 44, 46-47, 49-52, 62-72, 74*

49 THREE-ON-THREE TRAPPING AND PASSING

Team • 3 minutes

SKILL FOCUS Dribble retreat (27), step-through (39), chest pass (44), bounce pass (44), overhead pass (44), fake passing (47), when to make which pass, trap (50), interception drill (50, 131), trap to follow dribble retreat (50, 157)

Intermediate

1. Players line up as shown in the figure. Divide squad into defenders and attackers. After 90 seconds, squads switch roles.
2. The player with the ball may pivot in any direction to complete passes. This player may also fake a pass in any direction before passing in the same or opposite direction. Player 1 is at the free-throw line; players 2 and 3 are on their respective big blocks. The two receivers stay at their positions until they receive the pass.
3. Defenders X1 and X2 trap 1 while X3 tries to intercept passes to either 2 or 3. Players X1 and X3 trap 3 while X2 tries to intercept passes to either 1 or 2. Players X2 and X3 trap 2 while X1 tries to intercept passes to either 1 or 3. The figure shows 1 passing to 3 and X1 and X3 going to trap 3 as X2 slides to a position to try to steal a pass to either 1 or 2.
4. The receiver does not have to hold the ball until the traps arrive. Players may pass immediately or wait for the double team. Player 3 may pass to either 1 or 2, and the drill becomes continuous.

Advanced

The squads cannot switch roles until defenders have deflected at least three passes by the attackers.

Options (all skill levels)

1. The player with the ball is allowed to step through the double team to pass.
2. The player with the ball is allowed to retreat dribble two dribbles as a simulation of trying to get free from a trap. When the player with the ball retreat dribbles, the two receivers are allowed to move toward the ball 3 to 5 feet (.9-1.5 m).

➲ TEACHING POINTS

1. Drill 27 elaborates on the dribble retreat. Drill 47 includes fake passing. Traps and interceptions receive full technical treatment in drill 50.
2. Attackers should fake pass to get the defenders' arms out of the lane of the intended pass. Check to be sure each pass is made away from the trappers' arms and away from the interceptors' movement. If not, correct your passers.

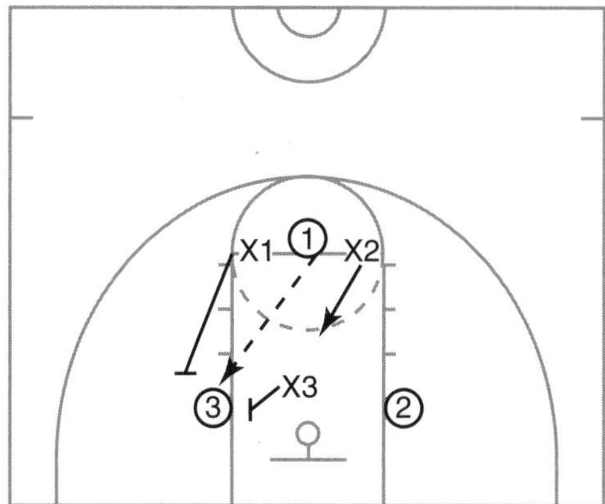

Related Drills *27, 41, 44, 46-48, 50-52, 62-72, 74, 155-160*

50

PASSING, DRIBBLING, TRAPPING

Team • 10 minutes

SKILL FOCUS Step-through (39), chest pass (44), bounce pass (44), overhead pass (44), two players trapping passer (50, 158), two defenders trapping dribbler (50, 157), passing out of traps, dribbling out of traps, run-and-jump traps (156)

Advanced

1. Divide squad into two teams: offense and defense (see figure).
2. Player 1 dribbles into the frontcourt, while X1 stays with 1 as a defender; 1 seeks to pass to 2. Player X2 plays off 2, encouraging 1 to pass to 2.
3. After 2 receives the pass from 1, X1 and X2 go to trap 2.
4. The coach moves around the court so defenders will not know where the coach is. Player 2 tries to pass to the coach, or the coach may have player 1 move about the court to receive the pass from 2.
5. When the trap is over, players X1 and 1 rotate to X2 and 2, respectively, and X2 and 2 go to the end of their lines. Player 3 becomes the new 1, and X3 becomes the new X1. After each attacker has had a chance to play both 1 and 2, and each defender a chance to play X1 and X2, the squads switch roles.
6. You can use the mechanics of this drill—(1) trapping the dribbler as the dribbler crosses the half-court line and (2) trapping the pass—to build your team man-to-man defense.

Options

1. Instead of X1 helping X2 trap the receiver, X2 races upcourt and helps X1 trap 1 to prevent the pass. Player 1 can keep the dribble alive or may pass to the coach or to 2. In this case, X2 must be in denial position on 2, rather than playing off 2.
2. In the original drill, instead of 2 passing to the coach, 2 tries to retreat dribble before passing to the coach or to 1, compelling X1 and X2 to continue their coverage.
3. Instead of the coach calling for the trap to be on passer 2 or dribbler 1, let defenders call for the trap by the way they play the dribbler. If X2 stays inside to help X1 on the dribbler, 1 passes to 2; then the defenders go to trap 2. If X2 denies 2 the pass, the defenders trap the dribbler, 1.

TEACHING POINTS

Trap With Dribble Alive

1. To trap a player with the dribble available (player 2 in figure), the defender must stay a few steps away from the ball handler. Player 2 still has the dribble alive and may split the two trappers by stepping through, but if defenders stay a step or so off the potential dribbler, the step-through is eliminated.

2. Defenders should be on both sides of player 2. Their feet should meet at a 90-degree angle; they should bend at the knee but keep their backs straight.
3. Defenders must keep arms and hands swinging in a windmill fashion, with hands always in the same plane as the ball, regardless of where 2 moves it. This compels 2 to fake again before passing to prevent a deflection.
4. If 2 decides to dribble instead of pass, X1 and X2 stay with 2. Player X1 is responsible for keeping 2 from dribbling by on 2's left side, while X2 has the same duties if 2 tries to dribble by on 2's right side. Both have the task of keeping 2 from splitting them and driving down the middle.
5. Should 2 escape either right, left, or down the middle, the two defenders follow 2 from behind and try to deflect the dribble away from 2 (called *flicking*).
6. To trap 1 while dribbling, X1 and X2 try to keep 1 between them. Player X1 refuses to allow 1 to dribble back to the left, and X2 must not let 1 escape around to the right. Both must keep 1 from splitting the two defenders with a dribble.

➜ Trap With Dribble Used

1. When the offensive player picks up the dribble, both defenders get up against the attacker, even bumping the ball handler slightly.
2. The defenders' arms and hands become even more active, trying to tie up the ball by reaching for it if possible. Defenders keep feet together at a 90-degree angle.
3. At the end of the dribble, either 1 or 2 can step through. Because the attackers cannot dribble, they may actually pick up the pivot foot to pass the ball. The defenders must be ready for this.
4. Defenders use the slide step while trapping, careful not to cross the feet.
5. Step-through mechanics are covered in drill 39, all passing techniques in drill 44, and slide steps in drill 46.

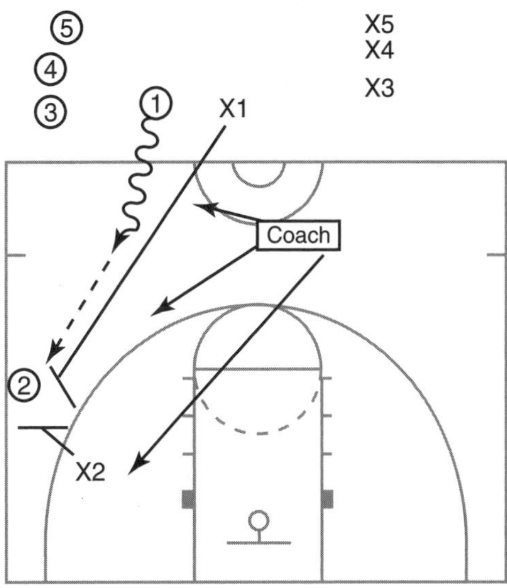

Related Drills *27, 41, 44, 46-49, 51-52, 62-72, 74, 155-160*

51

FOUR-CORNER PASSING

Team • 3 minutes

➲ **SKILL FOCUS** Chest pass (44), bounce pass (44), overhead pass (44), one-handed chest pass (44), one-handed bounce pass (44), pass receiving (44), fake passing (47)

Beginner

1. Players line up around the corners of the free-throw lane as shown in the figure.
2. Player 1 passes to 2 and goes to the end of 2's line. Player 2 receives the pass, passes to 3, then goes to the end of 3's line. Player 3 receives 2's pass, passes to 4, then goes to the end of 4's line. Player 4 receives 3's pass, passes to 1, then goes to the end of 1's line.
3. The coach dictates which pass to use.
4. After 90 seconds of passing to the right, switch directions and let every player pass to the left.

Intermediate

Use two balls instead of one. Let players 1 and 3 each start with a basketball.

Advanced

Use one ball and allow fake passes before passing. For example, player 1 could fake a pass to 4 or to 3 before passing to 2.

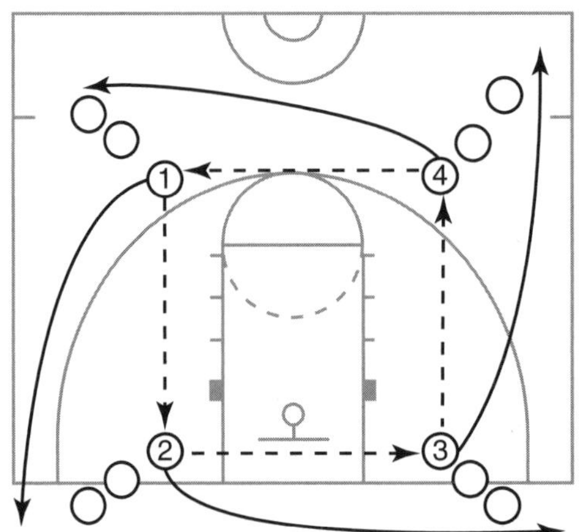

Related Drills *27, 41, 44, 46-50, 52, 62-72, 74*

TOUCH PASSING AND LAYUP

Team • 3 minutes

SKILL FOCUS Front pivot (35), reverse pivot (36), jump stop (37), stride stop (38), chest pass (44), bounce pass (44), overhead pass (44), one-handed chest pass (44), one-handed bounce pass (44), pass receiving (44), flash pivot (56)

Intermediate

1. Players line up as shown in the figure. Player 5 rotates to 4, and 4 rotates to the end of 5's line.
2. The team manager passes to a coach. On seeing this pass, 5 flash pivots to the free-throw line, and 4 steps out to the short corner. This gets players accustomed to moving on every pass, a rule of the motion offense. The coach can pass either to 4 or to 5.
3. If the coach passes to 5, 5 front pivots (or reverse pivots) to face 4. Player 4 cuts along the baseline for a pass from 5 and a layup. Player 5 should catch the pass from the coach, front pivot, and pass to 4 all in one motion.
4. If the coach passes to 4, 5 cuts down the free-throw lane for a pass from 4 for a layup. Player 4 should catch the pass from the coach and immediately flip the pass to the cutting 5.
5. In either step 3 or 4, the next player in line rebounds the layup and passes out to the manager, who passes to the coach, and the drill continues. This should be a speedy, spirited drill. The coach determines the passes to be used.

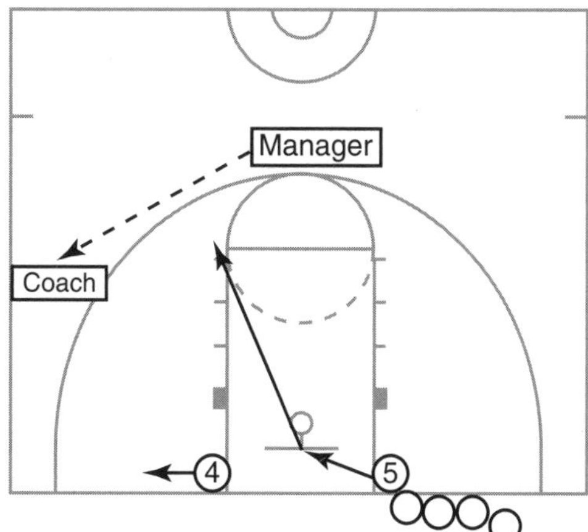

Related Drills *27, 35-51, 62-72, 74*

CHAPTER

6

Cutting

Your players have progressed with their masterful fakes, wonderful ballhandling, and superior passing. In fact your squad might have progressed so far in their offensive skills that opponents will be extra determined to disrupt your offensive game plan. By employing double-teams and traps, opponents may try to prevent certain players from getting the ball.

To combat the added defensive pressure, your players must be able to execute a variety of cuts. Drill 53 introduces the V-cut. Among other reasons, players use the V-cut to replace themselves (necessary in the motion offense), to get free from pressure, and to keep their defenders busy while teammates score. The options in drill 53 also progress your team offense from simple cutting into the beginning of faking, used within a team concept.

There are only two types of individual off-the-ball defensive coverage. Defenders can play more toward the basket, allowing the middle cut (drill 54), or they can play more toward the ball, conceding the backdoor cut (drill 55). These cuts are also available when a defender watches the ball or overplays the opposing player.

Anytime an offensive player is at a wing or lower, that player has the opportunity to flash pivot (drill 56). Drill 57 introduces work on combining various cuts and moves on offense; the focus here is not only on cutting but also on one-on-one play.

Drills 58 and 59 get your players thinking about the tactics of cutting—the *when,* not just the how. This is quite important when your squad begins to operate under motion offense rules.

Drill 60 combines cutting with dribble penetration as part of your motion offense rules. Drill 61 brings together passing and cutting while moving at full speed over the full court.

53

V-CUT

Individual or team • 3 minutes

SKILL FOCUS Triple-threat position (9), rocker step (11), in and out (12, 28), crossover (13, 29), spin (14, 30), half-spin (15, 31), control dribble (24), front pivot (35), stride stop (38), chest pass (44), bounce pass (44), pass receiving (44), slide step (46), fake passing (47), V-cut, swim technique, sealing technique

Beginner

1. Players line up as shown in figure 1.
2. Player 2 V-cuts to get open.
3. Player 1 passes to 2 and then goes to the end of 2's line.
4. Player 3 V-cuts to get open.
5. Player 2 passes to 3 and then goes to the end of 3's line.
6. Continue the drill as long as necessary.
7. Drill on the right side of the court one day and on the left side the next.

Option To teach the V-cut to an individual player, set up a cone for the player to cut around. Have the player make the cut, and then pass the ball to the player. Correct the player's cutting technique, get the ball back, and repeat the process as long as you think necessary.

Intermediate

1. Players execute the drill at various places over the half-court and the full court.
2. Players complete the V-cut by using a sealing maneuver.

V-Cut Into Triple-Threat Position

1. Players line up as shown in figure 2.
2. Player 2 makes a V-cut.
3. A coach passes 2 the ball. On receiving the ball, 2 front pivots into triple-threat position.
4. Player 2 executes the offensive fake the coach requests and then goes to the end of the line.
5. Drill on the right side of the court one day and on the left side the next.

Advanced

Add a defender to play only token defense. (Or a coach may serve as the defender.) This allows players to see how the V-cut should work in the course of an actual game.

V-Cut Into Triple-Threat Position

1. Add a token defensive player. Player 2 must read the defender's stance and actions and make a move according to what the defender has dictated.

2. The coach, without allowing a defender, calls for multiple options on the fakes (e.g., a jab-step crossover into a dribbling half-spin).

➜ TEACHING POINTS

1. This is the beginning of the development of the team motion offense.
2. The V-cut is used in four options:
    a. To get free for a pass, to continue the swing of the ball from one side of the court to the other
    b. To get open at the wing to begin the offense
    c. To keep defenders busy by players replacing themselves in the scheme of the motion offense while teammates attack
    d. To try to coax a defender into an individual defensive mistake, such as playing too far off the line of the ball (see backdoor cut) or playing too close to the offensive player (see middle cut)
3. To V-cut, you want to change your pace. In figure 2, for example, 2 would walk slowly toward the baseline. Once 2 decides to make a cut, 2 plants the inside foot (left foot in figure 2) and front pivots with a long step with the right foot in the direction he or she came from. Player 2 now races back outside, giving the left hand and arm as a target for 1 to make the pass. Or, instead of racing back outside, 1 could slide-step back outside. Player 1 should lead 2 a step or so and use either the chest pass or the bounce pass. Instead of walking in and then cutting hard back outside, 2 could jog in and then break hard outside. Any change of pace will do.
4. To use the sealing technique, 2 stops on the inside foot (the left foot in figure 2), using the stride stop. Player 2 then picks up the right foot and front pivots, bringing the right foot between the torso and the defender. Player 2 also uses the swim move with the right arm, meaning that 2 swings the right arm between the torso and the defender and then propels the right arm in a swim motion without pushing. Player 2 now holds this arm against the defender while sliding back outside to receive the pass.

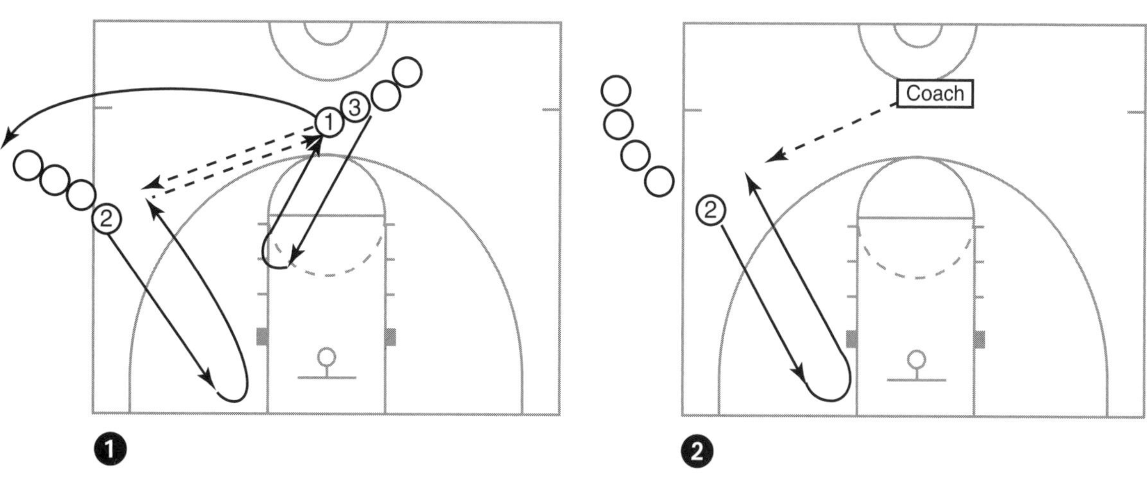

Related Drills *35, 38, 44, 46-47, 58-63, 65-66, 122-128, 147-148*

54

MIDDLE CUT

Individual or team • 3 minutes

SKILL FOCUS Basic layup (8), in and out (12, 28), crossover (13, 29), spin (14, 30), half-spin (15, 31), front pivot (35), stride stop (38), chest pass (44), bounce pass (44), overhead pass (44), pass receiving (44), slide step (46), middle cut, slide dribble (97)

Beginner

1. Players line up as shown in figure 1.
2. Player 1 makes a middle cut around a cone.
3. A coach passes the ball to 1, and 1 slide-dribbles to a point outside the lane and passes the ball back to the coach. Player 1 uses a chest, bounce, or overhead pass, whichever the coach wants to work on. (It is usually best to use either the bounce or the overhead, preceded by a fake of the pass the player does not intend to use.)
4. Player 1 goes to the end of the line, while the next player in line steps up to make the middle cut.
5. Drill on the right side of the court one day and on the left side the next.

Option To teach the middle cut to an individual player, set up a cone for the player to cut around. Have the player make the cut, and then pass the ball to the player. Correct the player's cutting technique, get the ball back, and repeat the process as long as you think necessary.

Intermediate

1. Instead of passing to the cutter, a coach fakes a pass and allows the cutter to cut all the way through to the corner.
2. Instead of using a cone, use a token defender. This defender should step in the direction of the fake and follow the attacker to the basket.

Middle Cut and Layup

1. Players line up as shown in figure 2.
2. Player 1 passes to 2 and then middle cuts.
3. Player 2 passes to 1 for the driving layup. A coach rebounds 1's shot and passes to 2, and then 1 goes to the end of 2's line.
4. Player 2 passes to 3 and then middle cuts.
5. Player 3 passes to 2 for the driving layup. The coach rebounds 2's shot and passes to 3, and then 2 goes to the end of 3's line.
6. Continue the drill as long as necessary.
7. Drill on the right side of the court one day and on the left side the next.

Advanced

Middle Cut and Layup

All players have their own basketball and take turns rebounding their own shots. They then dribble back out to the end of a designated line. While dribbling back out to the end of the designated line, each player executes a dribbling move (such as a spin).

TEACHING POINTS

1. The middle cut should be used anytime the cutter sees that the defender is *not* playing in a jump step toward the ball defensive position. That is the beauty of the motion offense: players may cut when they see the defender is making a mistake instead of having to wait for the pattern to develop.
2. When executing a middle cut, the cutter will usually receive the pass. But should the cutter not receive the pass, the cutter should continue on through the lane to the corner. This clears out the scoring area for the next cutter.
3. To execute the middle cut, player 1 first recognizes that the defender is not between him- or herself and the basketball. Player 1 then steps one step opposite the direction of the cut. This step should be a stride stop. In figure 1, 1 stops on the right foot and then takes a long step with the left foot, swinging the right foot in a front pivot between him- or herself and the defender. Player 1's defender should now be on player 1's back. Player 1 begins using slide steps to keep the defender on his or her back. Should 1 receive the pass, 1 uses the slide dribble and steps slightly into the defender as 1 drives for the layup. The defender is out of position and must foul 1 or concede the layup. If 1 jumps slightly back toward the defender, it usually ends in a three-point play.

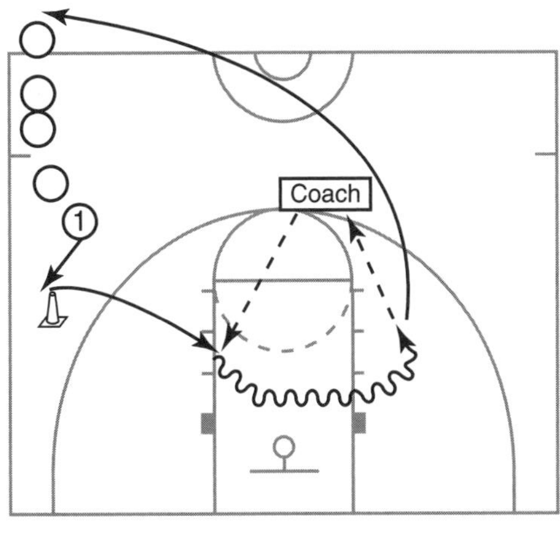

1

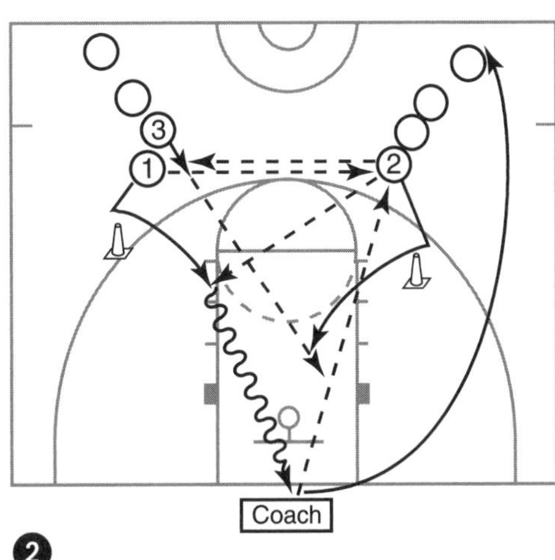

2

Related Drills *35, 38, 44, 46, 58-63, 65-66, 74, 97, 122-128*

55

BACKDOOR CUT

Individual or team • 3 minutes

SKILL FOCUS Basic layup (8), in and out (12, 28), crossover (13,29), spin (14, 30), half-spin (15, 31), front pivot (35), reverse pivot (36), jump stop (37), stride stop (38), chest pass (44), bounce pass (44), overhead pass (44), pass receiving (44), fake passing (47), swim move (53), V-cut (53), backdoor cut, fakes at end of dribble (96)

Beginner

1. Players line up as shown in figure 1.
2. Player 2 steps once or twice toward the cone and plants the outside foot (right foot in figure 1) using the stride stop.
3. Player 2 front pivots and crosses over the left foot, using the right foot as the pivot foot, then blasts hard toward the basket.
4. The coach passes to player 2, who gives a hand target, for the drive into the corner.
5. Player 2 passes to the coach and then goes to the end of the line.
6. Drill on the right side of the court one day and on the left side the next.

Option To teach the backdoor cut to an individual player, set up a cone for the player to cut around. Have the player make the cut, and then pass the ball to the player. Correct the player's cutting technique, get the ball back, and repeat the process as long as you think is necessary.

Intermediate

Backdoor Cut and Layup

1. Players line up as shown in figure 2.
2. Player 1 fakes and then backdoor cuts around the cone; 2 passes 1 the ball.
3. Player 1 drives for a layup. The coach retrieves the ball and passes to 3, while 1 goes to the end of line 2.
4. Player 2 fakes a step toward the cone and then backdoor cuts.
5. Player 3 passes to 2 for a driving layup. The coach retrieves the ball and passes to 4, while 2 goes to the end of line 3.
6. Continue the drill as long as necessary.

Advanced

Player 2 drives toward the corner and uses a dribbling move. After driving to the corner, 2 reverse pivots and passes back to the coach, using a pass designated by the coach.

➜ Backdoor Cut and Layup

Instead of shooting a layup, the cutter does a jump stop at the basket area, simulating the presence of a helping defender rotating over to stop the layup. At the end of the jump stop, the cutter uses a move at the end of the dribble (pump fake, pump fake crossover, pump fake spin, pump fake half-spin, all explained in drills 96 and 117).

➜ **Option** Instead of shooting the layup or doing the previous option, the cutter dribbles out to the corner, performs a dribbling move, and then throws an outlet pass to the same line he or she came from.

➜ TEACHING POINTS

1. Players should use the backdoor cut any time they are overplayed or when the area they are in needs to be cleared out to keep the motion offense going. Players may also use the backdoor anytime their defender has not dropped at least one step off the line between the cutter and the ball.
2. Players can get a layup if, during an overplay, their defender's knee comes over their toes. This means the defender is off balance and cannot recover to stop the backdoor cut.
3. If intending to go backdoor, players must give teammates a signal. The best signal is a closed fist. Players should give this signal with the hand on the side on which they are being overplayed.
4. To successfully execute the backdoor cut, a player steps toward the defender a step or two, then uses the stride stop, front pivoting with the back foot as the pivot foot. The player then cuts hard and in a straight line to the basket, using the front hand, open with palm pointing toward the passer, as a target hand.

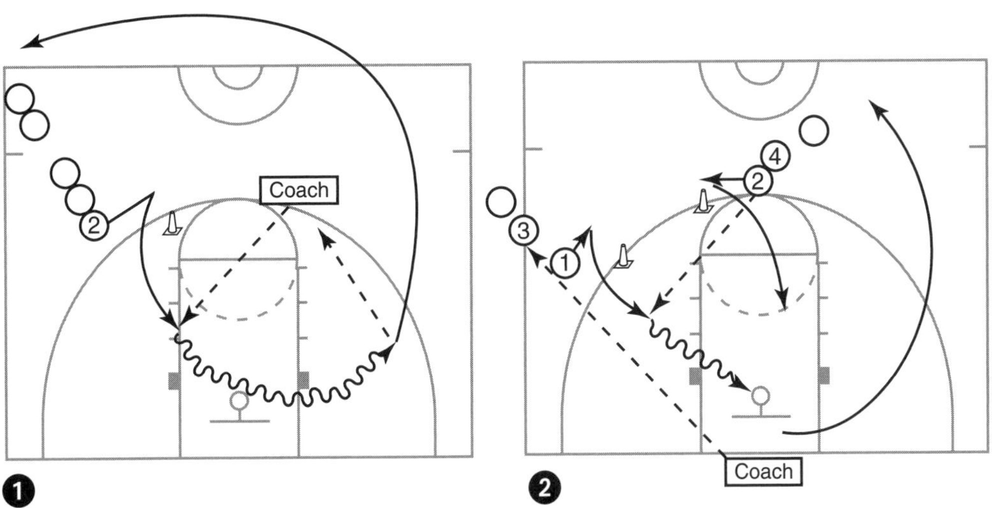

Related Drills *12-15, 27-30, 34, 36, 38, 44, 46, 54, 58-66, 74, 122-128*

56

FLASH PIVOT CUTTING

Individual or team • 3 minutes

SKILL FOCUS Triple-threat position (9), front pivot (35), reverse pivot (36), chest pass (44), bounce pass (44), overhead pass (44), pass receiving (44), slide step (46), swim move (53), middle cut (54), backdoor cut (55), flash pivot cut, drop step (96, 143), fence slide (128)

Beginner

1. Players line up as shown in figure 1.
2. Use a token defender to teach the correct spot to begin the flash pivot cut.
3. Player 1 walks in toward the basket until X1 is in a direct line between 1 and the passer (coach). At this point, 1 pushes off the outside foot (left foot in figure 1) and sprints out of the lane. This is the technique of the cut without a seal. The cutter could end up at the free-throw line, top of the key, or any high post-side position.
4. Player 1 receives the pass and passes back to the coach and then goes to the end of the line.

Option: Flash Pivot and Triple-Threat Position

1. Players line up as shown in figure 2.
2. Player 1 flash pivots and receives a pass from player 2.
3. Player 1 immediately front pivots into triple-threat position.
4. Then 1 passes to 4 and goes to the end of line 4; 2 goes to the end of line 3.
5. Player 3 flash pivots, and the drill continues until stopped by the coach.

Intermediate

1. Run the same drill, but allow the defender to overplay the cut to the free-throw line using the fence slide maneuver. This compels the receiver to run the middle cut and teaches the receiver to recognize when the middle cut is available. The coach then hits the cutter for a layup.
2. Run the same drill but allow the defender to overplay the cut by getting in the line between the receiver and the passer. This compels the cutter to immediately run the backdoor cut and teaches the receiver to recognize when the backdoor cut is available. The coach then hits the cutter for a layup.

Flash Pivot and Triple-Threat Position

1. The defender, X1 (a coach or manager), overplays as player 1 receives a pass from player 2. X1 simulates a steal. Upon reception, 1 drop-steps, using a reverse pivot, and drives for a layup.
2. X1 mixes up the coverage, one time overplaying and next time allowing the reception and playing straight up. Player 1 must recognize the coverage and react accordingly—drop step if overplayed, or triple threat if allowed to get the ball.

➔ TEACHING POINTS

1. To execute the flash pivot cut, players walk their defender to a spot at which the defender can no longer see both the passer and the cutter. At that exact moment, the player changes direction and pace by sprinting out to the high-post area. This can be at the top of the key, at the free-throw line, or at any high-post position. To change direction, the player pushes off the inside foot, makes incidental contact with the defender, front pivots, and uses the swim move. This is the cut using a seal. The sprint out to the high post should use the slide-step maneuver to keep the defender on the cutter's back.
2. Once reaching the area at which the pass is expected to be received, the player may either stride stop (one pivot foot) or jump stop (two pivot feet).

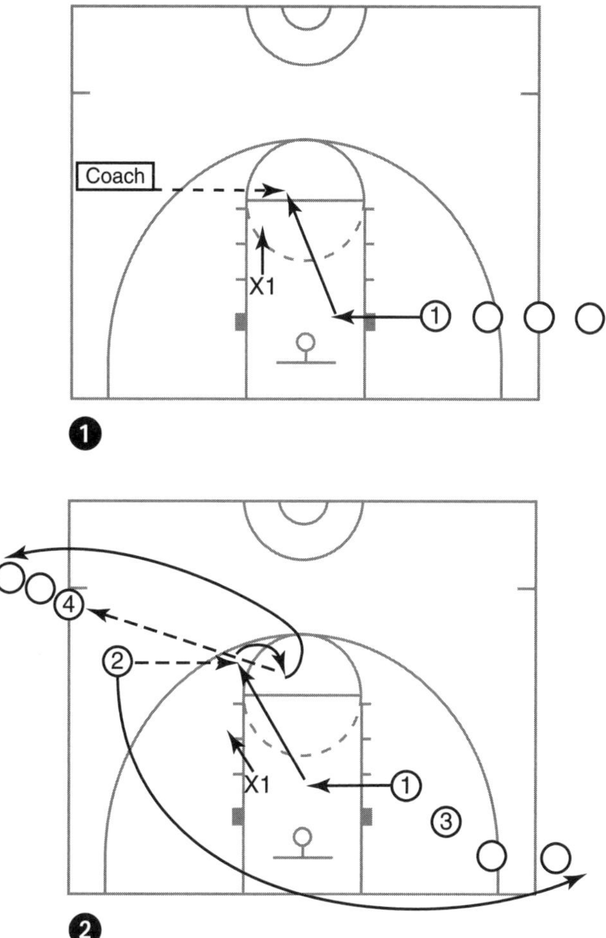

Related Drills *44, 46, 53-55, 57-59, 63-66, 122-128*

FLASH PIVOT, TRIPLE THREAT, AND OFFENSIVE MOVES

Individual or team • 10 minutes

SKILL FOCUS Triple-threat position (9), rocker step (11), in and out (12, 28), crossover (13, 29), spin (14, 30), half-spin (15, 31), front pivot (35), reverse pivot (36), jump stop (37), stride stop (38), chest pass (44), bounce pass (44), overhead pass (44), pass receiving (44), slide step (46), fake passing (47), swim move (53), middle cut (54), backdoor cut (55), flash pivot (56), pump fake (96, 117), pump fake crossover (96), slide dribble (97), fence slide (128), front foot to pivot foot (129), front foot to free foot (130), advance step (137), retreat step (137), swing step (137), close out receiver (148, 150-151)

Beginner

1. Players line up as shown in the figure.
2. Player 1 flash pivot cuts, and player 2 passes to 1 while X1 tries to prevent 1 from getting the pass.
3. Player 1 uses fakes designated by the coach; X1 plays front foot to pivot foot defense. Player 1 makes moves while X1 offers token defense.
4. As 1 goes to the end of line 2, 2 goes to the end of X2's line, and X1 goes to the end of 1's line.

Intermediate

Instead of step 3 in the beginner procedure, X1 plays defense and 1 must read X1's defensive techniques and use the move that counteracts X1's tactics.

Advanced

Run the intermediate drill, but require that player 1 takes a jump stop at the end of the dribble near the basket and use a move at the end of the dribble. The move might be a pump fake, a pump fake crossover, a spin, or a half-spin, among others.

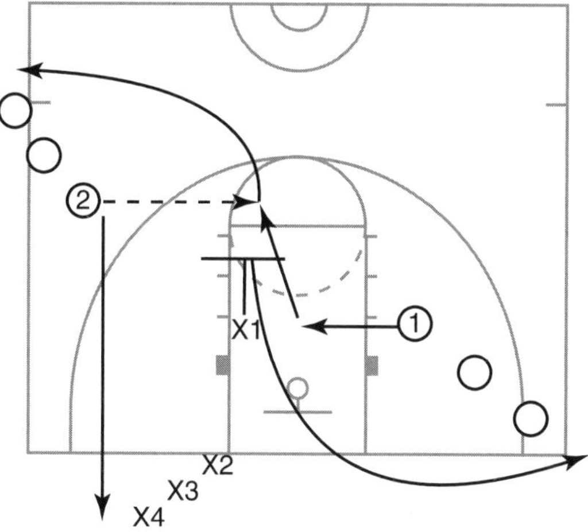

Related Drills *9, 11-15, 28-31, 35-37, 44, 46-47, 53-56, 58-59, 63-66, 96-97, 122-137, 148, 150-151, 154*

58

TWO-PLAYER CUTTING

Team • 3 minutes

SKILL FOCUS Triple-threat position (9), rocker step (11), in and out (12, 28), crossover (13, 29), spin (14, 30), half-spin (15, 31), front pivot (35), reverse pivot (36), jump stop (37), stride stop (38), chest pass (44), bounce pass (44), overhead pass (44), pass receiving (44), slide step (46), fake passing (47), V-cut (53), middle cut (54), backdoor cut (55), flash pivot (56), motion offense rules (122)

Beginner

1. Players line up as shown in the figure. In this drill, you will begin to teach the rules of the motion offense. There is no structure for either 1 or 2. Each chooses a cut, makes the cut, then tells which cut he or she makes and the reason for the cut. Place six cones at different spots on the court from day to day. To cut between the passer and a cone is a middle cut. To cut behind a cone is a backdoor cut. To replace oneself or to V-cut to any spot on the court, a player says "V-cut." Players must maintain 15-foot (4.5-m) spacing, even if they have to dribble to do so.
2. Player 1 passes to 2 (see figure). The following describes the action in the figure; in your drills, the action should differ from player to player and from time to time. Let the players decide.
3. Player 1 executes a middle cut (and calls out "middle cut"). Reason: "Defender did not jump to the ball when I passed."
4. Player 2 sees that player 1 is more than 15 feet (4.5 m) away, so 2 dribbles toward 1. Reason: "To keep proper spacing."
5. Player 2 passes to 1 and backdoor cuts (and calls "backdoor cut"). Reason: "My defender overplayed the passing lane."
6. The drill continues for 1 minute with players making V-cuts, middle cuts, and backdoor cuts, and dribbling to keep 15-foot (4.5-m) spacing. Then players go to the end of the line and two new players come forward.

➲ TEACHING POINTS

1. The first rule of motion offense is to *use the cut your defender gives you.*
2. The second rule is to *maintain 15-foot (4.5-m) spacing.*
3. Players may use rocker steps and dribbling moves to drive to the basket and pass back outside. In drills, players must explain their reasons for their chosen maneuvers.

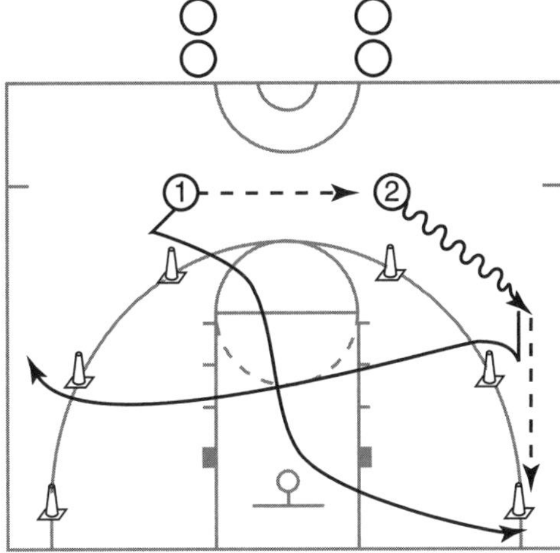

Related Drills *9, 11-15, 28-31, 35-37, 44, 46-47, 53-57, 59, 63-66, 96-97, 122-127*

59

THREE-PLAYER CUTTING

Team • 9 minutes

SKILL FOCUS Triple-threat position (9), rocker step (11), in and out (12, 28), crossover (13, 29), spin (14, 30), half-spin (15, 31), front pivot (35), reverse pivot (36), jump stop (37), stride stop (38), chest pass (44), bounce pass (44), overhead pass (44), pass receiving (44), slide step (46), fake passing (47), V-cut (53), middle cut (54), backdoor cut (55), flash pivot (56), motion offense rules (122)

Beginner

1. Players line up as shown in the figure. Three-player cutting is used here to teach two more rules of the motion offense: *Every player must move on every pass,* and *when a player dribbles toward you, you must cut or fade.*
2. The following describes the action shown in the figure; in your drills, the action should differ from player to player and from time to time. Let your players decide. They must state what they did and why they did it. Five cones are used in this description, but you may use more or less (but change cone locations from day to day).
3. Player 2 passes to 3 and calls out "middle cut." Reason: "The defender didn't jump to the ball when I passed."
4. Meanwhile, player 1 V-cuts, calling out "V-cut." Reason: "Every player must move on every pass," or "To keep 15-foot [5-m] spacing."
5. Player 3 dribbles toward player 1, and 1 calls out "fade." Reason: "On any dribble toward a properly spaced player, that player must cut or fade."
6. When player 3 passes, 3 must tell what she did and why. The drill continues, using the four cutting rules, dribbling, and any rocker step or dribbling move players wish to make.
7. One group operates for 3 minutes and then goes to the end of the line. Another group steps out and works for 3 minutes.

➲ TEACHING POINTS

1. Remind players of the first two rules of the motion offense: *Use the cut your defender gives you* and *maintain 15-foot spacing.*
2. Introduce two new rules: *Every player must move on every pass*, and *when a player dribbles toward you, you must cut or fade.*
3. Players may use rocker steps and dribbling moves to drive to the basket and pass back outside. In drills, players verbally state their maneuvers and the reasons for them.

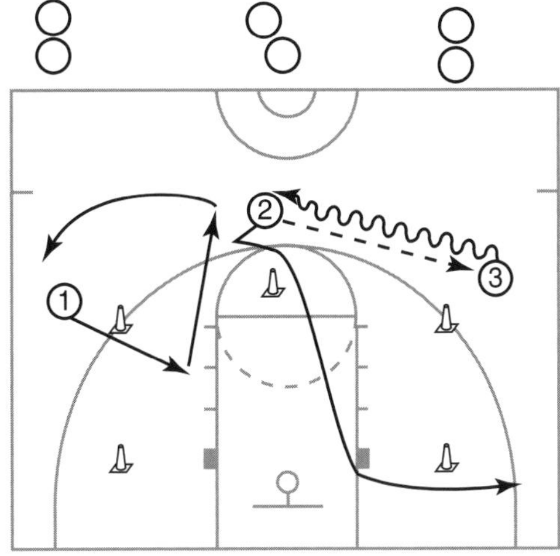

Related Drills *9, 11-15, 28-31, 35-37, 44, 46-47, 53-58, 63-66, 96-97, 122-127*

60

DEFEAT HELP AND RECOVER

Team • 7 minutes

SKILL FOCUS Hand quickness (5), rocker step (11), in and out (12, 28), crossover (13, 29), spin (14, 30), half-spin (15, 31), Paye drill (17), ball control (24), hesitation dribble (26), defensive fakes (33), jump stop (37), stride stop (38), bounce pass (44), chest pass (44), overhead pass (44), one-handed chest pass (44), one-handed bounce pass (44), V-cut (53), middle cut (54), backdoor cut (55), flash pivot cut (56), straight-stick shooting (84-88), slide-step dribble (97), penetration drill (113), defensive footwork (129-131, 139-144), close out (132, 149-150), help-side defense (133-135), draw the charge (141), one-on-one multiple skills (152)

Beginner

1. Players line up as shown in the figure.
2. A coach begins the drill by passing to player 1. When learning the drill, X1 plays only token defense, allowing 1 to drive to the middle.
3. X4 must stop 1 or 1 will drive all the way to the basket for a layup. X4 is on the help side defensively (see drill 133).
4. When X4 slides over to close the gap and stop 1's penetration, 4 has three options: 4 can stay put and be ready to receive a pass from 1 for a jump shot (A in the figure); 4 can cut backdoor for a pass and a layup (B in the figure); or 4 can cut behind the dribbling 1 for a handoff and a jump shot (C in the figure).
5. At the end of the drill, players rotate from offense to defense to the end of the opposite line.

Intermediate

Have X1 play real defense on player 1 instead of being a token defender. Now 1 must use the rocker-step sequence to get the drive. You might want to add a player and a defender on the strong side of the court so 1 can drive to the right as well as to the left. This compels X1 to play 1 straight up instead of an overplay.

Advanced

1. X1 can deny player 1 receiving the pass from the coach. Player 1 must use a V-cut or a backdoor or middle cut to get free for the pass from the coach.
2. Should 1 be unable to get free from X1, 4 should either flash pivot cut or V-cut outside to receive the pass from the coach. Now 1 and 4 exchange duties. Player 4 becomes the dribbling driver while 1 takes on 4's duties (stay, cut backdoor, or cut behind the dribbling 4).

➜ Options (all skill levels)

1. If you do not plan on using dribbling penetration in your motion offense, you do not want to use this drill. But if you plan on using dribbling penetration, this drill can be adjusted by using only one part at any time. You can allow penetration with 4 staying, receiving the pass, and shooting the 3-shot; or you can allow 4 to cut backdoor; or you can allow 4 to cut behind the dribbling 1. This is a great teaching drill for the dribbling penetration part of your motion offense.
2. You can add trapping of the ball handler when two players cross (if that is part of your defensive scheme). This eliminates 4 cutting behind 1 for the handoff.
3. You want X4 to draw the charge if possible.

➜ TEACHING POINTS

1. Your players are learning to play your man-to-man defense and your motion offense. This drill runs the entire sequence of offensive and defensive maneuvers. You may want to break the drill down into one or two parts. Then after several days of teaching you can allow players to use all the offensive and defensive maneuvers they have learned.
2. You may want to stop the action whenever a mistake is made and have players explain what they should have done instead. You are teaching player savvy and want to make corrections while the movement is still fresh. Turnovers will always occur and do not need be corrected. Bad decisions need to be corrected.

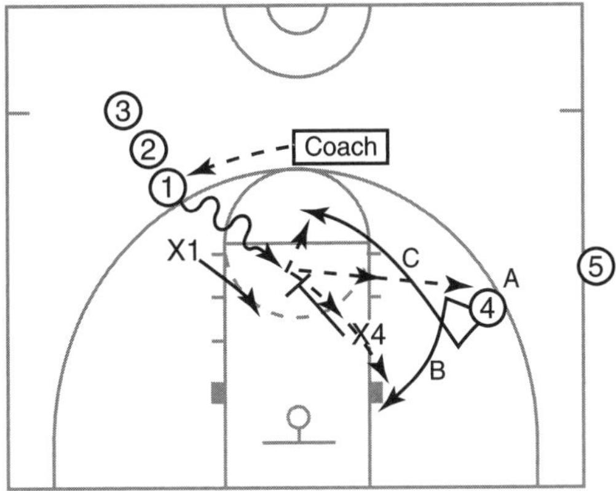

Related Drills *5, 11-15, 17, 24, 26, 33, 37-38, 44, 53-56, 84-88, 97, 113, 124-131, 132-135, 139-144, 149-150, 152*

61

FULL-COURT CUTTING

Team • 2 minutes

SKILL FOCUS Layup, conditioning, catching the ball (44), bounce pass (44), chest pass (44), overhead pass (44), one-handed chest pass (44), one-handed bounce pass (44), passing drills (44-52), cutting drills (53-60), middle cut (54), backdoor cut (55), flash pivot cut (56)

Beginner

1. Line players up as shown in the figure.
2. Player 1 begins with a basketball. Player 2 cuts into the court. Player 1 passes to 2. Player 1 immediately replaces 2.
3. Meanwhile player 3 cuts into the court. Player 3 must time the cut to be ready to receive the pass from 2 immediately. Player 2 replaces 3.
4. Meanwhile player 4 has cut onto the court. Player 3 passes to 4. Player 3 replaces 4.
5. Player 5 meanwhile has begun a V-cut to the perimeter. When 4 receives the pass, 5 cuts backdoor or uses a middle cut for a pass from 4 and a layup.
6. Player 6 rebounds the layup shot and begins the same passes back down the court. Player 6 passes to 3; 3 passes to 2; 2 passes to 1; and 1 passes to 7 for the layup.
7. Player 8 rebounds, and the procedure is repeated as the passing and cutting go back downcourt. Player 7 rotates to the end of the line.
8. This action is easily taught if you tell passers to always replace the players they pass to. In the figure, the broken circles around the player show where the player has rotated for the trip back down the floor.

Intermediate

When the passer passes the ball to the cutter, the passer runs a V-cut to replace the receiver.

TEACHING POINTS

1. Focus on the pass that needs the most work (bounce, chest, or overhead passes).
2. Focus on the cut that needs the most work (middle cut, backdoor cut, flash pivot cut, or V-cut).

3. You can add the front and reverse pivots to the drill. For example, when player 2 receives the pass from 1, 2 front pivots before passing to 3. Player 3 does likewise, and so on.
4. Players must concentrate on making their cuts and passes sharply. You want the drill to be constant motion so that the action also develops conditioning.

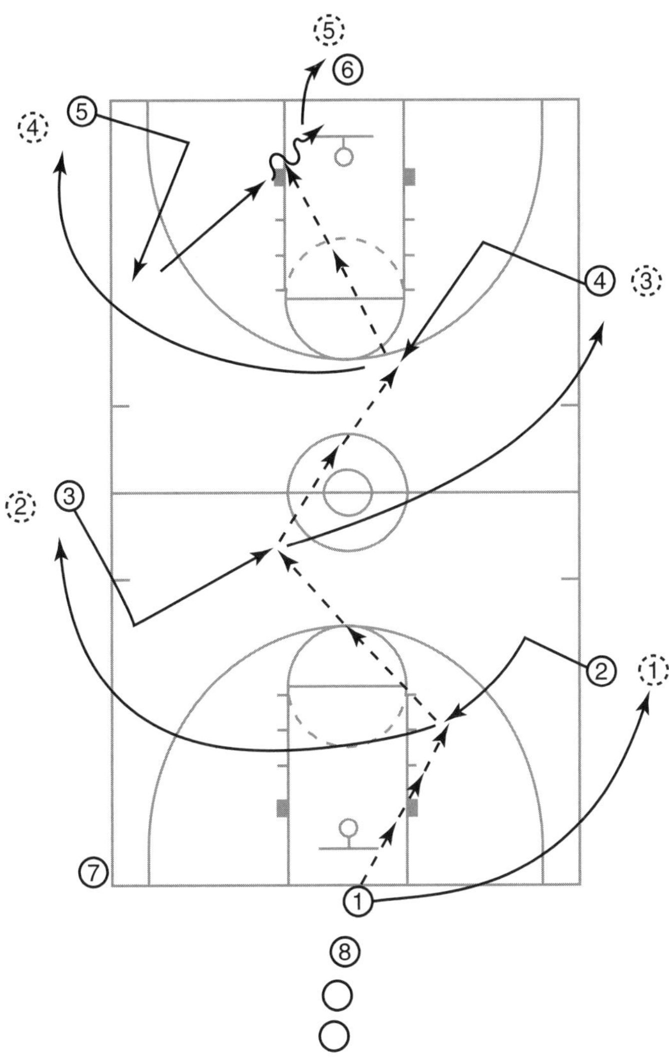

Related Drills *44-52, 53-60*

CHAPTER

7

Passing and Cutting

In this chapter we cover not only passing and cutting but also activating parts of the motion offense rules and combining several rudiments. Although cuts off a pass are our primary focus here, recognizing when to cut, when to dribble, and when to space properly also receive extensive treatment.

Attackers within the motion offense quickly learn that they must maintain 15-foot (4.5-m) spacing. They repeatedly rehearse cuts to learn proper timing. They learn to read and react to what their defenders give them. They commit to mental and muscle memory that they must cut or fade when a dribbler moves toward them and that they must cut every time the ball moves.

In each drill, players must learn first and foremost *to use the cut the defender gives them*. Never, ever allow a backdoor cut when a middle cut should have been used. Reading the defender must be stressed in all drills. In each drill where screening is involved, the passer and the receiver must read the defender. This proper pass must be stressed. Never allow an incorrect read (see chapter 8 for the key to reading the primary and secondary receivers).

In drill 62 we combine passing, dribbling, the middle cut, the backdoor cut, and the V-cut. Now your players are really beginning to play team basketball.

Drill 63 puts two attackers against two defenders, making it easy for coaches to see who makes mistakes in judgment as players continue to practice both *when* to make their maneuvers as well as *how* to make them.

Spacing is added to passing and cutting in drill 64, as are a third attacker and a third defender. Drill 65 adds dribbling to spacing, passing, and cutting. Again, three attackers and three defenders make it easy for coaches to see who commits errors of judgment and miscues of technique and tactics.

Drill 66 offers a three-on-three recognition of *when* as well as how to perform tactics of passing, dribbling, cutting, and spacing.

Drills 67 through 70 give attackers opportunities to learn passing and cutting techniques under various gamelike circumstances. For example, drill 67 adds offensive and defensive rebounding. Drill 68 promotes full-court passing and cutting. Drill 69 adds defensive pressure by not allowing attackers to dribble, compelling passers to be accurate and cutters to be crisp with their cuts. Drill 70 brings it all together and adds shooting to the mix.

TWO-ON-TWO PASS, DRIBBLE, AND CUT

Team • 3 minutes

SKILL FOCUS Triple-threat position (9), rocker step (11), in and out (12, 28), crossover (13, 29), spin (14, 30), half-spin (15, 31), front pivot (35), reverse pivot (36), jump stop (37), stride stop (38), chest pass (44), bounce pass (44), overhead pass (44), pass receiving (44), slide step (46), fake passing (47), V-cut (53), middle cut (54), backdoor cut (55), motion offense rules (122)

Beginner

1. Players line up as shown in figures 1, 2, and 3. Figure 1 shows the middle cut, figure 2 shows the backdoor cut, and figure 3 shows the V-cut. In this drill, each cut needs to be run separately. The defense simulates the coverage that activates the one particular cut. This teaches attackers to recognize when to run each cut. After a minute, offense rotates to defense, and defense goes to the end of the line.
2. In each figure, players 1 and 2 create their own cuts based on the way the defense plays them; unlike in previous drills, they do not have to explain their moves. You will notice in each instance players do not have to pass to make a cut. Players may cut any time the ball moves by pass or dribble.
3. Player 1, in all figures, can use fakes, rocker steps, and dribbling moves to drive to the basket, and then pass back out to 2. Player 1 cuts, and 2 can use fakes, rocker steps, or dribbling moves.
4. The following steps describe the action shown in figure 1, but your drill sequences should vary every time because they are based on the way play evolves. For clarity's sake, defenders are not shown following their assignments in the figures.
5. Defenders should drop away from their assignment instead of jumping toward the ball. This signals the middle cut (figure 1).
6. Player 2 dribbles into the frontcourt. Player 1 sees that the defender is not playing 1 properly, so 1 middle-cuts. Player 2 can then hit 1 for the driving layup, and the play starts over.
7. In figure 1, 2 passes to 1 after 1 has come back out to a wing. Player 2 middle-cuts; if 1 could have hit 2 for a layup, they would start over.

(continued)

Backdoor Cut

1. Players repeat steps 1 through 3. Defenders should overplay between the ball and their assignment, sometimes exaggerating their knees coming over their toes. This beckons the backdoor cut.
2. Player 2 dribbles into the frontcourt (figure 2). Player 1 sees that the defender is not playing 1 properly, so 1 backdoor cuts. A cutter may backdoor cut any time the defender overplays between the passer and the cutter, or when the cutter sees the defender's front knee going in front of the toes, or when the defender takes eyes off the cutter to watch the ball handler. Player 2 can hit 1 for the driving layup, and the play starts over.
3. But in figure 2, 2 passes to 1 after 1 has come back out to a wing.
4. Player 2 backdoor cuts. If 1 could have hit 2 for a layup, they would have started over. But 2 cuts into the corner, and defender X2 follows.

V-Cut

1. Players repeat steps 1 through 3 in the beginner drill. When defenders play proper denial defense, middle and backdoor cuts are not available, so V-cuts provide ways for teammates to reverse the ball even under pressure. Remind players of the motion offense rule: *Every player must move on every pass.* The V-cut permits players to follow this rule by simply replacing themselves. This is the purpose of this drill—to recognize *when* to use the cuts as well as how to make them.
2. Player 2 dribbles into the frontcourt (figure 3). Player 1 sees that no advantage is gained by a middle or backdoor cut, so 1 V-cuts. A player may V-cut any time the ball moves by pass or by dribble. A player may V-cut to keep the 15-foot (4.5-m) spacing required by motion offense rules. So player 1 V-cuts to replace herself, and 2 hits 1 after 1 has come back out to a guard position.
3. Then player 2 V-cuts toward the corner; 1 could hit 2 for a layup if X2 does not cover 2 properly.

TEACHING POINTS

1. Reinforce the two cutting rules of motion offense: *Use the cut your defender gives you,* and *maintain 15-foot (4.5-m) spacing.*
2. Reinforce the other two motion offense rules: *Every player must move on every pass* and *when a player dribbles toward you, you must cut or fade.*
3. Players may use moves, rocker steps, and dribbling moves to drive to the basket to pass back outside.

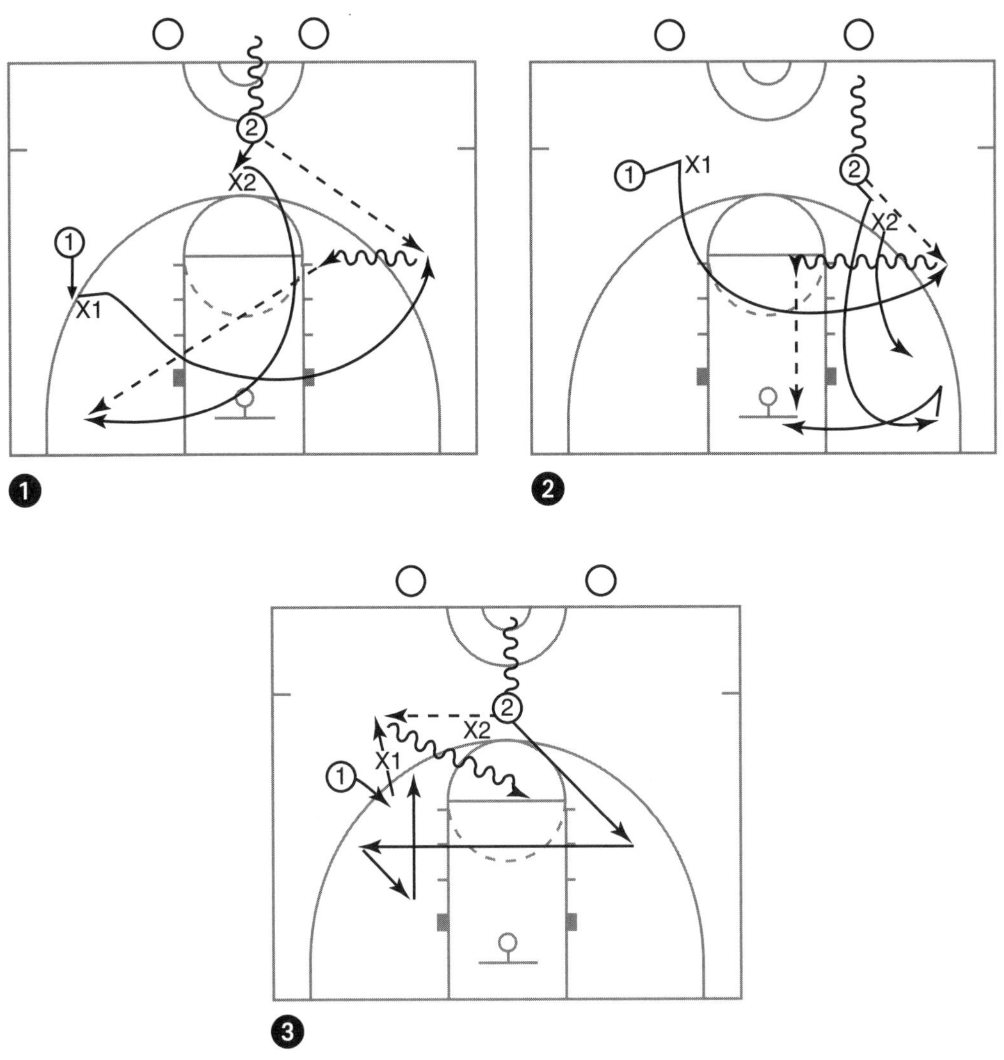

Related Drills *9, 11-15, 28-31, 35-37, 44, 46-47, 53-59, 63-66, 96-97, 122-127*

63

TWO-ON-TWO RECOGNITION

Team • 6 minutes

SKILL FOCUS Triple threat (9), rocker step (11), in and out (12, 28), crossover (13, 29), spin (14, 30), half-spin (15, 31), front pivot (35), reverse pivot (36), jump stop (37), stride stop (38), chest pass (44), bounce pass (44), overhead pass (44), pass receiving (44), slide step (46), fake passing (47), V-cut (53), middle cut (54), backdoor cut (55), flash pivot cut (56), motion offense rules (122)

Intermediate

1. Players line up as shown in the figure. After 2 minutes, the offense rotates to defense, and the defense goes to the end of the line.
2. You should have run drills 53 through 62 before using this drill. After drilling on 53 through 62, cutters will have run their cuts with no defenders, and cutters must recognize and react. Here players X1 and X2 play live defense, and 1 and 2 must take advantage of what X1 and X2 dictate. You may run this drill before teaching man-to-man defense, but the drill is more effective if you have run all your defensive drills.
3. The following steps describe the action shown in the figure, but your drill sequences should vary each time, based on the way play evolves.
4. Player 2 dribbles into the frontcourt, and 1 sees X1 sagging to help on the dribbling 2. Therefore, 1 middle-cuts. Player 2 does not pass 1 the ball, so 1 comes back out to the wing.
5. Now 2 passes to 1; X2 jumps toward the pass, giving 2 the backdoor cut.
6. Player 1 does not pass 2 the ball, so 2 cuts to short corner.
7. Player 1 starts to dribble outside; 2 sees this dribble and flash pivots. Then 1 passes to 2; X1 turns to look at this pass, and 1 races backdoor.
8. Throughout this set of cuts, the offense is trying to score, so if players can pass for a driving layup, they should.
9. At the end of 2 minutes, rotate your players and explain where any mistakes were made.

Option Players call out reasons for their moves while making them.

Advanced

1. Limit the number of cuts and passes the offense may make before they must score. If the defense can keep the offense from scoring during that number, the teams rotate. A good number to start with is five passes. If the defense forces a turnover, the teams rotate.
2. Call for more cuts by allowing the offense to score only on layups—no jump shots.

➔ TEACHING POINTS

1. Reinforce the two cutting rules of motion offense: *Use the cut your defender gives you* and *maintain 15-foot (4.5-m) spacing.*
2. Teach the other two motion offense rules: *Every player must move on every pass* and *when a player dribbles toward you, you must cut or fade.*
3. Players may use moves, rocker steps, and dribbling moves to drive to the basket to pass back outside.

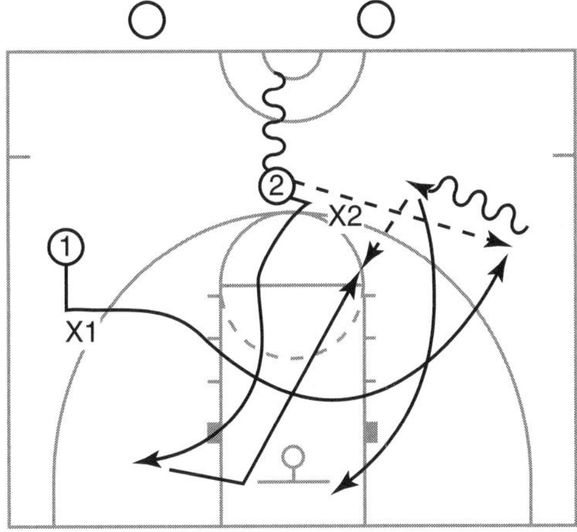

Related Drills *9, 11-15, 28-31, 35-37, 44, 46-47, 53-59, 64-66, 96-97, 122-127*

64 THREE-ON-THREE PASSING, CUTTING, AND SPACING

Team • 4 minutes

SKILL FOCUS Chest pass (44), bounce pass (44), overhead pass (44), pass receiving (44), slide step (46), fake passing (47), V-cut (53), middle cut (54), backdoor cut (55), flash pivot cut (56), motion offense rules (122)

Intermediate

1. Use three offensive and three defensive players (see figure). For clarity's sake, defenders are not illustrated in the figure.
2. Defenders play live defense. Offense players make the cuts dictated by the play of the defenders.
3. Do not allow dribbling in this drill; players must score by cutting, adhering to motion offense rules.
4. After 2 minutes, offense and defense switch roles.
5. In the figure (which is just one of an infinite number of sequences of cuts), player 1 V-cuts to the side high post. Player 2 passes to 1 and immediately cuts backdoor. Meanwhile, 3 has cut backdoor on the baseline. (Remember: Every player must move on every pass.)
6. Meanwhile, 2 has V-cut back away from the basket to a side post position. On this second pass, both 1 and 3 must make another cut (not shown). This continues until the offense scores.
7. This is a live three-on-three drill with no dribbling. Each player must be aware of proper spacing (15 feet, or 4.5 m).

Options

1. Designate a maximum number of passes; the offense must score or else change place with the defense.
2. Require that the defense stop the offense two consecutive times before the defense rotates to offense.
3. Emphasize a certain cut by allowing points each time the offense can maneuver and get that particular cut.
4. Allow only layups; this will result in many more cuts.
5. Give the offense the ball five times, and then the defense gets the ball five times. The team that scores the most in their five turns wins.

➔ TEACHING POINTS

1. Reinforce the two cutting rules of the motion offense: *Use the cut your defender gives you* and *maintain 15-foot (4.5-m) spacing.*
2. Reinforce that *every player must move on every pass.*

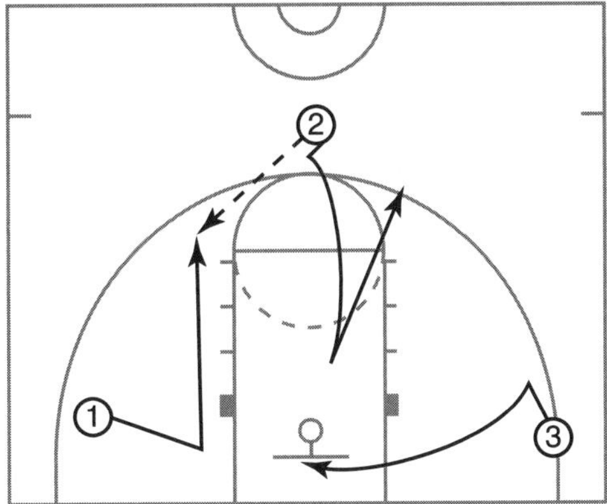

Related Drills *35-37, 44, 46-47, 53-63, 65-66, 122-127*

65

THREE-ON-THREE PASSING, CUTTING, DRIBBLING, SPACING

Team • 6 minutes

➲ SKILL FOCUS Triple-threat position (9), rocker step (11), in and out (12, 28), crossover (13, 29), spin (14, 30), half-spin (15, 31), front pivot (35), reverse pivot (36), jump stop (37), stride stop (38), chest pass (44), bounce pass (44), overhead pass (44), pass receiving (44), slide step (46), fake passing (47), swim move (53), V-cut (53), middle cut (54), backdoor cut (55), flash pivot cut (56), pump fake (96), pump fake crossover (96), motion offense rules (122)

Intermediate

1. Use three offensive and three defensive players (see figure). Defenders are not shown in the figure.
2. Defenders play live defense. Offensive players make the cuts dictated by the play of the defenders.
3. Dribbling is added in this drill, so players cut, pass, and dribble, activating all the dribble moves as well as the rocker step. Players can score by cutting, faking, and driving, adhering to motion offense rules.
4. After 3 minutes the offense and defense switch roles.
5. In the figure (which is just one of an infinite number of cut sequences), player 2 dribbles toward 1, who is overplayed by X1. This is called a *dribbling entry* into the motion offense. Player 1 may fade or cut, and in this case chooses to backdoor cut. If 2 can pass to 1, and 1 can get the layup, a new sequence begins. Player 3 V-cuts to keep 15-foot (4.5-m) spacing, per motion offense rules.
6. In the figure, 2 passes back to 3, which means all players must now move again, per motion offense rules. So 1 flash pivot cuts; 2 replaces himself, using the V-cut; and the moves continue.
7. This is a live three-on-three drill with dribbling. Receivers can square up to triple-threat position on receiving the pass. Players can drive off the rocker step or a dribbling offensive move. Moves can also be made at the end of the dribble to get off either a jump shot or a layup.

➜ Options

1. Designate a maximum number of passes; the offense must score or else change places with the defense.
2. Require that the defense stop the offense two consecutive times before the defense rotates to offense.
3. Emphasize a certain cut by allowing points each time the offense can maneuver and get that particular cut.
4. Allow only layups; this will result in many more cuts.
5. Give the offense the ball five times, and then the defense gets the ball five times. The team that scores the most in their five turns wins.

➲ TEACHING POINTS

1. Reinforce the two cutting rules of the motion offense: *Use the cut your defender gives you* and *maintain 15-foot (4.5-m) spacing.*
2. Reinforce the other two motion offense rules: *Every player must move on every pass* and *when a player dribbles toward you, you must cut or fade.*
3. Players may use moves, rocker steps, and dribbling moves to drive to the basket to pass back outside.

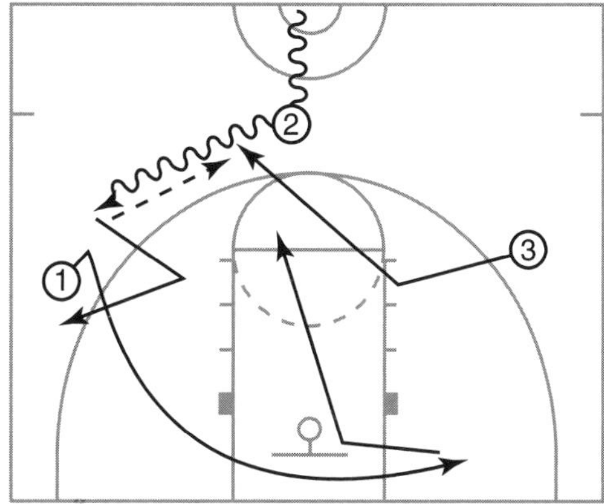

Related Drills *9, 11-15, 28-31, 35-37, 44, 46-47, 53-64, 66, 96-97, 122-127*

66

THREE-ON-THREE PASS, CUT, AND RECOGNITION

Team • 6 minutes

SKILL FOCUS Triple-threat position (9), rocker step (11), in and out (12, 28), crossover (13, 29), spin (14, 30), half-spin (15, 31), front pivot (35), reverse pivot (36), jump stop (37), stride stop (38), chest pass (44), bounce pass (44), overhead pass (44), pass receiving (44), slide step (46), fake passing (47), swim move (53), V-cut (53), middle cut (54), backdoor cut (55), flash pivot cut (56), pump fake (96), pump fake crossover (96), motion offense rules (122)

Intermediate

1. Players line up as shown in the figure. After 3 minutes, offense and defense switch roles. For clarity's sake, defensive moves are not shown in the figure.
2. Players should have run drills 53 through 65 before using this drill. After drilling on 53 through 65, cutters will have run their cuts with no defenders, and they will have run their cuts separately with only predetermined defense. Here defenders (X1, X2, and X3) play live defense. Offense players (1, 2, and 3) must take advantage of what the defenders dictate. Cutters must recognize and react. You may run this drill before teaching man-to-man defense, but the drill is more effective if you have run all your defensive drills.
3. We will describe here what happens in the figure, but this is only a typical sequence of cuts. Never should the same series of cuts occur again during the drilling. Let your players create based on how defenders play them.
4. Player 1 dribbles into the frontcourt and passes to 2. Every player moves on every pass.
5. Player 1 middle-cuts because the defender did not jump to the ball; 3 V-cuts to keep proper 15-foot (4.5-m) spacing.
6. Player 2 passes to 1, who has cut to the corner strong side. This again activates cuts by all players.
7. Then 2 backdoor cuts because X2 looked at the pass; 3 again V-cuts to keep proper spacing.
8. Throughout this set of cuts, the offense is trying to score; if they can pass for the driving layup, they should.
9. At the end of 3 minutes, rotate players and explain where mistakes were made.

Option Have players call out their reasons for their moves while making them.

Advanced

1. Limit the number of cuts and passes the offense may make before they must score. If the defense can keep the offense from scoring during that number, the teams rotate. A good number to start with is five passes. If the defense forces a turnover, the teams rotate.
2. Call for more cuts by allowing the offense to score only on layups—no jump shots. Moves at the end of a dribble can be used near the basket as part of the layup.
3. Designate one player to be allowed to score, but don't tell defenders who this player is. This compels the offense to try to get that player open for the jump shot or layup. It also has the advantage of working players who are not as offensively advanced as their teammates.

TEACHING POINTS

1. Reinforce the cutting rules of motion offense: *Use the cut your defender gives you* and *maintain 15-foot (4.5-m) spacing.*
2. Reinforce the other two motion offense rules: *Every player must move on every pass* and *when a player dribbles toward you, you must cut or fade.*
3. Players may use moves, rocker steps, and dribbling moves to drive to the basket to pass back outside.

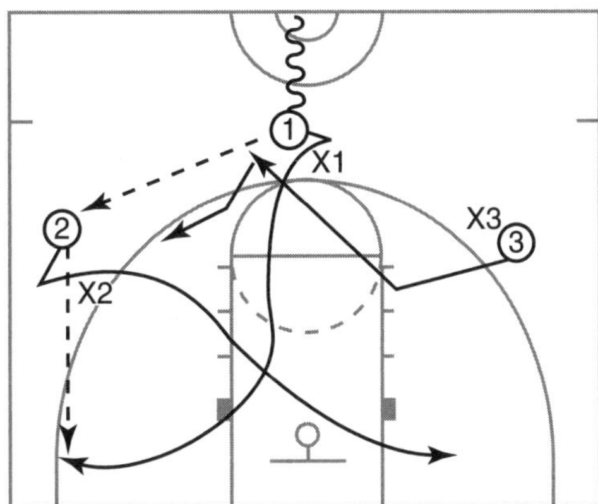

Related Drills *9, 11-15, 28-31, 35-37, 44, 46-47, 53-65, 96-97, 122-127*

67

PASS, CUT, AND REBOUND

Team • 4 minutes

SKILL FOCUS Front pivot (35), reverse pivot (36), jump stop (37), stride stop (38), catching the ball (44), bounce pass (44), chest pass (44), overhead pass (44), one-handed chest pass (44), one-handed bounce pass (44), fake passing (47), V-cut (53), middle cut (54), backdoor cut (55), jab step and roll rebounding (78), swim technique (81), straight-stick shooting technique (84-88), pump fake series (96), pass and blast (122)

Intermediate

1. Line players up as shown in the figure.
2. Player 2 begins the drill by dribbling into the frontcourt.
3. Both 1 and 3 V-cut to get open for the pass from 2. Player 2 passes to 1 in the figure (or 2 can pass to 3, and the drill is run from the other side of the court).
4. Player 2 dips on the V-cut and cuts behind 1. Player 2 continues around 1 and goes to touch the sideline with one hand.
5. Meanwhile, player 3 has either middle-cut or backdoor cut for a pass from 1; 3 takes a jump shot.
6. Player 2 races toward the basket for a weak-side rebound. Player 1 races to block 2 off the boards. Players 1 and 2 battle for the rebound.
7. Rotation: Player 2 goes to the end of 3's line; 1 goes to the end of 2's line; and 3 goes to the end of 1's line.

Advanced

1. Player 2 can execute a dribbling move before passing to 1.
2. Player 3 can make a dribbling move before shooting.

Options (all skill levels)

1. Allow the offense to begin on either side of the court. This requires players to concentrate more because their duties change.
2. If 2 gets the offensive rebound, 2 can use the pump fake series to shoot a layup. If 1 gets the defensive rebound, 1 can throw an outlet pass (overhead) to the next player in 2's line, and the drill continues.
3. You are teaching the rules of the motion offensive: pass and blast footwork, for example, between 1 and 2. Or have 2 stop the dribble, fake pass to 1, and pass to 3.

➲ TEACHING POINTS

1. Emphasize offensive rebounding. Make sure offensive rebounders know the jab step and roll, the jab step and go, and the swim technique (see drills 78 and 81). You want to stress getting the second shot.
2. Also emphasize defensive rebounding. Make sure every attacker is boxed out on every shot. Defensive rebounders should use the slide step and box out or the immediate box out techniques of drill 79. Allowing one shot per possession should be the goal.
3. Almost 72 percent of shots taken will rebound to the weak side of the court (side away from the shot). This is called primary rebounding position. Both 1 and 2 must fight for this position. Those weak-side rebounds also come off at the same angle as the shot (in other words, a shot taken from the corner will rebound to the opposite corner, a shot taken at a 45-degree angle will rebound at a 45-degree angle). This is the rebounding savvy you want to emphasize in this drill.
4. Of course you also want to make sure cuts are done correctly, passes are made accurately, and shots are taken in correct form. Teach relentlessly during drills. Players remember best what the coach emphasizes.

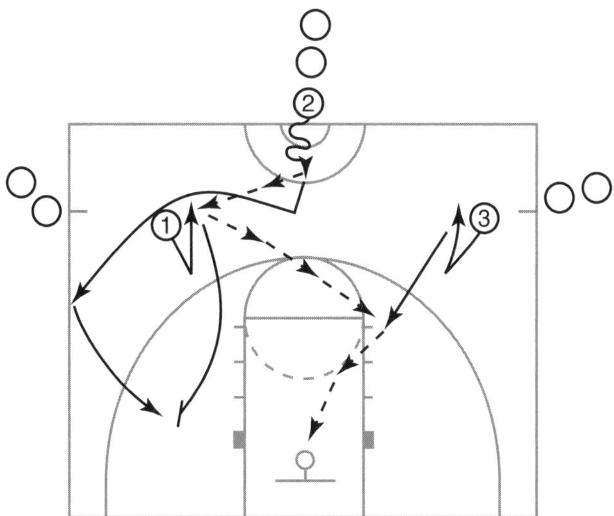

Related Drills *35-38, 44, 47, 53-55, 78, 81, 84-88, 96, 122*

68

OUTLET PASS, CUTTING, SHOOTING

Team • 6 minutes

SKILL FOCUS Conditioning, layup (8), post positioning (10), rocker step (11), perimeter moves (12-15), speed dribble (23), change of pace (25), dribbling move (28-31), front pivot (35), reverse pivot (36), jump stop (37), stride stop (38), overhead pass (44), pass receiving (44), bounce pass (44), chest pass (44), one-handed bounce pass (44), one-handed chest pass (44), V-cut (53), middle cut (54), backdoor cut (55) flash pivot cut (56), straight-line shooting (84-88), post moves (96-103), pass and blast (122)

Beginner

1. Pair up your players. In figure 1, 5 is paired with 1; 4 is paired with 2.
2. Player 5 tosses the ball off the board; 5 rebounds and pivots while in the air.
3. Player 5 throws an outlet pass (overhead) to 1. Player 1 meanwhile has executed the V-cut to come back to the ball to receive the pass.
4. Player 1 dribbles to the other free-throw line. Player 5 sprints down the outside lane and cuts to the basket at the free-throw line extended (figure 1).
5. Player 1 passes to 5 for a layup.
6. Players step off the court because the next pair (4 and 2) began their movement when 5 and 1 crossed the half-court line.
7. After 1 and 5 have finished the drill, they step off the court. When all groups have completed the drill, the groups execute the same drill going back down the floor. After one complete revolution, have 1 and 5 exchange duties.

Intermediate

1. Add another player to the drill (3). Now 1, 3, and 5 are grouped together. Player 3 lines up on the baseline and sprints the length of the court, stopping between the free-throw line extended to the corner. Figure 2 shows a spot where 3 can stop.
2. Instead of racing down floor for a layup, 5 cuts into the low-post area. Player 1 passes to 3 at the wing; 3 can shoot, make a one-on-one move, or pass to the low-post player, 5.
3. Player 5 uses the post techniques to get open (see drill 10). On receiving the pass from 3, 5 uses a low-post move (see drills 114 and 115).

Advanced

1. Player 1 can use a dribbling move while dribbling down the floor.
2. If 3 is in the drill, 3 can use a perimeter move before shooting or passing to the low post.
3. Player 3 can race down the floor on the opposite side of 5. Player 5 would then have to use a flash pivot cut to get to 3's side of the court.
4. Player 5 could stay on the perimeter and 3 could cut to the low post.

➔ Options (all skill levels)

1. You can put two defenders (or three if three attackers are used) on the court for an offense-against-defense drill.
2. Break the drill down into parts and drill only on the part you want to focus.

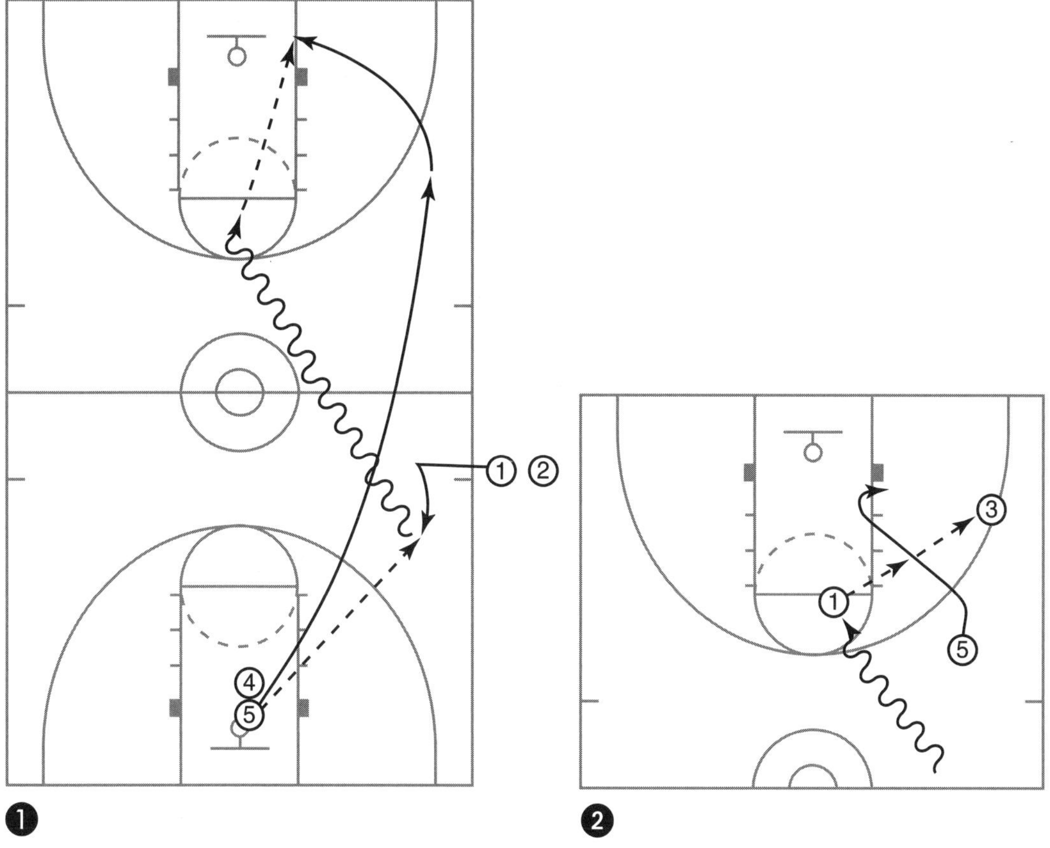

Related Drills *8, 10-15, 23, 25, 28-31, 35-38, 54-56, 84-88, 96-103, 122*

69 FULL-COURT PASSING, CUTTING

Team • 6 minutes

SKILL FOCUS Conditioning, front pivot (35), reverse pivot (36), jump stop (37), stride stop (38), passing and receiving (44), traps (50), V-cut (53), middle cut (54), backdoor cut (55), flash pivot cut (56) screening (71), passing out of trap (157-158)

Beginner

1. Line players up as shown in the figure.
2. Players 1, 2, and 3 go down the floor passing and cutting until they reach the other end of the floor. Each player has a defender.
3. No dribbles are allowed—just cutting and passing.
4. Limit the type of passes and cuts your beginners can make. For example, allow only chest and bounce passing. Cuts should be limited to V-cuts and middle cuts. Cuts should be made to advance the ball down the floor. If the middle cut does not allow the cutter to receive the pass, the cutter may have to V-cut back toward the ball. On receiving the pass, the cutter cannot dribble but must pass to another teammate.
5. When 1, 2, and 3 have successfully passed the ball without a turnover to the other end of the court, they become the defenders, and X1, X2, and X3 become the offense. The drill continues back to the end of the court where it began.
6. After a complete revolution, A, B, and C step on the floor as the attackers, and 1, 2, and 3 stay as defenders. This rotation continues.
7. If a turnover occurs, the offense must sprint down the floor and back. They then begin again against the same defenders.

Intermediate

1. All passes may be used. All cuts may be used.
2. If the ball is successfully advanced into the frontcourt, the three players on offense may attack the three players on defense for a shot. Still allow no dribbling, but do allow screens.

Option (all skill levels) If traps have been taught and are going to be part of your defense, you may allow trapping. This would require a trap and one defender trying to intercept the pass to one of the other two. Remember: no dribbling.

➲ TEACHING POINTS

1. Make sure players execute sharp cuts; defenders can overplay the reception with no fear because the player receiving the ball cannot advance it by dribbling.
2. Pass receivers must come to meet the pass.
3. Passes must be crisp and accurate.
4. This drill requires teamwork. Players depend on each other, which builds a team concept.

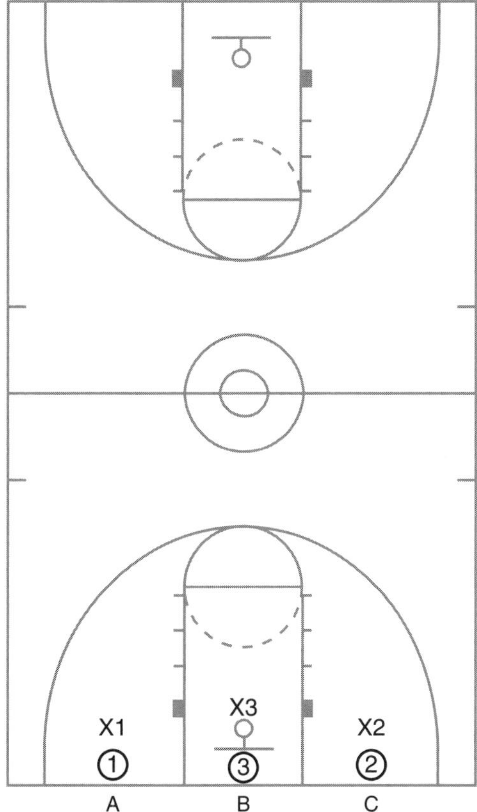

Related Drills *35-38, 44-52, 53-61, 62-68, 71, 157-158*

70

INDIVIDUAL COMBO

Individual or team • 4 minutes

SKILL FOCUS Layup (8), triple threat (9), rocker step (11), in and out (12, 28), crossover (13, 29), spin (14, 30), half-spin (15, 31), control dribble (24), change of pace (25), hesitation dribble (26), jump stop (37), stride stop (38), bounce pass (44), chest pass (44), one-handed chest pass (44), one-handed bounce pass (44), receiving pass (44), V-cut (53), middle cut (54), backdoor cut (55), shooting technique (84-88), end-of-dribble moves (96, 116-117), passing off dribble (113), motion offense rules (122)

Beginner

1. Line players up as shown in the figure.
2. This drill will be run in seven steps: (1) layup, (2) 8-foot (2.4-m) bank shot, (3) catching ball on wing, fake shot, one dribble baseline and shoot, (4) catching ball on wing, fake shot, one dribble middle and shoot, (5) catching ball on wing, rocker step series into a dribbling move, jump shot, (6) shoot the three, and (7) shots at the end of the dribble.
3. Beginners do only steps 1, 2, and 6. Of the steps listed, only steps 1 and 6 are shown in the figure.
4. Players 1, 2, 3, 4, and 5 each has a basketball. These players make a pass to A, B, C, D, and E.
5. Players A, B, C, D, and E make a cut before they receive the pass. In the figure, (1) shows a backdoor cut by A. A then receives a bounce pass from 1. A shoots a layup in step 1. Next time, A can shoot an 8-foot (2.4-m) bank shot.
6. Step 6 is shown in the figure. A makes a V-cut and receives the chest pass from 1. A shoots the three-point shot. Beginners do only steps 1, 2, and 6.
7. The shooter rebounds the shot, passes back to the passer, and moves to the same spot on the other side of the floor. The same shot is repeated on the other side of the floor before the second shot is attempted. For example, the backdoor cut and the layup are run from both sides of the floor before the 8-foot (2.4-m) bank shot is run from both sides of the floor.
8. After the seven shots listed (in step 2) have been attempted from both sides of the floor, the players 1, 2, 3, 4, and 5 exchange places with players A, B, C, D, and E. A coach should run through a choice of cuts, moves, passes, and shots several times in the 4 minutes allotted for the drill.

Intermediate

1. Intermediate players execute the three steps described for beginners and add to those three shots steps 3, 4, and 5 (not 7). In step 3, A receives a pass at the wing, fakes a shot, one dribbles baseline, and shoots. In step 4, A receives the pass, fakes a shot, one dribbles to the middle, and shoots. In step 5, A receives the pass, performs a rocker step move into a dribbling move, and shoots a jump shot.

2. Alter the cuts, fakes, and passes. For example, in step 1, have players middle-cut, throw a chest pass, and dribble-drive for the layup.

Advanced

1. Advanced players do all six steps described for beginner and intermediate players.
2. Advanced players add the moves and shots at the end of the dribble. This adds the pump fake, the pump fake crossover, and the pump fake up-and-under.
3. Advanced players can also add moves by the passer. In this case, the passer begins at half-court, uses a dribble move to dribble to the head of the key, and makes a pass off the dribble, such as a one-handed bounce pass. This requires cutters to time their moves with the passer.

Options (all skill levels)

1. Alter in any step the passes to be used, the cuts to be used, the moves to be used, and the shots to be taken. For example, request the rocker step crossover move be used one time and the rocker step direct drive move be used the next.
2. Drill on the cuts, moves, passes, and shots you intend to use in your motion offense. Stress the motion offense rules.

TEACHING POINTS

1. Explain the sequence you intend to use.
2. Explain how this sequence is part of your team's motion offense rules.
3. Make sure each cut, pass, move (both stationery and dribbling), and shot is made using proper fundamentals.

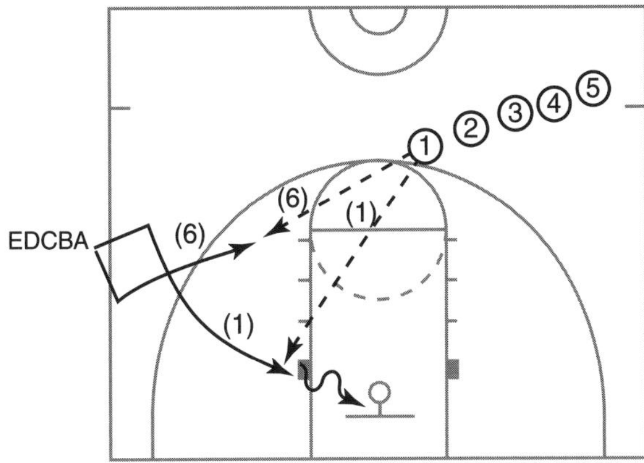

Related Drills *8, 9, 11-15, 24-26, 28-31, 37-38, 44, 53-56, 84-88, 96, 113, 116-117, 122*

CHAPTER

8

Screening

The purpose of this chapter is twofold: (1) to teach proper individual screening techniques and (2) to add screening to your motion offense. Your players should now be adept at passing, cutting, dribbling moves, the rocker step, and spacing. Add screening to that repertoire, and your motion offense becomes almost unstoppable.

In this chapter we integrate the individual techniques and tactics of screening into a team concept. We also incorporate the screening game into the motion offense, giving your squad another offensive weapon.

A major point of emphasis in each drill should be: *When setting a screen for a teammate, call out the teammate's name.* This coordinates the fundamentals of the art of screening and accepting the screen into a team concept. All players, including the passer to the cutters coming off of the screen, hear this communication and know what is about to occur. Never allow a screen to be set without this communication technique.

Pass and screen away is covered in drill 71. Players learn how to set this screen, when to roll, when to fade, and when to replace themselves. The teammate with the ball will learn how to determine who is the primary receiver and who is the secondary receiver. (An unmistakable key determines this.)

Drill 72 covers passing and screening on the ball, which includes the screen-and-roll as well as the unstoppable explosive blast. The drill illustrates how these maneuvers are added to the motion offense.

Drill 73 displays three attackers running, running again, and running yet again all the screening techniques and tactics so coaches can determine who needs further improvement. The *when* is emphasized as well as the *how.*

Drill 74 brings all the screening techniques and strategies together in one drill. Players learn how to cooperate to free themselves and their teammates with a screening game. Adding the screening game to their one-on-one game, dribbling game, and cutting game will make for a formidable motion offense.

Drill 75 adds four basic screening techniques to the screening options of your motion offense. Drill 75 allows players to continuously use two-player techniques on one side of the court and three-player techniques on the other side of the court.

PASS AND SCREEN AWAY

Individual or team • 10 minutes

➲ SKILL FOCUS Triple-threat position (9), rocker step (11), in and out (12, 28), crossover (13, 29), spin (14, 30), half-spin (15, 31), control dribble (24), reverse pivot (36), jump stop (37), chest pass (44), bounce pass (44), overhead pass (44), fake passing (47), pass and screen away, screen away and roll, screen away and fade, pump fake (96), pump fake crossover (96)

Beginner

1. Players line up as shown. Rotation is from 1 to X1 to 2 to X2 to 3 to the end of the line. Player 1 passes to 3 and goes to set a screen on X2.
2. Player 2 sets up the screen by taking a step or two away from the screen. Player 1 must set the screen on the upper half of X2's body, requiring X2 to go beneath 1's screen if X2 is to stay with 2. Player 1 then rolls into the path of X2 going underneath the screen.
3. Player 2 reads X1's coverage. If X1 switches, 2 goes high for a pass from 3. Because of X1's switch, 2 is now the secondary target. Player 1 is the primary target on the roll. If 1 executes the roll correctly, X2 is behind 1 and 1 can receive the pass for a layup.
4. Player 3 reads X1's switch and passes to 1 for the layup.
5. All defensive teams teach only one coverage of the screen-and-roll. If you know the technique, you can predrill your squad to exploit it.
6. Set this drill up at different areas of the court each day.

Intermediate

1. Players line up as shown in figure 2. Rotation is from 1 to X1 to 2 to X2 to 3 to the end of the line. Player 1 passes the ball to 3 and goes to screen X2.
2. Player 2 sets up the screen by taking a step or two away from the screen. Player 1 must set a screen on the upper half of X2's body. This requires X2 to go beneath 1's screen if X2 is to stay with 2. Player 1 rolls into the path of X2 going underneath the screen.
3. Player 2 reads X1's coverage. There is no switch. X1 opens up to let X2 slide through and maintain coverage on 2. Player 1 rolls slightly into X2's path before breaking back toward the ball. Player 2 has a middle cut to the basket for a layup, 2 is the primary receiver and 1 the secondary receiver.
4. Player 3 reads X1's opening maneuver and passes to 2 for the layup.

(continued)

Advanced

1. Players line up as shown in figure 3. Rotation is from 1 to X1 to 2 to X2 to 3 to the end of the line. Player 1 passes to 3 and goes to screen X2.
2. Player 2 sets up the screen by taking a step or two away from the screen. Player 1 sets a screen on the upper half of X2's body, which requires X2 to go beneath the screen in order to stay with 2. Player 1 then rolls into the path of X2 going underneath the screen.
3. Player 2 reads X1's coverage. There is no switch. Both X1 and X2 have sagged to the basket to prevent a layup, so 2 cuts toward 3 for a pass and possible jump shot. Player 1 fades away from the area, allowing 3 to pass to 1 for a jump shot. This fade also clears the area should X2 or X1 not close properly on 2. An improper defensive closing maneuver permits 2 to fake and drive to the basket.
4. Player 3 reads X1 and X2's sagging techniques and passes to 2 for the jump shot or proper use of fakes.

TEACHING POINTS

1. Player 2 always sets up the screen by moving away from the place of the screen.
2. Player 1 always sets the screen on the upper half of X2's body. This compels X2 to go underneath the screen or fall behind coverage.
3. Player 1 sets the screen as close as possible to X2 without contact.
4. Player 1 jump stops just before setting the screen.
5. Player 1 reverse pivots into X2 as X2 decides to go beneath the screen.
6. All offensive players, including the passer, key off X1's movement.
7. Any time a screen is set under the motion offense rules, the screener calls out the name of the teammate intended to set the screen for.

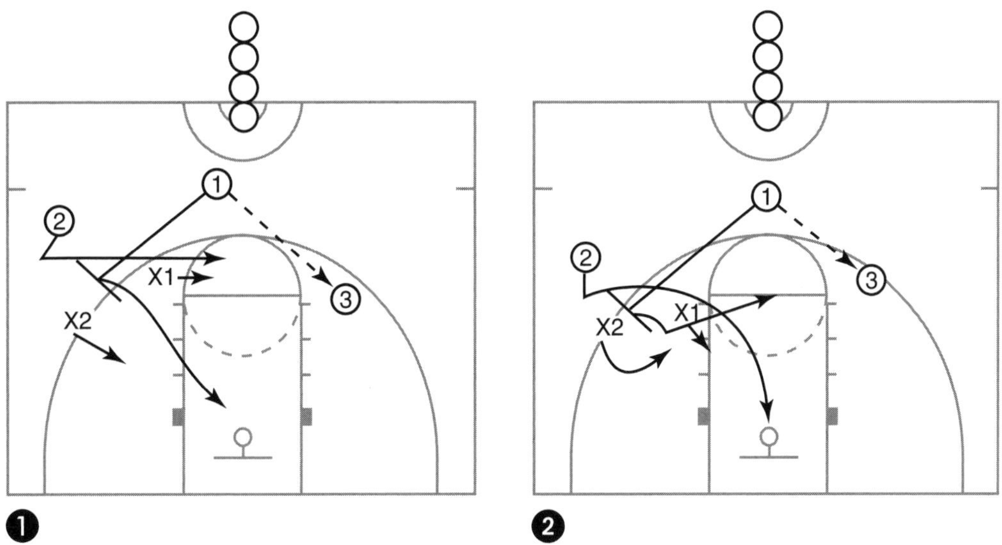

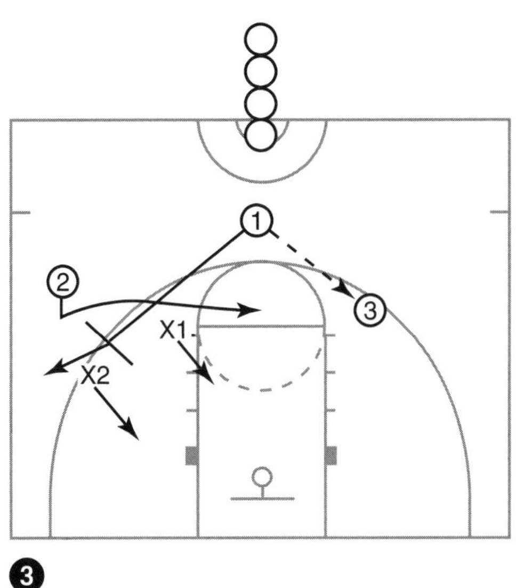

Related Drills *72-75, 122-127*

72

PASS AND SCREEN ON BALL

Individual or team • 6 minutes

➲ SKILL FOCUS Control dribble (24), reverse pivot (36), jump stop (37), chest pass (44), bounce pass (44), overhead pass (44), slide steps (46), fake passing (47), pass and screen away (71), screen away and roll (71), screen away and fade (71), pump fake (96), pump fake crossover (96)

Intermediate

1. Players line up as shown. Rotation is from 1 to X1 to 2 to X2 to the end of the line.
2. Player 1 passes to 2 and goes to screen X2. (Use the same techniques as described in drill 71.)
3. Player 2 drives off the screen, looking to either drive all the way to the basket or to pass back to 1, who has rolled to the basket.
4. Player 2 drives to the basket if X2 tries to fight over the screen.
5. If there is a switch, 1 gets X2 on 1's back and uses slide steps to keep X2 there. Player 2 passes to 1 for a layup; 1 might have to use fakes at the end of a dribble to get a shot off, and 2 might have to use a fake pass to get the ball to 1. Once 1 has X2 on 1's back, 1 goes at least parallel to X2's line to the basket. In fact, 1 might even veer back into X2 without charging.
6. If there is a mismatch in size when X1 and X2 switch, 2 dribbles farther outside while 1 posts up.
7. There does not have to be a pass during the motion offense for a player to screen on the ball; 2 can start with the ball, and 1 can come screen on the ball.
8. Player 1 must communicate, yelling out 2's name when 1 goes to set the screen.

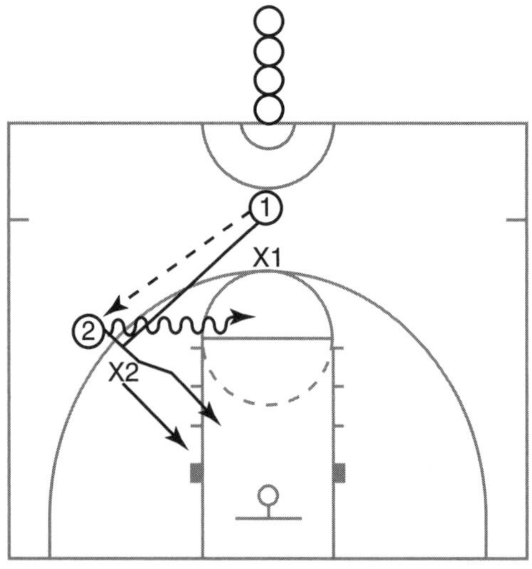

Related Drills *71, 73-75, 122-127*

THREE-PLAYER SCREENING DRILL

Team • 4 minutes

SKILL FOCUS Front pivot (35), reverse pivot (36), jump stop (37), stride stop (38), chest pass (44), bounce pass (44), overhead pass (44), pass receiving (44), slide step (46), V-cut (53), middle cut (54), backdoor cut (55), flash pivot cut (56), screen away (71), screen-and-roll (71), screen and fade (71), motion offense rules (122)

Beginner

1. Players line up as shown. One team runs screens for 1 minute or until they score a layup. That team goes to the end of the line, and the next team steps out. There are no defenders in this drill.
2. No sequence of cuts or screens should be the same from group to group. Players are learning the motion offense using screens. In the figure, 1 dribbles into the frontcourt, passes to 2, and calls out 3's name to set a screen for 3. Player 3 dips to set up the screen, then breaks off the screen but calls out a defensive switch. This tells 1 that 1 is the primary receiver, so 1 breaks back to the ball. Player 2 passes to 1, calling out 1's name, and goes to set the screen, calling out "screen and roll." Player 1 dribbles off 2's screen while 2 rolls. Meanwhile, following the rules of the motion offense, 3 has replaced himself with a V-cut. Player 1 sees a mismatch, calls it out, and dribbles outside. Player 2 posts up the mismatch; 3 on hearing this, flash pivot cuts to take 3's defender out of help position.

TEACHING POINTS

1. Remind players to call the name of the player they intend to screen for.
2. Players tell the reason they are doing what they are doing as they do it.

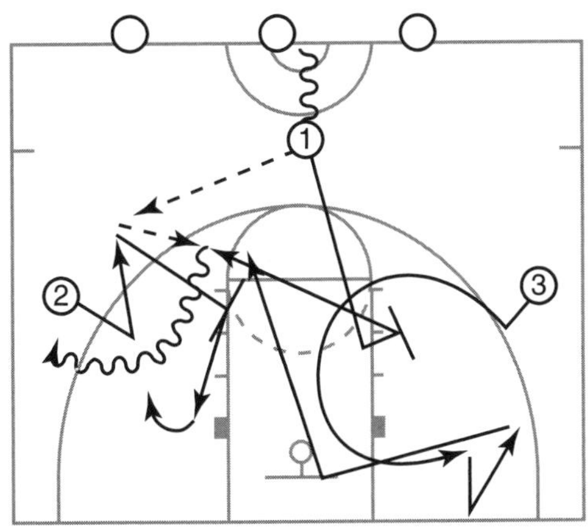

Related Drills *71-72, 74-75, 122-127*

74

THREE-ON-THREE PASS, SCREEN, AND RECOGNITION

Team • 4 minutes

➲ **SKILL FOCUS** Triple-threat position (9), rocker step (11), in and out (12, 28), crossover (13, 29), spin (14, 30), half-spin (15, 31), control dribble (24), reverse pivot (36), jump stop (37), chest pass (44), bounce pass (44), overhead pass (44), fake passing (47), V-cut (53), middle cut (54), backdoor cut (55), flash pivot cut (56), pass and screen away (71), screen away and roll (71), screen away and fade (71), pump fake (96), pump fake crossover (96), motion offense rules (122)

Intermediate

1. Players line up as shown (for clarity's sake, defense is not shown). Defense and offense switch roles after a specified period.
2. No two sequences of cuts should be the same. Let players decide what cut or screen to make and when—as long as they follow the motion offense rules.
3. In the figure, 1 dribbles into the frontcourt, passes to 2, and goes to screen for 2.
4. Player 3, meanwhile, has run the V-cut, and 1 and 2 activate the screen-and-roll. Player 3's defender has helped on 2's dribble, so 2 has passed to 3 and gone to screen for 1. Then 1 comes around 2's screen, and 2 thinks 1 will be open, so 2 fades instead of rolling. At this point, 3 has begun a rocker-step fake.

Advanced

1. Limit the number of screens and passes the offense can make before they must score. (A good number to start with is five screens.) If the defense can keep the offense from scoring, or forces a turnover, teams rotate.
2. Call for more screens by allowing the offense to score only on layups—no jump shots. Players can use moves at the end of a dribble near the basket as part of the layup.
3. Designate one player to be allowed to score, but don't let defenders know who this player is. This compels offensive teammates to try to get that player open for the jump shot or layup. It also has the advantage of working a player who may not be as offensively advanced as the player's teammates.

➲ TEACHING POINTS

1. Teach the cutting rules of motion offense: *Use the cut your defender gives you* and *maintain 15-foot (4.5-m) spacing.*
2. Teach the other two motion offense rules: *Every player must move on every pass* and *when a player dribbles toward you, you must cut or fade.*
3. Teach a new motion offense rule: *When setting a screen for a teammate, call out the teammate's name.*
4. Players may use moves, rocker steps, and dribbling moves to drive to the basket to pass back outside.

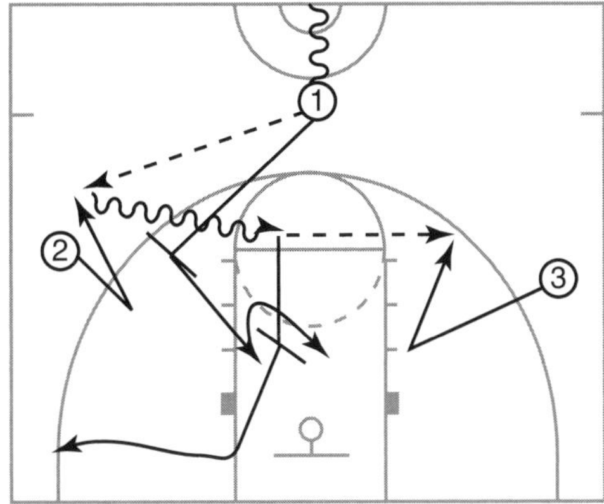

Related Drills *9, 11-15, 28-31, 35-37, 44, 46-47, 53-73, 75, 122-127*

75

THREE-PLAYER CONTINUOUS SCREENING

Team • 8 minutes

➲ SKILL FOCUS Front pivot (35), reverse pivot (36), jump stop (37), stride stop (38), bounce pass (44), chest pass (44), receiving pass (44), fake pass (47), V-cut (53), middle cut (54), backdoor cut (55), flash pivot cut (56), pass and screen away (71), screen away and roll (71), screen away and fade (71), down screen, back screen, screen the screener, screen on the ball, pass and blast (122), motion offense rules (122)

Advanced

1. Line players up as shown in figure 1: three players on one side of the court and two on the other side of the court. Shooting is not allowed. This drill runs continuous screening and cutting only.
2. Players are adding down screens, back screens, and screen-the-screener moves to their offensive repertoire. Remind them of the motion offense rule: *When setting a screen for a teammate, call out the teammate's name.*
3. Stress that each player must move when the ball moves (pass) and when the player with the ball moves (dribble). They accomplish this movement of the motion offensive rules by using only screens and cuts.
4. When 1 passes to 2, all players must move (figure 1). Player 1 uses the pass and screen away technique. Player 1 goes to screen for 3. Player 3 has set up 3's defender by using the V-cut. Player 1 could have cut. Player 1 could have screened for 5. Player 1 could dip and come off a screen by 3. Or use any other combination 1 wishes to use. Players 3 and 5 can execute different techniques from those shown in figure 1. Screens and cuts are limited only by the player's knowledge and imagination.
5. After 1 passes to 2, 1 immediately goes to screen for 3. Then 1 screens down for 5.
6. Meanwhile on the new ball side, 4 has kept 4's defender busy by using a V-cut to replace herself.
7. For explanation purposes, the drill continues: Player 2 passes to 4 (see figure 2), activating another series of cuts and screens: *Every player must move on every pass* is the motion offensive rule. All players on the weak side (side away from the ball) also move. Figure 2 shows player 3 screening down for 5 and 1 setting a back screen for 3 (screen for the screener).
8. Meanwhile 2 has screened down for 4. Player 4 uses 2's down screen to dribble. Player 2 chooses to fade after the screen.
9. Figure 3 shows 3 on ball side after cutting off 1's back screen. Player 4 passes to 5. Now 1 and 5 are ball side, and 3 has joined 2 and 4 on the new weak side. Players 2, 3, and 4 now continuously screen on the weak side, just as 1, 3, and 5 did in figure 1. But in figure 3, 4 backdoor cuts while 2 sets a down screen for 3 and fades. Player 3 uses the screen for a possible pass and three-point shot. Meanwhile 1 has dipped and made way to set a back screen for 5 to use in the screen on the ball and roll technique.

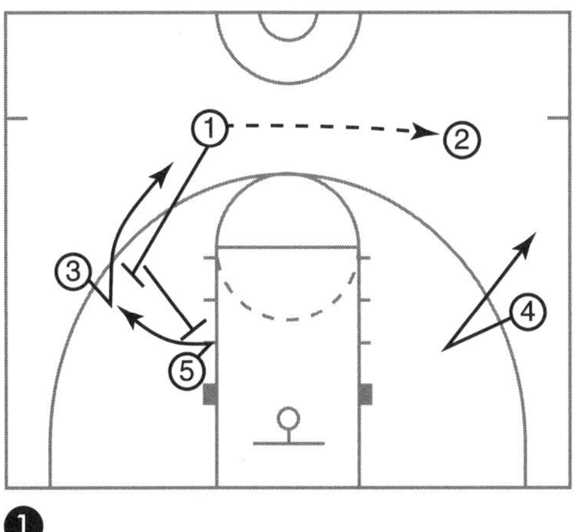

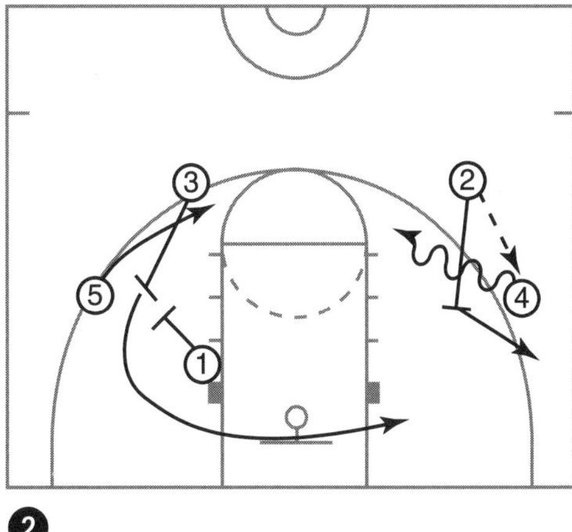

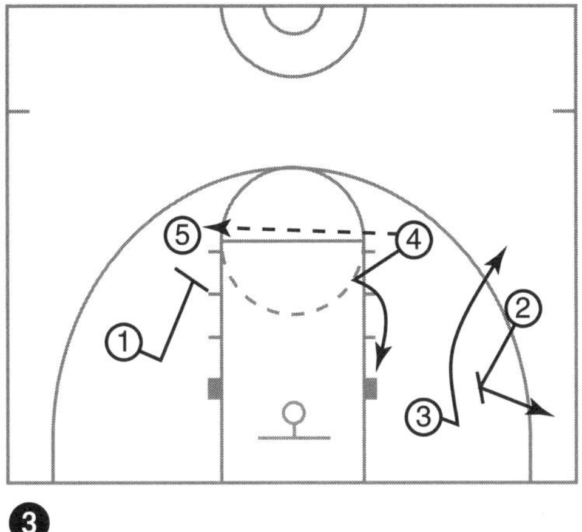

➜ Options

1. These are just a few of the screening options available in the motion offense. You should make sure many options are used.
2. To avoid confusion, you can name only a few screening techniques you will allow on the ball side and a few screening techniques you will allow on the weak side. You can also name just a few cuts you will allow. You do not want to overwhelm your team.
3. Players have the option to use the techniques in any order, but *all* players must move each time the player with the ball moves (dribbles) or the ball moves (pass).
4. It is easy to see you have a weak side with three players continuously screening and cutting, and you have a ball side with two players. This is the essence of your motion offense. Your only rule in this drill: *When a player cuts off a back screen to the ball side, the player with the ball on the ball side must pass to the weak side.* This keeps two players on ball side and three players continuously screening and cutting on the weak side.

(continued)

5. You can divide the 8 minutes into four 2-minute drills. You can use these 2 minutes one after the other in your practice schedule, or you can space the 2 minutes at four different intervals in your practice schedule (see appendix).
6. You can put five defenders against the five attackers. You still do not allow any shots except the layup. If you do this, you have in effect taught a stall game using your motion offense.

TEACHING POINTS

1. First, make sure there are always two players on the ball side and three players on the weak side.
2. Second, make sure players call out the names of the players they intend to screen for. Make sure the player receiving the screen always dips (V-cuts) before using the screen. This sets up the cutter's defender for a perfect screening angle. The screener and the player receiving the screen must work hand in hand, creating perfect team play in the motion offense.
3. Add screening on the ball to the motion offense. This should occur only on the side where the two players are. You do not want congestion on the ball side for the screen-and-roll activities.

Screen on the Ball

1. To screen on the ball, the screener must execute the screen about a half-body on the high side of the dribbler's defender. This compels the defender on the dribbler to go below the screener, allowing the dribbler to gain an advantage.
2. Dribblers must fake away from their intended direction. They can do this with a simple ball fake, or use a direct-drive fake or crossover fake from the rocker step series.

Down Screen

1. Screeners should set their screens where they know their teammates will be after the teammate has dipped to set up a defender for the screen. A few times drilling will allow the screener and the teammate receiving the screen to work together to make this screen successful.
2. Down screens are usually used to free a jump shooter coming off the down screen.

➜ Back Screen

1. The screener should set the screen at least a few feet from the defender, or else this type of screen can easily be called illegal. The screener sets the screen and remains motionless, letting the player using the screen to set up the defender.
2. The player using the back screen should dip to set up the defender. The player then cuts off the screener as close as possible (with a shoulder rub). This compels a defensive switch or an easy layup will result.
3. After setting the screen, the screener steps outside, using the fade technique.

➜ Screen the Screener

1. The player who sets the screen for the screener knows where this action will occur.
2. Figure 2 offers a perfect illustration. Player 1, who will screen for the screener, knows where the screen is going to occur. Player 1 can easily see 5 dip before using 3's down screen. Player 1 should set a screen on 5's defender if the defensive team is switching all screens. Player 1 should set a screen on 3's defender if the defensive team is fighting through all screens.

Related Drills *35-38, 44, 47, 53-56, 71-74, 122-127*

CHAPTER

9

Rebounding

Not every perfect cut, accurate screen, or precise one-on-one move leads to a basket. In fact, over half of all field goal attempts are missed. When those misses occur, someone needs to be there to grab the ball. There is a science to being in the right place when the carom comes off the board, and there is an art to keeping opponents from gaining that position on the floor.

First, your players must learn proper offensive footwork and how to use their hands to tip the ball until it can be secured. Drill 76 provides this instruction.

Second, players need to know proper defensive footwork to keep opponents from gaining proper rebound positioning on the floor; this skill is introduced in drill 77.

Third, you need alternatives in case opponents have studied your squad's primary techniques. To progress to the next level, your players will add more offensive and defensive footwork. They will learn the variances that occur depending on trajectories of the ball, shooting angles, and shot lengths. Using this knowledge, your players can coax opponents into mistakes, allowing them to get to exactly the right spot at precisely the right time. In drill 78 we reveal these techniques and strategies.

Drill 79 provides competition between players rebounding offensively and defensively. Drill 80 is a conditioning drill, both physically and mentally. Drill 80 gets your players going after the second, third, fourth rebound without stopping.

Drill 81 teaches savvy. Your players must know primary rebounding angles for every shot taken so they can head straight toward that area on any shot. Drill 82 adds more techniques and further savvy. Players learn about secondary rebounding and are introduced to the blast-out technique.

Drill 83 brings it all together, requiring your players to make offensive moves, shoot, and rebound. You can also add more strategies to your motion offense plan.

76

TIP BALL OFF THE WALL AND PIVOT

Individual • 1 minute

SKILL FOCUS Jab step (11), reverse pivot (36), jab step and roll (78), jab step and go (78), agility, balance, quick jumping, conditioning

Beginner

1. Player faces a wall, holding a basketball.
2. The player tips the ball off the wall five times right-handed and then catch the ball with both hands.
3. The player does a complete (360-degree) turn using the left foot as the initial pivot foot. This should place the player a yard (a meter) or so from the start spot. (Beginners might need more than two steps to do this turn; if so, let them do more steps.)

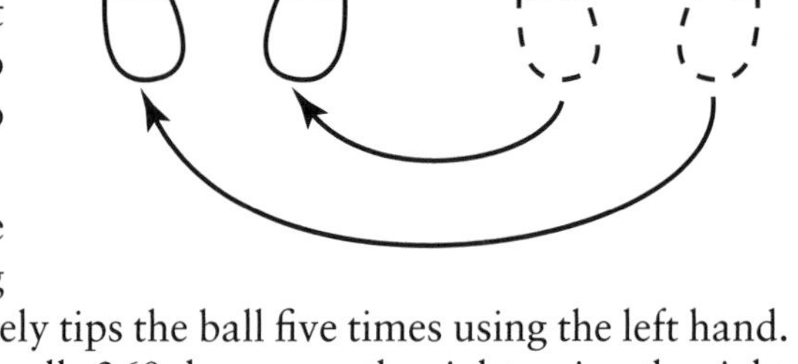

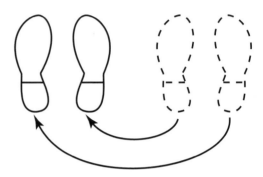

4. After completing the turn, the player should again be facing the wall. The player immediately tips the ball five times using the left hand. After five tips, the player now rolls 360 degrees to the right, using the right foot as the pivot foot.
5. Continue this action for 1 minute.

Advanced

1. Instead of having the player tip five times and then catch the ball, have the player tip two times and then tip the ball a little higher and to the left one yard (one meter). The player executes the 360-degree roll and then tips the ball twice with the left hand before tipping it a yard (meter) to the right. The player then rolls to the right and tips the ball twice with the right hand. This continues for 1 minute.
2. Same as step 1, but before pivoting the player does a jab step in the same direction as the roll.

TEACHING POINTS

1. To perform the roll, the player pivots strong on the foot in the direction desired to roll. The player might even jump into the air somewhat while trying to do a twist in the air.
2. All tips should be executed with the front two joints of the fingers. The tip should be like a catch and then a flip of the wrist.

Related Drills *11, 36, 77-78*

BULL IN THE RING

Individual or team • 4 minutes

➔ SKILL FOCUS Jab step (11), reverse pivot (36), swim move (53), jab step and roll (78), jab step and go (78), pump fake (96), pump fake crossover (96), agility, balance, quick jumping, conditioning, mental toughness

Beginner

1. Players line up as shown in the figure.
2. Players 1, 2, and 3 begin in the lane while a coach shoots the basketball.
3. The rebounder may put the carom back up, or pump fake and shoot, or use the jab step and roll and then shoot. The other two may bump the player with the ball slightly with their bodies. If the player misses the shot, the three again fight for the rebound.
4. When a player scores three baskets, that player rotates out of the lane to the end of player 4's line.
5. Player 4 steps into the lane, and the drill continues. All players begin again with the total rebounds they have already scored.
6. Should a shot ricochet outside the lane, the ball is tossed to the coach, and the coach shoots again.

Intermediate

1. Execute the drill as described for beginners.
2. When player 4 steps into the lane and the drill continues, all players' scores are wiped out; each begins with 0 scored rebounds.
3. Should a shot ricochet outside the lane, the ball is tossed to the coach, and the coach shoots again.

Advanced

Instead of the coach shooting, the coach tosses the basketball to one of the three players, and the player who catches it shoots. If the shot is made, that counts as one of the three shots made to get out of the circle.

(continued)

TEACHING POINTS

1. If possible, players should catch the rebound with both hands and shoot before landing with the basketball.
2. If catching and shooting is not possible and they are capable of tipping the ball into the basket, they should try to tip it. Tipping should be done with the fingertips.
3. When rebounders come down with the ball, they might need to use pump fakes to get the other two players off balance before taking another shot.

Body Positioning

1. Players lean slightly forward in direction of the basket. They want to be able to move quickly forward, backward, or sideways. They lift their heels first, putting their weight on their toes. They push off the toes as the body leaves the floor.
2. Balance and agility are extremely important.
3. Players lower their hips to a semicrouched position. This gives them catlike quickness to explode toward the missed shot.
4. Knees should be flexed at no greater than a 135-degree angle. Body weight is on the balls of the feet. Players should be prepared to jump.
5. Elbows should be out and away from the body. Arms are used to prevent opponents from getting better positioning; arms should be free to move in any direction.
6. Fingers point up toward the rim and should be spread widely apart for better grip on the basketball. Hands should be relaxed and flexible.
7. On defense, players keep their eyes on their assignments until they have completed their boxout. On offense they use peripheral vision to locate opponents so they can pick up their opponent's first intentions to box them out. Rebounders move to the spot at which the ball will carom (see drills 81 and 82).

➔ Approaching the Rebound

1. Players are able to move in all directions.
2. Elbows are fully extended.
3. Players time their jump to touch the ball at the highest point of the jump.
4. They use two hands to catch the ball. They do not slap at the ball to bring it to the other hand. The ball is always caught with two hands.
5. After catching the ball, the rebounder brings the ball down in a quick, jerky motion, such as when plucking an apple from a tree. On the way down, the player begins to spread feet and legs in a spread-eagle fashion and pivot the body toward the outside of the court.
6. The rebounder lands in a spread, balanced position, holding the ball overhead if on defense, prepared to throw an overhead outlet pass. If on offense, the rebounder secures the ball in the chest area and is prepared to pump fake to get a taller defender off balance before shooting. The ball should be swung low if the rebounder is on defense or if on offense and intending to blast out with a dribble.

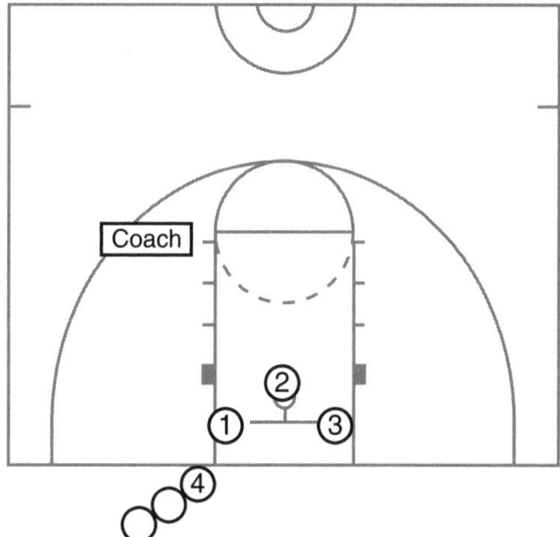

Related Drills *11, 36, 76, 78*

78

JAB STEP AND ROLL

Individual or team • 2 minutes

SKILL FOCUS Jab step (11), front pivot (35), reverse pivot (36), swim move (53), jab step and roll, jab step and go, pump fakes (96), pump fake crossover (96), agility, balance, mental toughness

Intermediate

1. Players line up as shown in figure 1. After 1 minute, offense and defense switch roles.
2. A coach lays the ball in the middle of the free-throw circle. On a signal from the coach, Xs try to block the Os from getting to the ball. The Os try to touch the basketball.
3. The defense keeps the offense from getting the ball for a count of five (counting "one thousand one, one thousand two . . . " and so on).
4. The defense may front pivot or reverse pivot (coach's call). Defenders may pivot immediately, or slide a step and then pivot. This is called a defensive blockout or boxout.
5. The offense uses the jab step and roll or the jab step and go, depending on the defense. The swim move should be used with either technique.

Advanced

1. Instead of using the circle, the coach may shoot the ball at the goal. In this case, the boxouts must be held until the ball hits the floor. If an offense player gets the ball, the player uses pump fakes or pump fake crossovers to put the ball back in the basket.
2. Instead of allowing the ball to hit the floor, the defense may play it live. And if the defenders get the rebound, they can outlet pass to the coach or blast out with the dribble.

TEACHING POINTS

1. Figure 2 shows the offensive jab step and the defensive blockout using the reverse pivot. The reverse pivot should be used when the defender is near the basket and needs to get a view of the rebound sooner; the front pivot should be used when the defender is out on the perimeter and needs to keep an eye on an assignment longer. The slide one step/pivot defensive technique is used when the attacker is an exceptional offensive rebounder. This requires the attacker to use a combination of two or more moves to get open.
2. Figure 3 adds the roll off the jab step. Because the defender blocked out, the roll was used. This enables the offensive player to get alongside the defender. The swim move should be used when the attacker gets alongside the defender.

3. Figure 4 shows the jab step and go. When the defender does not react, the attacker brings the right foot up even with the jab step (left foot). The swim move is used as the attacker brings the right foot forward.
4. Rebounds tend to ricochet away from where the ball is shot. A ball shot from the left corner usually caroms toward the right corner. A ball shot at a 45-degree angle will usually rebound at a 45-degree angle on the other side of the basket.

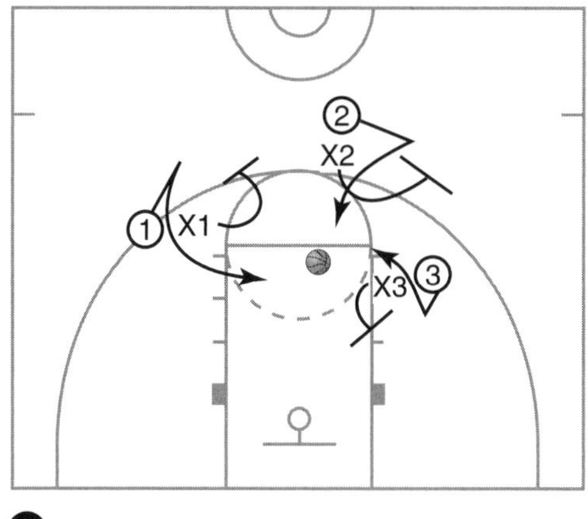

❶

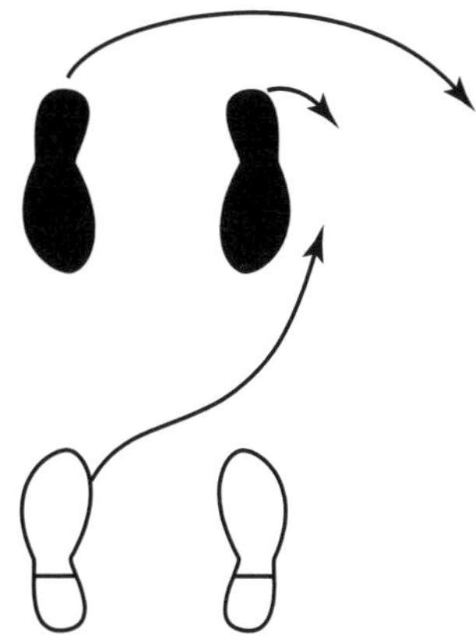

❷ Jab step for offensive rebound. Reverse pivot blockout by the defender.

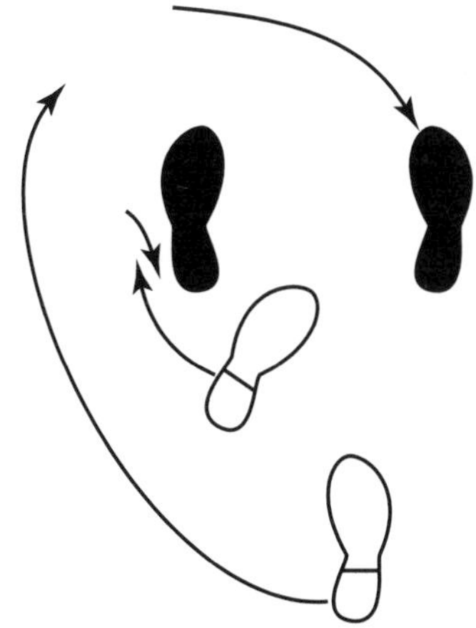

❸ Jab step and roll. The jab step has been completed, and the defender has reverse pivoted for the blockout. As the defender completes the blockout maneuver, the attacker begins the roll.

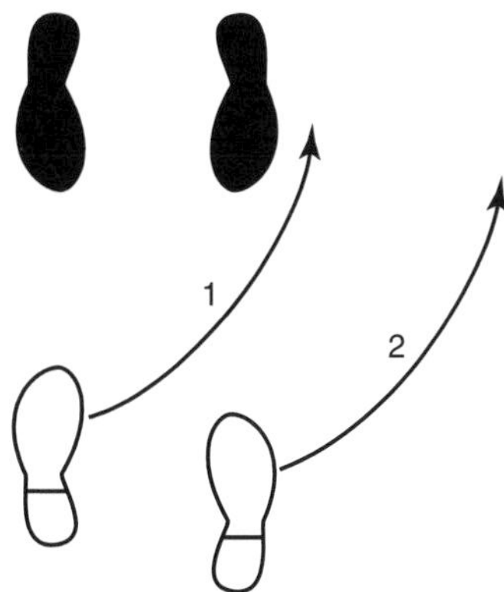

❹ Jab step and go. The offensive rebounder has jab stepped (1). When the defender does not block out, the attacker goes (2).

Related Drills *11, 36, 76-77*

79

ONE-ON-ONE BLOCKOUTS

Individual or team • 1 minute

SKILL FOCUS Balance, front pivot (35), reverse pivot (36), jump stop (37), stride stop (38), slide and boxout, immediate boxout, jab step and roll (78), jab step and go (78), swim technique (81)

Beginner

1. Line players up as shown in the figure.
2. Place the basketball in the middle of the circle.
3. On signal, defenders try to keep attackers from touching the ball.
4. Defenders use one of their two techniques to prevent attackers from touching the ball: slide and boxout or immediate boxout.
5. Attackers use the jab step and go or the jab step and roll techniques to touch the ball.
6. Defenders must keep attackers from touching the ball for 3 seconds.

TEACHING POINTS

1. Constantly check body positioning for offensive and defensive rebounding.
2. The defensive technique of slide and boxout or immediate boxout must be fundamentally sound. These techniques are described in drill 81.
3. The jab step and roll and jab step and go are described in drill 78. The swim technique is described in drill 81.
4. Savvy is described in drills 81 and 82.

Slide and Box

1. Great offensive rebounders anticipate the boxout and move quickly around it. Defensive rebounders must use the slide and box technique to keep these offensive rebounders under control.
2. To slide and box, players simply use the slide step for the first two steps of their assignment's movement. They do not turn to the basket when the ball is shot. They watch their assignment. When their assignment moves in one direction, defenders slide. If their assignment's second step is in the opposite direction, defenders slide again. If the assignment is in the same direction, defenders slide and begin to box out.
3. After the two-step slide, defenders front pivot, making contact with their assignment. They legally hold this position until the rebound is retrieved.

➔ **Immediate Boxout** When the ball is shot, players immediately reverse pivot, making contact with their assignment. They hold this positioning until the rebound is retrieved.

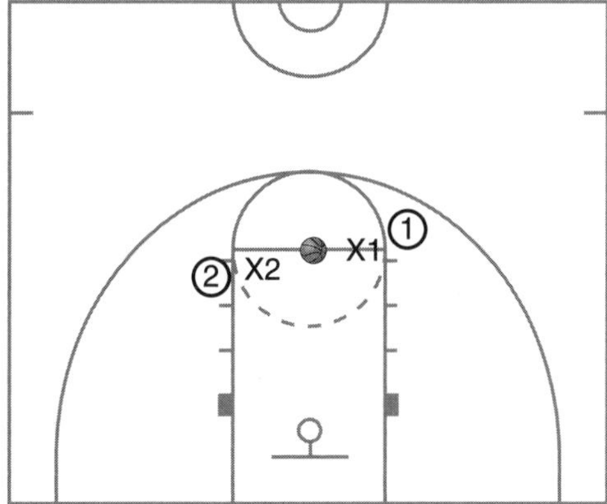

***Related Drills** 35-38, 76-83*

80

SUPERMAN

Individual • 1 minute

SKILL FOCUS Quickness, balance, agility, conditioning, slide step (37)

Beginner

1. A player with a basketball begins on a big block near the basket.
2. The player tosses the ball off the board so it caroms to the other side of the basket.
3. The player slide-steps into the lane to the other side of the basket, leaps into the air, and grabs the rebound. The player turns in the air while coming down.
4. The player immediately tosses the ball off the board so it ricochets to the opposite side of the basket. The player slide-steps into the lane to the other side of the basket, leaps into the air, grabs the rebound, turns while in the air, and lands.
5. The player immediately tosses the ball off the board to the other side of the basket, and the drill continues.
6. Begin with half-minute sessions; work up to a full minute by the end of the season.

Intermediate

1. Place a lid over the basket so the ball will roll off the lid when the ball lands on it.
2. The player tips the rebound, lands, tips again, lands, and tips again.
3. Continue this drill for 30 seconds.

TEACHING POINTS

1. Make sure the player's body positioning from tips of toes to tips of the arm is in perfect rebounding form (see drill 79).
2. Make sure the player goes immediately back up. No resting. You are trying to condition your player to go after the second, third, and fourth rebounding opportunity.

Related Drills *76-79, 81-83*

COUNT-SLIDE-PIVOT-SAVVY

Individual or team • 4 minutes

SKILL FOCUS One-on-one moves (12-15, 28-31), front pivot (35), reverse pivot (36), jump stop (37), stride stop (38), bounce pass (44), chest pass (44), skip pass (44), overhead pass (44), swim technique (53, 81), jab step and roll (78), jab step and go (78), body positioning for rebound (79), approaching the rebound (79), slide and boxout (79), immediate boxout (79), rebounding primary position (81), savvy (81, 82), rebounding secondary position (82), blast-out technique (82), shooting techniques (84-88), pump fakes (96, 117), pump fake crossover (96), post moves (96-103), defense of post (99-101), pump fake up-and-under (116), defense of perimeter (129-131, 137-144)

Beginner

1. Line up one offensive player and one defensive player near the basket as shown in the figure.
2. A coach (or a third player) shoots from each spot designated by a letter. The coach shoots from spot; players rebound. If the defensive player gets a rebound, the player outlet passes back out to the coach with an overhead pass. If the offensive player gets the rebound, the player pump-fakes and goes back up for a power layup.
3. After shooting from area A, the coach moves to area B (and then to area C, D, E, F, and G). The defensive player and offensive player begin in the same spot on each shot. This allows players to rebound on the weak side (areas A, B, and C) and on the strong side (areas E, F, and G). Area D is straight on—no weak side, no strong side.
4. After the coach has shot from all positions, the two rebounders rotate.
5. The defensive player should use the technique the coach requests—the immediate boxout, slide-step boxout, or a mix of the two.

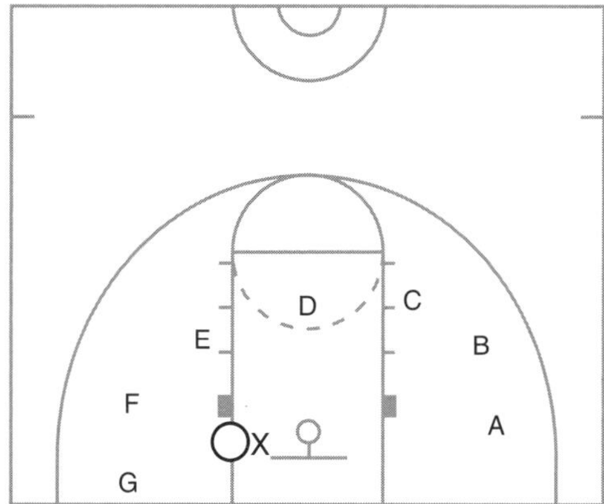

(continued)

➜ Options

1. A coach (or a player if using three players in the drill) should alter the arc of the shot—one time shoot a flat shot and the next time a high-arcing shot.
2. Alter the distance of the shot (coach can move back to 3-point area or come into the lane from any of the spots).
3. Alter the position from which the players begin. By moving the offensive player out to the wing when shooting from areas A, B, and C and keeping the defender in near the basket, you get the actual game situation of a defender playing on the weak side. But by starting both players low, you get a much better feel of the physical aspect of rebounding.
4. The coach can always pass to the offensive player. The offensive player could then go one on one. This keeps the defensive player from cheating and getting better rebounding position.
5. The offensive player should use the jab step and go or the jab step and roll along with the swim technique to try to get inside position on the defender.
6. You can take the defensive phase of keeping the offensive player from getting the basketball out of the drill by merely saying "passes cannot be made into the offensive player as long as the defender is in reasonable position defensively."

Intermediate

You can have two players passing the ball before shooting. For example, locate a player at areas A and C (both on the strong side). Now the offensive player and the defensive player must constantly adjust their positions to prevent the pass to the offensive player and to get primary rebounding position.

Advanced

You can place two shooters on the court: one on the weak side (area F, for example) and one on the strong side (area B, for example). These players can pass the basketball back and forth until one of them takes the shots. They can pass inside to the offensive player should the defensive player get out of position defensively. This requires both players to constantly gauge the correct defensive and offensive positioning as well as to calculate where the primary rebounding position is.

➜ Primary Rebounding Position Rules (Savvy)

1. **The higher the arc, the shorter the rebound.** A low arc will ricochet further out on the court than a high-arcing shot. A high-arcing shot will ricochet higher, taking it longer to come down.
2. **The further the distance from the goal, the longer the rebound.** A shot taken from the 3-point arc will rebound further out on the court than a shot taken from 8 feet (2.4 m), for example.

3. **The shot will usually rebound at the exact angle it is shot from but on the opposite side of the court.** In other words, shots from area A will rebound toward area G. Shots from area B will rebound toward area F. Shots from area C will rebound toward area E. Shots from area D will rebound toward area D.
4. **The Wilson Jet is more lively than the Spalding 100.** Check the ball before the game begins. The livelier ball will rebound further and higher than the less lively ball.
5. **A basketball with more air in it will carom further and higher than a ball with less air.** Again, check the ball before the game begins.

➲ TEACHING POINTS

1. Make sure the body position of the defender is always correct for rebounding. Make sure defensive position on the court is always correct (your man-to-man defense).
2. Make sure the defensive rebounder uses the immediate boxout techniques when the attacker is near the basket. The rebound comes quickly, so the defender does not need to use the slide-step technique. The carom will be there quickly.
3. Because the carom comes quickly when defenders are near the basket, they should use the reverse pivot, which allows them to see the ball more quickly. They will lose sight of their assignment quicker, but the attacker cannot move much because the ball is there in a hurry.
4. Make sure defensive rebounders use the slide step and the front pivot when boxing out on the perimeter. The slide step allows defenders to see their assignment longer. The front pivot allows them to see the opponent's move longer.
5. Offensive players should use the jab step and go or the jab step and roll to try to get even or in front of the defender. They should make ample use of the swim technique.
6. Both offensive and defensive rebounders should develop a count system. For long shots, a count of *one thousand one, one thousand two* usually suffices. Before long, your players will develop an innate timing mechanism.

Related Drills 12-15, 28-31, 35-38, 44, 53, 76, 79-82, 84-88, 96-103, 116-117, 129-131, 137-144

82

TWO-ON-TWO REBOUNDING

Team • 4 minutes

➲ **SKILL FOCUS** Balance, agility, conditioning, post positioning (10), front pivot (35), reverse pivot (36), jump stop (37), stride stop (38), passing (44), jab step and roll (78), jab step and go (78), body positioning (79), approaching the rebound (79), slide and boxout (79), immediate boxout (79), primary rebounding area (81), swim technique (81), secondary rebounding area, blast-out technique, shooting techniques (84-88), low-post moves (96-103), pump fake series (96, 116-117), low-post half-spin move (115), low-post spin move (115), up-and-under (116)

Intermediate

1. Line players up as shown in the figure. Players A, B, C, D, and E are offensive players. Only one attacker has a basketball.
2. Players 1 and 2 are offensive post players. X1 and X2 are defensive post players. A rebounder is under the goal.
3. The play is five on five. Players A, B, C, D, and E make up one team; players 1, 2, X1, X2, and the rebounder under the basket make up the other team. The five players outside exchange positions with the five players inside after 2 minutes of drilling. The inside attackers rotate after each shot. Their rotation is 1 to X1, 2 to X2, X1 to 1, X2 to the rebounder under the goal, and the rebounder under the goal to 2. This rotation occurs after each shot. When a basket is made, the rebounder under the goal retrieves the ball and passes outside.
4. The outside five players pass the ball around the perimeter, including skip passing, until one of them either passes inside to a post player (1 or 2) or takes a shot.
5. When the pass goes inside, the post player performs a low-post move and shoots the basketball.
6. Whether the ball is shot from the perimeter or from the post, X1 and X2 must use defensive boxout techniques. If X1 or X2 secures the rebound, the player blasts out before passing to a perimeter player, and the drill begins again.
7. Players 1 and 2 use offensive rebounding techniques to secure either primary or secondary rebounding position. If either 1 or 2 get an offensive rebound, they use the pump fake series to go back up for a power layup.

Advanced

1. Instead of a blast out on a defensive rebound, the defensive rebounder can throw an overhead outlet pass.
2. Once the ball is passed inside, the two low-post offensive players can pass among themselves until one of them shoots or passes back out to the perimeter.
3. Post players can screen for each other inside, if screening is part of your motion offense.

➜ Secondary Rebounding Area

1. The secondary rebounding area is the area back toward the shooter. This is the area at which the second most missed shots carom (usually because the shot comes up short).
2. The same rebounding principles apply to the secondary area as to the primary area (see drill 81). For example, the higher the arc, the higher the ricochet (but not longer). The lesser the arc, the longer the carom.

➜ Blast-Out Technique

1. After securing a missed shot, the rebounder brings the ball low in both hands, as near the floor as possible, and swings the ball out in front.
2. At the same time as swinging the basketball low, the rebounder executes a long crossover step.
3. The rebounder then immediately tosses the ball slightly out in front, goes to get it, and dribbles down the floor until passing off.

➲ TEACHING POINTS

1. Make sure defenders maintain a proper defensive stance throughout the drill.
2. Make sure the low-post attackers try to gain legal position on their defenders.
3. Check all low-post moves to make sure they are fundamentally sound.
4. Check both offensive and defensive rebounding techniques. Don't let any player get lazy!

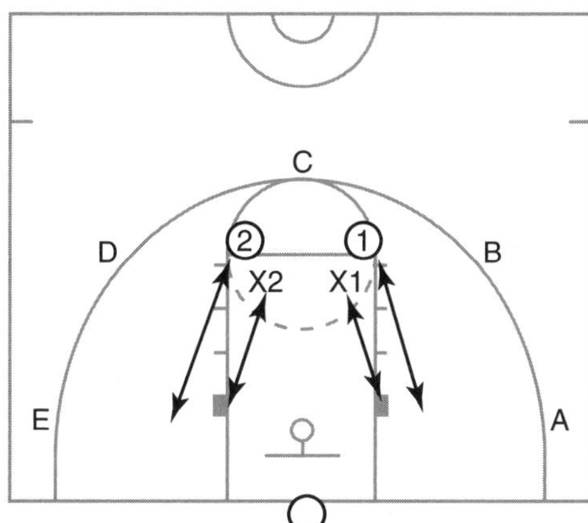

Related Drills *10, 35-38, 44, 76, 79, 81, 84-88, 96-103, 116-117*

83

POST MOVES: PASSING-SHOOTING-REBOUNDING

Team • 4 minutes

➲ SKILL FOCUS Post positioning (10), front pivot (35), reverse pivot (36), jump stop (37), stride stop (38), flash pivot cut (56), jab step and roll (78), jab step and go (78), body rebound positioning (79), approaching the rebound (79), slide and boxout (79), immediate boxout (79), primary rebounding area (81), swim technique (81), secondary rebounding area (82), blast-out technique (82), shooting techniques (84-88), low-post moves (96-103, 115-116), pump fake series (96, 116-117), low-post defense (98-101), help-side defense (133-135), drawing charge (141), flash pivot defense (148)

Intermediate

1. Line players up as shown in the figure. Players 4 and 5 are low-post players. X4 and X5 are low-post defenders. Player 3 is a perimeter player to help the coach outside. After a score or defensive rebound, rotate from 3 to 4 to 5 to X4 to X5 to 3.
2. A coach begins with the basketball. The coach may immediately shoot or pass to 3 or to the flash pivot cutter, 5.
3. If X4 is not in proper help-side defensive position, the coach can pass to 4. This keeps the weak-side defender concentrating.
4. If post player 5 cannot get open, player 3 and the coach pass the ball until they can get it inside to 5. If 5 receives the ball, 5 makes a low-post move and shoots. X4 and X5 must box out. Players 4 and 5 use offensive rebounding techniques to get the rebound. Instead of passing inside to 5, either the coach or player 3 can shoot an outside shot.
5. If after 3 seconds (the motion offensive rules) 5 has not received the pass, 5 rolls down the lane and through the basket area. Player 4 then begins a flash pivot cut to get open. The drill continues until a shot is taken and the rebound is secured.
6. At any time, the coach (or preferably player 3) can take a shot. The inside four fight for the rebound using correct offensive and defensive rebounding techniques.
7. At any time a pass is made inside, the post receiver must make a move to score. If unable to get the shot off, the post player should not take a bad shot. The post player with the ball either passes back outside and the drill continues, or the ball is passed to the other post player.

Advanced

1. The posts can screen for each other if this is part of your motion offense.
2. You can limit this screen to before the inside pass is made, or the screening action can occur once a post player has received the ball.

➲ TEACHING POINTS

1. Make sure all rebounding techniques are fundamentally sound. Make sure two players go to the primary rebounding area and two go to the secondary rebounding area.
2. Watch for the flash pivot cut being executed correctly and that it is properly defended. You want to drill these fundamentals tougher than anything your team will face in a game.
3. Make sure the post player receiving the pass executes an immediate low-post move. Check for proper footwork.

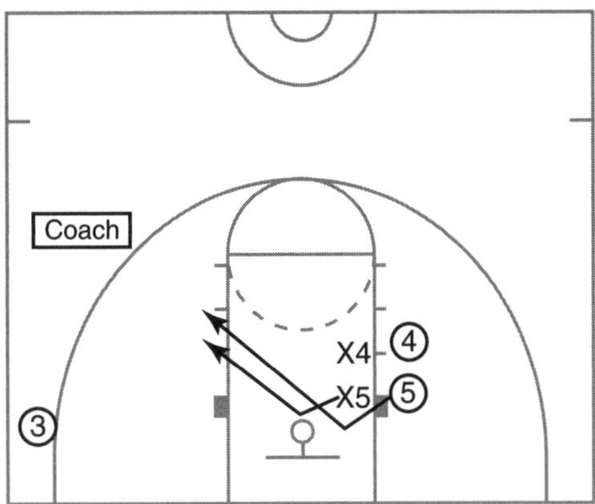

Related Drills *10, 35-38, 56, 76, 79, 81-82, 84-88, 96-103, 115-117, 133-135, 141, 148*

CHAPTER 10

Shooting

Shooting a basketball is one of the most challenging skills to master in all of sport. And once this skill has been mislearned and practiced incorrectly, it is very difficult to correct. Shooting is the most difficult technique in basketball. It requires precision of muscular movement for the greatest accuracy; these activities come from the hand, wrist, lower arm, upper arm, torso, upper leg, lower leg, and even the toes. Muscles must memorize these motion patterns so they can be repeated over and over again.

With so many parts of the body involved in shooting, it is easy to see how any component can get out of alignment. Thus we present the *straight stick* concept in this chapter so that alignment can be corrected easily. Players simply put all elements in a straight line, and the alignment is fine tuned.

Once perfectly aligned, the shooter must propel the ball forward and upward. *Lift, extend, flip* delivers the ball in the same manner as a catapult did in ancient times, flinging rocks at stationary targets. In this case, the basket is the target. The last shot Michael Jordan took in the NBA (as well as his first shot, and all his shots in between) was a picture-perfect *lift, extend, flip*—a model of keeping the elbow in, a flawless execution of all body parts that should be studied by all aspiring shooters.

In drill 84 your players will practice proper hand and wrist action. Drill 85 covers the actual flip. Drill 86 provides the catapult step. Drill 87 combines all these skills into one drill. Drill 88 allows you to check alignment and thrust. Drill 89 lets you progress to a fun drill, actually using the basket as the target. Drill 90 advances your squad by requiring greater concentration on the shot. Drills 91 and 92 present two more practice techniques to develop muscle memory for the entire shot process.

Drill 93 presents drilling on the baby hook—the proper shot to take when your low-post player drop-steps to the middle of the floor.

Drill 94 adds passing, cutting, and rebound training to shooting practice. Drill 95 is a shooting drill that allows players to get off a great number of shots in a short amount of time. Here you must be careful that your players do not concentrate on the number of shots instead of focusing on correct mechanics.

At any time that either alignment or thrust becomes a problem, you can go back to the appropriate drill to correct the snag. Once righted, you can go to another drill to accelerate muscle memory learning. With younger players use a smaller ball. Too often, young players create bad muscle memory by using a ball that is too heavy for them. Also, younger players should have the baskets lowered to about 8 feet (2.4 m).

84

WAVE GOOD-BYE

Individual or team • 1 minute

SKILL FOCUS Straight-stick shooting techniques (84-88)

Beginner

1. Line your entire team up facing you or another coach; spread players out about 15 feet (4.5 m) apart.
2. Each player waves good-bye to the coach and holds the position after one wave. Divide the wave into two steps: *cock the wrist* and *wave good-bye*.
3. Repeat until all players can use and practice correct technique.

TEACHING POINTS

1. Players hold their shooting hand up and spread their fingers until the hand hurts. Then they relax. The position the hand naturally falls in after relaxing is the proper shooting cup.
2. The arm should be held in front of the face, with upper arm parallel to the floor and lower arm perpendicular to the upper arm.
3. Before players wave good-bye, the coach should give the command "cock the wrist." Players hold their hand in this cocked position until the coach confirms that all players have a wrinkle behind the wrist. The wrist should be cocked to a position parallel to the ground.
4. Then the coach gives the "wave good-bye" command. Players hold this wave position after completion. The wrist should be straight in line with the lower and upper arm, and the arm should be extended toward the coach. The fingers should be pointing down toward the floor.

Related Drills *85-95*

FLIP-BALL DRILL

Individual or team • 1 minute

➲ SKILL FOCUS Straight-stick shooting techniques (84-88)

Beginner

1. Line players up scattered around the floor about 15 feet (4.5 m) apart.
2. Give each player a ball. Each player holds the ball in the shooting hand only, using only the pads and fingertips, not the palms.
3. Lower arms are perpendicular to the upper arms; upper arms are parallel to the floor.
4. The wrist is cocked, and the ball is in the shooting hand. The ball should be in front of the face or slightly to the shooting-hand side of the face.
5. Players flip the ball very slightly into the air and catch it with only the shooting hand when it returns.
6. A piece of tape around the center of the ball makes a good shooting aid, making it easy to see whether the ball has perfect backspin. Any spinning that shows the tape whirling from side to side means the ball has not been released properly.
7. Continue for 1 minute.

➲ TEACHING POINTS

1. The ball cannot stay in the hand unless the alignment is correct. If the parts of the arm are not correctly aligned, the player cannot hold the ball. It will roll off the side that is slanted or crooked.
2. The elbow must be in or else the arms will be crooked and the ball will not stay in the hand.
3. If the wrist is not cocked, the ball will roll out of the hands. So you need only to watch the ball to see if alignment is correct.

Related Drills *84, 86-95*

86

LIFT, EXTEND, FLIP

Individual or team • 1 minute

➲ SKILL FOCUS Straight-stick shooting techniques (84-88)

Beginner

1. Line players up facing each other as shown in the figure.
2. Give a verbal cue: "lift." Players raise their upper arms to a position no greater than 45 degrees from parallel to the floor (no ball is used).
3. Say "extend." Players extend their upper arms so there is very little sway at the elbow. The wrist remains cocked.
4. Say "flip." Players respond by waving bye and leaving palms down with fingers pointing toward the floor.
5. After repeating steps 2 through 4 several times, put the cues together: "lift, extend, flip." The cues should be so close together that they sound like one word.
6. After repeating step 5 a few times, add a basketball. One side of players lifts, extends, and flips the ball to the other side. The sides should be about 10 feet (3 m) apart. The ball should reach its apex about two-thirds the distance from the shooter to the receiver. The ball should also be flipped at least 15 feet (4.5 m) high. The receiver should receive the ball with both hands.
7. The shooter steps forward only slightly with the same foot as the shooting hand.

Intermediate

Allow the receiver to catch the ball with only the shooting hand, keeping it balanced so the ball will not fall to the floor.

➜ TEACHING POINTS

1. Check positions of the arm: Is lower arm perpendicular to the upper arm? Upper arm parallel to the floor?
2. Check to see that the wrist is cocked—there should be a wrinkle behind the wrist.
3. Be sure the ball is on the pads of the hand. Players should spread and then relax the shooting hand to form the perfect cup.
4. The ball should be in front of the face or slightly to the shooting-hand side.
5. Check for straight-stick alignment; the ball should be in a straight line with the elbow, the knee, and the toe of the front foot.
6. Players catapult the ball by lifting the upper arm, extending the lower arm, and flipping the wrist.

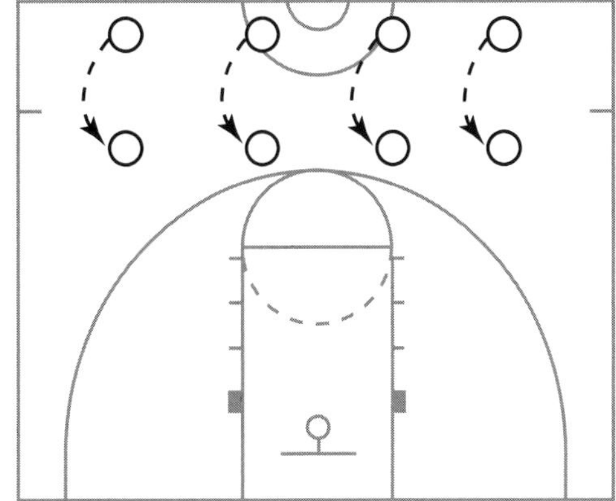

Related Drills *84-85, 87-95*

87

LYING-DOWN FLIP-BALL DRILL

Individual or team • 1 minute

➲ SKILL FOCUS Straight-stick shooting techniques (84-88)

Beginner

1. Players lie on the floor about 15 feet (4.5 m) apart.
2. Each player has a basketball.
3. On command from coach, every player shoots the basketball 8 to 10 feet (2.4-3 m) into the air using the lift-extend-flip technique.
4. The ball should be held directly in front of the face, with elbows in, not out to the side.
5. Players should hold the ball only in the shooting hand but may catch the ball from its downward flight with both hands.

Intermediate

Players execute the beginner drill but now catch the ball from its downward flight with only the shooting hand.

Related Drills *84-86, 88-95*

FLIP THE BALL OFF THE WALL

88

Individual • 1 minute

SKILL FOCUS Straight-stick shooting techniques (84-88)

Beginner

1. Player (or entire squad) stands in front of a wall.
2. Let's say these instructions are for right-handed shooters. They place their right toe against the wall, with their left foot about 18 inches (45 cm) behind their right foot. They place their right knee and entire lower right arm against the wall. They cock their right wrist, with the end of the wrist against the wall. They hold a ball in the right hand. The wrist should be slightly to the right of their face with the thumb almost over the right eye. A straight line could be drawn from the wrist, down the lower arm, through the elbow, to the knee, and down to the toe. This is straight-stick shooting technique (figure 1), the perfect alignment for the basketball shot.
3. The players take a few steps back from the wall and shoot the ball about 10 feet (3 m) into the air, letting the ball hit off the wall.
4. They may catch the return with both hands.
5. They step to the wall again and repeat the steps, focusing on correct alignment each time.

Intermediate

Players execute the beginner drill but catch the return with only the shooting hand.

TEACHING POINTS

1. Check players' straight-stick positioning for proper alignment each time.
2. Check the lift-extend-flip techniques for proper catapulting.
3. Make sure the elbow stays in throughout the shot. A crooked shooting elbow is the worst fault in all of basketball.
4. Figure 1 shows proper alignment. Figure 2 illustrates the coordination between the eyes, shoulders, elbow, and legs on the jump shot. Notice the legs go straight after the jump, and toes point to the floor. Figure 3 displays the front view.

(continued)

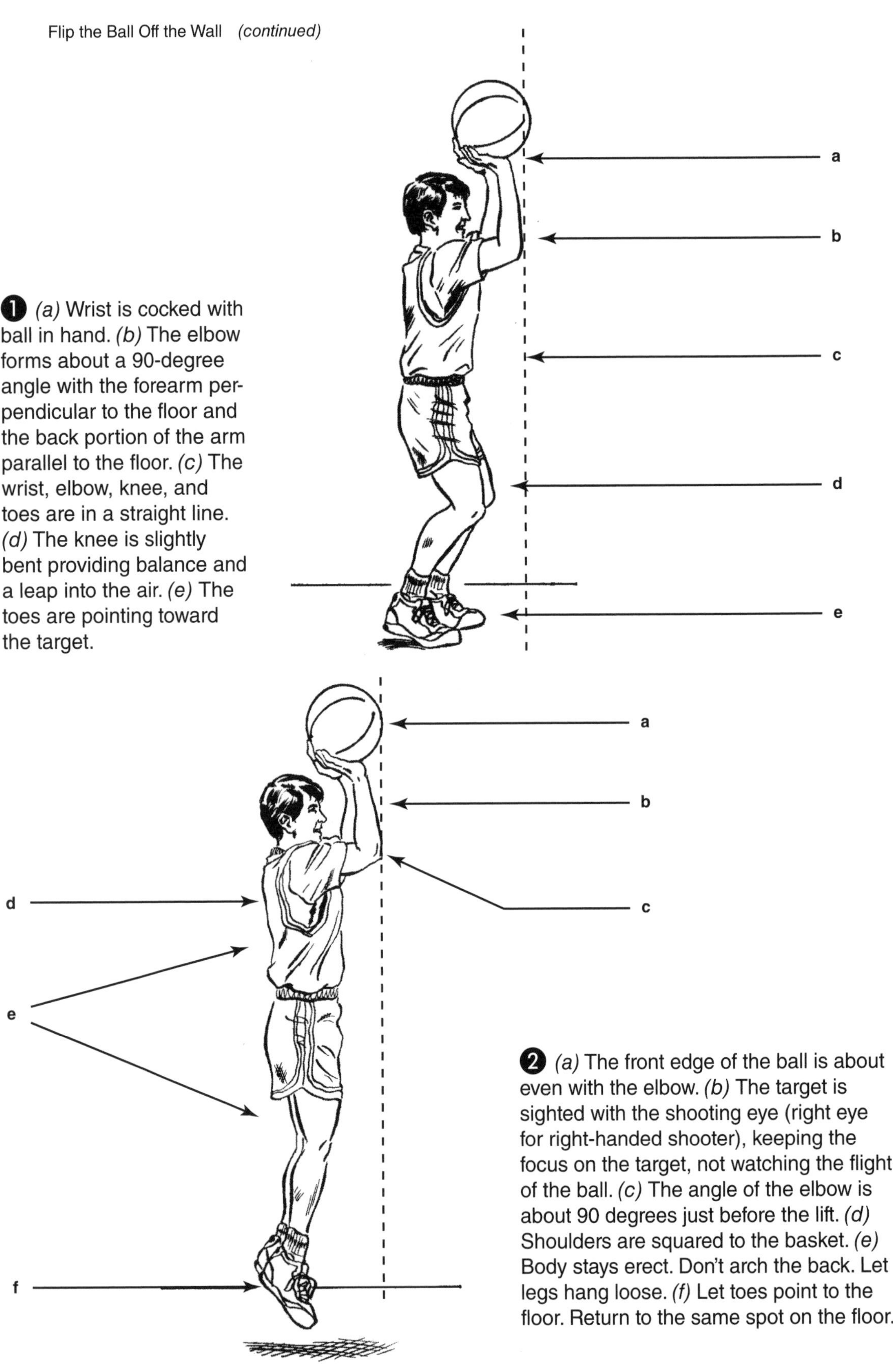

❶ *(a)* Wrist is cocked with ball in hand. *(b)* The elbow forms about a 90-degree angle with the forearm perpendicular to the floor and the back portion of the arm parallel to the floor. *(c)* The wrist, elbow, knee, and toes are in a straight line. *(d)* The knee is slightly bent providing balance and a leap into the air. *(e)* The toes are pointing toward the target.

❷ *(a)* The front edge of the ball is about even with the elbow. *(b)* The target is sighted with the shooting eye (right eye for right-handed shooter), keeping the focus on the target, not watching the flight of the ball. *(c)* The angle of the elbow is about 90 degrees just before the lift. *(d)* Shoulders are squared to the basket. *(e)* Body stays erect. Don't arch the back. Let legs hang loose. *(f)* Let toes point to the floor. Return to the same spot on the floor.

❸ *(a)* The wrist is cocked with ball on fingertips, not palms. *(b)* The elbow is on line to the target. Slight lateral shift of the elbow, if more comfortable, is allowed. *(c)* The opposite hand is comfortable but lightly on the ball. *(d)* Eyes are focused on the target, not on the flight of the ball. *(e)* Shoulders are squared to the basket.

Related Drills *84-87, 89-95*

89

AROUND THE WORLD

Individual or team • 10 minutes

➲ SKILL FOCUS Straight-stick shooting techniques (84-88)

Beginner

1. The player shoots from the seven spots in figure 1 and then back around. (This is called Little Around the World.)
2. The player must make shot 1 before moving to shot 2, and so forth all the way around. When the player reaches shot 7, you may require the player to stop, or to go all the way back to shot 1 in reverse order—from 7 to 6, to 5, and so on. Players can compete against each other. The first player to complete all the shots wins the game.
3. The shot spot numbers are . . .
    a. Big block, left side of basket
    b. Second line, left side of basket
    c. Corner of free-throw line and lane line, left side of basket
    d. Middle of free-throw line
    e. Corner of free-throw line and lane line, right side of basket
    f. Second line, right side of basket
    g. Big block, right side of basket

Intermediate

1. Execute the beginner drill but now allow players to "chance" any first shot at any of the shots except 1 or 7—those must be made on the first try. Players say "chance," and if they make the second ("chance") shot, they go on to the next shot spot. But if they miss the "chance" shot, they return to 1.
2. Put team A at one end of the court and team B at the other. Players on each team rotate shooting the spots. The first team through wins.
3. Again put team A at one end of the court and team B at the other. One player from each team tries to go around the world. Then the second player from each team tries to go around the world, and so on. The first team with a player who goes around the world wins.
4. Again put team A at one end of the court and team B at the other. Each of the five players on each team is given one of the shot spots. Players shoot in order of the numbers. If a shot is missed, the player may "chance" it. The first team with all five players hitting from their spot wins the game.

Advanced

1. Add Big Around the World (figure 2) to the drill. Players now have five new spots to shoot from (8, 9, 10, 11, and 12 in the figure). Players execute the drill in any of the ways that have been described.
2. Have players play only Big Around the World. The shot spots are . . .
    a. Right corner where the 3-point line is marked
    b. At a 45-degree angle to the basket, where 3-point line is marked on right side of basket
    c. Top of key where 3-point line is marked
    d. At a 45-degree angle to the basket, where 3-point line is marked on left side of basket
    e. Left corner where 3-point line is marked

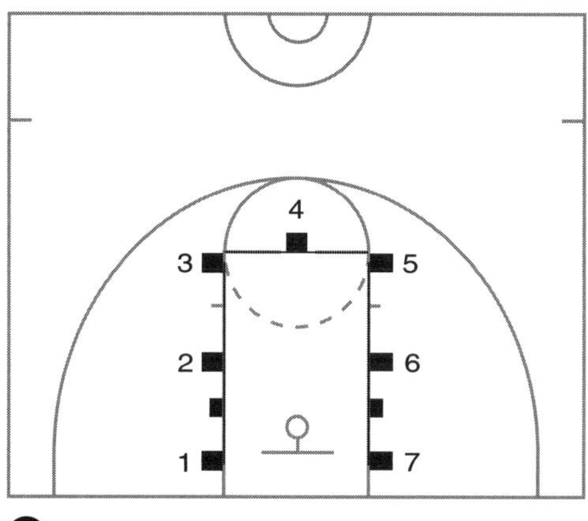

1

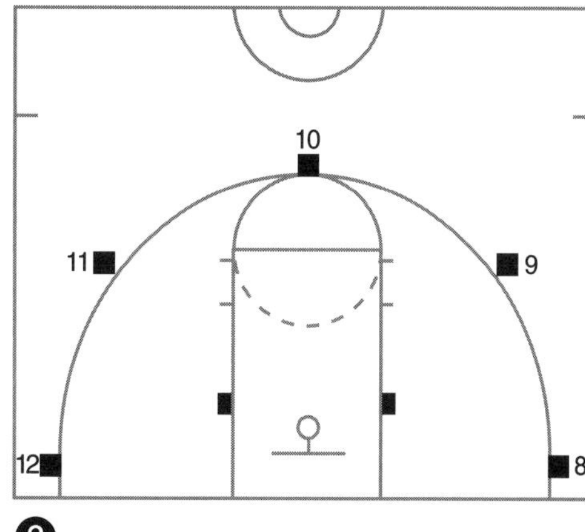

2

Related Drills *84-88, 90-95*

90

NO RIM

Individual or team • 10 minutes

SKILL FOCUS Straight-stick shooting techniques (84-88)

Beginner

1. Put two players at each basket. (If necessary, you may put four players at each basket.) Two players act as a team: One team shoots, and the other rebounds.
2. There are five shooting angles (see figure):
   a. Out the left baseline
   b. 45-degree angle on the left side of the basket
   c. Up the middle of the court
   d. 45-degree angle on the right side of the basket
   e. Out the right baseline
3. One shooter starts at angle a, about 3 feet (1 m) from the basket, and shoots until making a shot without the ball touching the rim.
4. The shooter steps back one full step, now about 6 feet (1.8 m) from the basket, and shoots until making a shot without the ball touching the rim. Continue until the shooter has stepped back three times. Then the shooter moves to angle b, c, and so on.
5. One player shoots, and the other rebounds. Let one player complete one angle before the players switch roles.

Advanced

Instead of stepping back three times, step back five times. This changes the last shot of each angle from 9 feet to 15 feet (2.7 to 4.5 m).

➜ Options (all skill levels)

1. Play teams of two against each other. Teams must shoot more quickly with accuracy. The first team through wins.
2. Make all shots bank shots, except the angle directly down the floor, angle c, without shots touching the rim.

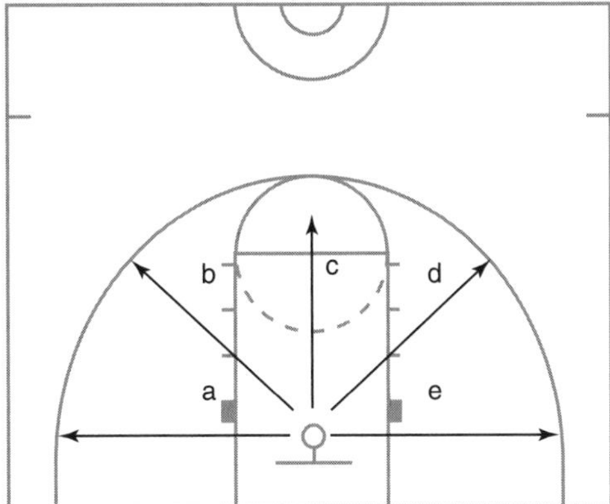

Related Drills *84-89, 91-95*

91

21

Team • 6 minutes

➲ **SKILL FOCUS** Chest pass (44), bounce pass (44), overhead pass (44), pass receiving (44), straight-stick shooting techniques (84-88)

Beginner

1. Line two teams up as shown in the figure. From day to day, change the area of the court the teams shoot from, but make sure each team shoots from equal areas. In the figure, both teams are at the corner of the free-throw line and the free-throw lane line.
2. The first player in line for both teams shoots and then rebounds the shot (whether the shot is made or missed). The player then passes outside to a teammate and goes to the end of the team's line. (You may designate which pass you want teams to work on.)
3. The second player shoots, rebounds, and passes to a teammate. This continues until one team scores 21 baskets. Teams count their score aloud as they make their baskets.
4. Teams switch places and go to 21 again so that players get practice shooting from both sides of the court.
5. If a member of team A touches team B's basketball, team B is awarded a basket, and vice versa.

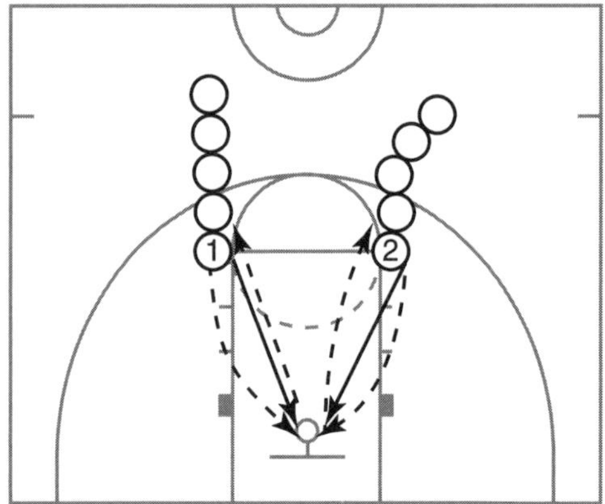

Related Drills *44-50, 52, 58-74, 84-90, 92-95*

NBA SHOOTING DRILL

Individual • 2 minutes

SKILL FOCUS Straight-stick shooting techniques (84-88), pump fake (96, 116-117), pump fake crossover (96), pump fake up-and-under (116)

Beginner

1. A player shoots from beyond the 3-point line. If made, the shot counts 3 points.
2. Whether the shot is made or missed, the player goes to get the rebound. If the ball is rebounded out on the court, the player makes a move, takes one dribble, and then shoots a jump shot. If made, it counts 2 points. If the shot is rebounded under the basket, the player does a pump fake, pump fake crossover, or pump fake up and under for the score. This shot counts 2 points.
3. The player then goes to the free-throw line. If made, the shot counts 1 point.
4. Each player is given five possessions each half, which means five 3-point attempts, five short jumpers or layups, and five free throws. This gives a total of 30 points per half, or 60 points for the game.
5. The goal is to score at least 50 percent of the time. Thus to win the game, a player must score 30 points. From week to week, players keep adding to the number of points they have to score to win the game. Play a regular NBA schedule, using your favorite team.

Related Drills *84-91, 93-96, 116-117*

93

MIKAN DRILL FOR BABY HOOK

Individual • 1 minute

SKILL FOCUS Agility, balance, conditioning, post positioning (10), reverse pivot (36), jump stop (37), stride stop (38), post moves (96-103), pump fake series (96, 116-117), half-spin (115), spin (115), up-and-under (116)

Beginner

1. One player stands under the basket with a basketball (see figure).
2. The player begins on the left side of the floor.
3. The player shoots a baby hook on the left side using the left hand, rebounds the missed or made shot, and slide-steps to the other side of the basket.
4. The player immediately turns back to the opposite direction, again doing step 3 but now from the right side, shooting the baby hook using the right hand.
5. The drill continues for 1 minute.

Intermediate

1. After the player makes the first baby hook, the player rebounds the ball and jump-stops outside the lane on the opposite side from where the player began.
2. The player immediately drop-steps to the middle and shoots another baby hook.
3. The player continues this from one side of the basket to the other for 1 minute.

Option (intermediate only) The player executes the three immediate steps, but instead of shooting the baby hook each time, the player pump-fakes and follows with the pump fake series (see drills 116-117).

➲ TEACHING POINTS

➔ **Baby Hook** Players begin on the left side of the goal (facing midcourt) with back to the basket. They turn slightly until their back is parallel to the backboard and their right shoulder pointing to the opposite side of the court. Players land on the right leg and raise the left leg as high as possible while remaining balanced. Players transfer the ball from both hands to only the left hand as they begin their jump. The left arm extends until straight. They flip the ball gently over the rim.

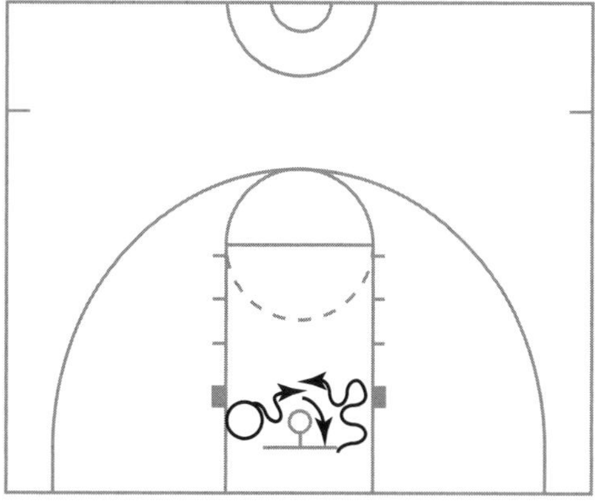

Related Drills *10, 36-38, 96-103, 114-117*

94

REBOUND-PASS-SHOOT

Team • 4 minutes

SKILL FOCUS Agility, conditioning, rocker step (11), in-and-out (12, 28), crossover (13, 29), spin (14, 30), half-spin (15, 31), front pivot (35), reverse pivot (36), jump stop (37), stride stop (38), passing (44), V-cut (53), middle cut (54), backdoor cut (55), flash pivot cut (56), slide and boxout (79), immediate boxout (79), straight-stick shooting method (84-88), shooting drills (89-93, 95)

Beginner

1. Line players up as shown in the figure. Player 1 is the shooter, 2 is the passer, 3 and 4 are the rebounders.
2. Player 1 shoots for 30 seconds; then the players rotate from 1 to 2 to 3 to 4 to 1.
3. After a complete rotation, the shooter lines up on the opposite side of the floor. Each player shoots for 30 seconds. The drill continues for another 2 minutes.
4. Both 1 and 4 begin with basketballs. As soon as 1 shoots, 4 passes to 2. Player 2 passes to 1 for another shot. Meanwhile 3 or 4 has rebounded 1's first shot and passed to 2. Player 2 again passes to 1, who shoots, and the drill continues.

Intermediate

1. Instead of just shooting the basketball, player 1 makes a cut before receiving a pass and shooting.
2. Instead of making a cut before shooting, player 1 uses a rocker-step move or a dribbling move, followed by a shot.
3. Instead of just facing the basket and rebounding, both 3 and 4 face outside on each shot. Player 3 then executes a reverse pivot and rebound, and 4 executes a front pivot and rebound.

➔ TEACHING POINTS

1. Getting the shot off fast and the number of shots taken are not as important as proper shooting technique. Make sure all players have perfect shooting fundamentals. Don't let shooters be lazy.
2. If emphasizing rebounding technique, watch for proper execution of body positioning and pivots. Note there is one strong-side rebounder and one weak-side rebounder. Both the primary and the secondary rebounding areas should be covered.
3. Quickness, not speed, is most important. Don't count the number of shots taken, for example. This might encourage bad technique.
4. If allowing shooters to cut before shooting, tell them to dip before the cut. Make sure all cuts are crisp and quick.

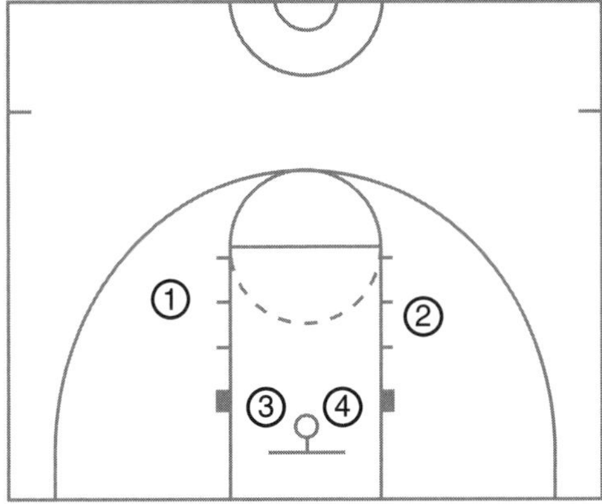

Related Drills *11-16, 28-31, 35-38, 53-56, 79-83, 84-93, 95*

95

QUICK SHOOTING DRILL FOR TWO PLAYERS

Team • 2 minutes

SKILL FOCUS Chest pass (44), bounce pass (44), rebounding (79-83), straight-stick method (84-88), shooting drills (89-95)

Beginner

1. Line players up as shown in the figure. Both players begin with a basketball.
2. Player 1 begins with a shot.
3. Player 2 chest-passes to 1 as soon as 1 has landed on the floor.
4. Player 2 rebounds 1's first shot.
5. The drill continues in this sequence for 15 seconds. Players alternate roles.
6. Player 1 changes spots on the floor, and the drill continues from that spot for 30 more seconds (15 seconds of shooting for 1, 15 seconds of shooting for 2).
7. Four areas are used on the floor to make up the 2-minute drill.

Options

1. Require player 1 to use a slide step for a step or two in either direction before receiving the second pass for a jump shot.
2. Player 2 can use the bounce pass instead of the chest pass.

TEACHING POINTS

1. Make sure all passes are crisp.
2. Make sure rebounders use proper rebounding technique.
3. Don't let shooters get lazy! Make sure all shots are picture perfect.

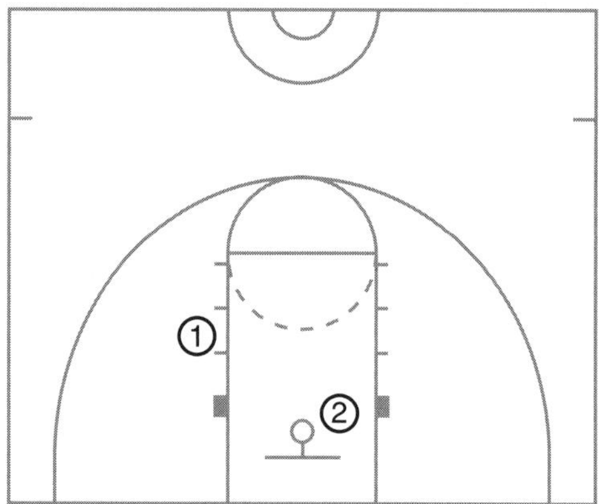

Related Drills *44, 79-83, 84-93, 94*

CHAPTER 11

Post

There are many similarities between perimeter movement and post movement. After all, in today's motion offenses, perimeter players slide into post positions with impunity. A great one-on-one player must be able to operate in the post as well as on the perimeter.

When perimeter players dribbling to the basket are cut off by defenders just shy of scoring and pick up the dribble, they are in the same position as post players who have used the dribble inside. We call this situation *scoring at the end of the dribble*. Pump fakes are used, and the pump fake crossover is a countermove.

Perimeter dribblers use the spin and half-spin dribbling techniques. The same footwork is practiced by post players with back to the basket.

When perimeter players square up in triple-threat position, they use a rocker step as the first fake. Post players can front pivot (or reverse pivot) and face the basket. We call these *face-up moves*. The face-up moves involve much the same movement as the rocker step.

The eight post drills in this chapter cover all of these techniques. These drills also incorporate the defensive coverage of each move. This makes one-on-one play at the post very intense. Drill 96 demonstrates the fakes.

Players cannot dribble outside their legs when in the post position because outside defenders sink to help force the ball back outside. A dribble outside the legs by a post player would lead to a sagging perimeter defender deflecting the dribble. Drill 97 shows how to avoid this.

Drill 98 teaches fronting defense and the type of attack players need against it. Drill 99 explains the most common defensive coverage, the two-step, and the offensive tactics to be used against it.

Drill 100 presents the unstoppable roll step, an offensive maneuver all post players must have in their repertoire. Drill 101 illustrates the three-quarter defensive maneuver and how to attack it. Drill 102 practices the high-low offensive attack used by two post players cooperating against defenders. Drill 103 adds post screening as another option to your squad's motion offense.

POST-UP MECHANICS

Individual or team • 5 minutes per fake

SKILL FOCUS Triple-threat position (9), rocker step (11), crossover (13, 29), spin (14, 30), half-spin (15, 31), front pivot (35), reverse pivot (36), jump stop (37), post moves, pump fake, pump fake crossover, post-up position, drop step, face-up moves, slide-step dribble (97), fronting post defense (98), one-step defensive post (99), two-step defensive post (99), three-quartering defensive post (101), pump fakes series (116-117)

Advanced

1. Players line up as shown in figure 1.
2. A coach instructs players to execute a post technique. Players execute the skill and then go to the end of the line. Work on only one technique per day, or on two or three at one time—for example, post-up position, drop step, and a pump fake for a layup. The following steps explain different post techniques.
    a. *Posting up:* The coach tells players they are defended on the upper side. Players use their bodies to push their defenders a step up from the big block. The coach passes inside, and players use a drop-step technique (see part b) to score. If a defender plays low side, the player pushes the defender a step or so lower. If fronted, the defender is pushed outside a step or two by the attacker. The body push creates a greater area for the pass. If the defender plays directly behind the post player, the post player gets low as if sitting in a chair and holds hands out in front for a pass. The post player keeps the defender at bay by keeping buttocks protruding out back into the defender.
    b. *Drop step:* Placing the front foot in front of the defender's front foot, the post player puts an arm in the defender's torso, bending the elbow 90 degrees. The arm keeps the defender from stepping around the front foot and intercepting a pass. When the coach passes inside, the player moves the back foot toward the basket, still holding off the defender with the front foot and arm, receives the pass, and shoots the layup, using a slide-step dribble, if needed (see drills 97 and 114).
    c. *Pump fake:* The post player (who must be near the basket) squares shoulders up to the basket and, using both hands to control the ball, violently throws both arms up toward the basket. A player may pump-fake up to three times but should shoot anytime the defender leaves the floor to block the shot. Pump fakes must look like the shot. More than three pump fakes usually result in a 3-second violation. Players can use the pump fake at the end of a dribble near the basket, at the end of a post move near the basket, or after getting an offensive rebound.
    d. *Pump-fake crossover:* When a defender reacts to the pump fake by coming up on the toes, the post player then uses the crossover move to step by the defender for the layup. It is important to always end

the post move or dribble with a jump stop in order to have two pivot feet, enabling the attacker to cross over in either direction. Instead of a pump fake crossover, the player may use a pump fake direct step, called the *up and under.* Players should use whichever maneuver the defender gives them (for more detail, see drills 116-117).

e. *Face-up moves:* A post player front pivots or reverse pivots, ending up facing the basket. Now the attacker can jump shoot immediately, or pump-fake and then shoot, or use a rocker step to drive directly or to crossover drive.

f. *Spin move:* Same as the dribbling spin move but executed by a post player with back to the basket (for more detail, see drill 115).

g. *Half-spin move:* Same as the dribbling half-spin move but executed by a post player with back to the basket (for more detail, see drill 115).

➔ Options

1. Put one defender on the post player and let the post player react to the way the defender is defending.
2. Put an offensive player at the free-throw line extended and another player in the corner (see figure 2; rotate from 1 to 2 to 5 to X5 to end of line). These two players pass the ball back and forth until the post player is able to get free for a pass from a perimeter player. X5 can front, use a one-step defensive technique or a two-step tactic, or play behind the attacker. The offensive post player reads and reacts to the defender.

➔ TEACHING POINT Make sure all mechanics, including footwork, are executed properly.

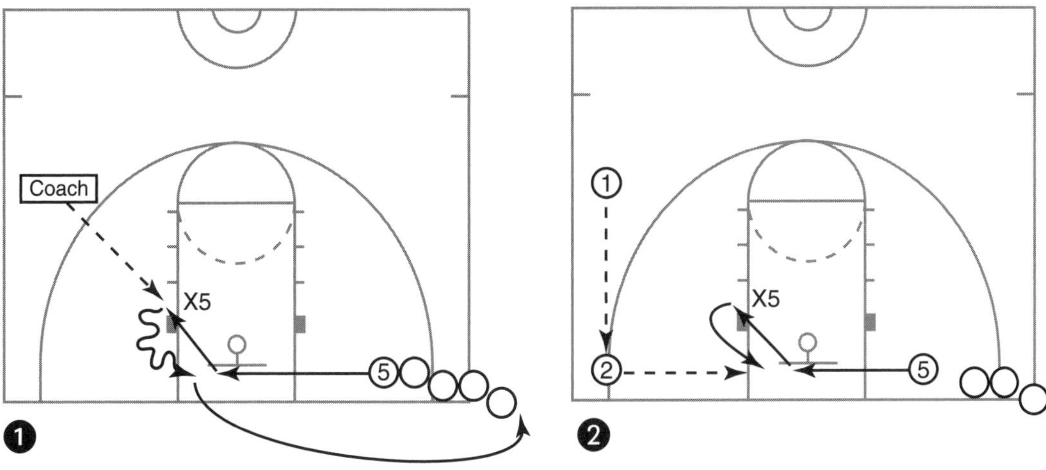

Related Drills *97-103, 114-121*

97

SLIDE-STEP DRIBBLE

Individual or team • 1 minute

SKILL FOCUS Slide-step dribble

Beginner

1. Players line up as shown in the figure. The first player in line does a single slide-step dribble—one step. This step ends at the second line marking on the free-throw lane line. The player picks up the dribble, executes one slide-step dribble to the middle of the lane, picks up the ball with both hands, and then does another slide-step dribble, which should take the player out of the lane. The player again picks up the ball with both hands and then does one more slide-step dribble, which should put the player at the big block on the opposite lane. The player goes to the end of the line.
2. In the post, players must dribble sparingly. The proper dribble is the slide-step dribble. The ball should be dribbled no higher than the knees. Players make one dribble, let's say to the right, by using the left hand, keeping the ball low and directly beneath their crouch. They slide-step to the right. To do the slide step, they pick up the right foot, step once, and then bring the left foot up to shoulder-width apart. They keep the ball low and between the legs so it cannot be slapped away. They should never dribble more than one step in the post area.
3. Practice going to the right one day, and to the left the next.

Advanced

After each slide-step dribble, have players do a move, such as any move in the pump fake series: pump fake, pump fake crossover, or up and under.

TEACHING POINT Make sure the dribble is directly between players' legs, not out in front of them.

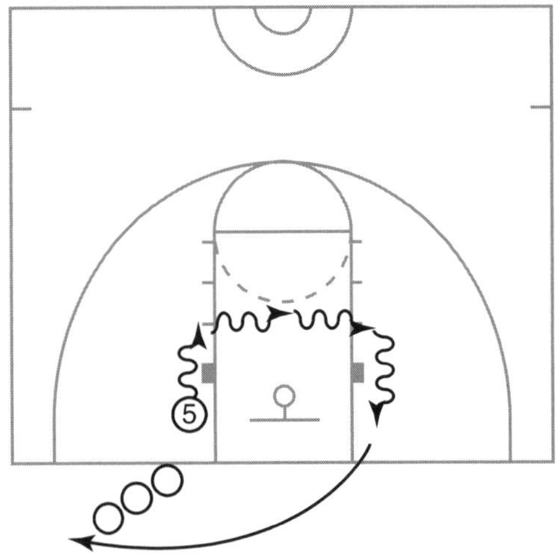

Related Drills *96, 98-103, 114-121*

FRONTING

Individual or team • 2 minutes

SKILL FOCUS Overhead flip pass (44), flash pivot cut (54), post-up offense (96), pump fake (96), fronting post defense

Intermediate

1. Players line up as shown in the figure. Rotation is from offense, 5, to defense, X5, to end of 3's line, and 3 to end of 5's line.
2. Player 5 flash pivots to the big block or slightly above. X5 fronts 5.
3. Then 5 uses the body to push X5 a step or so farther outside, but not so far that X5 moves behind 5.
4. Player 5 turns to face the baseline, placing the right arm against X5's lower back; 5's upper arm should be at a 90-degree angle with the lower arm. Player 5 raises the left arm and hand high overhead, giving 3 a target for the overhead pass. Player 5 waits until the pass is directly overhead, and then steps forward once toward the basket, catches the ball, and—without bringing the ball down—leaps toward the basket and lays the ball in.
5. Player 3 throws an overhead flip pass to 5. The pass should be about a step farther than where 5 holds a target hand.
6. If 5 needs to reestablish footwork, 5 can bring the ball down, then pump-fake, then lay the ball in.
7. X5 jumps back toward the basket as the ball is being thrown over his or her head. X5 is behind the attacker so must time the jump to try to block the layup. X5 does not want to foul.

TEACHING POINTS

1. Make sure the pass is properly thrown; it should be a semi-lob just slightly out of the reach of a jumping defender.
2. The attacker should face out of bounds; the step should be taken with the lead foot first (left foot in the figure).
3. The attacker should not bring the ball down; the attacker makes the catch, keeps the ball up high, and then lays it in.

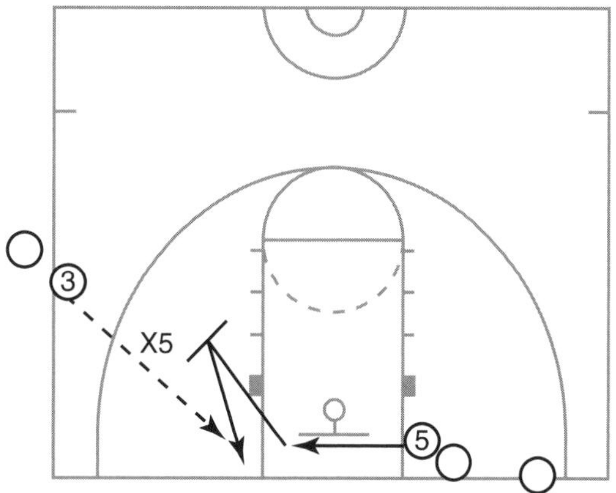

Related Drills *96-97, 99-103, 114-121*

99

TWO-STEP DRILL

Individual or team • 5 minutes

➲ SKILL FOCUS Triple-threat position (9), rocker step (11), crossover (13, 29), spin (14, 30), front pivot (35), reverse pivot (36), jump stop (37), flash-pivot cut (54), post moves (96, 114-121), pump fake (96), pump fake crossover (96), post-up position (96), drop step (96, 114), face-up moves (96), slide-step dribble (97), two-step defensive post

Intermediate

1. Players line up as shown in the figure. Rotation is from offense, 5, to defense, X5, to 1 to 3 to end of line.
2. Player 5 flash pivots to the big block area. X5 begins by playing above 5 because the ball is in 1's hands.
3. Player 1 passes to 3, and 5 tries to prevent X5 from doing the defensive two-step. Player 5 should have the front foot (right foot in the figure) even with or above X5's right foot. X5 should have the right foot half a body above 5 and the left foot slightly below 5's body. This should become a legal pushing match, with neither the offense nor defense using hands and arms.
4. When the pass is made from 1 to 3, X5 picks up the left foot and places it directly in front of 5's body. As the pass is caught by 3, X5 should be picking up the right foot and placing it slightly behind 5's body. X5's left foot should be half a body length above 5's body. Player 5 now should be trying to put the left foot up by X5's left foot, using the lower arm to establish proper post-up position.
5. Begin the drill with 5 being inactive and X5 just drilling on the two-step maneuver. Players 1 and 3 should hold each pass about two seconds while drilling on the two-step maneuver. Then make it live.

➜ **Option** Instead of doing a two-step drill, the defender does a one-step drill. As the ball is passed from 1 to 3, X5 pulls the left foot up and places it in front of 5's body. X5's shoulders should now be parallel to the passing line between 1 and 3. X5 keeps hands down and reaches back to feel the movement of 5. This puts X5 in a fronting position instead of a three-quarter position. When using the one-step technique, X5 would play three-quarters when the ball is in 1's hands and would front when the ball is in 3's hands.

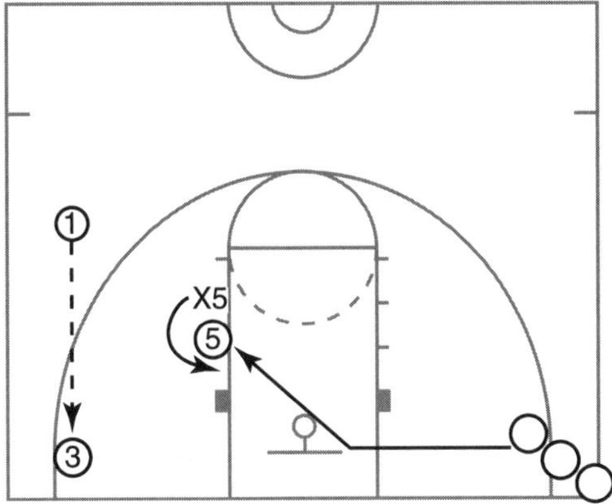

Related Drills *96-98, 100-103, 114-121*

100

ROLL STEP

Individual or team • 5 minutes

➔ **SKILL FOCUS** Triple-threat position (9), rocker step (11), crossover (13, 29), spin (14, 30), front pivot (35), reverse pivot (36), jump stop (37), post moves (96, 114-121), pump fake (96, 117), pump fake crossover (96, 117), post-up position (96), drop step (96, 114), face-up moves (96), slide-step dribble (97), defensive fronting (98), defensive two-step (99), offensive post roll step

Advanced

1. Line up players as if you were running drill 99 (figure 1). Rotation is the same as in drill 99.
2. Instead of trying to prevent the post defender from moving as the pass is thrown from 1 to 3, the post player allows the defensive two-step (or one-step) movement without interference. As the defender moves, the attacker turns to face the defender (figure 2). As 3 catches the ball, the post player reverse pivots. Now the defender cannot possibly recover. A quick pass back to 1 from 3 gives 1 a perfect passing angle into the post, where the post player is prepared to execute offensive moves.

➔ **Option** Make it a live one-on-one drill with the defender and post attacker reading and reacting to the developing situations.

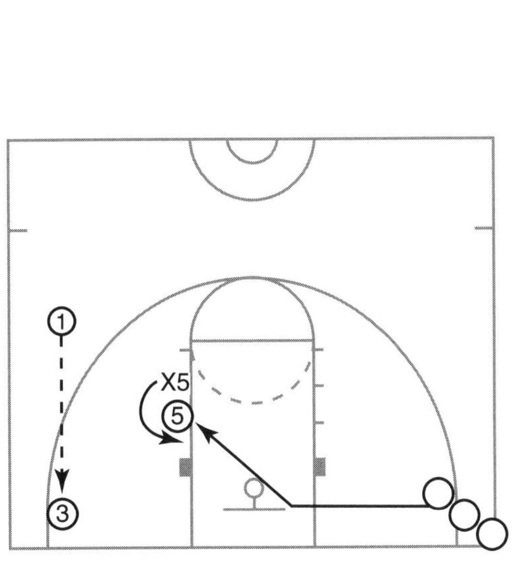

❶

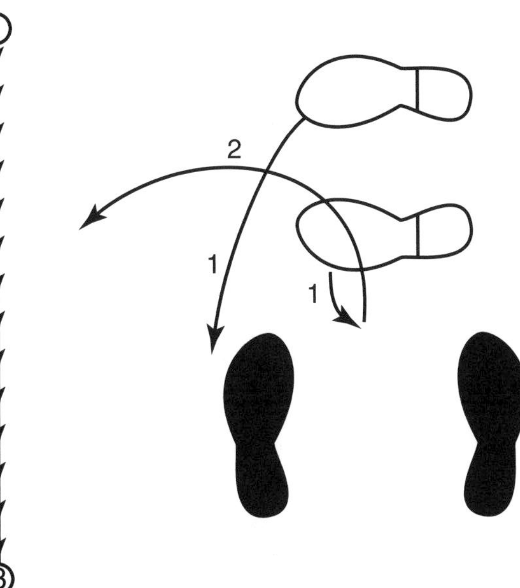

❷ The unstoppable roll. The post defender executes a two-step maneuver (or one-step maneuver) as the pass goes from player 1 to player 3. As the defender completes the maneuver, 3 does a 180-degree reverse pivot. The first step is with the foot away from the defender (right foot here), and the second step is the reverse pivot. Player 3 quickly passes back to 1, and the post defender cannot keep the pass from going into the post.

Related Drills *96-99, 101-103, 114-121*

101

THREE-QUARTER DRILL

Individual or team • 5 minutes

SKILL FOCUS Triple-threat position (9), rocker step (11), crossover (13, 29), spin (14, 30), front pivot (35), reverse pivot (36), jump stop (37), post moves (96, 114-121), pump fake (96), pump fake crossover (96), post-up position (96), drop step (96, 114), face-up moves (96), slide-step dribble (97), defensive fronting (98), defensive two-step (99), offensive post roll step (100)

Intermediate

1. Players line up as shown in the figure. Rotation is from 5 to X5 to 3 to the end of the line.
2. Player 5 flash pivots toward a coach. X5 defends from the three-quarter defensive position.
3. Player 5 tries to get the right foot ahead of X5's. X5 tries to keep the right foot in front of 5's. Both use slide steps to try to get this position on the floor. After several small steps, 5 will be out too far on the court, so X5 immediately tries to get behind 5. Player 5 tries to prevent this by sliding back toward the lane.
4. Allow this foot movement to continue until a defensive mistake is made. If X5 does manage to get behind 5, 5 should move into sitting position, receive the pass from the coach, and make an offensive move.
5. Should no mistake be made in a reasonable amount of time, the coach passes to 3. Player 5 releases toward the goal, trying to keep X5 on 5's back. Player 3 passes to 5, who tries to score. Player 5 may have to use pump fakes and a slide-step dribble to maintain balance.

Options

1. Use player 1 in place of the coach. Make it a live one-on-one post drill.
2. Play defenders X1 and X3 to try to prevent rapid ball movement outside while still drilling one on one in the post.

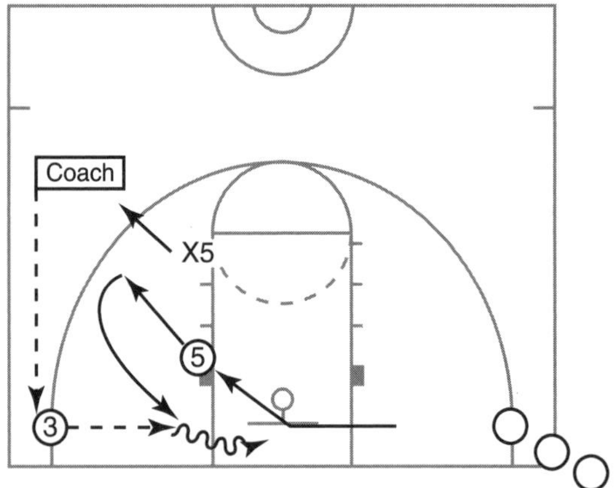

Related Drills *96-100, 102-103, 114-121*

HIGH LOW POST PASSING

Team • 6 minutes

➲ SKILL FOCUS Triple-threat position (9), rocker step (11), crossover (13, 29), spin (14, 30), front pivot (35), reverse pivot (36), jump stop (37), bounce pass (44), overhead pass (44), flash pivot (54), post moves (96, 114-121), pump fake (96), pump fake crossover (96), post-up position (96), drop step (96, 114), face-up moves (96), slide-step dribble (97), defensive fronting (98)

Intermediate

1. Players line up as shown in the figure. Rotation is from 4 to X4 to 5 to X5 to the end of the line.
2. Player 4 flash pivots to the free-throw line area. X4 defends this move. If X4 denies, 4 cuts backdoor for a lob pass from a coach. If 4 is successful with the flash pivot cut, the coach passes 4 the ball, and the high-low passing drill is activated.
3. When 4 receives the pass at the high post, 4 front pivots into triple-threat position.
4. Player 5 ducks into the lane and tries to post X5.
5. Players 4 and 5 must read X4 and X5's coverage to make the next pass. If X5 is behind 5, 4 bounce passes to 5, who uses post moves or dribble moves. If X5 fronts 5, 4 tosses the overhead lob pass to 5 for the layup. If X5 is sealed properly, 4 steps right and bounce passes to 5.
6. First run the drill without defensive pressure. After several run-throughs, the defense should become live.

Advanced

Put a perimeter player in the corner (or wing) on the same side as 5. When 5 seals X5, 4 could pass to the corner player, who has a perfect entry angle to 5.

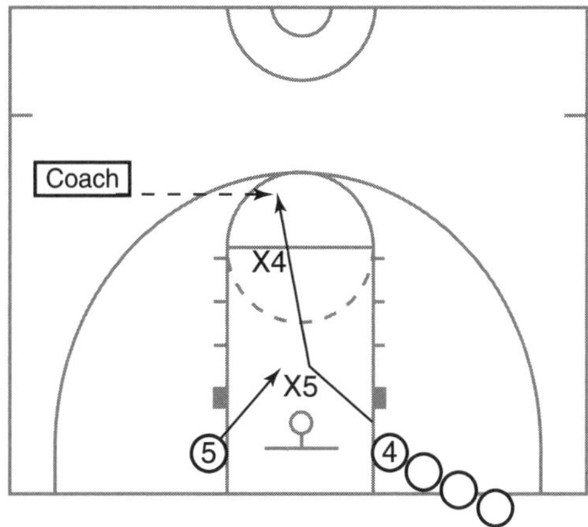

Related Drills *96-101, 103, 114-121*

103

POST SCREENING

Team • 10 minutes each phase

➲ SKILL FOCUS Triple-threat position (9), rocker step (11), crossover (13, 29), spin (14, 30), front pivot (35), reverse pivot (36), jump stop (37), bounce pass (44), overhead pass (44), flash pivot (54), screening (71), post moves (96), pump fake (96, 117), pump fake crossover (96), post-up position (96), drop step (96, 114), face-up moves (96), slide-step dribble (97), defensive fronting (98), defensive two-step (99), three-quartering (101), high-low (102)

Intermediate

1. This drill consists of two phases: post screening for perimeter players (figure 1) and post screening for post players (figure 2).
2. First phase: Players line up as shown in figure 1. Rotation is from 1 to X1 to 3 to X3 to 5 to X5 to 1. Be sure to let each player operate from each spot.
3. Player 5 can screen for either 3 or 1. Both 3 and 1 must try to set their defenders up for the screen. In figure 1, 1 is setting up X1, and 5 is screening for 1. Remember that 5 must call out 1's name when 5 goes to set the screen, and 5 must either screen and come back to the ball or screen and fade. In this case, 5 screens and comes back to the ball. The coach reads the defense of the screen and passes to the correct primary receiver.

Advanced

1. Second phase: Players line up as shown in figure 2. Rotation is from 4 to X4 to 5 to X5 to the end of the line (defenders are not shown). One post player screens for the other post player, and the screener rolls back high, creating a high-low passing post offense.
2. To play proper defense, X4 must always go over the top of the screen. X5 guards the big block until X4 can get there. Then X5 picks 5 back up. X5 can bump 4 slightly before going back to pick up 5.
3. The coach reads the defense of the screen and passes to the correct primary receiver.

➜ Options (all skill levels)

1. Instead of the coach making the entry pass, put an offensive player there and drill on reading the screen and making the entry pass.
2. When using a perimeter player and a pass is made into the high post (5 in figure 2), 4 can try to seal X4. You now have the high-low passing drill with a perimeter player to help pass the ball into the low post.

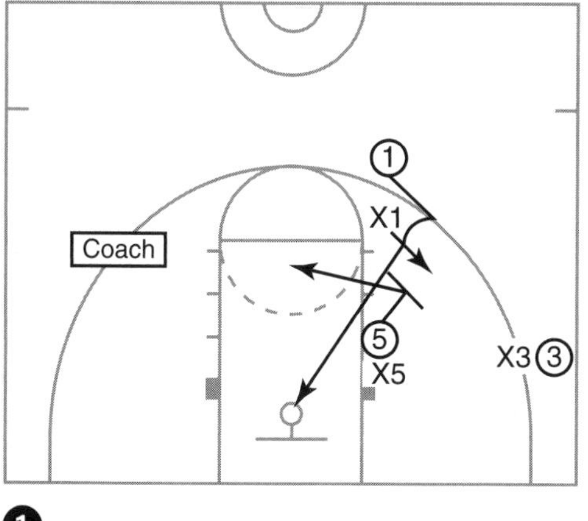

1

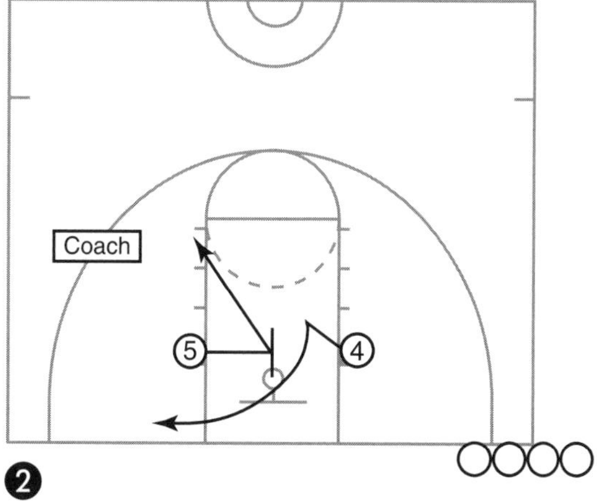

2

Related Drills *71, 96-102, 114-121, 149, 151-154*

CHAPTER

12

Perimeter

Now that your players are adept at one-on-one perimeter movement without a defender, we will add a defensive player. This will progress your players from knowing not only how to make a move but *when* to make a move. Patience is required (for both coaches and players) because players will make many mistakes before they become intelligent one-on-one players. Once players have developed this intelligence, they will make all other players on your squad better.

Kobe Bryant of the Lakers perfected his one-on-one moves at a very young age. Today he is among the best players in basketball at creating his own shot and passing off to teammates, thereby making them better. Grant Hill of the Phoenix Suns is so smooth at his one-on-one moves that it seems the ball is an extension of his movements. Grant was from South Lakes High School in Reston, Virginia. Because South Lakes is in our area, we got to see him play before he became famous. He was smooth then, but practice, practice, and more practice has made his one-on-one movement flawless.

Drill 104 requires players to stay in a 15-foot (4.5-m) lane to make their maneuvers. This is the required distance of the motion offense. Teammates will always be cutting to keep the proper 15-foot (4.5-m) spacing. But 15 feet (4.5 m) is enough space if technique is good and only one or two dribbles are used to create separation from defenders.

In drill 105, players learn not to take a bad shot out of their one-on-one play. Drill 106 is a highly competitive, fun drill, starting with recovering a loose ball. Drill 107 forces constant one-on-one play.

In drill 108, players practice never resting on the court. The bench is for resting; the court is for playing. In drill 109, defenders learn how to close out on a one-on-one breakaway dribbler, a scenario that occurs often in games.

Drill 110 is a great drill to end practice sessions; it is highly competitive and draws together all the components of one-on-one offensive and defensive techniques. This drill leaves your players in a positive, upbeat mood. In drill 111, defenders master how to close out on a weak-side pass receiver—one of the most frequent occurrences in any game.

Drill 112 adds cutting to perimeter play. Players learn to read defenders to determine which cut to use and when it is best to use that cut.

Drill 113 adds dribble penetration to your motion offense. Now your perimeter players should become adept at going one on one, screening, cutting, and penetrating with a dribble.

These individual and team drills will help perfect your motion offense.

104

ONE-ON-ONE LANE DRILL

Individual • 4 minutes

➲ SKILL FOCUS Triple-threat position (9), rocker step (11), in and out (12, 28), crossover (13, 29), spin (14, 30), half-spin (15, 31), control dribble (24), defensive fakes (33), jump stop (37), stride stop (38), pump fake (96), pump fake crossover (96), slide dribble (97), front foot to pivot foot (129), front foot to free foot (130), advance step (137), retreat step (137), swing step (137)

Beginner

1. Players line up as shown in the figure. Players 3 and X3 switch roles after a time.
2. Have several different groups going at one time at different baskets. Or use three groups at the same basket, each using a different 15-foot (4.5-m) space.
3. Offensive players must stay inside the 15-foot lane and must score within three dribbles. The offense begins with a rocker step and any dribbling move.
4. The defense tries to compel the offense to change direction as many times as possible during those three dribbles.
5. Offensive players must create separation from defenders to get their jump shots off.
6. Change the 15-foot lanes from day to day.

➜ Options

1. Limit offensive players to only one move (e.g., spin) or two moves.
2. Instead of forcing offensive players to change direction, defenders can play front foot to pivot foot defense and stay on the shooting shoulder.
3. The defense must stop the attacker twice in a row before rotating to offense.
4. Offensive players stay on offense as long as they create separation, whether they score or not.

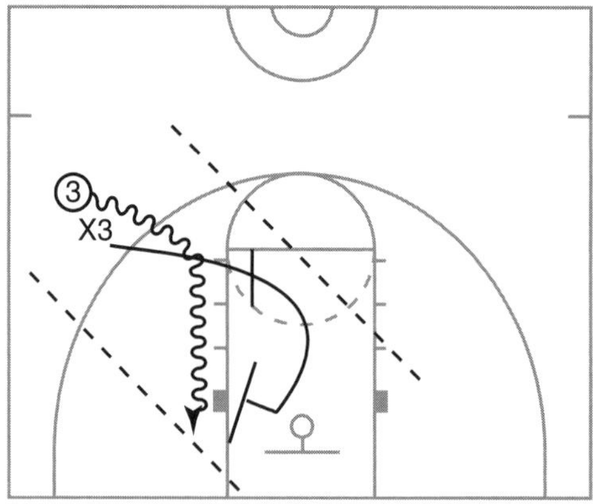

Related Drills *9, 11-17, 96, 105-109, 111, 137-139, 151-154*

ONE-ON-ONE RELIEF DRILL

Individual • 4 minutes

SKILL FOCUS Triple-threat position (9), rocker step 11), in and out (12, 28), crossover (13, 29), spin (14, 30), half-spin (15, 31), control dribble (24), defensive fakes (33), jump stop (37), stride stop (38), chest pass (44), bounce pass (44), overhead pass (44), V-cut (53), middle cut (54), backdoor cut (55), pump fake (96), pump fake crossover (96), slide dribble (97), front foot to pivot foot (129), front foot to free foot (130), advance step (137), retreat step (137), swing step (137)

Beginner

1. Players line up as shown in the figure. Player 3 rotates to X3, X3 to 4, and 4 to 3.
2. Have several groups going at one time.
3. When on offense, players must stay inside the 15-foot (4.5-m) lane. They may begin with a rocker step and any dribbling move. If they cannot create separation and get a shot, tell them not to take a bad shot. Instead they should pass to 4 and then V-cut, middle-cut, or backdoor cut (whichever the defense gives). Player 4 hits 3 with a pass, and 3 again operates one on one against X3.
4. Change the 15-foot lanes from day to day.
5. The defender must play solid defense, from stance to denying the shot.

Options

1. Limit offensive players to only one or two moves.
2. Defenders must stop attackers two consecutive times before rotating.

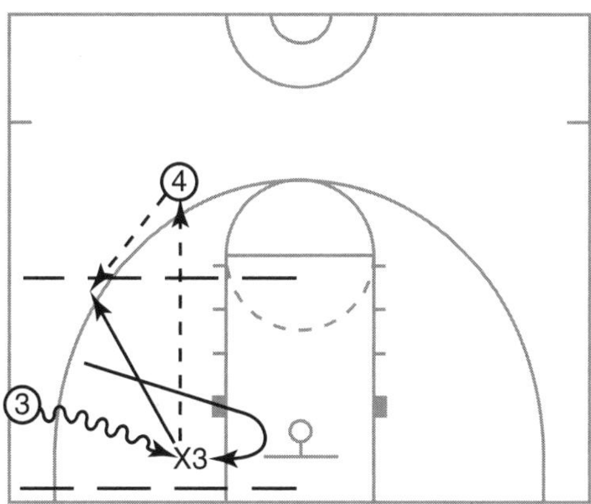

Related Drills *9, 11-17, 96, 104, 106-109, 111, 137-139, 151-154*

106

ONE-ON-ONE TEAM DRILL

Individual • 2 minutes

SKILL FOCUS Triple-threat position (9), rocker step (11), in and out (12, 28), crossover (13, 29), spin (14, 30), half-spin (15, 31), control dribble (24), defensive fakes (33), jump stop (37), stride stop (38), pump fake (96), pump fake crossover (96), slide dribble (97), front foot to pivot foot (129), front foot to free foot (130), advance step (137), retreat step (137), swing step (137)

Beginner

1. Players line up as shown in the figure. After 1 minute, offense and defense switch roles.
2. Player 1 begins with a basketball and may use any fake desired.
3. When first teaching the drill, don't let 1 dribble. Then advance to one dribble, and then to two dribbles. You may begin by allowing 1 to attack in only one direction, and then later in either direction.
4. Player 1 may shoot if 1 can get X1 off balance, but 1 shouldn't force the shot.
5. X1 begins in front foot to pivot foot stance.
6. X1 cannot move until 1 moves.

Options

1. Allow 1 to use any move, including several dribbles. X1 must react.
2. Have a coach stand where X1 cannot see the coach; the coach holds up numbers for fakes or dribbles to be used.
3. Player 1 uses the right foot as a pivot foot one time, and then the left foot as the pivot foot the next.
4. Player 1 stands under the basket and executes pump fakes and pump fake crossovers as if at the end of the dribble.

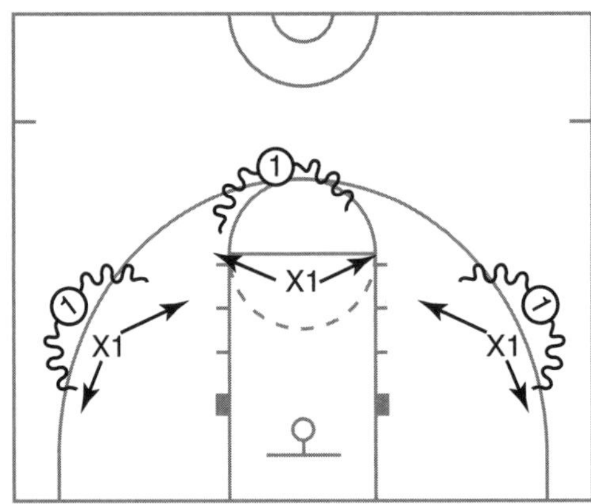

Related Drills *9, 11-17, 96, 104-105, 107-109, 111, 137-139, 151-154*

ONE ON ONE ON ONE ON ONE

Team • 4 minutes

SKILL FOCUS Triple-threat position (9), rocker step (11), in and out (12, 28), crossover (13, 29), spin (14, 30), half-spin (15, 31), control dribble (24), defensive fakes (33), jump stop (37), stride stop (38), pump fake (96), pump fake crossover (96), slide dribble (97), front foot to pivot foot (129), front foot to free foot (130), advance step (137), retreat step (137), swing step (137)

Beginner

1. Players line up as shown in the figure.
2. Player 1 plays one on one against X1 and may use any move.
3. If 1 scores, X1 goes to the end of the line while 2 comes out as the new defender on 1. If X1 stops 1 by getting a turnover or a defensive rebound, 1 goes to the end of the line, and X1 becomes the new offensive player, while 2 races out to defend. Whether 1 scores or X1 stops 1, the new attacker must race with the ball back to the head of the key. It is there that the new attacker reverse pivots or front pivots, establishing a pivot foot.
4. When reaching the head of the key and pivoting, the new attacker may immediately attempt a shot if the defender has not raced out there to defend.
5. Score is kept for each attacker. First player to 10 wins.

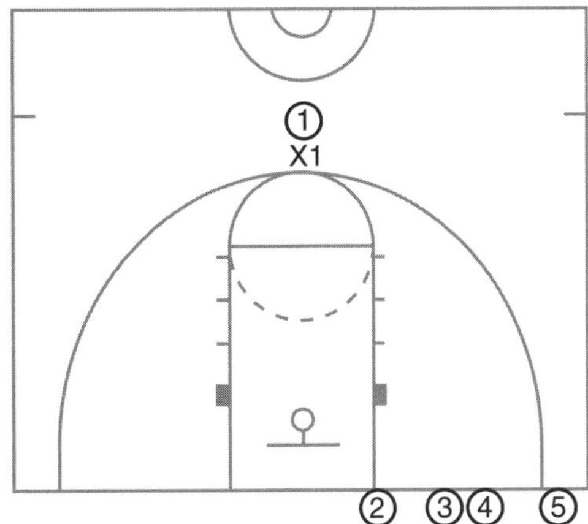

Related Drills *9, 11-17, 96, 104-106, 108-109, 111, 137-139, 151-154*

ONE-ON-ONE FULL-COURT GAME

Individual or team • 5 minutes

SKILL FOCUS Triple-threat position (9), rocker step (11), in and out (12, 28), crossover (13, 29), spin (14, 30), half-spin (15, 31), control dribble (24), defensive fakes (33), jump stop (37), stride stop (38), pump fake (96), pump fake crossover (96), slide dribble (97), front foot to pivot foot (129), front foot to free foot (130), advance step (137), retreat step (137), swing step (137), conditioning

Beginner

1. This drill is nearly as much fun as a real game. Players line up as shown in the figure.
2. Players 1 and X1 begin the drill by "inbounding the ball," which in this case means player 1 tossing the ball onto the backboard. The two players then fight for possession. The winner tries to score, and the other defends. In the figure, the offensive player, 1, gains the "inbounds" pass, and takes off one on one full court. It is best to use smaller side-court baskets if available.
3. If 1 scores, 1 goes to the end of the line on the side of the court scored on. If X1 stops 1, X1 begins to drive to the far basket to score against 1. If 1 scores, X1 quickly tosses the ball off the backboard ("inbounding the ball"). X2 then steps on the floor to fight for possession of this inbounded ball, and X1 and X2 go full court one on one. This pattern continues for 5 minutes. The player who scores the most baskets in 5 minutes wins.
4. If you have baskets at the side courts, you can have two groups drill at once.

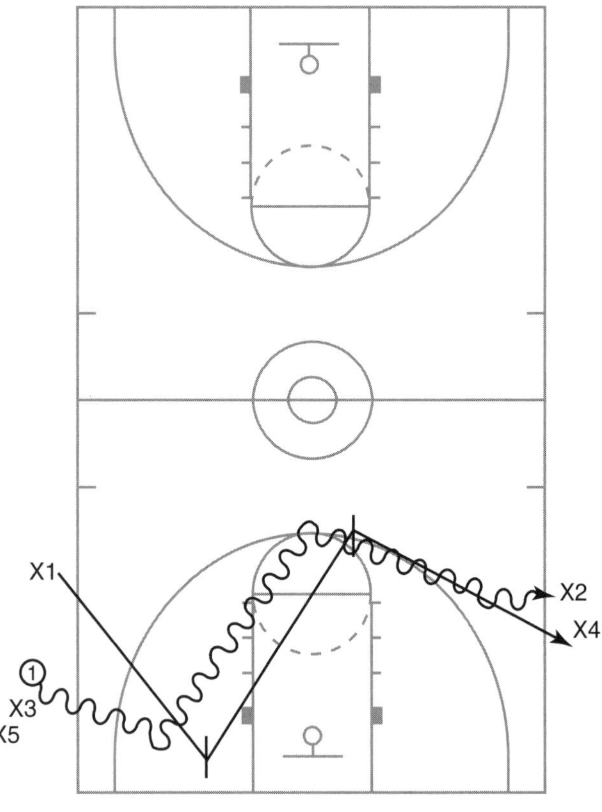

Option Do not use substitutes. Only players 1 and X1 play a full-court one-on-one game for 2 minutes. The player with the most points wins. Two other players then take the court and play full-court one on one.

Related Drills *9, 11-17, 96, 104-107, 109, 111, 137-139, 151-154*

RECOVERY DRILL

Individual or team • 6 minutes

SKILL FOCUS Triple-threat position (9), rocker step (11), in and out (12, 28), crossover (13, 29), spin (14, 30), half-spin (15, 31), control dribble (24), defensive fakes (33), jump stop (37), stride stop (38), pump fake (96), pump fake crossover (96), slide dribble (97), front foot to pivot foot (129), front foot to free foot (130), advance step (137), retreat step (137), swing step (137)

Beginner

1. Players line up as shown in figure 1 or 2; these are two types of alignments for the same drill.
2. A coach rolls the ball down the middle of the floor, varying speed and distance on each roll.
3. The first two players in figure 1 race out to recover the ball. In figure 2, the coach calls out a number (in this case, 3) and those two like numbers race out to recover the ball.
4. The player who recovers the ball becomes the attacker and the other the defender. They play one on one back to the basket; then they go to the end of the line in figure 1 and to their former spots in figure 2.

Options

1. Make the drill competitive and keep score to a set number of baskets. Put guards on one team and big men on the other, starters on one team and substitutes on the other, and so on.
2. To make this a full-court transition-type drill, designate the basket at the opposite end of the court as the one-on-one basket after the recovery.
3. Use figure 1 and place two cones equidistant from each line somewhere on the court, such as in the corners; players must race around these cones before recovering the basketball.

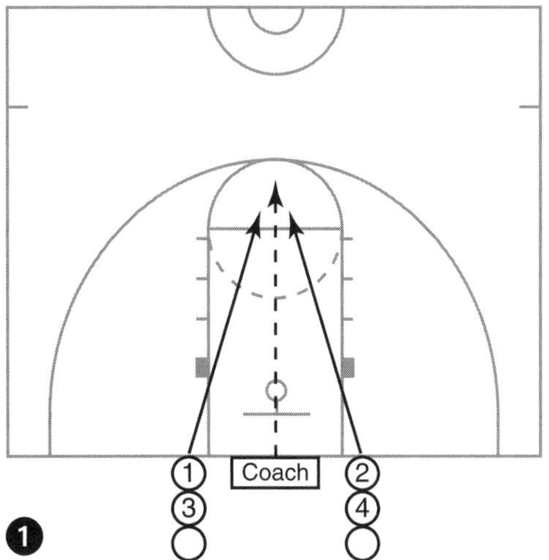

1

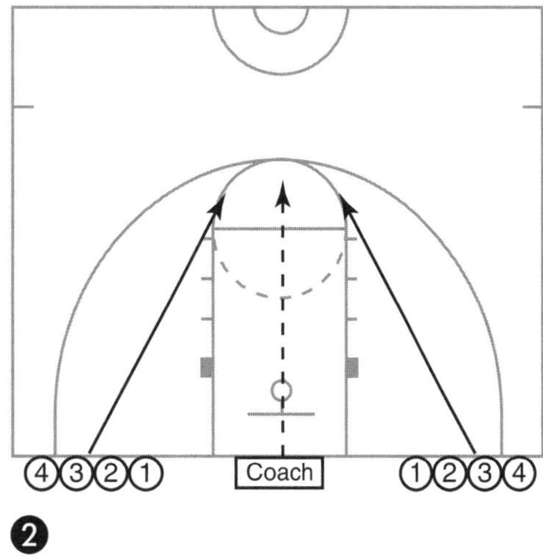

2

Related Drills *9, 11-18, 96, 104-108, 111, 137-139, 151-154*

110

ONE ON ONE ON ONE

Team • 3 minutes

SKILL FOCUS Rocker step (11), perimeter moves (12-15), change of pace (25), hesitation (26), dribbling moves (28-31), front pivot (35), reverse pivot (36), jump stop (37), stride stop (38), offensive and defensive rebounding (78-83), jump shots (84-88), baby hook (93), pump fake series (96, 116-117), post moves (114-121)

Intermediate

1. This is a fun, highly competitive drill.
2. The three players shoot free throws. The first missed free throw is out. The second missed free throw becomes the first defender. The player who did not miss begins on offense.
3. In the figure, 1 is on offense, 2 is on defense, and 3 is the next player on the floor.
4. Player 1 begins anywhere along the 3-point line. Player 2 defends. As long as 1 scores, 1 gets to keep the basketball. Should 1 not score and 2 get the defensive rebound, 2 becomes the new offensive player, and 3 rushes out to play defense on 2. Player 1 goes to wait for the next turn. Should 1 score, either on a move or an offensive rebound, 3 rushes out to defend 1. Player 2 goes to wait for the next turn.
5. If 1 scores, 1 makes a dribble move back to the 3-point line. Player 3 must get out there to defend 1 or 1 will have a wide-open 3-point shot. If 2 gets the rebound, 2 makes a dribble move back to the 3-point line. Player 3 must get out there to defend 2 or 2 will have a wide-open 3-point shot. If 2 fouls 1, 1 calls the foul. Player 1 makes a dribble move back to the 3-point line while 3 rushes out to play defense.
6. Each 3-point shot equals 3 points. Jump shots and layups equal 2 points. A foul disqualifies the defender for that turn, and the offensive player gets 1 point.
7. The first player to 10 points wins.

Options

1. Have the offensive player call out the scoring move while dribbling back to the 3-point line.
2. Limit the number of dribbles the attacker can use; three is a good number.
3. The attacker's move must create space or the shot is no good, even if it goes in. (Created space means the attacker has no defender's hand in the face or on the ball when the shot is taken.)

➲ TEACHING POINTS

1. Make sure to go over the offensive moves with each player as the game continues.
2. Correct any defensive mistake that allows space enough for the player to get the shot off.
3. Make sure each player knows when to shoot (at the exact moment space is created). If space has been created, the shot is a quality shot. The winner of nearly every basketball game is the team that takes the most quality shots.

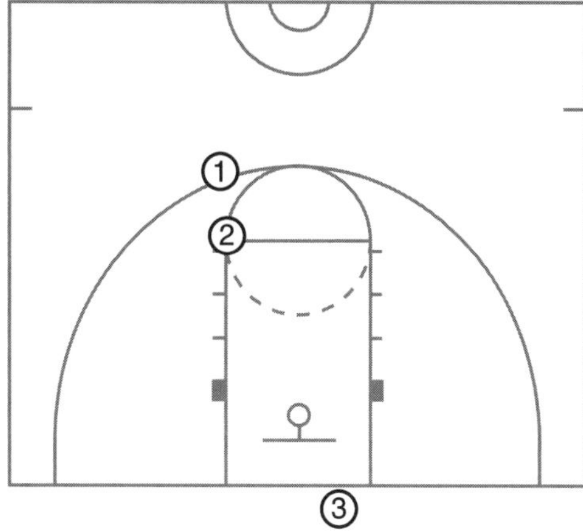

Related Drills *11-15, 25-26, 28-31, 35-38, 78-83, 84-88, 93, 96, 114-121*

111

APPROACH AND CLOSE OUT

Individual or team • 6 minutes

SKILL FOCUS Triple-threat position (9), rocker step (11), in and out (12, 28), crossover (13, 29), spin (14, 30), half-spin (15, 31), control dribble (24), defensive fakes (33), jump stop (37), stride stop (38), pump fake (96), pump fake crossover (96), slide dribble (97), front foot to pivot foot (129), front foot to free foot (130), advance step (137), retreat step (137), swing step (137), closeout (149-151)

Beginner

1. Players line up as shown in the figure. Rotation is from offense to defense to end of the line. The first player in line becomes the next attacker.
2. X1 rolls the ball to 1; 1 fakes and drives.
3. X1 must close out on the dribbler and bring the dribbler under control. Then X1 and 1 play one on one.

Option X1 rolls the ball to 1. X1 must get to 1 and close out on the pass receiver before 1 begins a drive.

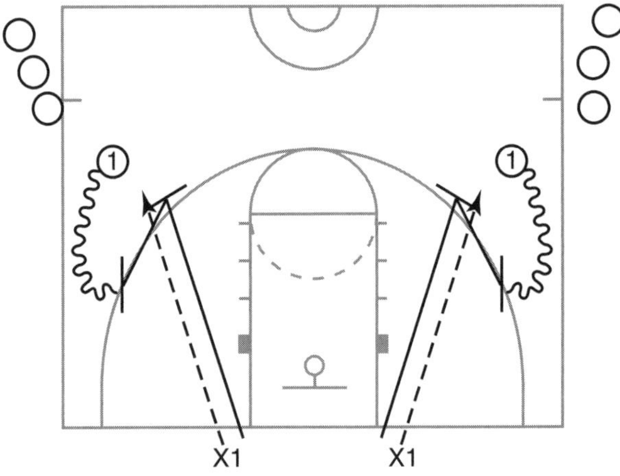

Related Drills *9, 11-18, 96, 105-109, 137-139, 149-154*

BASIC THREE-STEP READ

Individual or Team • 2 minutes

➲ SKILL FOCUS Triple threat (9), jab step (11), jab-step pullback (11), jab-step crossover (11), jab-step direct drive (11), dribbling moves (12-15, 28-31) in and out (12, 28), crossover (13, 29), spin (14, 30), half-spin (15, 31), passing and receiving (44), cuts (53-55), V-cut (53), middle cut (54), backdoor cut (55), offensive and defensive rebounding techniques (81-83), recovery (109), approach and closeouts (111), interception stance (131), help-side defense (133-135), drawing charge (141), rotation (143), closeouts (149-151)

Beginner

1. Line players up as shown in figures 1, 2, and 3.
2. Player 1 has a basketball. X2 is defending 2. X2 is a help-side defender. Player 2 moves up and down the side until X2 makes a coverage mistake.
3. Player 2 reads X2's coverage. If X2 is playing two-thirds of the distance from the ball to the attacker (player 2), X2 is in proper defensive *spacing*. If X2 is playing one step off the straight line from the ball to player 2 in an interception stance, X2 is in proper *alignment*. If X2 is not in this spacing and alignment position, 2 takes advantage with the appropriate cut.
4. Figure 1 shows X2 in proper spacing and alignment. Thus there is no attacking cut available to 2. Player 2 uses the V-cut to replace him- or herself. This V-cut keeps X2 busy and unable to offer great help from the weak side—a basic tenet of your motion offense.
5. Figure 2 illustrates X2 in improper alignment. X2 is not in the straight line between the ball and the attacker (player 2). X2 is too deep. Player 2 sees this, dips, and middle cuts for the layup. Player 2's dip likely compelled X2 to drop even deeper, opening up the middle cutting lane even more.
6. Figure 3 displays X2 in improper alignment. X2 is too high, above the straight line between the ball and the attacker (player 2). X2 must use a swivel head to check both the ball and player 2. Player 2 sees this and dips toward the high side, encouraging X2 to go even higher. Player 2 plants the right foot, pushes off, and sprints backdoor for the pass and a layup. (To tell the passer that the cut will be backdoor, player 2 can use a closed fist as a signal.)
7. For beginners, begin the drill by walking them through each of the three phases. Cutting is extremely important to the success of the motion offense. Once your players understand which cut they should use and under what defensive coverage, progress to the second phase of the drill.
8. Players always rotate from 1 to 2 to X2 to 1.

(continued)

Intermediate

1. Allow player 1 to dribble up and down the frontcourt and for 2 to move up and down the side of the court. This compels X2 to constantly change positioning to remain two-thirds of the distance from the ball to the attacker and always one step off the line between the attacker and the ball.
2. Once X2 makes a mistake, player 2 immediately executes the appropriate cut. If X2 maintains proper position for several seconds, 1 can drive toward the basket. This compels X2 to stop the dribble (rotation drill 143) and try to draw the charge (drill 141). Player 1 can shoot either the layup or the jump shot, or can pass to 2 for the shot.

Advanced

1. You can put a defender on 1, called X1. Now you have a strong-side defender (side of the ball) and a weak-side defender (side away from the ball). Player 1 uses the rocker step move into a dribbling move while 2 slides up and down the court. If 1 gains an advantage on X1, 1 shoots or drives. If 1 chooses, when 2 V-cuts to replace him- or herself because X2 did a perfect job on weak-side coverage, 1 can pass to 2 (drill 113).
2. Once 1 passes to 2, 1 becomes the weak-side cutter, and 2 becomes the strong-side player with the ball. Player 1 now looks for X1 to make a mistake on either spacing or alignment. Should X1 make this mistake, 1 uses the appropriate cut.
3. If either X1 or X2's spacing is not correct, 1 and 2 must take advantage of this. If the defender is closer to the ball than two-thirds the distance, the attacker with the ball passes to the opposite player. The defender is too far away from the receiver and cannot close out properly. The receiver can fake a shot and drive. Or the receiver can shoot before the defender gets there. (See drills 149 and 150 for closeout discussions.)
4. If the defender is too close to the receiver, the receiver moves into the defender and then chooses the proper cut (middle cut or backdoor cut) for the easy layup.

➲ TEACHING POINTS

1. Constantly watch your defenders to see if they make a stance (interception), spacing, or alignment mistake. Correct these immediately.
2. Have an assistant coach watch carefully to see if the attacker takes advantage of defensive mistakes. If not, this too must be corrected immediately.
3. This drill helps players see how the weak side works (either screening or cutting maneuvers) to keep the motion offense working top notch.

4. Make sure the appropriate pass is made. Make sure the pass leads the cutting receiver.
5. Make sure all players execute proper rebounding techniques after a shot is taken.
6. This drill is great for two-on-two play inside the rules of the motion offense. It is easy for coaches to see and correct mistakes because of the few number of players.
7. Any time a defender takes an eye off the attacker and looks at the ball, the attacker must make a middle cut or a backdoor cut.

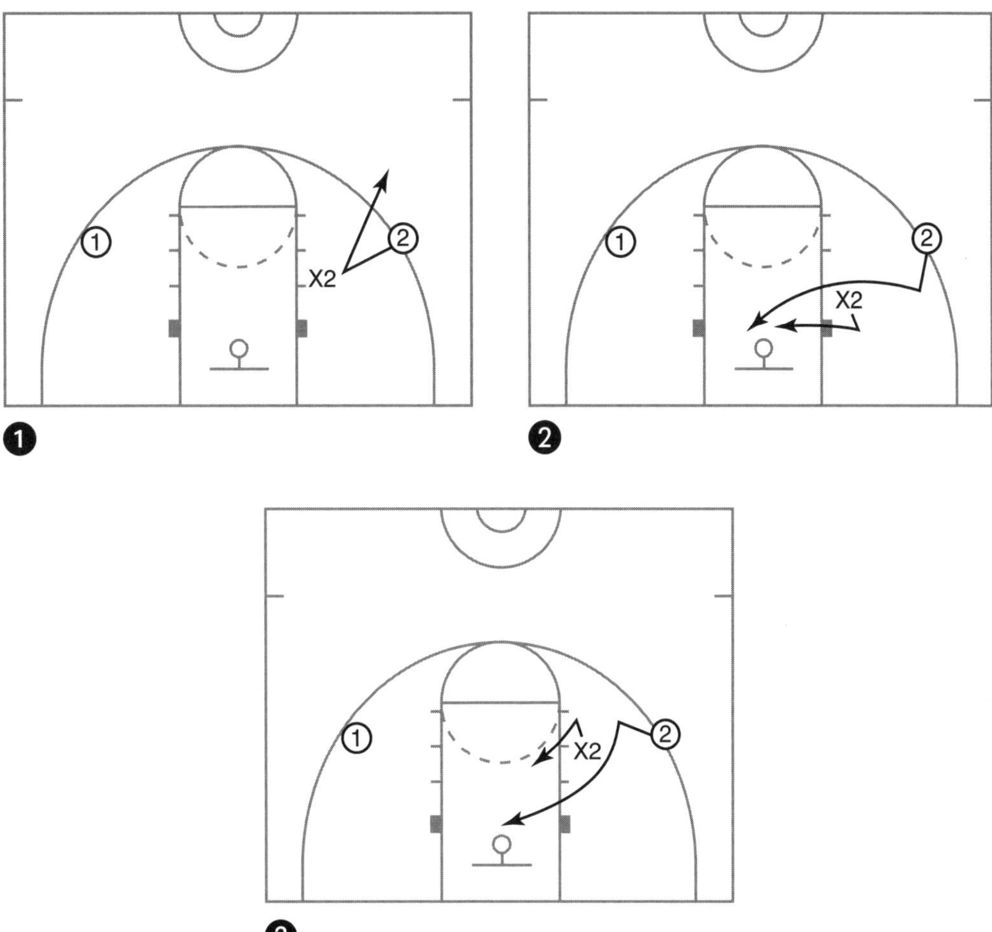

Related Drills *9, 11, 12-15, 28-31, 44, 53-55, 81-83, 104-109, 111, 131, 133-135, 141, 143, 149-151*

113

PENETRATION DRILL

Team • 6 minutes

SKILL FOCUS Triple threat (9), rocker step series (11), dribbling moves (12-15, 28-31), pivots (35-36), stops (37-38), cuts (53-56), passing and receiving (44), interception stance (131), close the gap (132), help side (133-135), draw charge (141), rotation (143), jump to ball (146), closeouts (149-150)

Intermediate

1. Line players up as shown in the figure.
2. A coach begins with the basketball and passes to one of the attackers to begin the drill. In the figure, the coach passes to player 1. All players are stationary until the coach passes the ball.
3. Once player 1 has the ball, all defenders must make their necessary adjustments so they will be two-thirds of the distance from the ball and one-third of the distance from their assignment. All defenders jump to the ball (drill 146).
4. Player 1 dribble penetrates to either the right or left. In the figure, 1 dribbles left. The off- the-ball attackers, players 2 and 3 in the figure, stay motionless until the coach signals that all can move. The coach keeps the drill motionless until convinced defenders get to their proper positioning. Then player 1 passes to 2 or to 3, and the drill continues.
5. Players rotate after three repetitions. Rotation is from offense to defense to end of line. Player 1 rotates to the end of 2's line, player 2 rotates to the end of 3's line, and player 3 rotates to the end of 1's line.
6. Once convinced defenders are playing properly, allow some cuts. In the figure, 2 has the option of staying where put, cutting backdoor, or cutting behind the dribbling 1 (see drill 60). Player 3 V-cuts to keep the defender busy.
7. Once either 2 or 3 gets the ball, they do a dribbling penetration move. The two remaining offensive players make the same moves described earlier for players 2 and 3. The player nearest the penetration drive executes as player 2 did in step 6. The other player executes as player 3 did in step 6.

Option Allow only layups for more dribbling penetration practice.

➲ TEACHING POINTS

1. You are teaching your motion offensive rules by adding dribbling penetration to your cuts and screens and one-on-one play. This drill is excellent for adding the dribble penetration.
2. Make sure defenders close the gap properly (drill 132).
3. Make sure defenders close out properly (drills 149 and 150).
4. Make sure attackers execute proper dribble penetration and that the penetration results in a layup, an easy jump shot (after separation), or a perfect pass to a teammate. Don't let attackers get lazy with their execution.
5. You are teaching your motion offensive rules by adding dribbling penetration to your cuts and screens and one-on-one play.

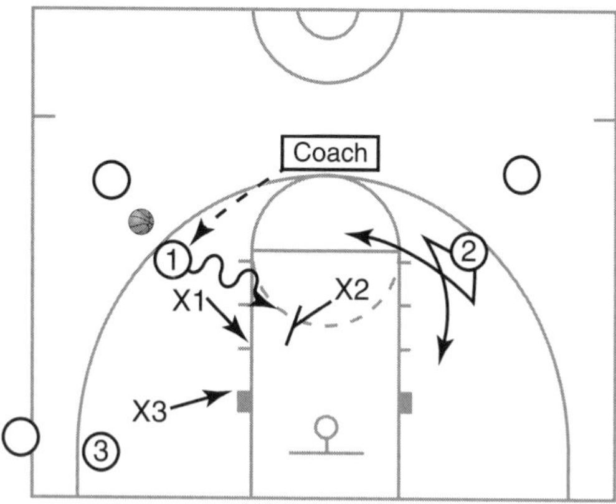

Related Drills *9, 11-15, 28-31, 35-38, 44, 53-56, 110, 131-135, 141, 143, 146, 149-150*

CHAPTER

13

Low-Post Fakes and Moves

There are six rules to the motion offense. One of those rules, *no player may stay in the post area longer than 3 seconds*, keeps the area around the low post open and clear for cutting, screening, driving, and posting up in the low post. Cutting received complete treatment in chapters 6 and 7, chapter 8 covered screening, and driving was the focus of chapter 12, so these skills are already part of your motion offense. The only skill remaining to be discussed is low-post play. That is the subject of this chapter.

In chapter 2, drill 10 introduces the fundamentals of post play. In drill 93 (chapter 10), you learned the importance of the baby hook shot in low-post play. In chapter 11, the subject of positioning at the low post was fully developed. Now in this chapter we give you the *moves* your players need to defeat their defenders in the low post.

Players have 3 seconds to receive the pass in the low post. If they have not received a pass in three seconds, they must clear the low post for their teammates. Three seconds is plenty of time to get position on a defender and receive the pass (see the roll step, drill 100). This chapter deals with what players do with the ball once they have received it. They may take more than 3 seconds once they get the ball into the big block area. Remember that by rule players have only 3 seconds to operate inside the lane.

Drill 114 covers the footwork of the drop step, both to the baseline and to the middle. Drill 115 adds the footwork of the spin move and the half-spin move. These moves are counters to each other, preventing defenders from overplaying either move without surrendering the layup. Drill 116 adds the up-and-under move.

Drill 117 demonstrates the pump fake, which is actually a series of moves. Players learn not only the moves involved but also how and when to use them. They also learn how to incorporate the other moves into the pump fake series.

Drill 118 is a hard conditioning drill as well as a continuous one-on-one battle in the low post. Drill 119 is a continuous team drill, teaching not only continuous footwork but forcing players to concentrate and intensify. They must be constantly on their toes or be left out. Drill 120 combines posting techniques, moves, shots, and rebounding, just as in a regular game, but here with only four players.

Drill 121 allows players to practice on their own in a driveway, park, or gym when you, the coach, are not available. Players learn best by doing, and this drill shows your players how to work out on their own to improve footwork in the low post.

114

DROP-STEP BASELINE/MIDDLE

Individual • 5 minutes

SKILL FOCUS Balance, post positioning (10), front pivot (35), reverse pivot (36), jump stop (37), stride stop (38), V-cut (53), flash pivot cut (56), post-up position (96), slide-step dribble (97), drop-step baseline, drop-step middle

Beginner

1. Line players up as shown in figure 1. This figure displays player 1 breaking along the baseline into the low-post position. The cutting angle should be changed daily. Because in the motion offense cutters cut into the low post from all perimeter positions, you should drill from different areas on the court from day to day.
2. Player 1 cuts and lands a step or so above the big block and executes a jump stop. Why the jump stop? It gives the attacker the choice of pivot feet. In figure 1, 1 has cut from the right side of the court to the left side of the court. Thus if 1 were to drop-step baseline, 1 would drop-step with the left foot. If 1 were to drop-step middle, 1 would drop-step with the right foot.
3. Any time an offensive player drop-steps baseline, the player wants to dive toward the basket for a power layup (see figure 2). If the offensive player drop-steps middle, the player wants to use a baby hook (see figure 3). If the offensive player needs another step to gain balance or get closer to the basket, the player wants to use a slide-step dribble (drill 97).
4. In all low-post fakes, the attacker wants to use the same method to determine where the defender is. This keeps things simple and consistent. The method the attacker should use is to *always check baseline first*. When checking baseline, the attacker turns the head slightly to check on the location of the defender's shoulder. Peripherally, the attacker should check the foot placement of the defender.
5. If the attacker sees the defender's shoulder clearly, the attacker cannot drive baseline. The attacker must either use a fake to compel the defender toward the middle of the floor, or consider using a drop-step middle move. The drop step cannot be circuitous but must be a direct drive. The beginner should use the drop-step middle as the counter to the drop-step baseline. The attacker wants the drop-step baseline first because there is no defensive help there. This is why the attacker always checks baseline first. But if the baseline is not available, the drop-step middle must be there.
6. Coaches should break the beginner's drill into two parts: (1) Cut to the low-post block area and execute the jump stop. The player then goes to the end of the line, and the next player cuts to the low-post block area and executes the jump stop. (2) Add on the actual drop-step techniques. Both the drop-step baseline and the drop-step middle are discussed at the end of this drill.
7. In the motion offense, *all* players must learn to cut to the low-post block and use low-post moves. Don't teach these moves only to your post players.

8. After player 1 has successfully learned the drop-step baseline, 1 goes to the end of the line, and 2 cuts toward the coach; the drill continues. After all players have learned the drop-step baseline, progress to the drop-step middle.
9. Change sides of the court the next day and reteach both moves. (Note that now the opposite foot is the drop-step foot.)

Intermediate

1. Intermediate players should be allowed to use ball fakes and head and shoulder fakes to augment their drop-step moves. To execute the ball fakes and the head and shoulder fakes correctly, the attacker throws the head slightly backward and to the right if intending to use the drop-step baseline left. At the same moment the attacker looks to the middle of the court and raises the ball up slightly over the right shoulder. The attacker turns the shoulder and torso quickly toward the middle of the floor, but the feet do not move. It looks as if the attacker is going to drop-step middle to the defender. If the attacker sees even the slightest movement by the defender toward the middle of the court, attacker picks up the left foot and places it beyond the left foot of the defender. Then the attacker drop-steps baseline.

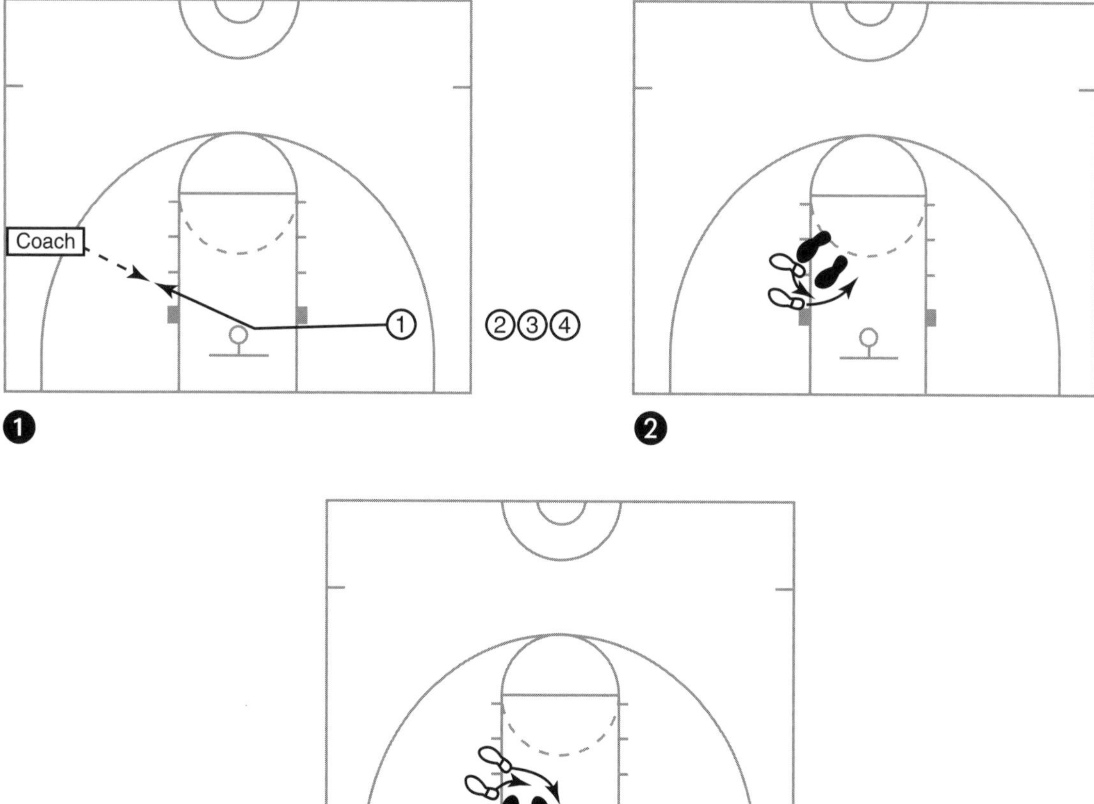

(continued)

2. If you are going to teach the ball and the head and shoulder fakes, you should teach this sequence in two parts. First, teach the ball and head and shoulder fakes. Second, teach the picking up of the left foot (if using the side of the court shown in figure 1; if on the other side of the court, the right foot would be used to drop-step baseline).

➜ Options

1. Teach the entire movement in three phases. Teach the drop-step phase. Teach the ball and head and shoulder fakes in another phase. Then teach the shot in the third phase. If you choose, you can use only one of these phases in this drill and leave the other two phases for another day.
2. Use drill 117 to teach the pump fake before adding the pump fake to this drill. For example, a player can drop-step baseline, slide-step dribble, pump-fake, and then shoot the power layup.
3. The player can drop-step middle, slide-step dribble, and shoot the baby hook, *or* can drop-step middle, slide-step dribble, pump-fake the baby hook, and execute the up-and-under move (once learned). You can see how your players are beginning to develop their low-post moves.

➜ Drop-Step Baseline

1. To execute the drop-step baseline (figure 2), the player (P) first jump-stops.
2. P drop-steps (left-foot drop-step is shown) as far as possible while maintaining balance. P wants to place the left foot at least equal to (and hopefully further than) the defender's left foot. P then squares up parallel to the baseline.
3. P dives toward the basket with a power layup, keeping both hands on the ball until laying it on the backboard. P may even throw P's buttocks out toward the middle of the court, making slight contact with the defender and getting the defender on P's back. P wants to make slight contact so the defender cannot jump and try to block the shot.
4. If P is too far away from the basket on the drop-step, P holds position physically and uses the slide-step dribble technique to get closer to the basket. If the defender is taller than P and still on P's back, P should consider using the pump fake series (drills 116 and 117) to get the defender off balance, maybe even leaping into the air before the shot. P may choose to use the nondribbling arm to secure position. If so, the arm should be kept straight and strong. Hooking the nondribbling arm around the defender would likely result in a turnover.

➔ Drop-Step Middle

1. Figure 3 displays the drop-step middle. The attacker checks baseline and sees the defender's shoulder. The attacker knows a charge will be called if a drop-step baseline is attempted, so the attacker chooses to drop-step middle.
2. The attacker drop-steps with the right foot as far as possible while maintaining balance. Again, if the attacker is too far from the basket, the slide-step dribble is used to prevent a perimeter defender from deflecting the dribble. The attacker can use finesse to spring into the air and shoot a baby hook over the front of the rim.
3. If the attacker feels the defender is not enough off balance, the attacker can use a pump fake instead of a baby hook. If the defender bites, the attacker can execute the up-and -under (drill 116). If the defender does not bite, the attacker might resort to a second pump fake before shooting a power layup.

➔ TEACHING POINTS

1. Make sure the V-cut or flash pivot cut is executed properly.
2. Make sure the attacker lands in a jump stop.
3. Make sure the attacker checks baseline quickly.
4. Make sure the drop step is executed properly and quickly.
5. If you teach the ball and head and shoulder fakes, make sure they look like the real drop-step middle is coming (or make sure the ball and head and shoulder fakes look like the drop-step baseline is coming if the player intends to drop-step middle).
6. Make sure both shots—the power layup and the baby hook—are executed properly.

Related Drills *10, 35-38, 53, 56, 96-101, 115-121*

115

POST SPIN AND HALF-SPIN

Individual • 6 minutes

➲ **SKILL FOCUS** Balance, post positioning (10), spin (14, 30), half-spin (15, 31), front pivot (35), reverse pivot (36), jump stop (37), stride stop (38), V-cut (53), flash pivot cut (56), slide-step dribble (97), drop-step baseline (114), drop-step middle (114), spin, half-spin

Intermediate

1. Line players up as shown in figure 1 in drill 114. You use the same format to teach your post moves from the drop steps through the up-and-under move. This makes the teaching simple.
2. Player 1 flash pivot cuts or V-cuts toward a coach. The coach calls out the moves for the player to run. For example, the coach might say "drop-step middle" and that is all the player does. But if the coach wants to teach the spin and half-spin, the coach must say something like, "drop-step middle spin move," or "drop-step middle half-spin move."
3. After player 1 has completed a successful spin or half-spin move, 1 goes to the end of the line and 2 cuts toward the coach. The drill continues until all players have learned both the spin and the half-spin move.
4. You want to teach your players the drop-step middle spin move first. Then teach them the drop-step middle half-spin move. Do not teach drop-step baseline spin or half-spin moves because your players would be out of bounds. Once your players have mastered and practiced the drop-step middle spin and half-spin, you can teach the drop-step baseline spin and half-spin moves toward the middle of the court. You want to always teach the spin and half-spin back toward the middle of the floor regardless of the original drop-step used.
5. The spin and the half-spins are counters to each other. They are used to create separation from the defender. They are used to get the defender off balance so the attacker can shoot a jump shot, power layup, or baby hook.
6. Teach the spin move before teaching the half-spin. These two moves may be used whether players are initially drop-stepping to the middle or to the baseline. They will be discussed here by continuing the drop-step middle into the spin.
7. Teach the steps in sequence, walking through each step. First, do just step 1 (the drop-step). Then add step 2 from the drop-step (see figure 1 and spin move steps). Go very slowly at first. Then add quicker movement but never faster movement. Quickness is the key, not speed.
8. Drill the spin move several days on both sides of the court before progressing to the half-spin. Once you begin teaching the half-spin move, go one step at a time. Note that step 1 (the drop-step middle move) will be learned quickly. Step 2 isn't bad either because it involves going only halfway on

the spin move. Players spin only until their body is perpendicular to the baseline (see half-spin move steps and figure 2). Steps 3 and 4 are only the spin move going in the other direction. Players will pick these skills up quicker than you think.

9. Drill only on one side of the court until players have mastered both moves. This could take a few days. Then move to the other side of the court.

➜ Spin Move (figure 1)

1. The attacker has executed the drop-step middle but is not fully open. The defender has reacted well. The attacker merely continues by fully turning the body toward the basket after pivoting far away from the defender (see figure 1).
2. The steps are shown in sequence, both by the number on the arrow and the number inside the foot. (Defense is left out of the figure because adding it would cause too much clutter and hinder understanding of the footwork. Just imagine the defender staying close on step 1.)
3. Step 1 shows the end of the drop-step middle. Attackers may use the slide-step dribble to get into these same foot positions. Step 2 displays a half turn of the body, 180 degrees. This is the full-spin move. The attacker is now facing the basket. It is important for the attacker to remember that the defender is now more than half a body behind because the defender had to wait to see if the attacker used a half-spin back in the other direction or another drop-step in the other direction. Thus the defender will always be tardy. The attacker's full-spin move leaves the body parallel to the basket and the baseline.
4. If the defender guesses right and the attacker has not created separation, the attacker may pump fake and use the up-and-under move (drills 116 and 117).
5. Also, before the attacker started the full-spin move (step 2 in figure 1), the attacker could have faked back left with the body as if intending to execute a half-spin or drop step with the left leg. This slows down the overly aggressive defender.
6. The attacker wants to end the spin move with a jump stop, if possible, to allow choice of pivot foot.

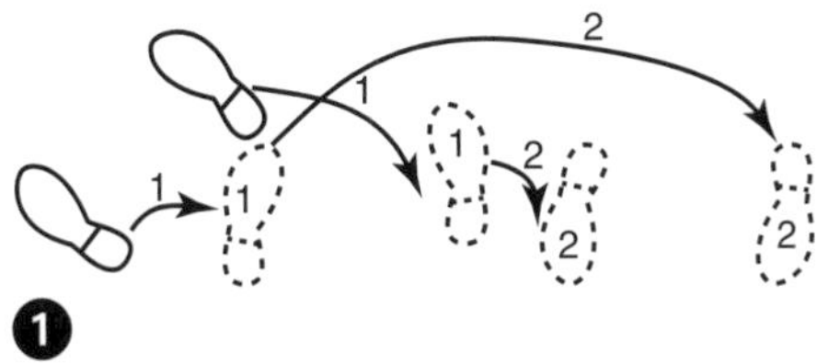

(continued)

→ Half-Spin (figure 2)

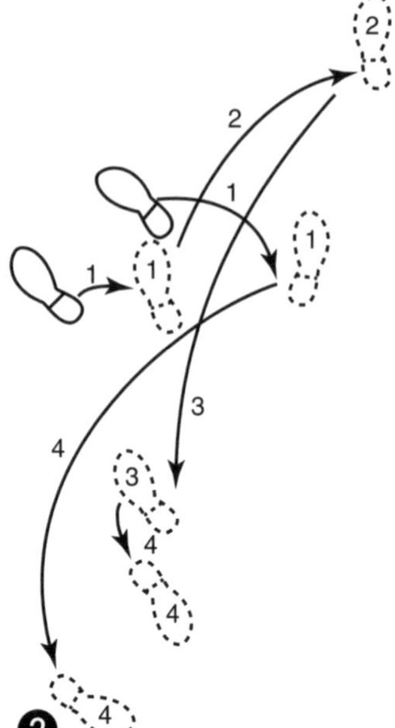

1. Again we will use no defenders because that would clutter up the instruction.
2. Figure 2 shows the first step as being the drop-step middle. In step 2, the attacker does not go to the full spin but stops when body is perpendicular to the basket. The defender can only guess if the attacker is going to pick up the left foot and continue the full spin. If the defender anticipates the full spin, the attacker's half-spin move will place the attacker two body lengths away from the defender. If the defender plays straight up, the attacker's half-spin techniques will still take the attacker at least a step and a half away from the defender (creating separation).
3. In step 3, the attacker pivots on the right foot, swinging the left foot all the way back around as though executing a drop-step baseline. The attacker executes this step as far as possible while still maintaining balance.
4. In step 4, the attacker swings the right foot into a complete 180-degree turn. The attacker is now facing the basket for an easy jump shot or power layup.
5. The last steps of the half-spin move, as you can see, are exactly like the last steps of the full-spin move, just in the opposite direction.
6. The attacker wants to end the move with a jump stop, if possible, because this allows choice of pivot foot.

➲ TEACHING POINTS

1. Make sure in the spin move that the attacker pivots quickly into a parallel body position to the baseline.
2. Make sure in the half-spin move that the attacker stops on the toes at a position perpendicular to the basket.
3. Make sure the attacker does not pick up the pivot foot in either after completing the dribble. The attacker should pivot on the pivot foot, keeping it in contact with the court.
4. Make sure the attacker has created separation. If so, the attacker should shoot. That's what creating separation is all about. If separation is not created, the attacker should make liberal use of pump fakes.
5. Make sure the attacker ends the move in a jump stop.
6. Make sure if the attacker has picked up the dribble that the pivot foot is not lifted and then replaced on the floor. This is a travelling violation.

Related Drills *10, 35-38, 53, 56, 96-101, 114, 116-121*

POST UP-AND-UNDER

116

Individual • 5 minutes

SKILL FOCUS Balance, post positioning (10), spin (14, 30), half-spin (15, 31), front pivot (35), reverse pivot (36), jump stop (37), stride stop (38), V-cut (53), flash pivot cut (56), slide-step dribble (97), drop-step baseline (114), drop-step middle (114), post spin (115), post half-spin (115), up-and-under (116), pump fake (117)

Intermediate

1. As long as you are teaching the post moves, use the simple format post drill format presented in drill 114. Line players up as shown in drill 114, figure 1.
2. The up-and-under move is easily taught after players have learned the spin and half-spin post moves. The up-and-under move is merely a crossover step after a pump fake (a pump fake is a shot fake near the basket).
3. The player must land on both feet simultaneously at the end of either the spin move or the half-spin move. The player should land on both feet at the end of any dribble from the perimeter that takes the player near the basket. This allows the pump fake, up-and-under move to be used at the end of a dribble.
4. In figure 1 in drill 114, player 1 V-cuts or flash pivot cuts toward the coach. Player 1 lands on both feet in a jump stop. The coach passes to 1 and calls out how far along the move's trail the player should go; for example, the call "drop-step baseline" means the player stops at drop-step baseline, power layup. But to teach the up-and-under move, the coach should say something like "drop-step baseline, spin move, up-and-under."
5. After 1 makes the up-and-under move, 1 goes to the back of the line and 2 flash pivot cuts toward the coach, and the drill continues.
6. The next day do the drill from the other side of the court.
7. Teach all the moves presented in this chapter in parts. Make sure each part is fully mastered before moving to the next part.

Advanced

1. Instead of using a pump fake, up-and-under move, the advanced player can use the step-back jump shot technique.
2. The player lands on both feet (jump stop) so has either the pump fake or the immediate step-back jump shot available. These moves are counters to each other.
3. If you intend to teach the step-back jump shot techniques, you need to teach the pump fake, up-and-under until mastered before teaching the step-back jump shot.

(continued)

➜ Up-and-Under

1. This move is used at the end of a dribble move; it can be used by either a post player or a perimeter player.
2. The attacking player first lands on both feet (jump stop).
3. The attacker pump-fakes (see drill 117).
4. When the defender gets off balance, either via a movement toward the attacker to stop the jump shot (pump fake is a shot fake) or when rising on the toes in anticipation of a shot, the attacker merely crossover-steps in the opposite direction from where the defender is coming. The figure displays the simple crossover step.
5. The attacker lays the ball in the basket. The attacker is allowed a step to shoot, but the pivot foot (the opposite foot from the crossover step) must not return to the floor or else traveling will be called.

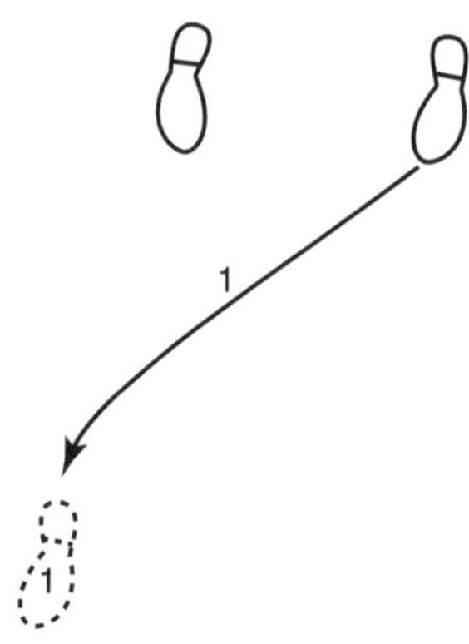

➜ Step-Back Jump Shot

1. The attacker stops in a jump stop when using the dribble drive off of either the drop-step baseline or the drop-step middle. If not using the jump stop, the attacker can use the step-back jump shot described in the Paye drill (drill 17). The Paye drill's step-back jump shot is the same except the one described here is for attackers very close to the basket. The techniques are the same, but the dribble is kept alive in the Paye drill, allowing the attacker to use a step back onto the left foot before shooting.
2. The attacker pushes off the right foot and leaps slightly backward. If the dribble is not picked up before landing on the right foot, the attacker may step back onto the left foot, as in the Paye drill. This allows better balance even when shooting very close to the basket.
3. The attacker shoots a jump shot.
4. This is a difficult shot to master and requires practice, practice, and more practice.
5. Players want to have both the step-back jump shot and the pump fake up-and-under in their repertoire. They are counters to each other. Imagine you are a defender: Your assignment, the attacker, has just completed a spin move and picked up the ball in both hands. Is the attacker going to step back and jump shoot? Or is the attacker pump-faking and planning on going up and under? No way to tell, and impossible to stop—as a defender this is all you can conclude.

➔ TEACHING POINTS

1. Make sure players stop in a jump stop.
2. Make sure pump fakes look exactly like jump shots (see the next drill for proper pump fake techniques).
3. Make sure players never let the pivot foot touch the floor after executing the crossover step. The crossover step and ensuing layup should look exactly like any other layup.

Related Drills *10, 35-38, 53, 56, 96-101, 114-115, 117-121*

117

PUMP FAKE

Individual or team • 2 minutes

SKILL FOCUS Balance, post positioning (10), jump stop (37), post moves (96-103, 114-116), pump fakes (96, 116-117), slide-step (137)

Intermediate

1. Line two players up at each basket as shown in the figure.
2. Place a basketball on each big block.
3. Player 1 picks up the ball on one of the big blocks. Player 1 pump fakes and then shoots a power layup. Player 1 immediately slide-steps to the opposite big block and 1 picks up that ball. Player 1 pump fakes and then shoots a power layup.
4. After each shot 1 takes, 2 rebounds and places the basketball back on the big block.
5. Player 1 goes for 30 seconds, and then 1 and 2 exchange positions. Repeat the drill for another minute.

Options

1. Instead of placing the basketball on a big block, player 2 keeps one of the balls and 1 keeps the other.
2. Player 1 executes a dribble from the perimeter or a post move, ending the dribble further out on the court but within 5 feet (1.5 m) of the basket. Player 1 pump-fakes at the end of the move or dribble. Player 1 then cross-over steps and shoots a layup, the up-and-under move.
3. Player 1 rebounds the shot and moves back outside to repeat the sequence.
4. Player 2 does the three steps above, beginning as player 1 shoots.

Pump Fake

1. The pump fake occurs at the end of an inside move or at the end of a dribbling move from the perimeter.
2. The pump fake is simply a shot fake.
3. To execute the pump fake, players throw arms up until they are fully extended.
4. Both hands remain on the ball.
5. From the crouched position at the end of a dribble or at the end of a post move, the player quickly straightens the legs to give the appearance of a jump.
6. The player throws the shoulders into the air as if truly jumping. But feet remain on the floor to avoid a travel call.
7. The player maintains balance and prepares to go up and under.

➲ TEACHING POINTS

1. Make sure offensive moves are done correctly, whether perimeter moves or post moves.
2. Make sure the pump fake looks like a real shot.
3. Make sure there is no walking violation on the crossover step.

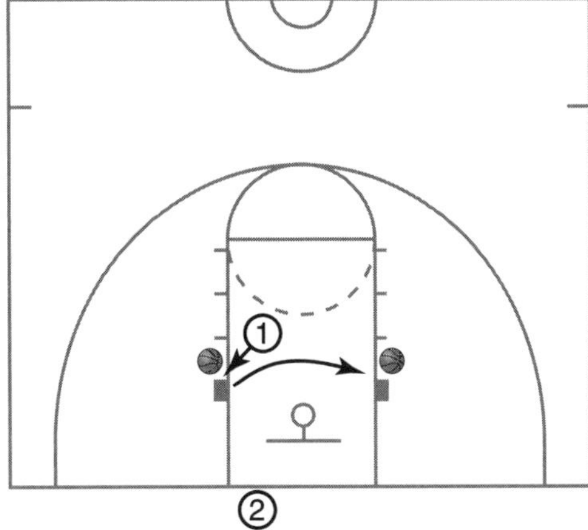

Related Drills *10, 37, 96-103, 114-116, 118-121, 137*

118 BULL-IN-THE-RING POST DRILL

Individual or team • 8 minutes

➲ SKILL FOCUS Balance, agility, conditioning, post positioning (10), jump stop (37), passing and receiving (44), V-cut (53), flash pivot cut (56), baby hook (93), post-up position (96), drop step (96-103, 114), slide-step dribble (97), post up and roll (100), power layup (114), half-spin (115), spin (115), up-and-under (116), pump fakes (116-117), step-back jump shot (116)

Beginner

1. Line players up as shown in the figure.
2. Player 3 is the initial bull in the ring. Player 3 receives a pass from 1, makes a move, and shoots. Player 4 rebounds and passes out to 1. After 3 shoots, 3 immediately cuts toward 2. Player 3 receives a pass from 2, makes a move, and shoots. Player 4 rebounds and passes out to 2. The drill continues.
3. After 3 has gone through an entire repertoire of moves, players rotate from 1 to 2 to 3 to 4 to 1.
4. The post player should in the beginning do the moves in the following order:
    a. Drop-step baseline with power layup
    b. Drop-step middle with baby hook
    c. Drop-step middle spin move
    d. Drop-step middle half-spin move
    e. Drop-step middle up-and-under move
    f. Drop-step baseline spin move to middle
    g. Drop-step baseline half-spin to middle

Pump fakes can be added anywhere along the move:

1. Beginners should do only the moves they have been taught. They may be limited to drop-step baseline and drop-step middle only.
2. Player 3 goes for 1 minute before rotation begins, which means each player goes 1 minute for a total of 4 minutes. Then players go again for a total of 8 minutes in the drill.
3. Players should do the drop-step baseline from both sides. Then they should execute the drop-step middle from both sides. Then they do the drop-step middle spin move from both sides, and so on.

Intermediate

Intermediate players should be able to do all the post moves just listed except the drop-step baseline spin and the half-spin move to the middle.

Advanced

1. Advanced players should add the step-back jump shot.
2. Advanced players should add the drop-step baseline spin or half-spin move to the middle.

➜ Options (all skill levels)

1. Player 3 can execute the entire repertoire as listed or can do only one move as instructed by a coach (in which case 3 should go 30 seconds instead of a full minute). This option is meant to really improve the player in a single move.
2. When doing option 1, each player would drill on four different moves during the 8 minutes allocated for the drill.
3. A coach can call out the move to be used as player 3 flash pivots (cuts before receiving the pass). This requires 3 to concentrate, execute, and react with a quick move.
4. After players are very good at executing the moves and shots, add a fifth player to defend the post. Now the rotation is 1 to 2 to 3 to 4 to 5 to 1. Extend drill time to 10 minutes.

➲ TEACHING POINTS

1. Make sure each cut (flash pivot or V-cut) is done correctly and with enthusiasm.
2. Make sure the move is done correctly, including pump fakes.
3. Make sure shots are fundamentally sound. It does players no good to make a great move and then shoot a sloppy shot. Always stress finishing.
4. Make sure all moves begin and end with a jump stop.

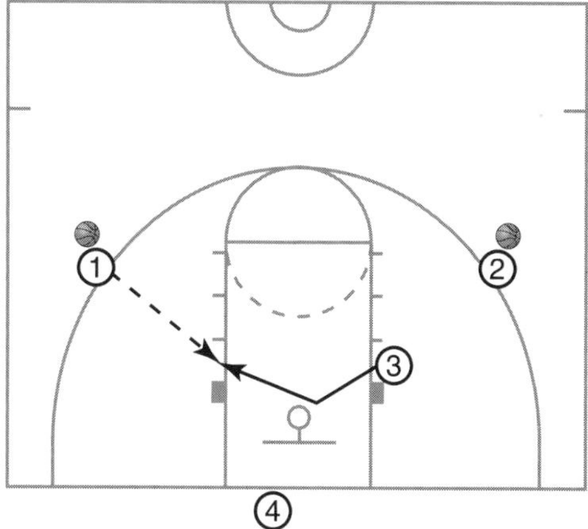

Related Drills *10, 37, 44, 53, 56, 93, 96-103, 114-117, 119-121*

119 THREE-PLAYER CONTINUOUS LOW POST

Individual or team • 4 minutes

SKILL FOCUS Balance, agility, conditioning, post positioning (10), jump stop (37), passing and receiving (44), V-cut (53), flash pivot cut (56), baby hook (93), post-up position (96), drop step (96-103, 114), slide-step dribble (97), post up and roll (100), power layup (114), half-spin (115), spin (115), up-and-under (116), pump fakes (116-117), step-back jump shot (116)

Intermediate

1. Players 3 and 4 both begin with a basketball (see figure).
2. Player 5 begins the drill by flash pivot cutting toward 4 (move 1 in the figure). Player 4 passes inside to 5. Player 5 executes the move the three players are working on—for example, drop-step baseline (shown in the figure) or something as complex as drop-step middle, spin, up-and-under (not shown). Player 5 rebounds the shot and replaces 4 (move 2 in the figure).
3. Meanwhile, player 4 has cut with a flash pivot toward 3 after passing to 5 (move 3 in the figure). Player 3 passes to 4. Player 4 executes the same move 5 just made (drop-step baseline in the figure). Player 4 rebounds the shot and replaces 3.
4. Meanwhile, player 3 has cut with a flash pivot toward 5 (move 4 in figure; remember that player 5 has replaced 4). Player 3 makes the same move both 4 and 5 just made. Player 3 rebounds the shot and replaces 5. Player 5 begins the flash pivot cut. The drill continues.

Options

1. Instead of all players making the same move, call for a different move each time a player receives a pass. This requires players to concentrate and intensify because they never know until the last second which move to execute.
2. Let players decide which move they will make.
3. Before the perimeter player passes into the post, require the post player to use proper posting mechanics against an imaginary defender (drills 10 and 96).
4. Put a defender out on the cutting post player. If you do this, there has to be a rotation, so rotate from offense to defense; the defender rebounds the shot and replaces the outside passer. Then all four players are in the offensive cutting phase, the execution of the move, the shot, and the defense.

➔ TEACHING POINTS

1. Don't let the post player execute a sloppy flash pivot cut.
2. Make sure all moves are fundamentally sound.
3. Check for proper footwork.
4. The four points of emphasis should be flash pivot cut, jump stop, post move, shot (power layup, baby hook, step-back jump shot).

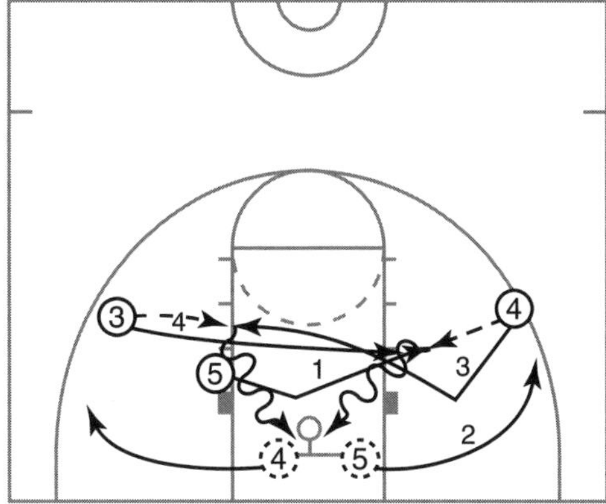

Related Drills *10, 37, 44, 53, 56, 93, 96-103, 114-118, 120-121*

120

POST TO POST

Team • 4 minutes

SKILL FOCUS Balance, agility, conditioning, post positioning (10), jump stop (37), passing and receiving (44), V-cut (53), flash pivot cut (56), rebounding techniques (78-83), baby hook (93), post-up position (96), drop step (96-103, 114), slide-step dribble (97), post up and roll (100), power layup (114), half-spin (115), spin (115), up-and-under (116), pump fakes (116-117), step-back jump shot (116)

Intermediate

1. Line players up as shown in the figure.
2. Begin the drill by letting 1 and 2 skip pass back and forth for a few passes. This compels 4 and 5 to get position on their defenders. The ball is constantly changing X4 and X5 from weak-side defenders to strong-side defenders.
3. Players 4 and 5 try to establish proper positioning on both their defender and on the court.
4. Once the ball is passed in to a post player, the post player executes the move read by the way the defender is playing him. The post player shoots. All four players—4, 5, X4, and X5—fight for the rebound.
5. Rotate from 1 to 4 to X4 to end of opposite line. Rotate from 2 to 5 to X5 to end of opposite line.

Options

1. Allow 1 and 2 to cut into their post positions when rotations occur. If either receives a pass on their cutting maneuvers, they immediately execute a post move. This requires 4 and 5 to become defenders immediately after scoring.
2. Allow 4 and 5 to screen for each other to try to get the other open.
3. Allow 1 and 2 to shoot at any time, compelling the four inside players to immediately make use of offensive rebounding techniques and defensive rebounding block outs (drills 76-83).

➲ TEACHING POINTS

1. Make sure all post mechanics are followed correctly. Make sure attackers have gained proper position on defenders; ensure they have created larger space on the floor.
2. Make sure moves are executed properly. Proper footwork is a point of emphasis.
3. Make sure shots are fundamentally sound.
4. Make sure when the shot is taken that attackers crash the boards and defenders block out.

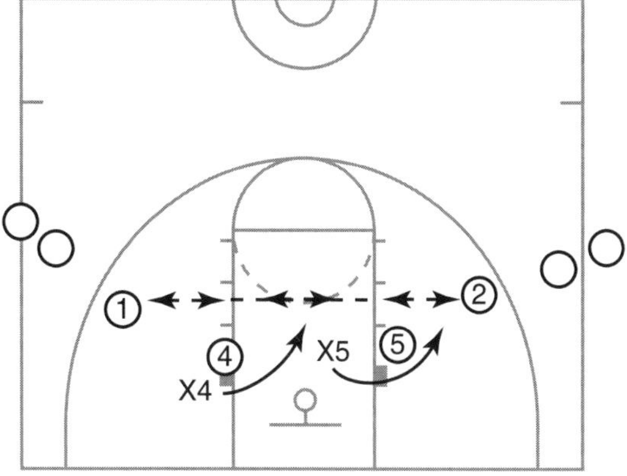

Related Drills *10, 37, 44, 53, 56, 78-83, 93, 96-103, 114-119, 121*

121

DEVOE DRILL

Individual • No time limit

SKILL FOCUS Balance, agility, conditioning, post positioning (10), jump stop (37), passing and receiving (44), V-cut (53), flash pivot cut (56), baby hook (93), post-up position (96), drop step (96-103, 114), slide-step dribble (97), post up and roll (100), power layup (114), half-spin (115), spin (115), up-and-under (116), pump fakes (116-117), step-back jump shot (116)

All Players

1. Players practice on their own. All they need is a basketball and a low-post marking on the driveway or gym floor.
2. This drill is named after Coach Don DeVoe, who once coached at the University of Tennessee. We first learned this drill from him.
3. While cutting across the lane, the player tosses the ball out in front with backspin.
4. The player jump-stops, catches the ball in both hands, and executes a move and a shot.
5. Players repeat one move over and over or mix up moves in any manner they wish.

Related Drills *10, 37, 44, 53, 56, 93, 96-103, 114-117, 119-121*

CHAPTER 14

Team Offense

Maintain 15-foot (4.5-m) spacing. This is rule number one for the motion offense. It not only keeps your teammates away from you while you play one on one but also keeps your teammates' defenders away from you. By having a teammate only 15 feet (4.5 m) away, you always have the option of reversing the ball.

Every player must move on every pass. This keeps the motion attackers moving, and more important, it keeps all defenders engaged, allowing the one-on-one player to operate against only one defender.

If your motion offense consists of only one-on-one play, your squad must adhere to these two rules. This is as simple as the motion offense gets. You may add any or all of the rules listed in this chapter. The more you add, the more complicated your offense gets, and the more practice time you must devote to each option—and the harder it is for defensive teams to stop you.

Use the cut your defender gives you. Players read their defender to determine the cut they wish to use (see chapters 6 and 7 for details). Tell players to communicate with passers by giving signals before they cut. A closed fist can signal a backdoor cut; an open hand can signal a middle cut. This eliminates guesswork for the passer. By adding this principle to your motion offense, you now have one-on-one play and cutting maneuvers. This is enough to make your club solid offensively.

When a player dribbles toward you, you must cut or fade. This allows the one-on-one player to penetrate toward a teammate and pass the ball to that teammate if the teammate's defender helps.

When setting a screen for a teammate, call out the teammate's name. This practice keeps your motion offense organized and allows you to add screening on the ball and screening away from the ball to the offense.

No player may stay in the post area longer than 3 seconds. This keeps the scoring area open for driving, cutting, screening and rolling, and post-up play.

Drill 122 activates screening on the ball for your motion offense. Drill 123 does the same for screening away from the ball. Drill 124 stresses cutting, posting up, and moving without the ball. Drill 125 gives you a chance to work on any phase or combination of movements in your motion offense. Drill 126 compels players to follow any rules you wish to introduce or improve on. Drill 127 allows your team to display knowledge of the rules of your motion offense.

ON BALL: SCREEN-AND-ROLL, SCREEN-AND-FADE, PASS AND BLAST

Team • 10 minutes

➲ SKILL FOCUS Triple-threat position (9), rocker step (11), in and out (12, 28), crossover (13, 29), spin (14, 30), half-spin (15, 31), control dribble (24), defensive fakes (33), jump stop (37), stride stop (38), chest pass (44), bounce pass (44), overhead pass (44), pass receiving (44), fake passing (47), V-cut (53), middle cut (54), backdoor cut (55), flash pivot (56), screen away (71), screen-and-roll (71), screen-and-fade (71), pump fake (96), pump fake crossover (96), slide-step dribble (97), pass and blast, motion offense, post mechanics (96-103), dribble penetration (113), low-post moves (114-117), fence slide (128), front foot to pivot foot (129), front foot to free foot (130), advance step (137), retreat step (137), swing step (137), jump to the ball (146), deny the wing (147), deny flash pivot (148), closeouts (149-150)

Intermediate

1. Figure 1 shows the screen-and-roll between players 1 and 5. It shows 2 screening for 4 and fading, and 3 replacing herself with a V-cut. (Defenders are omitted to prevent clutter in the figure.) This is a five-on-five drill following the rules of the motion offense. (For explanation of the screen-and-roll and screen-and-fade, see drill 71.)
2. Figure 1 shows one of many variations players can make up within the motion offense.

Advanced

1. The explosive blast is almost unstoppable by a man-to-man defense. The blast is shown in figure 2; the footwork is shown in figure 3. Players rotate from 1 to 5 to the end of the line so everyone gets to learn the blast from all positions.
2. Player 1 passes to 5, who has flash pivoted to the side of the key. Player 1 then dips and runs directly at the left shoulder of 5. Yes, the left shoulder. In other words, 1 is going to run over 5 if 5 does not pivot. Just as 1 gets to 5, 5 reverse pivots. Now 5 can hand off to 1, if X5 stays with 5. Then 1 can drive for the layup. If X5 switches off to 1, 5 dribbles one time and lays the ball in. X1 would be on 5's back if the explosive blast has been executed properly. Player 5's read is X5. If X5 stays with 5, 5 hands off to 1. If X5 leaves 5, 5 drives, using only one dribble.
3. Run the blast several days without defense. Then add the defense so players can learn when to hand off and when to keep the ball. As you drill other two-player offensive tactics, you can use this drill's format to add the newly learned two-player plays to your motion offense.

➜ Options (all skill levels)

1. Put five players on the court and run each section of this drill separately. Example: Two players will be running the screen-and-roll after every pass. The other three players must be screening away and replacing themselves.
2. On the next series, two players will be running the screen-and-fade while the other three players will be backdoor cutting or middle-cutting.
3. Then two players run the blast while the other three are V-cutting or screening away. These are just three of the many combinations you can drill. Don't drill any to the extent they become set plays. You want a true motion offense.
4. Run five offensive players and no defenders. Players may run any screen on the ball they wish. Players cannot try to score (you want more options run until they learn the motion offense); they must screen at different places on the court, calling out their screens as they set them.

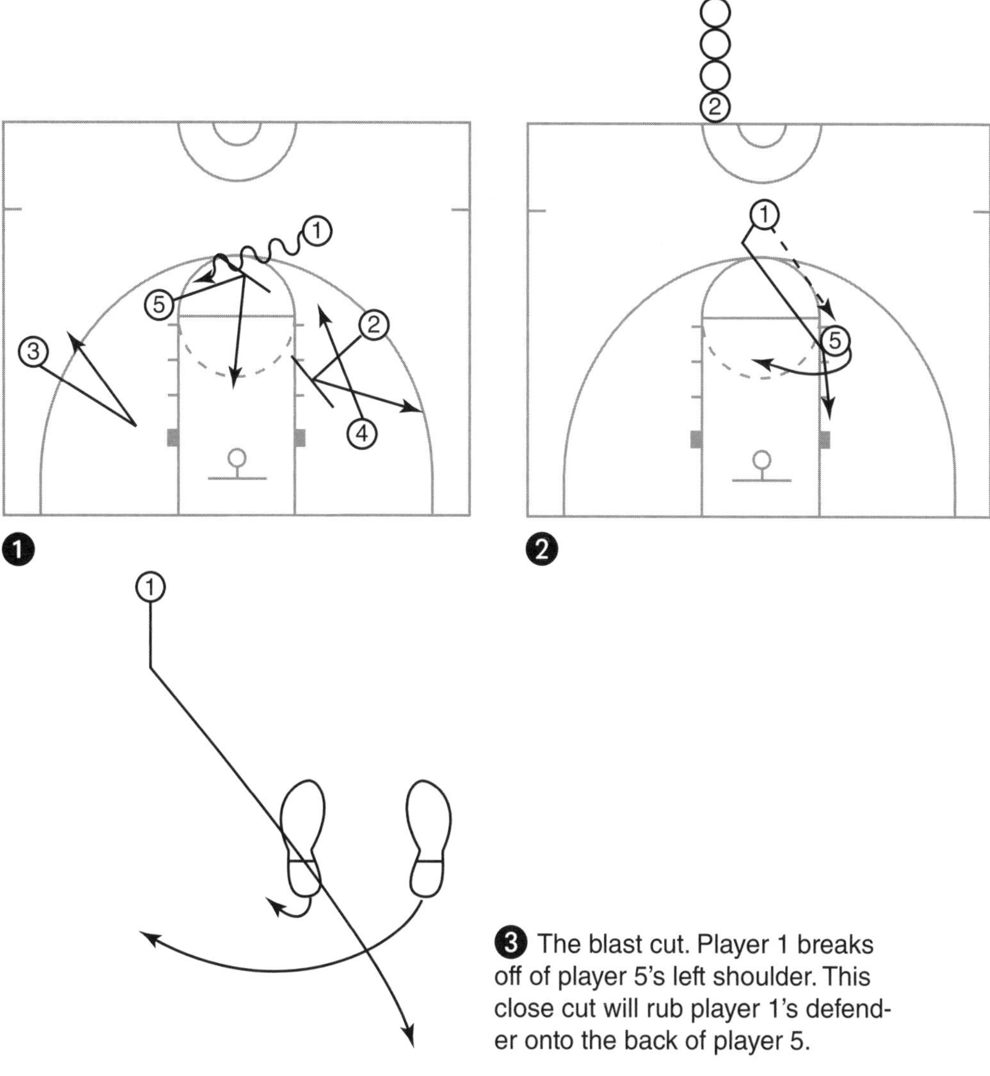

3 The blast cut. Player 1 breaks off of player 5's left shoulder. This close cut will rub player 1's defender onto the back of player 5.

Related Drills *9, 11-18, 71, 96, 104-109, 111, 114-121, 123-130, 137-139, 148, 151-154*

AWAY FROM BALL: SCREEN-AND-REPLACE OR REPLACE YOURSELF

Team • 10 minutes

SKILL FOCUS Triple-threat position (9), rocker step (11), in and out (12, 28), crossover (13, 29), spin (14, 30), half-spin (15, 31), control dribble (24), defensive fakes (33), jump stop (37), stride stop (38), chest pass (44), bounce pass (44), overhead pass (44), pass receiving (44), fake passing (47), V-cut (53), middle cut (54), backdoor cut (55), flash pivot (56), screen away (71), screen-and-roll (71), screen-and-fade (71), pump fake (96), pump fake crossover (96), slide-step dribble (97), pass and blast (122), motion offense (122), fence slide (128), front foot to pivot foot (129), advance step (129), retreat step (129), swing step (129), front foot to free foot (130), jump to the ball (146), deny the wing (147), deny flash pivot (148), closeouts (149-150)

Intermediate

1. The figure illustrates the running of screens and the V-cut, replacing yourself. For clarity's sake, no defenders are pictured. However, this should become a five-on-five drill. Notice players in the figure start from the same position as players in figure 1 in drill 122. This is so you can see all the potential options your players can create in the motion offense.
2. Begin by running the drill without defenders. Then add defenders. Players do not run these options from the same position on the court. Vary the positions; otherwise players begin to make the options set plays instead of a motion offense.
3. Player 5 screens for 1 and replaces him- or herself (see figure); in figure 1 in drill 122, 5 screened for 1 and rolled. Player 2 screens for 4 and rolls back to the ball (see figure); 3 V-cuts, replacing him- or herself.

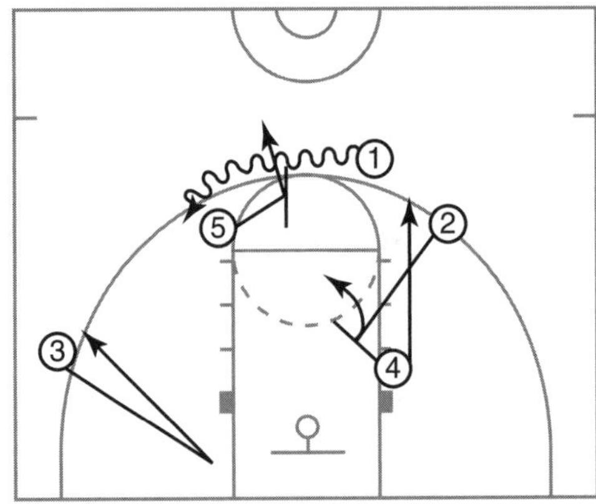

Related Drills *9, 11-18, 71-72, 96, 104-122, 124-129, 137-139, 148, 151-154*

THREE-ON-THREE NO-DRIBBLE DRILL

Team • 5 minutes

➲ SKILL FOCUS Triple-threat position (9), rocker step (11), jump stop (37), stride stop (38), chest pass (44), bounce pass (44), overhead pass (44), pass receiving (44), fake passing (47), V-cut (53), middle cut (54), backdoor cut (55), flash pivot (56), screen away (71), screen-and-roll(71), screen-and-fade (71), motion offense (122), fence slide (128), front foot to pivot foot (129), front foot to free foot (130), advance step (137), retreat step (137), swing step (137), jump to the ball (146), deny the wing (147), deny flash pivot (148), closeouts (149-150)

Beginner

1. Begin without a defense. After several practices, add the defense. The purpose of this drill is to add the screening maneuvers to the cutting maneuvers in the motion offense. No dribbling compels attackers to cut and to screen.
2. During the early drilling, don't let players score. They are to just hold the ball a few seconds, and then pass. After a few drills, allow scoring. On any score, teams switch roles.
3. The figure shows 1 passing to 2 and 1 middle-cutting to the basket, and then to the corner. Player 3 V-cuts to the top of the key.
4. Then 2 passes to 3, and 2 sets a screen for 1. Player 2 rolls, and 1 comes around 2's screen for a jump shot. This is one of many sequences the players can develop.
5. Begin with the rule that players cannot have more than two passes without a screen being set; otherwise players will just pass and cut instead of pass and cut and pass and screen.

➜ Option The defensive team must stop the offensive team twice in a row before they can rotate to offense.

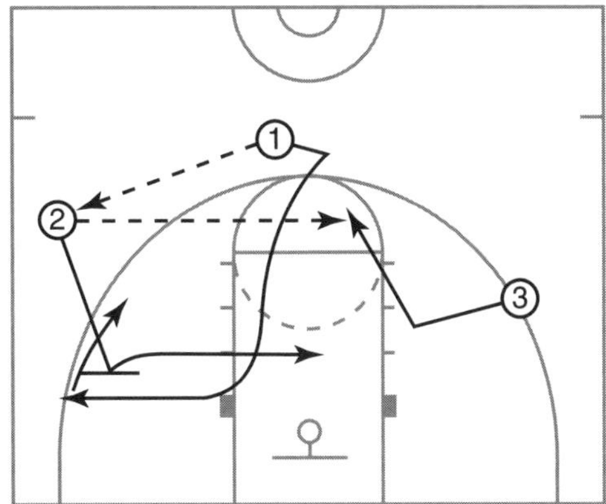

Related Drills *9, 11, 71-72, 96, 104-123, 125-129, 137-139, 148, 151-154*

125

THREE-ON-THREE NAME MOVE

Team • 6 minutes

SKILL FOCUS Triple-threat position (9), rocker step (11), in and out (12, 28), crossover (13, 29), spin (14, 30), half-spin (15, 31), control dribble (24), defensive fakes (33), jump stop (37), stride stop (38), chest pass (44), bounce pass (44), overhead pass (44), pass receiving (44), fake passing (47), V-cut (53), middle cut (54), backdoor cut (55), flash pivot (56), screen away (71), screen-and-roll (71), screen-and-fade (71), pump fake (96, 117), pump fake crossover (96, 117), slide-step dribble (97), pass and blast (122), motion offense (122), fence slide (128), front foot to pivot foot (129), front foot to free foot (130), advance step (137), retreat step (137), swing step (137), jump to the ball (146), deny the wing (147), deny flash pivot (148), closeouts (149-150)

Beginner

1. Players line up as shown in the figure. Rotation is from offense to defense to end of line.
2. Huddle together the three offensive players, telling them which maneuver they must run before they can score (e.g., the screen-and-roll). These tactics can be cuts, screens, individual moves (e.g., a rocker step), and so on.
3. You may require players to run two distinct maneuvers before they can score.

Option The defense must stop the attackers twice before they go to the end of the line. Tell the attackers which maneuver they must run before scoring. The defense would then know that tactic for the second stopping, and the defense could attempt to stop that maneuver from being run, making offensive execution a premium.

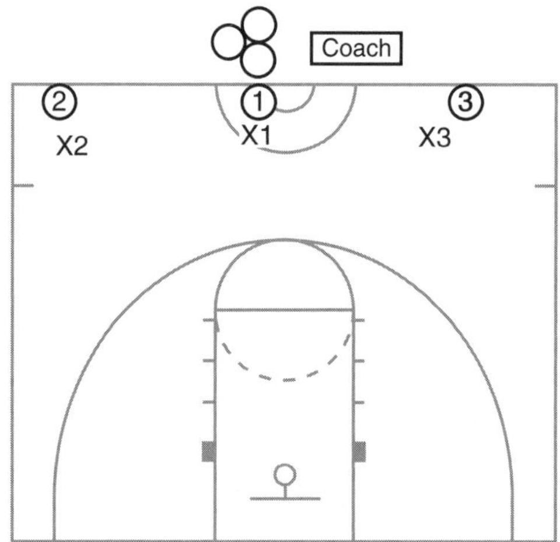

Related Drills *9, 11, 71-72, 96, 104-124, 126-128, 137-139, 148, 151-154*

FOLLOW THE RULES

126

Team • 9 minutes

SKILL FOCUS Triple-threat position (9), rocker step (11), in and out (12, 28), crossover (13, 29), spin (14, 30), half-spin (15, 31), control dribble (24), defensive fakes (33), jump stop (37), stride stop (38), chest pass (44), bounce pass (44), overhead pass (44), pass receiving (44), fake passing (47), V-cut (53), middle cut (54), backdoor cut (55), flash pivot (56), screen away (71), screen-and-roll (71), screen-and-fade (71), pump fake (96, 117), pump fake crossover (96, 117), slide-step dribble (97), pass and blast (122), motion offense (122), fence slide (128), front foot to pivot foot (129), front foot to free foot (130), advance step (137), retreat step (137), swing step (137), jump to the ball (146), deny the wing (147), deny flash pivot (148), closeouts (149-150)

Intermediate

1. Players line up as shown in the figure. Begin the drill with no defense; then add defense after several repetitions. Rotation is from offense to defense to end of line.
2. Write the six rules of the motion offense on a chalkboard in any order. Players must practice those rules in the order listed. Players may execute rule 3, for example, several times before they move to rule 4. But they must not call out rule 5 before they call out rule 4. The purpose of the drill is to get your players to really learn the rules of the motion offense.

Advanced

Instead of listing the rules of the motion offense, list several different tactics. The offense must execute these tactics in the order listed and tell where they fit into the rules of the motion offense.

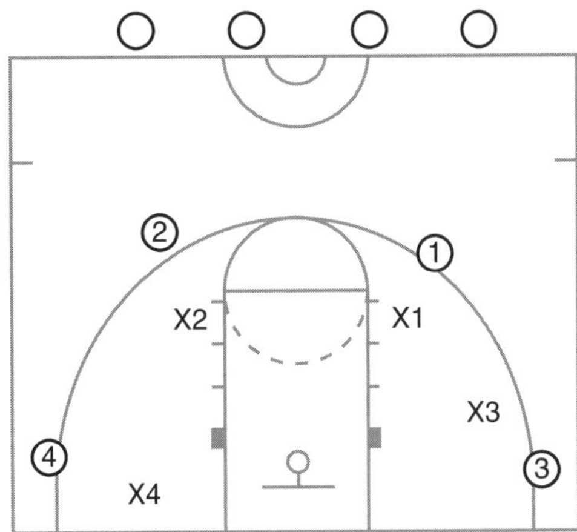

Related Drills *9, 11, 71-72, 96, 104-125, 127-128, 137-139, 148, 151-154*

127

FIVE-ON-FIVE WITH NO DEFENSE

Team • 6 minutes

➲ **SKILL FOCUS** Triple-threat position (9), rocker step (11), in and out (12, 28), crossover (13-29), spin (14-30), half-spin (15, 31), control dribble (24), defensive fakes (33), jump stop (37), stride stop (38), chest pass (44), bounce pass (44), overhead pass (44), pass receiving (44), fake passing (47), V-cut (53), middle cut (54), backdoor cut (55), flash pivot (56), screen away (71), screen-and-roll (71), screen-and-fade (71), pump fake (96, 117), pump fake crossover (96, 117), slide-step dribble (97), pass and blast (122), motion offense (122), fence slide (128), front foot to pivot foot (129), front foot to free foot (130), advance step (137), retreat step (137), swing step (137), jump to the ball (146), deny the wing (147), deny flash pivot (148), closeouts (149-150)

Beginner

1. Five players begin in any formation and run the offense for a full minute without scoring. They mix up their techniques and tactics, creating new sequences at all times.
2. After 1 minute, the team finishes with a score. The next team steps onto the floor and follows the same procedure.
3. Sequences will vary, but the figure shows 1 passing to 2 and going to screen away for 3, and then fading into the corner. Player 4 screens for 5 and rolls back to the basket. Let's say 2 passes to 5 (not shown) and runs the blast with 5. Meanwhile, 4 could V-cut to the corner and 3 could V-cut to a wing while 1 backdoor or middle cuts the defender. Or 2 could replace him- or herself while 5 and 4 play high-low. Player 3 could still V-cut to a wing, and 1 could still backdoor or middle cut. You get the idea.
4. This movement continues for 1 minute. Have teams start from different formations. The figure starts with a 1-3-1 formation. Let the next formation be a 2-1-2, for example. Then a 1-2-2. Then 1-4, and so on.

Advanced

Put five defenders on the five offensive players. Start with token defense and allow attackers to read for their cuts and other maneuvers. Then make it live five on five. When it is live five on five, the defense must stop the offense two consecutive times before they rotate to offense.

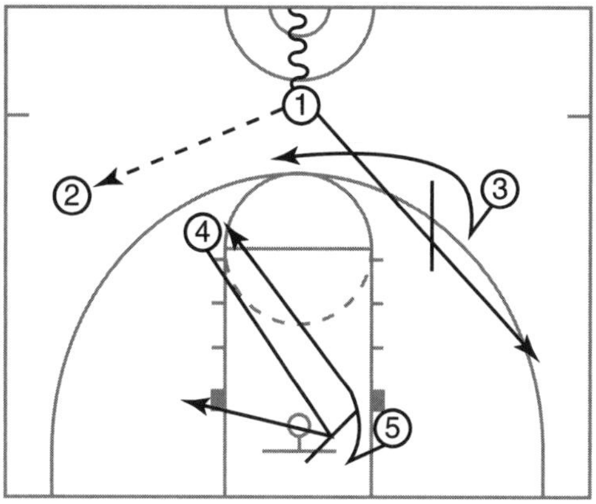

Related Drills *9, 11, 71-72, 96, 104-126, 128, 137-139, 148, 151-154*

PART II

DEFENSIVE Skills and Drills

CHAPTER 15

Stance and Footwork

If you can keep your assignment from getting the basketball, that player cannot score on you. In this chapter, drill 128 helps your players practice this very important principle.

Once a defender's assignment has the ball, if the defender can dictate where the offensive player will go, the defender has a leg up on eliminating opportunities to score. Drill 129 gives your players the chance to command where they want their assignments to go. Drill 130 has the same objective as drill 129, except drill 130 allows defenders to begin in a different stance.

But it is not enough for your players to defend their own assignments; they must also be willing to help teammates stop their assignments. Drill 131 gives them opportunity to practice this all-important individual tenet of team defensive play.

Drill 132 shows how to switch the pressure point from one foot to another so players can close the gap on breakaway dribblers. This helps teammates keep their dribbling assignments under control.

Drill 133 covers many of the variables a help-side defender must recognize and adjust to on defense. Executing skills and strategies necessary to counter the offense will make your team man-to-man defense unbeatable by dribbling penetration.

Drill 134 shows how the help-side defender must accomplish two or three fundamental techniques at the same time. Drill 135 brings all the previously worked techniques and tactics together in one drill. Finally, drill 136 is a fun drill that players love to end practice with.

Add the individual defensive rudiments learned in this chapter to the art of stopping the dribbler (chapter 16), and your squad has all the ingredients they need to become a great defensive one-on-one unit.

128

FENCE SLIDE

Individual or team • 1 minute

SKILL FOCUS Triple-threat position (9), rocker step (11), fence slide (128), front-foot-to-pivot-foot stance (129), front-foot-to-free-foot stance (130), advance step (137), retreat step (137), swing step (137), conditioning

Beginner

1. Players line up as shown in figure 1. Rotation is to the end of the line, and five new players step out.
2. Players go the length of the court and back in the fence-slide position. Have players begin with left side up one time and right side up the next.

Intermediate

1. Figure 2 shows the drill from a wing spot. The defender is in denial fence-slide position. Player 1 uses the V-cut to get open. Once 1 receives the pass, 1 front pivots or reverse pivots into triple-threat position and then passes to the coach.
2. The coach can allow rocker step movement once 1 receives the pass, compelling X1 to use retreat step, advance step, and swing step.

Advanced

From triple-threat position in figure 2, 1 and X1 play one on one.

TEACHING POINTS

1. Let's say the right side is up. Then the right foot should be pointing straight ahead just underneath the right shoulder. The left foot should be perpendicular to the right foot with the heels of both feet in the same straight line. To get into this proper foot position, players should put their heels together at a 90-degree angle to each other, and then step one full step out with the right foot. Now they are in fence-step position.
2. The first step forward is with the right foot. Players step out about 2 feet (.6 m). Then they bring the left heel up near the right heel. They use slide steps.
3. The defender's ear should be on an the imaginary attacker's chest.
4. If the right foot is forward, the right arm should be extended out about shoulder high or slightly lower.

5. The palm should be pointing outward with thumb pointing to the floor.
6. Imagine a taut string between 1 and X1 in figure 2. When 1 steps toward X1, the string becomes loose. X1 should immediately step back to keep the string tight.
7. Once you extend the drill into the one-on-one situations, you need to review triple-threat position (9), rocker step (11), and so on for the fakes, and the advance step (137), retreat step (137), and so on for the defense.

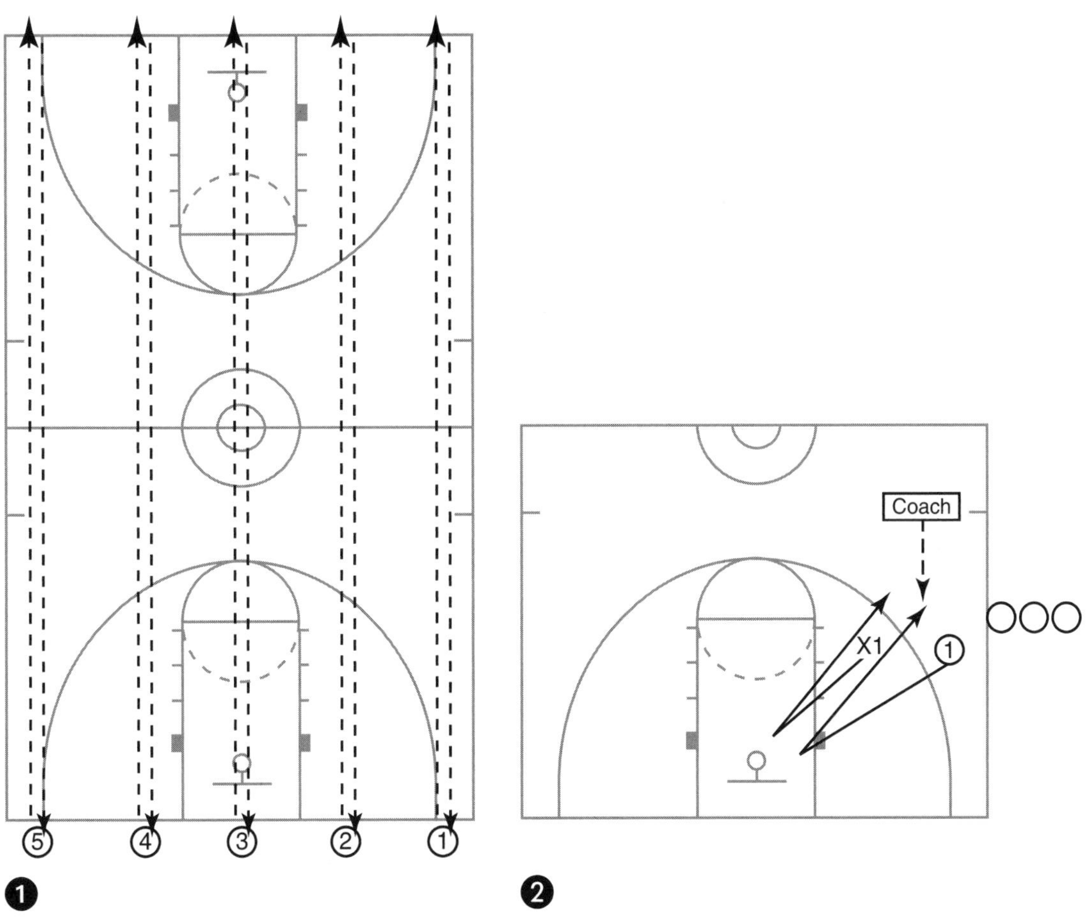

Related Drills *145, 149, 151*

129

FRONT FOOT TO PIVOT FOOT

Individual or team • 3 minutes

SKILL FOCUS Triple-threat position (9), rocker step (11), reverse pivot (36), front-foot-to-pivot-foot stance, front-foot-to-free-foot stance (130), advance step (137), retreat step (137), swing step (137), slide step (137)

Intermediate

1. Players line up as shown in figure 1. Make sure you can easily observe players' footwork. Rotation is from offense to defense to end of line.
2. Player 1 breaks to the free-throw line. Player 1 is told by the coach which foot to establish as the pivot foot. X1 rolls the ball to 1. X1 must put front foot up near 1's pivot foot.
3. Player 1 uses a jab step, jab-step crossover, and reverse pivot, in that order. Observe X1's footwork.
4. Go over the drill's footwork as many times as it takes to get it perfect.

TEACHING POINTS

1. Figure 2 shows the defender's front foot up against the attacker's free foot. A simple crossover by the attacker defeats the defender.
2. Figure 3 exhibits proper front-foot-to-pivot-foot stance. On a jab step by the attacker, the defender does not need to react. The defender is already in a retreat-step position, just close enough not to permit the uncontested jump shot. On a jab-step crossover, the defender uses the swing step. The attacker cannot shoot because the body is sideways to the basket (shoulders not square to the basket). And the attacker cannot get the front foot in front of the defender's swing-step foot.
3. Figure 4 demonstrates the reverse pivot. Notice the defender uses a swing step to begin (1 in figure). Then the defender puts the left foot up against the attacker's pivot foot (2 in figure).
4. Under *no* circumstances would the defender ever want the front foot up against the attacker's free foot. The attacker could create separation merely by using a jab step and shooting because the defender would have to retreat a step or give the attacker a jab-step direct drive to the basket.
5. The use of front-foot-to-pivot-foot stance also gives the defender the added advantage of being on the shooting shoulder of the attacker should the attacker decide to drive toward the pivot foot, which is the only direction the attacker can go to get any type of advantage.
6. Attackers with the ball have three things they can do: Drive away from the pivot foot, drive toward the pivot foot, or jump shoot. Front-foot-to-pivot-foot stance eliminates the jump shot and the drive away from the pivot foot because the attacker can gain no advantage with either move. The defender has dictated to the offense what move is allowed.

7. The defender wants to be in a crouch, bending at the knees to almost a sit-down position. The defender should be able to touch the floor with the palms. The head is directly over the crouch and straight up, beneath the armpits of the attacker. Body is bent slightly at the waist with torso leaning slightly forward. Hands and arms should be out to both sides of the body, discouraging any offensive movement in either direction.

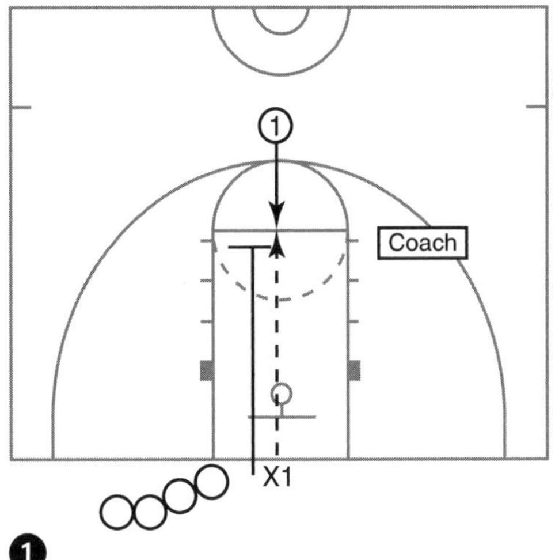

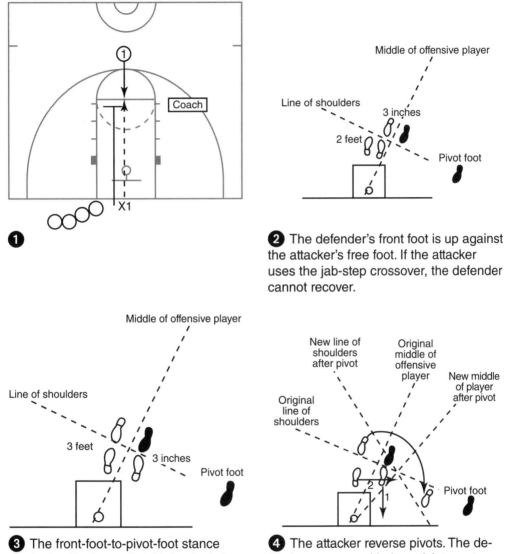

1

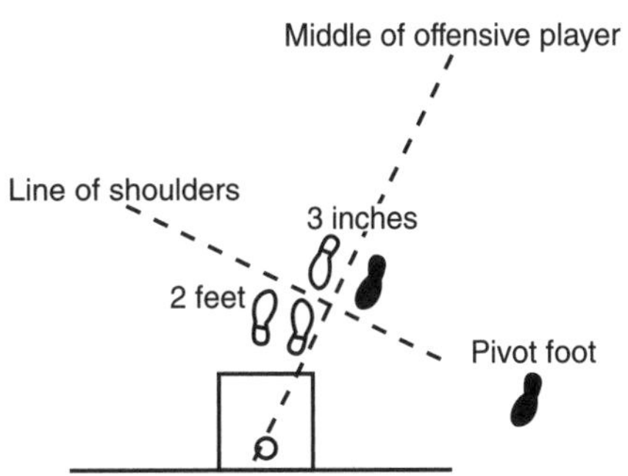

2 The defender's front foot is up against the attacker's free foot. If the attacker uses the jab-step crossover, the defender cannot recover.

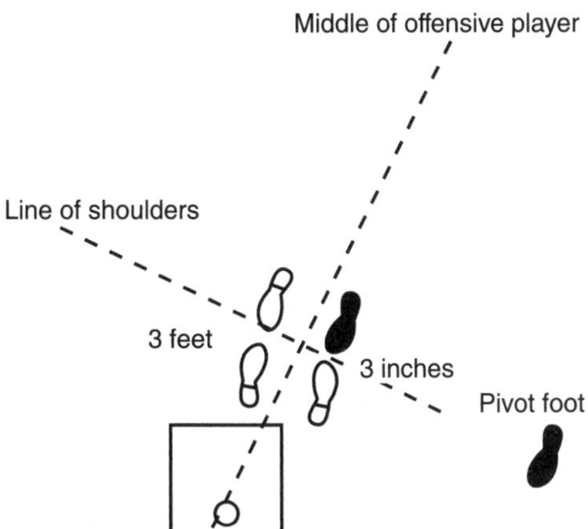

3 The front-foot-to-pivot-foot stance eliminates the jump shot (defender is too close). It also discourages the jab step (defender is already in retreat position).

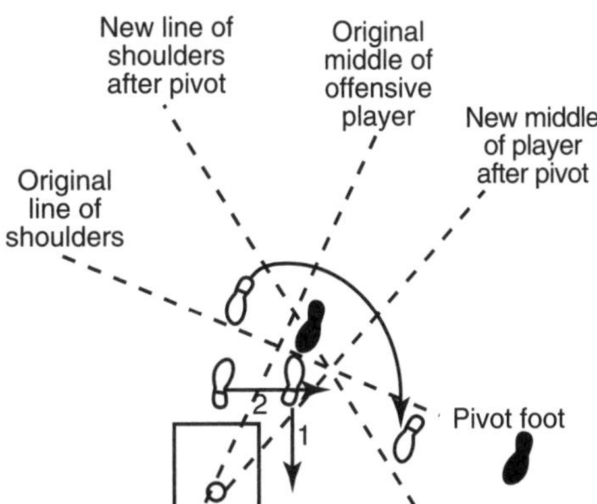

4 The attacker reverse pivots. The defender recovers with the quick two-step maneuver. Attacker must put ball on the floor; but then the defender would be on the attacker's shooting shoulder. The defender is back into front-foot-to-pivot-foot stance before the dribble would begin.

Related Drills *11, 17, 130, 137-139, 144-145, 148-149, 151-152*

130

FRONT FOOT TO FREE FOOT

Individual • 3 minutes

SKILL FOCUS Triple threat (9), rocker step (11), reverse pivot (36), front-foot-to-pivot-foot stance (129), front-foot-to-free-foot stance (130), parallel stance, advance step (137), retreat step (137), swing step (137), slide step (137)

Beginner

1. Line players up as shown in figure 1 in drill 129. Make sure you can easily observe the footwork. Rotation is from offense to defense to the end of the line.
2. Player 1 breaks to the free-throw line. The coach tells player 1 which foot to establish as the pivot foot. X1 rolls ball to 1. X1 must put front foot up near 1's free foot and outside 1's free foot by half a body—this is the overplay (see figure 1).
3. Player 1 uses jab step, jab-step pull-back, jab-step crossover, and reverse pivot, in that order. Observe X1's footwork:
    a. If player 1 uses the jab step, 1 must get the free foot outside the overplay or X1 does not react. If 1's free foot is outside X1's overplay, 1 must use a circuitous route to dribble. A slight swing step might be required of the defender.
    b. If player 1 uses the jab-step pull back, X1 does not need to react. A jump shot under tight coverage is not available.
    c. If player 1 uses the jab-step crossover (see figure 2), X1 uses a slight slide step and a slight retreat step. X1's first step coincides with the attacker's first step. X1 moves the right foot slightly to the right. Then X1 slides the left foot to regain balance.
    d. If player 1 reverse pivots (see figure 3), X1 uses a slight slide step and a slight retreat step, using the same foot movement as in step c.
4. Go over the drill's footwork as many times as it takes to get it perfect.

Front-Foot-to-Free-Foot Stance

1. The front-foot-to-free-foot stance is the simplest of the three options the defender has before an attacker begins the dribble. Figure 1 displays front-foot-to-free-foot stance initial stance. If the attacker has jump-stopped, there is a choice of pivot foot. The defender should meet the jump stop with a parallel stance and a slight overplay, compelling the attacker to choose a pivot foot. Usually it is best to overplay right-handed players to their right and left-handed players to their left.
2. An effective initial stance must force the attacker to use only one of the three options available. The attacker's three options are to drive right, drive left, or shoot. The defensive stance must take away two of these options. To be effective, defenders must dictate.

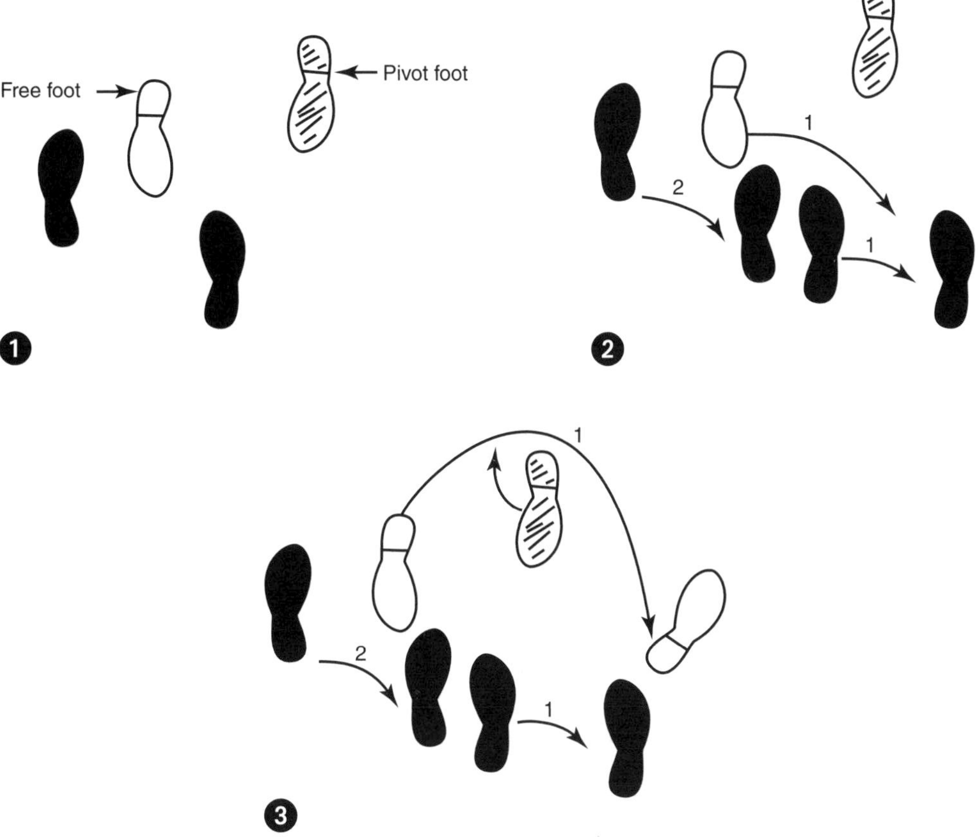

3. The only effective front-foot-to-free-foot stance is the overplay on the side of the free foot.
4. Remember the attacking principles of drill 17: *The attacker should always attack the defender's front foot.* So if the defender is not in an overplay position, this is what happens:
   a. If the defender tries to play even to the attacker's free foot and pivot foot with the defender's front foot being on the side of the free foot, the attacker would simply direct drive to the basket for a layup. This would be unstoppable.
   b. If the defender tries to overplay the pivot-foot side, this opens a direct drive by the attacker to the basket. This, too, is unstoppable.
   c. If the defender plays in a loose coverage with the front foot being the foot on the side of the free foot, the attacker shoots. This, too, is unstoppable in the front-foot-to-free-foot stance with loose coverage.
5. Thus the only stance and coverage that is logical when using the front-foot-to-free-foot stance is the overplay on the side of the free foot. This can be a reasonably tight coverage.

(continued)

6. The tight coverage eliminates the shot. The overplay by at least half a body eliminates the drive to the attacker's right (see figure 1). Thus the overplay and front-foot-to-free-foot stance achieves the objective of the defender: He takes away two of the attacker's three options.
7. The attacker's only achievable advantage is to make a move left. The attacker can do this by using jab-step crossover or reverse pivot. The attacker could pick up the free foot (right foot in figure 1) and try to put it beside the defender's right foot. But a simple small slide step with a slight retreat step would prevent this (see figure 2). And the attacker would be turned sideways to the basket and could not shoot. The attacker could reverse pivot (see figure 3). Now the defender need do nothing. If the attacker does a full spin, the attacker's back is to the basket—no shot available. The defender need only slide half a step to prevent a drive. The attacker has back to the basket—hardly a shooting position. Thus the attacker must put the ball on the floor to attack. Neither the jab-step crossover nor the reverse pivot gains an advantage because the defender's right foot is already back away from the attacker. This is why this is the simplest of the initial stances; even beginners have no trouble understanding and using this stance.
8. The attacker will have to put the ball on the floor to attack.
9. The great disadvantage is the defender must play between a tight and loose coverage. Too tight coverage results in the attacker being able to get the free foot outside the defender's front foot and get an unstoppable drive to the basket. Too loose coverage results in an easy jump shot.

TEACHING POINTS

1. The defender wants to be in a crouch, bending at the knees to almost a sit-down position. The defender should be able to touch the floor with the palms. The head is directly over the crouch and straight up, beneath the armpits of the attacker. The defender's body is bent slightly at the waist with torso leaning slightly forward. Hands and arms should be out to both sides of the body, discouraging any offensive movement in either direction.
2. A coach needs to be in a position to see the defender's footwork against the jab step, the jab-step pull back, the jab-step crossover, and the reverse pivot. Make sure the defender executes each defensive technique correctly.
3. Make sure the defender's body position is always correct. Should the defender have to slide slightly, the coach must make sure the defender's head does not bob. The defender's head should always be level, as if carrying a bowl of water on top.

Related Drills *11, 17, 137-139, 144-145, 148-149, 151-152*

INTERCEPTION STANCE

Individual or team • 3 minutes

SKILL FOCUS Front pivot (35), backdoor cut (55), fence slide (128), interception stance

Beginner

1. Players line up as shown in figure 1. Rotation is from 1 to X2 to 2 to end of line.
2. Player 2 uses V-cuts to make X2 use fence slides.
3. Player 1 passes toward 2. X2 pivots on front foot and intercepts the pass.

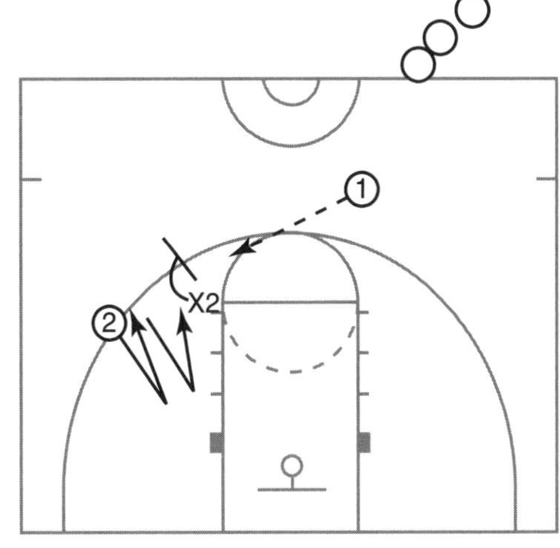

1

Intermediate

Allow 2 to cut backdoor, compelling X2 to use the other advantage of the interception stance—namely, pushing off the front foot to cover the backdoor cut.

TEACHING POINTS

1. By having pressure on the front foot and being in fence-slide position, a simple front pivot puts the defender in the passing lane for the interception (figure 2).
2. By having pressure on the front foot and being in fence-slide position, the defender picks up the back foot and slide-steps with 2 on any backdoor cut.
3. By being in fence-slide position, 2 cannot step toward X2 and gain the advantage of the middle cut.

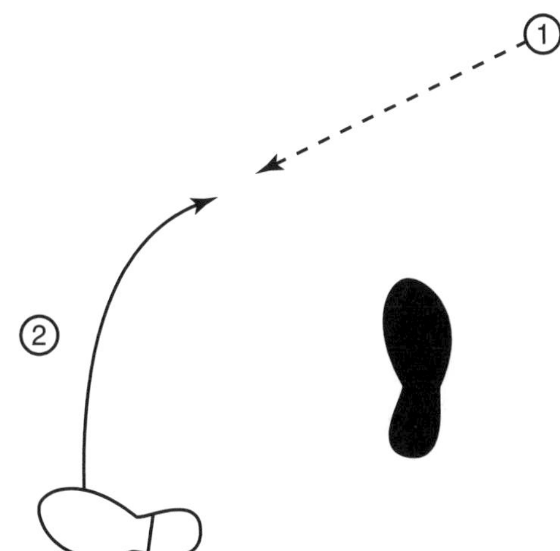

2 Interceptor's stance. Pressure on the front foot (black) permits the defender to front pivot into the passing lane for the interception. Should player 2 elect to use the backdoor cut, pressure on the front foot allows the defender to fence slide to keep player 2 from receiving the backdoor pass.

Related Drills *35, 44, 46, 55, 128, 140-144, 146-151*

132

CLOSE-THE-GAP STANCE

Individual or team • 3 minutes

SKILL FOCUS Front pivot (35), fence slide (128), interception stance (131), close the gap (132), ball-you-man (133), slide step (137), drawing the charge (141), jump to ball (146), deny the wing (147)

Beginner

1. Line players up as shown in figure 1. The squad is divided into groups of three around the court. Each player has a basketball.
2. Player 1 is being guarded by X1. Player 1 passes to player 2 and cuts three steps. X1 must readjust position to see both player 1 and the ball (player 2 has the ball). The ball-you-man principle is in effect here (see drill 133).
3. X1 is in an interception stance, using the fence slide should player 1 decide to move up and down the court a few feet (1-2 m) as though intending to receive a pass back from player 2.
4. After holding the basketball for 2 seconds, player 2 drives toward player 1. X1 must close the gap.
5. The players rotate from 1 to X1 to 2 to 1. The drill continues for 3 minutes.

Options

1. You can allow player 2 to pass back to player 1 before 1 cuts the three steps. This would require X1 to constantly be changing from ball-you-man coverage to deny-the-wing coverage by using a proper fence-sliding technique. Then allow player 1 to pass to 2 and take three steps.
2. When player 2 has the ball, but before the dribble-drives, player 2 tries to pass back to player 1. X1 uses deny-the-wing techniques.
3. When player 2 has the ball, player 2 can continue the dribble-drive until X1 draws the charge.

TEACHING POINTS

1. Check to make sure X1 is two-thirds the distance from player 2 and one-third the distance from the assignment, player 1. X1 should be in flat triangle, able to see both the assignment and the ball without moving the head (see drill 133).
2. Make sure X1 is in the interception stance with pressure on the foot nearest the ball. This not only allows X1 to intercept a sloppy pass back to player 1 but also allows X1 to move quicker in a fence slide to keep player 1 from getting the pass back should player 1 be moving to get the pass back.

3. When X1 sees player 2 begin to drive, X1 switches the pressure from the foot nearest the ball to putting pressure on the foot nearest the assignment (see figure 2). This allows X1 to open up and pivot directly into the dribbling path of player 2. This is called closing the gap. The open space (gap) between player 2 and player 1 has been closed. If player 2 continues to dribble, X1 can draw the charge.
4. Notice the difference between the interception stance and the closing-the-gap stance is merely where the defender puts the foot pressure to allow for quicker movement.

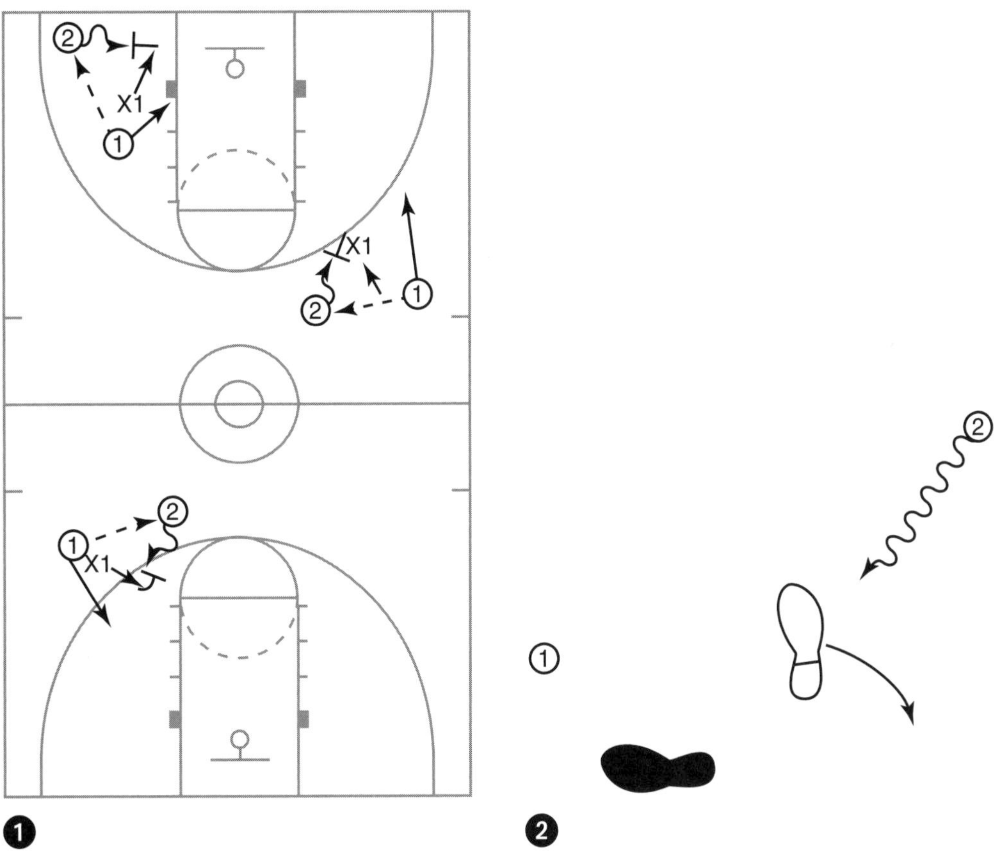

1

2

Related Drills *35, 128, 131-136, 141-144, 145-154*

133

HELP-SIDE DRILL

Individual or team • 2 minutes

SKILL FOCUS Fence slide step (128), front-foot-to-pivot-foot stance (129), front-foot-to-free-foot stance (130), interception stance (131), ball-you-man (134), flat triangle (134), help-side techniques (134-135), rotation (143), jump to the ball (146)

Beginner

1. Line players up as shown in the figure.
2. Player 1 begins with a basketball. X1 is in proper stance on the ball, either front-foot-to-pivot-foot stance, front-foot-to-free-foot stance, or parallel.
3. Player 1 skip passes to 2. X1 is no longer a strong-side defender (where ball is); now X1 is a help-side defender. As a help-side defender, X1 must always see both the assignment and the ball without moving the head (must use peripheral vision).
4. X1 first jumps toward the ball as the pass is being made. The proper distance is two-thirds distance from the ball and one-third distance from the assignment.
5. X1 next gets into a flat triangle in the interception stance.
6. After 2 receives the ball and holds it for 2 seconds, 1 can begin moving up and down the court. This compels X1 to constantly adjust the flat triangle.
7. Rotate from 1 to 2 to X1 to 1 after 10 seconds. Continue the drill until all three players have played all three positions several times.

Options

1. You can allow player 2 to dribble the ball up and down the sideline. X1 must adjust the flat triangle as the ball moves.
2. You can allow both movements: 1 can move up and down the court, and 2 can dribble the basketball up and down the sideline.
3. To keep X1 honest in help-side coverage, you can allow 1 to go one on one against X1.

Intermediate

1. You can allow 2 to drive to the basket. This compels X1 to activate the rotation drill (see drill 143).
2. You can allow 2 to drive to the basket and compel X1 to draw the charge (see drill 141).

➔ Flat Triangle

1. Draw a line between players 1 and 2.
2. Place X1 two thirds of the distance from 2 to 1.
3. Put X1 one step off this line. Now draw a line between 1 and X1. Now draw a line between 2 and X1. You have a flat triangle with X1 one step off the line between 1 and 2 and two-thirds of the distance from the ball (player 2).

➔ Ball-You-Man

1. *You* are the defensive player (X1 in the figure). *Ball* is where 2 is. *Man* is where 1 is. *Ball* you must see. *Man* you must see.
2. If players are in a flat triangle, they are in ball-you-man.

TEACHING POINTS

1. Check X1's initial stance.
2. Make sure as the ball is in the air from 1 to 2 that X1 is sliding into a flat triangle, two-thirds of the distance from the ball to X1's assignment.
3. Make sure X1 is in an interception stance.
4. When 1 begins to move up and down the sideline, make sure X1 uses the fence slide step.
5. Make sure X1 does not look at either the ball or X1's assignment. X1 must see *both* using peripheral vision.

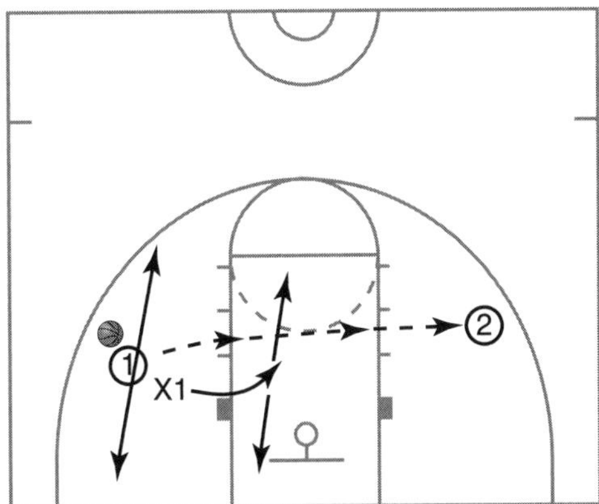

Related Drills *128-132, 134-135, 143, 145-154*

134

DUAL-HELP DRILL

Individual or team • 3 minutes

SKILL FOCUS Fence slide step (128), interception stance (131), ball-you-man (133), flat triangle (133), help-side techniques (134-135), draw the charge (141), rotation (143), jump to the ball (146)

Beginner

1. Line players up as shown in the figure.
2. A coach begins with two basketballs. The coach's first pass is a lob pass into the high-post area. X1 must deflect this pass (helping the imaginary high-post defender).
3. The coach's second pass is to 2 along the baseline. Player 2 immediately begins a drive toward the basket. Player 2 has defeated the defender (not shown in figure and not part of the drill—an imaginary defender) and drives along the baseline. X1 must hurry down and get position to draw the charge.
4. Help-side defense means just that: Players must *help* on anything that might be happening on the ball side that could lead to a score. Here X1 helped twice (dual help): on a lob pass to the high post and by drawing a charge on a breakaway dribbler.

Intermediate

1. Once your defenders know how to rotate, you can add another weak-side attacker along the free-throw line extended and run the rotation drill (see drill 143).
2. You can require 1 to move up and down the sideline, compelling X1 to constantly adjust and keep a flat triangle.
3. You can allow 1 to perform any offensive cutting technique, requiring X1 to know how to defend a player cutting from the weak side to the ball side (see drill 148).

➲ TEACHING POINTS

1. This is a hustle drill that requires the defender to constantly make adjustments and execute at least two (dual) techniques from the help side.
2. Your focus is the dual mandates of the weak-side helper, but make sure all stances and techniques are fundamentally sound.
3. Make sure the ball-you-man, flat triangle, and interception stances are executed perfectly. This is the heart of your help-side defense in man-to-man coverage.

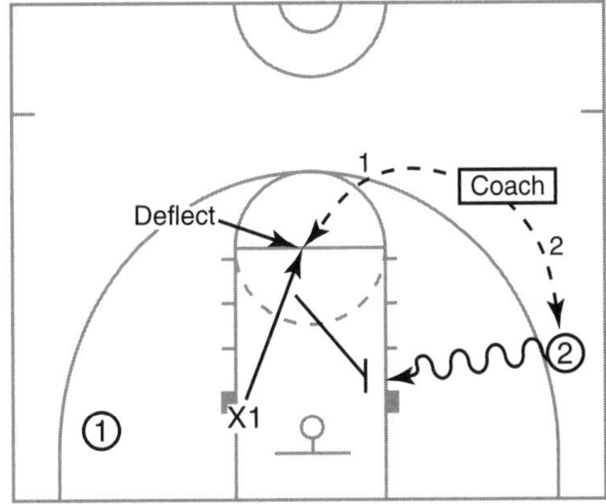

Related Drills *128-133, 135, 143, 145-154*

135 HELP THE HELPER

Individual or team • 6 minutes

SKILL FOCUS Triple threat (9), rocker step (11), in and out (12, 28), crossover (13, 29), spin (14, 30), half-spin (15, 31), defensive fakes (33), jump stop (37), stride stop (38), passing and receiving (44), offensive and defensive rebounding (78-81), fence slide (128), defensive footwork (129-131, 137-144), interception stance (131), close the gap (132), ball-you-man (133), flat triangle (133), help side (133-134), draw the charge (141), help and recover (142), rotation (143), jump to the ball (146), deny the wing (147)

Intermediate

1. Line players up as shown in the figure. Player 1 begins by bringing the ball into frontcourt under pressure from X1.
2. The drill is run in several phases. First phase: Have players 1, 2, and 3 pass the ball to each other. Each player holds the ball for 2 seconds before passing. This requires X1, X2, and X3 to constantly change positions to be in proper defensive positioning—denial stance, ball-you-man, and flat triangle.
3. Second phase: X2 and X3 use denial stances and fence slides to keep players 2 and 3 from receiving the basketball. This requires X2 and X3 to use deny-the-wing tactics and the fence slide.
4. Third phase: Whenever player 2 or 3 receives the pass, the player is required to drive to the middle of the court. This compels the defense to close the gap and to possibly activate the rotation drill. In the figure, player 2 drives to the middle of the court, forcing X1 to close the gap, a help-side tactic (drill 132). This is the first line of defense. X1 will not always be successful. Sometimes player 2 will penetrate between X1 and X2. This scenario compels X3 to activate the rotation drill (see drill 143). In the rotation drill, X3 would have to stop the ball (player 2). If player 2 continues the dribble, X3 would draw the charge. The ball scores, so it must be stopped. X1 would then rotate down to cover player 3 cutting along the baseline. For more details on the rotation drill, see drill 143.
5. When player 2 passes back to player 1, X3 must help the helper (X3 helps X1 get back to player 1 before player 1 can drive or shoot). X3 helps the helper by hedging toward player 1 and retreating (help and recover) to X3's own assignment, player 3.
6. Rotate from offense to defense. After players 1 and X1 have played the point, they must learn to play the wing. So rotate from 1 to 2 to 3 to 1, and X1 to X2 to X3 to X1. This allows all attackers to play point and wing and all defenders to defend the point and the wing.

Advanced

1. Instead of driving to the middle, player 2 can use moves and drive the baseline or shoot.
2. If player 2 drives the baseline, X3 must activate the rotation drill.
3. If player 2 shoots, all players must use offensive and defensive rebounding techniques.

➲ TEACHING POINTS

1. First phase: Make sure all defenders jump to the ball and end in a position two-thirds distance from the ball and one-third distance from their assignment. Defenders should be in a flat triangle and in an interception stance.
2. Second phase: Make sure X2 and X3 use the fence-sliding techniques to deny the wing the ball. X1 should help in this denial and possible interception of the pass by putting pressure on player 1 after 1 has picked up the dribble.
3. Third phase: X1 must close the gap properly. When player 2 picks up the dribble and passes back to player 1, X3 must hedge and recover. Make sure these techniques are done properly.
4. If the rotation drill has been taught and if player 2 is allowed to drive the baseline side of X2, make sure X3 rotates over and stops player 2's penetration. Also make sure X1 drops to cover player 3, who will probably be cutting to the basket for either a rebound or a pass from player 2.
5. Notice: Anytime player 2 has the ball, X3 is in help-side defense; anytime player 3 has the ball, X2 is in help-side defense.

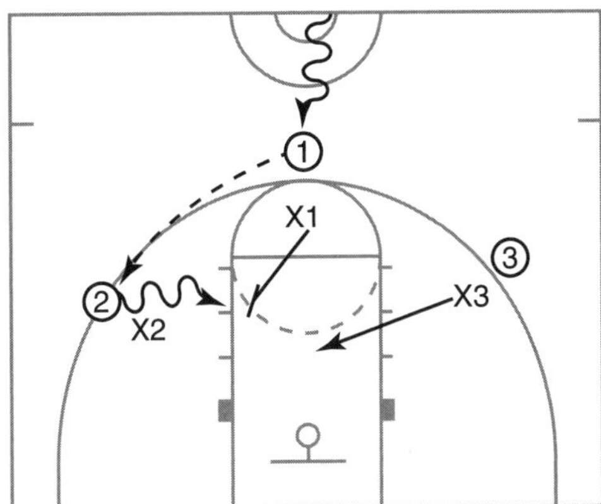

Related Drills *78-81, 129-134, 137-144, 146-154*

136

DEFENSIVE CONE

Individual • 1 minute

SKILL FOCUS Triple threat (9), rocker step series (11), dribbling moves (11-15, 28-31), speed dribble (23), control dribble (24), change of pace (25), hesitation dribble (26), retreat dribble (27), initial defensive stances (128-130), defensive steps before the dribble (137), defensive steps as dribbling (137)

Beginner

1. Line players up as shown in the figure. Player 1 begins at the wing. Player 2 begins in the corner.
2. This is a fun drill and highly competitive.
3. This drill uses all the one-on-one techniques of the offensive player and all the one-on-one tactics of the defender.
4. Players 1 and 2 each begin with a basketball. They have their dribble still alive.
5. The purpose of the drill: Player 1 wants to dribble past the cone for an easy shot. X1 wants to keep player 1 from dribbling past the cone. X1 wants to belly up to player 1 and draw the charge when possible. Players have 3 seconds to accomplish their purpose. Players 2 and X2 run these same sequences but not until after players 1 and X1 have finished.
6. Line other players up in the middle of the free-throw lane. These players count out "one-thousand-one, one-thousand-two, one-thousand-three." This count puts added pressure on the participating players. Have the other players cheer on the defense *loudly.* This builds team defensive spirit.

7. This drill makes defenders realize that all they have to do is control the attacker for 3 seconds to really help the team. The action compels the defender to concentrate and intensify.
8. Rotate from offense to defense to middle of free-throw lane. Don't let players 1 and 2 go at the same time. Let player 1 go. Then while rotation is occurring, let player 2 go.
9. Continue until all players have played both offense and defense. This is a great drill to end your practice session.

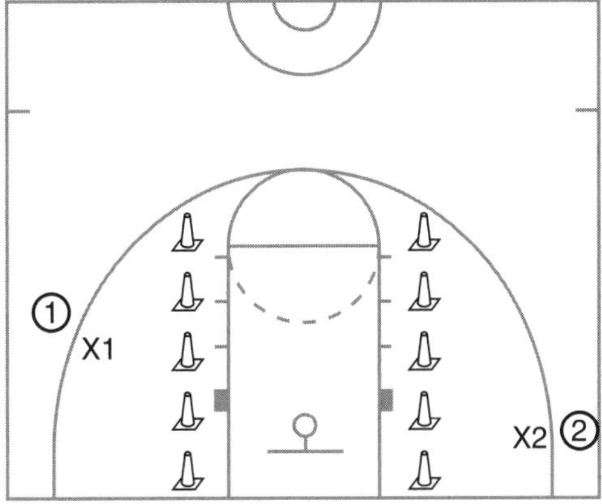

Related Drills *9, 11-15, 23-27, 28-31, 104-113, 128-130, 137*

CHAPTER

16

Individual Movement

Defenders begin in front-foot-to-pivot-foot stance; this way they dictate to the offense where they will allow the offense to go. However, front-foot-to-pivot-foot stance is not the only stance to use in defending an offensive player one on one. Defenders can also play parallel. They can overplay the front foot corresponding to the assignment's free foot. These are just three of a countless number of choices.

Regardless of the defender's beginning stance, all coaches agree that the defender must master three steps to control an attacker before the attacker dribbles the basketball. These steps are the advance step, the retreat step, and the swing step, all covered in drill 137. Each of these important steps has several drill variations devoted entirely to the step. Mastery of these steps is necessary for further individual development.

Once a defender forces the attacker to begin the dribble, the defender needs to execute other footwork to keep control of the attacker. The defender needs a slide step, covered in drill 137, and needs to decide whether to play a parallel slide or an overplay slide, both covered in drill 138.

All this coverage will be consolidated into one coverage drill (drill 139) for teaching purposes. Even if your players are beginners, they should have no trouble mastering the footwork they need to dictate to their assignments. But once your young defenders have forced their assignments in the direction they want, they must *dominate* that dictation. This is where attitude comes in.

Say a defender has his or her assignment under control. What about the attacker's teammates? Defenders must help on them, too. After all, man-to-man is a team defense—and team defense is only as good as the weakest defender. Helping teammates defend is covered in the second half of the chapter.

Drill 140 works individual aspects of the jump switch. Jump switching controls the screen on-the-ball tactics of the offense. Drill 141 teaches how to draw the charge.

Drills 142 through 144 divide the court into two sides. Draw a line from one basket to the other basket, and you have two sides of the court. Use one basketball in these drills. The ball is on one of the two sides, called the ball side. The other side is called the help side.

Drills 142 through 144 are all about help side. No help-side offensive players can score. Why? They do not have a ball. Drill 142 is a help-and-recover drill. Drill 143 shows the all-important rotation drill. Drill 144 works four individual defensive maneuvers with heavy emphasis on the help side.

DEFENSIVE STEP

Individual • 1 minute

SKILL FOCUS Rocker step (11), front-foot-to-pivot-foot stance (129), front-foot-to-free-foot stance (130), advance step, retreat step, swing step, slide step

Beginner

Advance Step

1. Players line up at the midcourt line: offense on one side of the line and defense on the other.
2. After 30 seconds, the offense and defense switch roles.
3. The attackers establish a pivot foot—right foot for 15 seconds, left foot for 15 seconds.
4. Attackers begin with the forward foot exaggerated forward. Defenders should be about a half-step back from front-foot-to-pivot-foot stance. Attackers bring their forward foot back to a semiparallel position (the centercourt line will show this). Pivot foot should be on one side of the line and the free foot on the other side. Defenders advance-step back into front-foot-to-pivot-foot stance.
5. Allow attackers to again exaggerate the front foot as if in jab-step position; repeat the first three steps in this procedure.

Retreat Step

1. Follow steps 1 and 2 as in the advance step.
2. The defender is in front-foot-to-pivot-foot stance. The attacker jab-steps, but farther away than normal from his pivot foot.
3. The defender must retreat-step slightly to counter the jab step.

Swing Step

1. Follow steps 1 and 2 as in the advance step.
2. The defender begins in front-foot-to-pivot-foot stance. The attacker uses reverse pivot. The defender reacts with the one-two tactic of the swing step.

Slide Step

1. Players line up as shown in the figure. Players slide-step around the court following the arrows in the figure.
2. On each slide step, the player taps palms on the floor. Have players always face the center of the court. Start from one side one day and the other side the next. Players may go around the court twice as the season progresses and they will get in better shape.

(continued)

Options

1. When the attacker steps back into shooting position, let the shooter jump shoot. The defender must raise an arm and a hand to discourage this shot.
2. Instead of going directly into the jump shot, the jump shooter pump-fakes and then shoots. The defender must not react to the pump fake but must respond to the jump shot.
3. The attacker may use all phases of the rocker step, and the defender must answer with intelligent defensive footwork.
4. Allow the attacker to jab-step, wait a second, and then dribble in the direction of the jab step. Defender must be in position to draw the charge.
5. Allow attacker to dribble a few steps to see if the defender is back in an overplay (or parallel).
6. Allow attacker to dribble a few steps and then shoot a jump shot. If in proper position, the defender will be on the shooting shoulder of the attacker.
7. If you teach the front-foot-to-free-foot stance instead of the front-foot-to-pivot-foot stance, go through the drill using all rocker step maneuvers against the front-foot-to-free-foot stance.

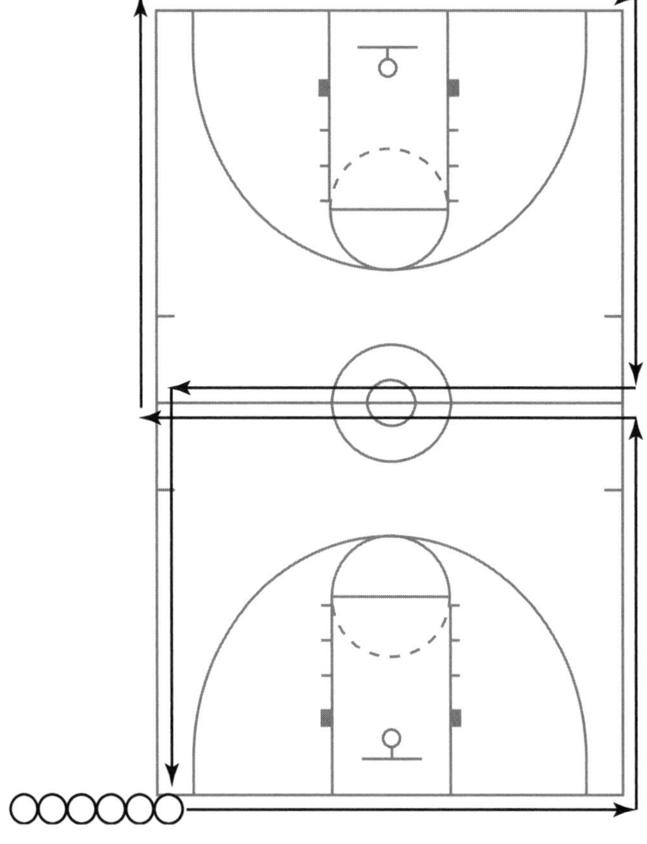

➲ TEACHING POINTS

1. The defender must step forward with the front foot to the attacker's pivot foot first, and then bring the trail foot back into a slightly wider base than the shoulders. The arm and hand that correspond with the front foot should be raised high to discourage the jump shot. The defender does not leave the floor until the assignment has left the floor on the jump shot; then the defender puts a hand between the arms of the shooter and goes straight toward the ball. If a jump is too difficult, the defender tries to cover the shooter's strong eye with a hand (usually the right eye for right-handed shooters). This completes the advance step.
2. In the retreat step, the defender starts with the trail foot dropping a half-step or so; the front foot then follows to maintain balance. If the attacker's jab step is away from the pivot foot, instead of forward, the defender's retreat step should be more in that direction. The defender stays low and places an arm and hand straight out in the direction of the fake. This completes the retreat step.
3. As the attacker spins, the defender swings. The defender's first step is with the front foot. This step should be wider than usual, occurring just as the attacker is half through a spin move. The defender's step should also be slightly backward because the defender is going to create a new front-foot-to-pivot-foot stance. The second step is to pull the former trail foot up to the attacker's pivot foot. This foot should also be slightly to the side of the attacker's other foot. The attacker cannot shoot while the defender swings because the attacker is sideways to the basket. This completes the swing step.

Related Drills *129-130, 139, 151-154*

138

OVERPLAY STEP

Individual • 2 minutes

SKILL FOCUS In and out (12, 28), crossover (13, 29), spin (14, 30), half-spin (15, 31), control dribble (24), defensive fakes (33), slide step (46, 137), defensive overplay

Beginner

1. Players line up as shown in the figure. An attacker dribbles downcourt and back; then the offense and defense switch roles.
2. Attackers must stay in their lane all the way down and back. Put the best dribblers in the center lane. The lane's boundaries are the sidelines and the free-throw lane lines extended full court.
3. Defenders must turn the opponents at least three times in each half-court.
4. You can allow attackers to use all four dribbling moves; or drill on only a specific move or two, such as the crossover and the spin move.
5. Begin by allowing dribblers to move slowly. After several attempts, permit dribblers to try to drive by the defender.
6. At the end of the dribble the attacker must put both hands on the ball. When the defender sees both hands go on the ball, the defender moves in tight on the attacker.

Option Make defenders put their arms behind their backs so arms and hands cannot be used. Movement of the feet then becomes key.

TEACHING POINTS

1. The defender's nose is on the basketball (the defender is in overplay). The dribble is out to the side of the dribbler, and the defender's nose is exactly equal to where the basketball is. Thus the overplay is about one half of a player.
2. The defender's head should be below the dribbler's armpits. The head should not bounce up and down; it should move as though it has a bucket of water on top.
3. Eyes should be on the belt buckle. This part moves less than any other during a fake.
4. Slide steps should be used; the front foot should be slightly behind parallel to the trail foot.

5. Arms and hands should be out to the side and constantly striking in toward the dribble. These strikes should as quick as a snake strike: in and back out.
6. Defenders should draw the charge if attackers continue dribbling into the overplayed defensive body position.
7. The defender's trail hand should be down and low, allowing the defender to deflect the crossover dribble.

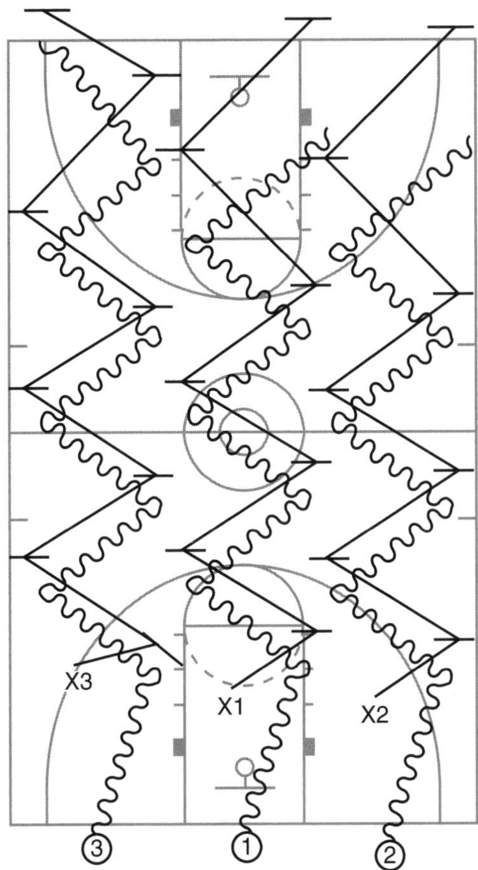

Related Drills *139, 145, 148, 150-154*

139

MIRROR STEP

Individual or team • 2 minutes

SKILL FOCUS Triple-threat position (9), in and out (12, 28), crossover (13,29), spin (14, 30), half-spin (15, 31), control dribble (24), slide step (46, 137), front-foot-to-pivot-foot stance (129), front-foot-to-free-foot stance (130), advance step (137), retreat step (137), swing step (137), overplay step (138)

Beginner

1. Players line up as shown in the figure. Attackers move parallel to the baseline.
2. Defenders mirror the movement of the offense by using the proper defensive step to counter the attacking move. Defenders begin in front-foot-to-pivot-foot stance or front-foot-to-free-foot stance.
3. Call out the attacking move and watch the defender's reaction. For example, a jab step is met with a defensive retreat step. Any dribble is overplayed, and when the dribbler changes direction, the defender reacts by sliding back into proper defensive overplay.
4. Begin with an offensive move and a defensive reaction. Analyze and discuss the move and its reaction.
5. Then permit the action to be continuous with one move following another.

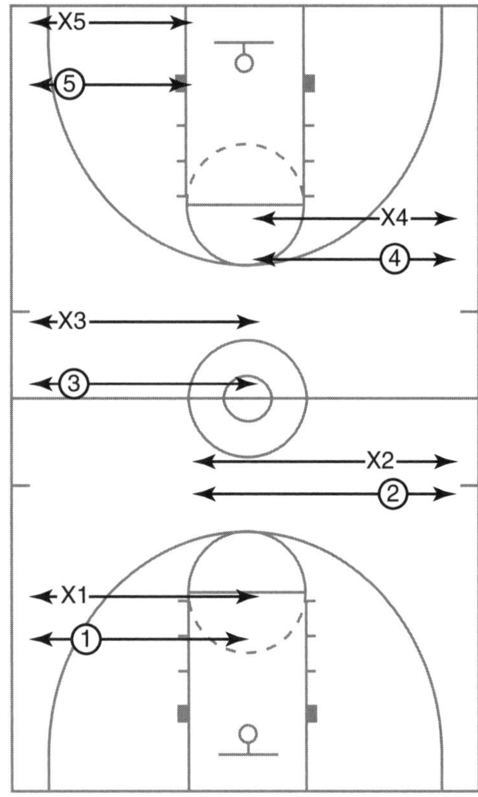

Option Allow attackers to choose the move to be used.

Related Drills *138, 145, 148-154*

JUMP SWITCHING

Team • 8 minutes

SKILL FOCUS Trapping (50), screening (71-75), fence slide (128), defensive footwork (129-131, 137-144), interception stance (131), close the gap (132), ball-you-man (133), flat triangle (133), help-side techniques (133-135), jump switch (140), draw the charge (141), rotation (143), jump to ball (146), deny wing (147)

Intermediate

1. Line players up as shown in the figure. Rotation is from offense to defense to end of the line after each defender has played at least one jump switch.
2. Player 1 passes to player 2, and player 1 goes immediately to screen for player 2. After player 1 screens, 1 rolls to the basket.
3. X1 aggressively jump-switches into the path of the dribbling 2. X2 must decide whether to slide through and below the screen or to fight over the top of the screen. Do not teach both techniques. Settle on one of the two and teach it to your entire team.
4. Defender X1 can hedge and recover back to assignment. This is a technique you want to teach to your entire squad. Or X1 can call "switch" to tell X2 to switch assignments. X3 must help inside on the rolling 1 in either case.
5. Player 1, for the sake of continuing the drill, goes to the baseline and then breaks back outside to the open wing. Now player 2 can pass to either 3 or back to 1 and go screen on the ball. This allows another jump switch to occur. The drill continues.
6. As long as you are teaching the jump switch, you should not allow a shot. You should not allow player 2 to pass to player 1 on the roll. This way you get more repetitions per minute.

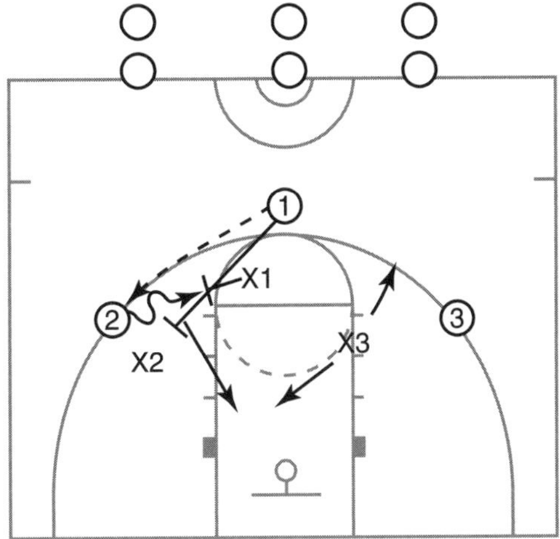

(continued)

➔ Options

1. Instead of jump switching, you can allow X1 to hedge and recover. This means X1 must jump out as if jump switching (using the techniques of jump switching) at least a half a body above the dribbling 2. You want X1 to compel dribbling 2 to dribble back toward the screener. Once X1 has hedged—and this should take only a fraction of a second—X1 hustles back to assignment. Within a fraction of a second, X2 should either go over the top of the screen or slide through the screen and hustle back to assignment. No switch occurred.
2. You can allow X1 and X2 to trap the ball handler, 2. This compels X3 to cover both player 3 and player 1.
3. You can play the drill live until player 1 makes a pass to either player 2 or player 3. This means X2 and X3 are in a deny-the-wing stance, using the fence slide.
4. If you are going to fast break, allow the defense to fast break on any steal. This teaches instant conversion from offense to defense and from defense to offense.

Advanced

1. Instead of player 2 driving in the direction of the screen, you can allow player 2 to drive the baseline. This activates the rotation drill (see drill 143).
2. Instead of player 2 allowing X1 to hedge and recover or to jump switch, player 2 can split the dribble and drive toward the basket. This activates the rotation drill.

➔ Jump Switching

1. To jump switch on a screen on the ball, X1 must align at least half a body higher than the dribbling 2 and in the direction player 2 is dribbling. X1 may align a full body higher. X1's purpose is to force player 2 to dribble further out on the court or to dribble back toward the screener.
2. Just before player 2 appears to change direction with a dribbling split of the two defenders and starts dribbling toward the basket, X1 fully recovers into a normal guarding position on player 2. X1 must anticipate this move by player 2. Player 2 might even try to create greater space for splitting the two defenders by dribbling even higher out on the court. This is a maneuver X1 must anticipate and recover to a normal guarding position.
3. X2 switches assignments. X2 covers player 1 on 1's roll to the basket.
4. X3, the help-side defender, must help on player 1 before getting back to assignment. X3 activates the help-side defender's tactics.

➲ TEACHING POINTS

1. Make sure the screen is set correctly (see drill 72).
2. Make sure the jump switch is aggressive and fundamentally sound.
3. Make sure the roll is fundamentally sound; player 1 should not take eyes off 2 on the roll (see drill 72).
4. Make sure help-side defenders offer help. This requires proper use of the flat triangle, ball-you-man, and the interception stance (see drills 131 and 133).
5. If you allow trapping off the screen on the ball, make sure the trap is set correctly and the interception techniques are properly played (see drill 50).

Related Drills *50, 71-75, 128-135, 141, 143, 145-147, 155-160*

141

DRAW THE CHARGE

Individual or team • 2 minutes

SKILL FOCUS Rocker step (11), interception stance (131), close-the-gap stance (132), ball-you-man (133), flat triangle (133), help-side techniques (133-135), draw the charge (141), slide-step (137)

Intermediate

1. Line players up as shown in the figure. Rotate from player 2 to player 1 to player 3 to end of line after each drawing of the charge.
2. Player 2 rolls the ball to player 1.
3. Player 2 hustles out to get in proper help-side defense: ball-you-man and flat triangle.
4. When player 1 receives the ball, player 1 executes one of the rocker step moves. Player 1 then drives directly to the basket.
5. Player 2 slides over to draw the charge.

Draw the Charge

1. To draw the charge, player 2 must have stopped the slide-step before player 1 leaves the floor to shoot the layup.
2. Player 2 pushes off the balls of the feet just before contact. Player 2 places both arms in front of the torso for protection as contact occurs. Player 2 lands on the buttocks.
3. Player 2 rolls over to the side after landing, raising the top leg.
4. This movement should prevent injury.

➲ TEACHING POINTS

1. Make sure the rocker step move is executed perfectly without speed but with quickness. Don't let the player hurry the move. You can determine which move or series you want used.
2. Make sure player 2 gets in proper help-side positioning. This means 2 must be two-thirds the distance from the ball and one step off the line between the ball and assignment in an interception stance. Player 2 shifts weight to the other foot as the drive begins (close-the-gap stance).
3. Make sure player 2 draws the charge by getting there on time and protects against injury by placing both arms in front of the torso.

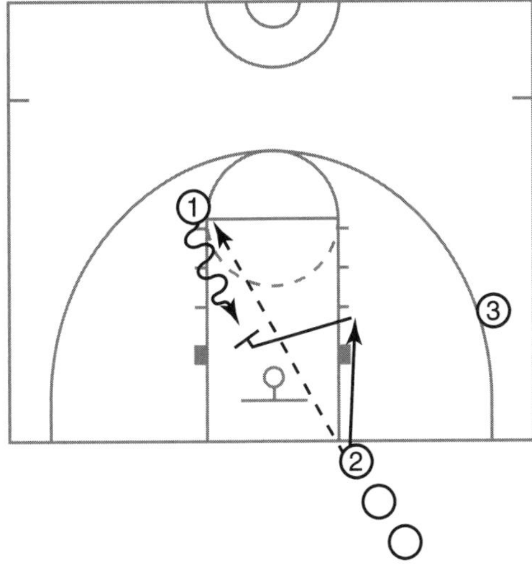

Related Drills *11, 131-135, 137-140, 142-144, 151-154*

142

HELP AND RECOVER

Individual • 2 minutes

SKILL FOCUS Rocker step (11), dribbling drives (23-27), defensive fakes (33), passing and receiving (44), fakes at the end of the dribble (96, 116-117), ball-you-man (133), flat triangle (133), help-side defense (133-135), defensive steps (137), draw the charge (141), hedging (142), help and recover (142), rotation (143), jump to the ball (146), closeouts (149-150)

Beginner

1. Line players up as shown in the figure. Rotation is from X4 to 4 to 1 to 3 to X4.
2. Player 3 begins with the basketball. Player 3 holds the ball until you are satisfied with X4's help-side positioning (flat triangle and ball-you-man).
3. Player 3 begins to drive. X4 hedges toward player 3, faking toward player 3, then dropping toward X4's assignment (4). X4 tries to slow player 3 down so X3 (imaginary in figure) can recover on X3's assignment (3).
4. You can allow player 3 to drive to the basket. In this case, X4 must rotate and pick up the charge.
5. At any time player 3 wishes, 3 can pass to player 1, who immediately passes to player 4. X4 must close out properly on 4.
6. Player 4 and X4 play one on one, which continues until X4 rebounds or player 4 scores.

Options

1. Allow player 1 to start with the basketball and pass to player 3. This means X4 must begin in denial stance using the fence slide to keep player 4 from getting the basketball.
2. Player 3 would begin to drive after receiving the pass. This forces X4 to get into proper help-side defense and then rotate to stop 3's drive or help and recover back to player 4.

Hedging To hedge, the defender fakes toward the ball, backs off, fakes back toward the ball, and then backs off until the help-side defender has brought the dribbler under control or until the help-side defender completely rotates to pick up the breakaway dribbler.

Help and Recover

1. To help and recover, the help-side defender keeps hedging but hurries back to assignment once sure the dribbler is under control.
2. Help and recover means the help-side defender helps and then goes back to assignment. Rotation means the help-side defender rotates to pick up the breakaway dribbler (see drill 143).

➲ TEACHING POINTS

1. Make sure X4's help-side defense on player 3 looks like the real thing. It should look as if X4 is going to pick up player 3.
2. Make sure X4 is in proper help-side positioning before player 3 drives. Help side is the side away from the ball, so X4 executes help-side defense. Ball-side defense is always denial and the fence slide.
3. Make sure the one-on-one game is played using proper fundamentals on both offense and defense. You want to make your drills more demanding than actual game conditions.

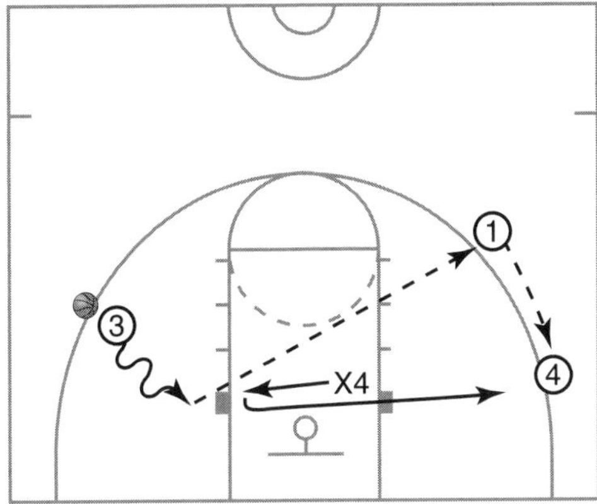

Related Drills *11, 23-27, 33, 96, 116-117, 128-135, 137-141, 143-154*

143

ROTATION

Team • 4 minutes

➲ SKILL FOCUS Trap (50), fence slide (128), help-side defense (132-142, 144), deny wing (147), dribble closeout (149), pass receiver closeout (150), trap dribble (157)

Intermediate

1. Line players up as shown in the figure.
2. A coach passes to player 1, who drives by the defender, X1. Player 1 can drive by X1 on either side. The rotation is the same.
3. On seeing player 1 become a breakaway dribbler, X4 slides across the lane to stop the ball. X3 immediately rotates down to cover the basket area. Player 4 is closing in to the basket for a pass and a layup.
4. Players rotate from offense to defense after each offensive player has played positions 1, 3, and 4 and after each defender has played X1, X3, and X4.
5. In the figure, X4 is responsible for the call. If X4 calls "hedge," X4 feels X1 can recover to keep player 1 from driving for the layup. In this case, all defenders keep their assignment. If X4 calls "rotate," the rotation drill occurs. X4 takes player 1, X3 covers 4, and X1 defends 3. If your squad has practiced the traps described in chapter 19, X4 can call "trap." If X4 calls "trap," then X4 and X1 trap the ball handler. In this case, X3 plays in an interception position, playing both 3 and 4 for a possible interception. X3 should shade more toward the basket area and 4. If a pass is successful out of the trap, X3 takes the pass receiver, X1 stays on 1, and X4 hurries to cover the open player.
6. Should player 1 drive to left, X3 is responsible to close the gap. Should player 1 still drive by X3, the rotation drill begins with X4 calling "rotate." X3 would drop toward the basket to pick up 4.

Advanced

1. You can begin the drill by allowing X1 to deny the pass to player 1. Denial defense brings into defensive play the fence slide and the deny-the-wing technique.
2. Allow player 1 and X1 to play one on one until player 1 creates separation and shoots or until player 1 drives either side of X1. This is more gamelike.
3. On a successful rotation, allow players to play three on three. Now all the aspects of the motion offense and man-to-man defense come into play.

Rotation

1. In man-to-man defense, there is the ball side and the help side. On ball side, the next pass should always be contested using the fence slide and by denying the wing. On the help side, defenders are to help stop the ball. The first line of stopping the ball is the defender on the ball. But sometimes the attacker with the ball will drive by the defender. Help-side defenders must stop this breakaway dribble drive. The first help-side defender is the one closest to the ball. This defender closes the gap (drills 131 and 132). The second help-side defender is the one nearest the basket. This is called rotation.
2. Two rules are always followed to call out rotation. Draw a line across the court about midway up the free-throw lane. Then follow these two rules:
   a. The help-side defender below the line rotates to stop the ball.
   b. The help-side defender above the line rotates to the basket to stop the pass for a layup.

TEACHING POINTS

1. Make sure all offensive and defensive techniques before the rotation are executed with perfect fundamentals.
2. Make sure the rotation is activated quickly enough to stop the ball outside the lane.
3. Make sure the rotation is correct.

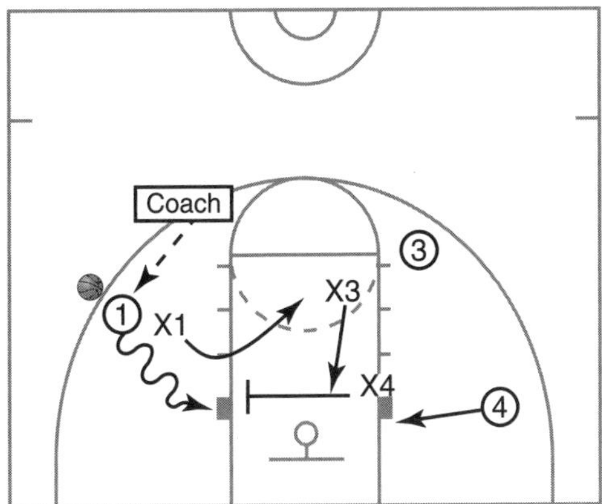

Related Drills *128-142, 144-154*

144

FOUR INDIVIDUAL DEFENSIVE TRAITS

Individual or team • 10 minutes

SKILL FOCUS Triple threat (9), rocker step series (11), dribbling perimeter moves (12-15, 28-31), control dribble (24), change of pace (25), hesitation (26), retreat (27), front pivot (35), defensive fakes (33), reverse pivot (36), jump stop (37), stride stop (38), passing and receiving (44), V-cut (53), offensive and defensive rebounding (78-81), pump fake (96), moves at the end of dribble (116-117), fence slide (128), defensive footwork (129-131, 137-144), close the gap (132), help-side defense (133-135), drawing the charge (141), help and recover (142), rotation (143), deny the wing (147), deny flash pivot cut (148), defensive close-outs (149-150)

1. Line players up as shown in the figure.
2. After X1 has run through the entire drill, rotation is from X1 to 1 to 2 to 3 to 4 to 5 to X1.
3. This drill can be run as a continuous drill covering all four parts, compelling X1 to work for nearly 2 minutes on defense before rotating; or the drill can be broken down into each of its parts and run in four phases. The parts are . . .
   a. Player 1 and X1 play one on one. Player 1 can use fakes before the dribble and then has only three dribbles to create separation. This phase ends when player 1 shoots, when player 1 does not create separation, or when X1 defensively rebounds. Whichever player ends with the basketball passes to player 2, and the second phase begins. Player 1 and X1 return to their original positions.
   b. Player 2 can do one of three maneuvers. First, 2 can try to make a pass to player 1 breaking up and down the sideline. X1 uses deny-the-wing defensive techniques, executing a fence slide. Second, 2 can dribble drive on the side where X1 is. This requires X1 to use close-the-gap techniques. Third, player 2 can shoot. This impels player 1 and X1 to fight for the rebound, using offensive and defensive techniques.

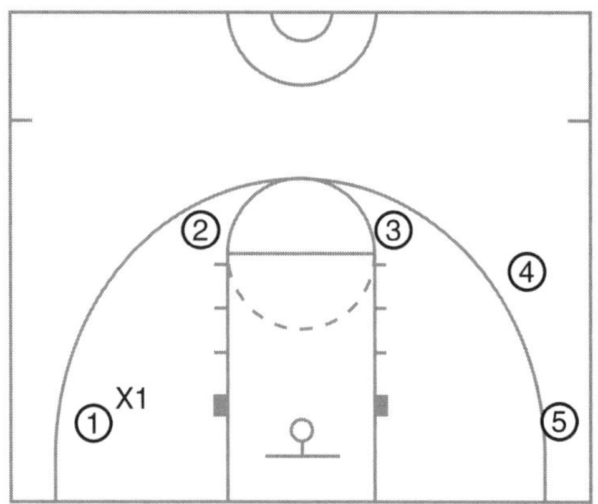

c. Whichever player ends up with the basketball passes to player 3. Player 1 and X1 have returned to their original positions. With player 3 with the basketball and player 1 and X1 in their original positions, X1 is on the help side. X1 immediately must get into help-side defensive tactics. X1 must use the flat triangle and ball-you-man techniques. Player 3 can do one of three things: (1) pass to 4, which compels X1 to adjust help-side positioning; (2) pass back to 2 and activate phase b, as just described; or (3) shoot, which ends the phase. Now player 1 and X1 fight for the rebound.

d. Whomever gets the rebound passes to player 4. Meanwhile, players 1 and X1 have returned to their original positions. X1 must get into proper help-side position. Player 4 has four options: (1) take a shot, which mandates X1 and 1 to fight for the rebound; (2) dribble drive a few steps and pass to player 1, which requires X1 to close out on the receiver; (3) motion for player 1 to flash pivot cut for a pass, which requires X1 to deny the flash pivot cut; or (4) pass to player 5, who drives the baseline, which requires X1 to rotate and draw the charge.

Beginner

1. Have the player choose from phases a, b, and c (only one option from each of the three phases).
2. The player does not have to tell the defender which of the options is chosen. This requires the defender to use savvy to play correct and fundamentally sound defense.

Intermediate

1. Players must choose one option from each phase.
2. This forces defenders to play four continuous defensive plays.

Advanced

1. You can allow players 2, 3, 4, and 5 to choose which options they intend to employ.
2. This requires defenders to use several techniques in each of the phases.

➜ Options (all skill levels)

1. Your choice of which option you intend to let the player use in each phase should depend on what you need to work on defensively.
2. You can limit each phase to one option or to two options.

(continued)

3. You can mix up the options you intend to use. For example, allow player 1 and X1 to play one on one (phase a), then player 2 shoots (phase b), and then player 3 passes to player 4 (phase c), who forces a closeout by the defender; then player 5 drives the baseline (phase d). Next time through the drill: Player 1 and X1 play one on one (phase a), then player 2 compels X1 to deny the wing (phase b), then player 3 shoots (phase c), and, last, player 4 forces X1 to hedge and recover before player 5 drives the baseline (phase d). There are all kinds of options, but by your choices you can require X1 to execute at least four individual defensive maneuvers.
4. You can take one phase and use it as the drill. For example, if you used only phase d, this would activate all four parts of phase d. The defender would have to use defensive rebounding techniques, closeout techniques, defense of the flash pivot, and all one-on-one defensive steps and tactics.

TEACHING POINTS

1. Make sure the defender is executing properly. This depends on which option in which phase you are using.
2. Early in the season you should stop the drill as mistakes occur. Later in the season you can let drill continue until the four phases have been run. Then you can discuss any mistakes with the defender.
3. Your team defense is only as good as your weakest defender, so make sure all tactics, techniques, and footwork are executed correctly by every player.

Related Drills *9, 11-15, 28-31, 24-27, 35-38, 44, 53, 78-81, 96, 110, 112-117, 128-135, 141-143, 147-152*

CHAPTER

17

Team Movement

Defensive team movement occurs when the ball moves (via the pass), when the player with the ball moves (via the dribble), or when a player's defensive assignment moves (via the cut). Thus players must know front foot to pivot foot, front foot to free foot, and parallel defense to force their opponents (assignments) to dribble. And they must know how to overplay their assignment to prevent the dribbling moves. These scenarios were discussed in chapters 15 and 16. A review of these individual steps is presented in a mass drill (drill 145).

But defensive players must know much more than this. They must also be able to stop their assignments from gaining an advantage via cutting and screening maneuvers, which can occur on either the strong side of the court (ball side) or the weak side (side away from the ball). The defense must always know where the ball is. Also, all of your players must know the rules of your squad's man-to-man defense.

On learning these defensive team tactics, your players in their defensive prowess can emulate Shane Battier of the Miami Heat, who played his college ball at Duke, setting all kinds of NCAA defensive records. Your players will learn to anticipate the opposition's movement and, like Battier, make stops on defense and draw many, many charges.

A first step on defense is to always make your assignment cut backdoor—no middle cuts allowed. Players do this by jumping to the ball (drill 146); they should always be two-thirds of the distance from the ball and one-third of the distance from their assignment. They also should be one step off a line between their assignment and the ball (tell your players "ball-you-man").

On the strong side (ball side), players never want to allow a penetrating pass, so they must deny any vertical pass (drill 147). On the weak side (help side), players want to offer help to teammates while remaining in position to prevent their assignment a direct cut to the ball (drill 148). Smart offenses take advantage of proper weak-side positioning. They try to gain shooting advantages for teammates by making a teammate's defender play them off their drive, which frees teammates up for open shots. Thus defenders must learn to close out on the breakaway dribbler (drill 149) and on the pass receiver (drill 150).

All individual offensive and defensive techniques and tactics will be drilled so that these moves become instinctive for your players (drill 151). They will then be ready to progress to team defensive maneuvers.

Drill 152 provides a review of the individual defensive fundamentals from the initial pass to the wing through help-side defense into low-post coverage. This is a great drill for late season check-ups on your individual defenders.

145

MASS WAVE SLIDING

Individual or team • 1 minute

SKILL FOCUS Defensive fakes (33), slide step (46, 137), interception stance (50, 131), fence slide (128), front foot to pivot foot stance (129), front foot to free foot stance (130), advance step (137), retreat step (137), swing step (137), jump to the ball (146), deny the wing (147)

Beginner

1. Players line up in staggered positions in the frontcourt where they all can see the coach, as shown in the figure.
2. The coach establishes a pivot foot. This should be changed from day to day.
3. All defensive players appoint the proper front foot to pivot foot, front foot to free foot, or parallel.
4. The coach jab-steps. Defenders react with a retreat step. The coach pulls back from the jab step. Defenders react with an advance step. The coach does a jab-step crossover; defenders react with a swing step. The coach uses a spin move; defenders react with a quick one-two step, creating a new front foot to pivot foot, front foot to free foot, or parallel stance.
5. The coach begins a dribble in one direction or the other. Players react by overplaying the dribble. The coach changes direction; players react with a retreat step with the trail foot and a quick movement into another overplay.
6. The coach picks up the dribble. When defenders see both hands go on the ball, they react with an advance step and a tight overplay.
7. The coach may have players gather in the frontcourt and run the movements again.

➜ **Option** Tell players they are on the weak side. Now you need an assistant coach to help you. In your first phase, pass the ball to your assistant coach, who is parallel to you. Defenders react by jumping to the ball. In the second phase, have your assistant move downcourt from you. Players react by denying the assistant the ball (fence slide position). In the third phase, the assistant coach moves to the weak side. Now throw a skip pass, and players close out to the ball. In the last phase, throw a line-drive pass; defenders execute an interception stance and intercept the pass.

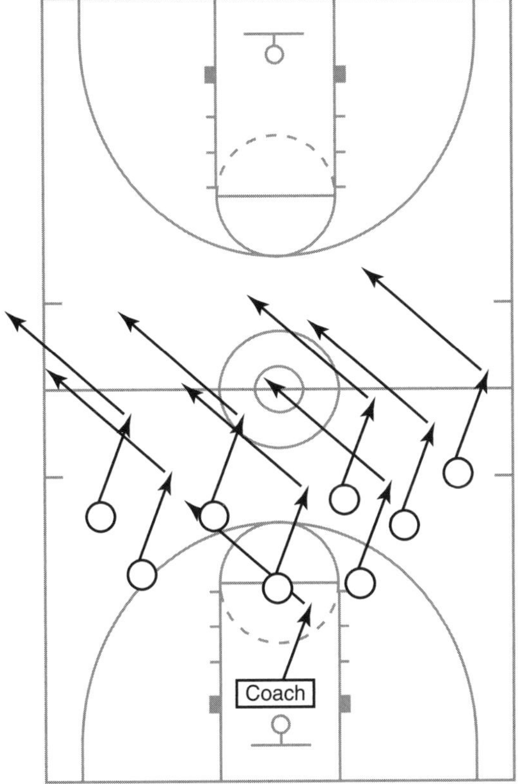

Related Drills *128-139, 146-154*

146

JUMP TO THE BALL

Team • 5 minutes

SKILL FOCUS Triple-threat position (9), rocker step (11), in and out (12, 28), crossover (13, 29), spin (14, 30), half-spin (15, 31), front pivot (35), reverse pivot (36), jump stop (37), stride stop (38), chest pass (44), bounce pass (44), V-cut (53), backdoor cut (54), pump fake (96), pump fake crossover (96), fence slide (128), front foot to pivot foot (129), front foot to free foot (130), advance step (137), retreat step (137), swing step (137), jump to the ball, deny the wing (147)

Beginner

1. Players line up as shown in the figure. Rotation is from offense to defense to the end of the line; the next player in each line moves out front to become the new attacker.
2. Player 1 passes to 2. X1 and X2 jump to the ball. Player 2 passes to 1. X2 and X1 again jump to the ball. This continues for several passes before rotation.

Options

1. The player with the ball does a jab step and jab-step crossover before passing the ball back to a teammate. Defenders react with the appropriate technique.
2. After several passes, the coach makes the drill live by allowing the weak-side attacker to middle-cut or backdoor cut into strong-side wing position. Now the defender on the wing plays denial defense. The wing V-cuts until getting open. Then the outside attacker jumps to the ball. The wing player with the ball and a defender play one on one.
3. After several passes, the coach sends the nonpass-receiver on a cut to the opposite corner. Now there is a help-side defender. This help-side defender lines up in a flat triangle with ball-you-man principles. You can allow the player with the ball to drive, activating the rotation drill. Or you can allow the player with the ball to skip-pass to the corner player. Now the help-side defender must close out to the pass receiver.

➲ TEACHING POINTS

1. When each player jumps to the ball, the player on the ball plays front foot to pivot foot, front foot to free foot, or parallel stance, and the off-the-ball player plays in the interception stance.
2. Defenders move while the pass is in the air; they do not jump to the ball on fake passes.
3. To "jump to the ball" does not mean a jump off the floor but rather a quick slide step or two toward the ball with toes grabbing at the floor.

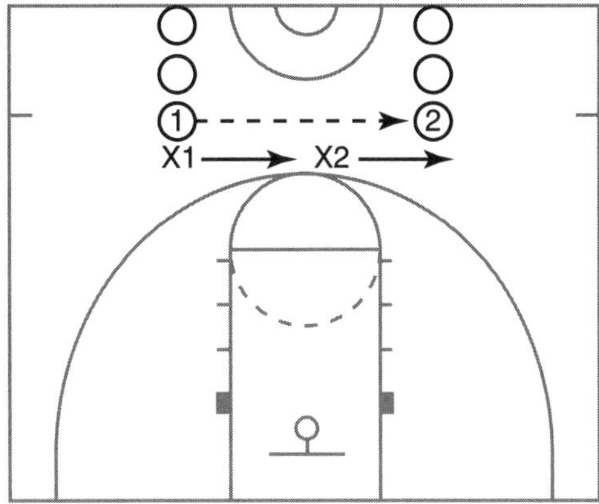

Related Drills *128-145, 147-154*

147

DENY THE WING

Team • 4 minutes

➲ SKILL FOCUS Triple-threat position (9), rocker step (11), in and out (12, 28), crossover (13, 29), spin (14, 30), half-spin (15, 31), front pivot (35), reverse pivot (36), jump stop (37), stride stop (38), chest pass (44), bounce pass (44), V-cut (53), backdoor cut (54), pump fake (96), pump fake crossover (96), fence slide (128), front foot to pivot foot (129), front foot to free foot (130), advance step (137), retreat step (137), swing step (137), deny the wing

Beginner

1. Players line up as shown in the figure.
2. Rotation is from 1 to 3 to X3 to end of line.
3. Player 3 runs the V-cut. X3 denies the pass to 3. Player 3 has the option of running a backdoor cut if X3 makes that available.
4. Once 3 receives the ball, 3 front pivots (or reverse pivots) into triple-threat position; 3 then passes the ball back to 1, and players rotate.

Intermediate

When 3 receives the pass, 3 front pivots into triple-threat position. Then the two players play one on one.

➲ TEACHING POINT X3 uses the fence slide to keep the ball from 3. X3 stays one full step toward the ball from 3 but in a straight line between 3 and the ball. X3, in other words, keeps an ear on the chest of 3. X3 keeps arm and hand in the passing lane between 1 and 3. X3 turns the palm of the hand toward 1 with thumb pointed down. X3 uses the off-arm and hand as leverage against 3. X3's off-arm should be straight out into the running lane of 3. When 3 makes contact, X3 stiffens, preventing 3 from moving at full speed. X3 must not initiate the contact.

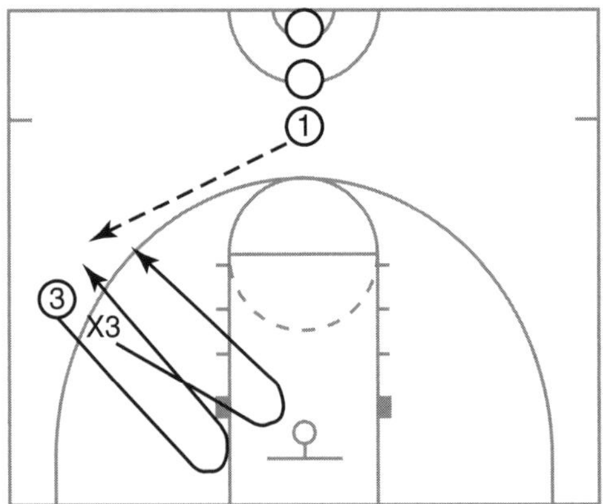

Related Drills *9, 11-15, 28-31, 35-38, 44, 53, 55, 96, 128-130, 137-139, 148-154*

DENY THE FLASH PIVOT

Team • 4 minutes

➲ SKILL FOCUS Triple-threat position (9), rocker step (11), in and out (12, 28), crossover (13, 29), spin (14, 30), half-spin (15, 31), front pivot (35), reverse pivot (36), jump stop (37), stride stop (38), chest pass (44), bounce pass (44), overhead flip pass (44), V-cut (53), backdoor cut (54), pump fake (96), pump fake crossover (96), fence slide (128), front foot to pivot foot (129), front foot to free foot (130), advance step (137), retreat step (137), swing step (137), deny the flash pivot

Beginner

1. Players line up as shown in the figure.
2. Rotation is from 1 to X5 to 5 to the end of the line.
3. Player 5 breaks on flash-pivot cut to the high-post area. X5 tries to deny this cut. Player 1 passes to 5; 5 can backdoor cut, and 1 can throw the overhead flip pass.
4. When 5 receives the pass, 5 front pivots (or reverse pivots) and gets in triple-threat position; 5 then passes to 1, and the rotation commences.

Intermediate

When 5 receives the pass, 5 front pivots and gets in triple-threat position. Then 5 and X5 play one on one.

➲ TEACHING POINT X5 first must body check 5 as 5 cuts across the lane. This should be a full torso against torso. The defense is allowed this position as much as the offense. The defense must get there first. Then when 5 cuts up the lane, X5 uses the techniques of the deny-the-wing pass in drill 147.

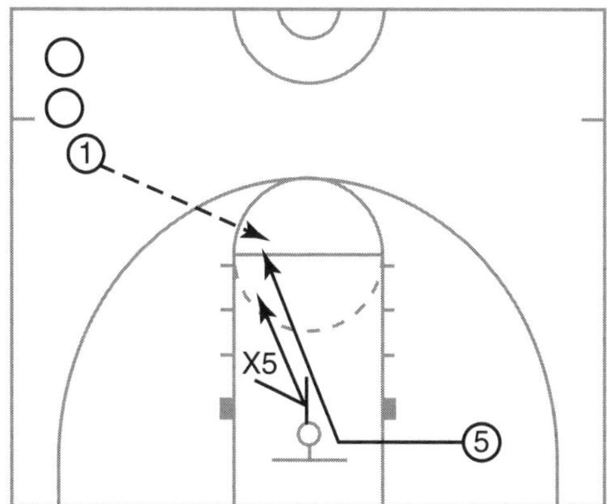

Related Drills *9, 11-15, 28-31, 35-38, 44, 53, 55, 96, 128-130, 137-139, 147, 149, 150-154*

DRIBBLE CLOSEOUT

Individual or team • 1 minute

SKILL FOCUS Speed dribble (23), control dribble (24), close out on dribbler

Beginner

1. Players line up as shown in the figure. Offense dribbles under control.
2. Defender goes to pick up dribbler and keeps dribbler under control.
3. Attacker dribbles a few steps before starting the drill again.

Intermediate

The offensive player uses a speed dribble. The defender still picks up the dribbler and keeps the dribbler under control.

Advanced

Start the drill at half-court and have the defender near the free-throw line. When the dribbler is closed out, the two players play one on one at the basket.

➲ TEACHING POINTS

1. The defender slide-steps a few steps toward the dribbler. She overplays half her body so that the dribbler must change direction, via either a crossover move or a spin move.
2. The defender uses a swing step and begins to use slide steps trying to get back into another overplay position, always keeping the dribbler in front of her.
3. This defense can occur on one's assignment or to help a teammate on a breakaway (free) dribbler.

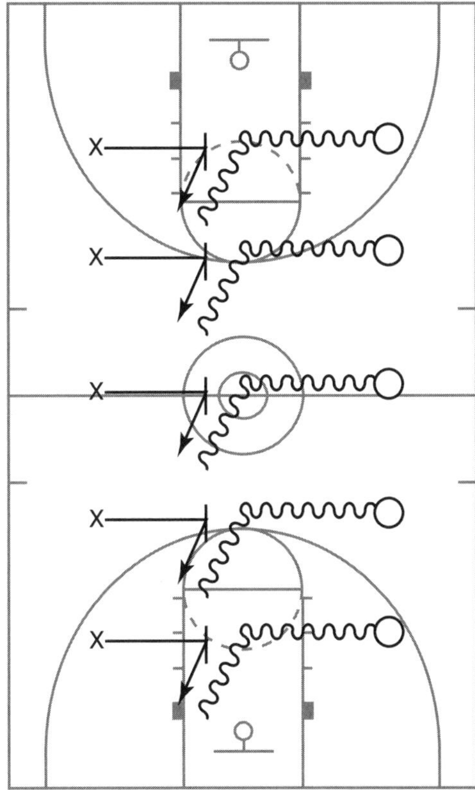

Related Drills *12-15, 23-24, 28-31, 46, 96, 137-139, 147-148, 150-154*

150

SKIP PASS AND CLOSEOUT

Team • 6 minutes

➲ SKILL FOCUS Triple-threat position (9), rocker step (11), in and out (12, 28), crossover (13, 29), spin (14, 30), half-spin (15, 31), front pivot (35), reverse pivot (36), jump stop (37), stride stop (38), chest pass (44), bounce pass (44), interception stance (50, 131), V-cut (53), backdoor cut (54), pump fake (96), pump fake crossover (96), fence slide (128), front foot to pivot foot (129), front foot to free foot (130), advance step (137), retreat step (137), swing step (137), skip pass and closeout

Intermediate

1. Players line up as shown in the figure. Rotation is from 1 to X3 to 3 to end of line.
2. Player 1 begins by throwing a line-drive pass, even underhanded, to 3. X3 must be in an interception stance and pick this pass off. X3 passes back to 1. Player 1 may repeat this as many times as desired to keep X3 honest.
3. Finally, 1 overhead lobs a pass to 3. X3 must close out on the pass receiver and keep the receiver under control.
4. Players 3 and X3 go one on one after a clean reception. Player 3 is allowed to move up and down the sideline, compelling X3 to continually readjust position.

➔ TEACHING POINTS

1. X3 is two-thirds the distance from 1 and one-third the distance from 3.
2. X3 is in an interception stance and is one step off the line between 1 and 3. X3 must see both 1 and 3 and must intercept any direct pass to 3.
3. To close out to a pass receiver, the defender runs straight toward the receiver, coming under control with slide steps the last few steps. The defender then slide-steps up the straddle of the receiver, overplaying on the free foot side of the receiver. This forces the receiver to crossover or spin (slower moves than a direct drive) toward the pivot foot. The defender uses the one-two swing-step maneuver (drill 129) to keep the potential dribbler under control. The defender must get to the receiver as the ball arrives.

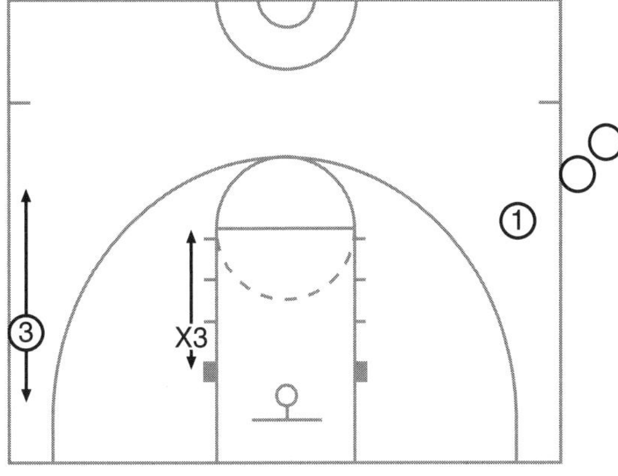

Related Drills ***9, 11-15, 28-31, 35-38, 44, 53, 55, 96, 128-130, 137-139, 147, 149, 151-154***

151

EIGHT-POINT DRILL

Individual or team • 10 minutes

➲ SKILL FOCUS Triple-threat position (9), rocker step (11), in and out (12, 28), crossover (13, 29), spin (14, 30), half-spin (15, 31), front pivot (35), reverse pivot (36), jump stop (37), stride stop (38), chest pass (44), bounce pass (44), interception stance (50, 131), V-cut (53), backdoor cut (54), pump fake (96), pump fake crossover (96), fence slide (128), front foot to pivot foot (129), front foot to free foot (130), advance step (137), retreat step (137), swing step (137), jump to the ball (146), flash pivot defense (148), dribbler closeout (149), skip pass and closeout (150)

Advanced

1. Players line up as shown in figure 1. Rotation is from 1 to X1 to the end of the line.
2. This is an eight-part drill: four strong side (figure 1) and four weak side (figure 2). You may drill on all eight points in one day, or strong side one day and weak side the next.
3. Player 1 passes to a coach. X1 must jump to the ball (part 1). This compels 1 to go backdoor. Player 1 stops in the post, and X1 plays post defense (part 2). If the coach can pass to 1, 1 and X1 go one on one inside. If so, 1 and X1 return to the low post to continue the eight-part drill. Player 1 breaks out to the corner, and X1 denies the corner (part 3); 1 can break backdoor if X1 makes this available. Anywhere 1 gets the ball, 1 squares up in triple-threat position, and the two players go one on one (part 4). This makes up the strong-side four.

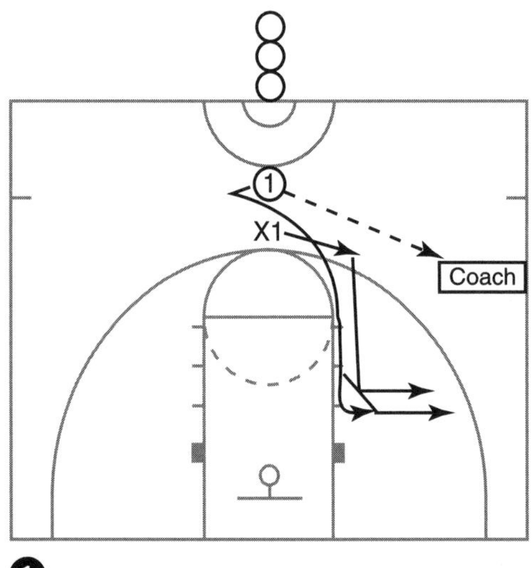

1

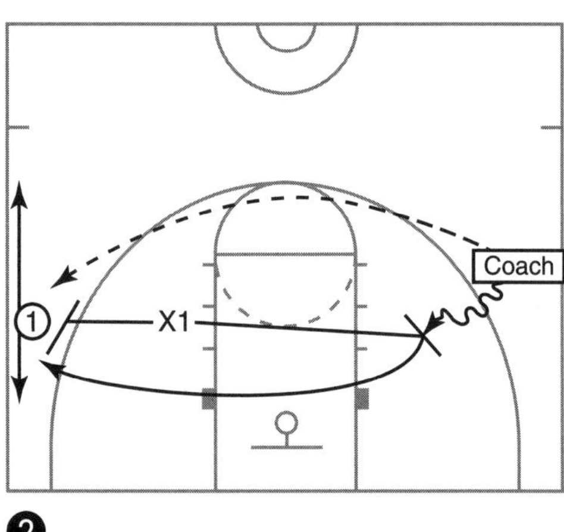

2

4. After drilling on the strong side, or when 1 initially cuts, the two end up again at the low post. From here, 1 breaks to the weak side, and the weak-side four begins. Player 1 may move up and down the sideline, inbounds only about 3 feet (1 m), to keep X1's coverage honest. First X1 must get in interception-stance position (part 1). X1 must be two-thirds the distance from the coach and one-third the distance from 1. X1 must also be one step off the line between 1 and the ball (coach). The coach rolls the ball hard toward 1, and X1 must pivot and intercept the pass. X1 gives the ball back to the coach, and the coach begins a drive baseline or middle. X1 closes out on the breakaway dribbler (part 2). Then the coach tosses a lob pass over to 1, and X1 closes out on the pass receiver (part 3). Player 1 squares up in triple-threat position, and the two play one on one. After this, the ball is tossed back to the coach, and 1 flash pivots. X1 must deny this flash pivot cut (part 4); 1 can go backdoor if X1 makes this available. When 1 gets the ball, X1 and 1 play one on one.

Related Drills *9, 11-15, 28-31, 35-38, 44, 53, 55, 96, 128-130, 137-139, 147, 149-150, 152-154*

152

ONE-ON-ONE MULTIPLE SKILLS DRILL

Individual or team • 6 minutes

SKILL FOCUS Defensive fakes (33), defensive rebounding (79), fronting (98), two-step post defense (99), three-quartering (101), front foot to pivot foot (129), front foot to free foot (130), interception stance (131), ball-you-man (133), flat triangle (133), help-side defensive techniques (133-135), advance step (137), retreat step (137), swing step (137), slide step (137), overplay step (138), drawing the charge (141), rotation (143), jump to the ball (146), flash pivot defense (148), close-outs (149-150)

Intermediate

1. Line players up as shown in figure 1. This drill teaches all the defensive mechanics of help-side defense and post defense.
2. You should allow the pass from player 1 to player 2 and walk through the coverage listed in sections a, b, and c in figure 1.
3. Then walk through the a and b coverage in figure 2.
4. Then cover the defensive post techniques you wish to install in figure 3.
5. Then run the drill live, stopping it after each one-on-one play to realign (see description, following).
6. Rotation is from 1 to X1 to 2 to 3 to end of line. The first player in line becomes the new 1.
7. In figure 1, three parts are presented. Player 1 passes to player 2. (a) X1 must jump to the ball. X1 must not allow a middle cut. Player 1 backdoor cuts to side away from the ball. (b) X1 is now a help-side defender. X1 must be in the flat triangle, using ball-you-man techniques. (c) Player 2 passes to player 3. X1 must adjust to get proper flat triangle and ball-you-man position. Player 3 drives to the basket. X1 rotates. If player 3 continues, X1 must draw the charge.
8. Figure 2 continues the drill from the positions players finished in figure 1. Player 3, instead of driving to the basket, dribbles back out to the corner and passes to player 2. X1 goes back to the help-side defender. (a) Player 2 skip-passes to player 1. X1 must close out on the pass receiver (drill 150). Player 1 and X1 play one on one. X1 must use all the defensive footwork of drills 129-131 and the defensive steps of drill 137. If player 1 can create separation and shoot, X1 and player 1 battle for the rebound. (b) After player 1 or X1 gets the rebound (or, if desired, player 1 can pass directly to player 2 while playing one on one), the pass is made to player 2. Player 1 then goes back to weak-side position and flash pivot cuts. X1 must deny the flash pivot cut. If the pass can be made inside to the flash pivot, player 1 and X1 again go one on one.
9. Figure 3 shows the last part of the drill. Player 1 moves back to the center of the lane before trying to establish position on X1 at the low post. X1 either fronts, does the two-step drill, or plays at a three-quarter position

(you should teach only one of these skills to your beginners, two or more to your intermediate and advanced players). Players 2 and 3 pass back and forth, back and forth, until one or the other can pass inside to the post. See drills 98-101 for defensive techniques. Player 1 then uses the low-post moves described in chapter 13 while X1 plays post defense.

➲ TEACHING POINTS Make sure all defensive positioning during the entire drill is correct at all times.

1. Make sure the offensive one-on-one moves are done with fundamentally sound techniques. These include the rocker step (drill 11) and perimeter dribbling moves (drills 12-16 and 28-31).
2. Make sure all defensive one-on-one techniques are fundamentally sound (from initial coverage on the attacker before the attacker dribbles through the dribble to the shot).

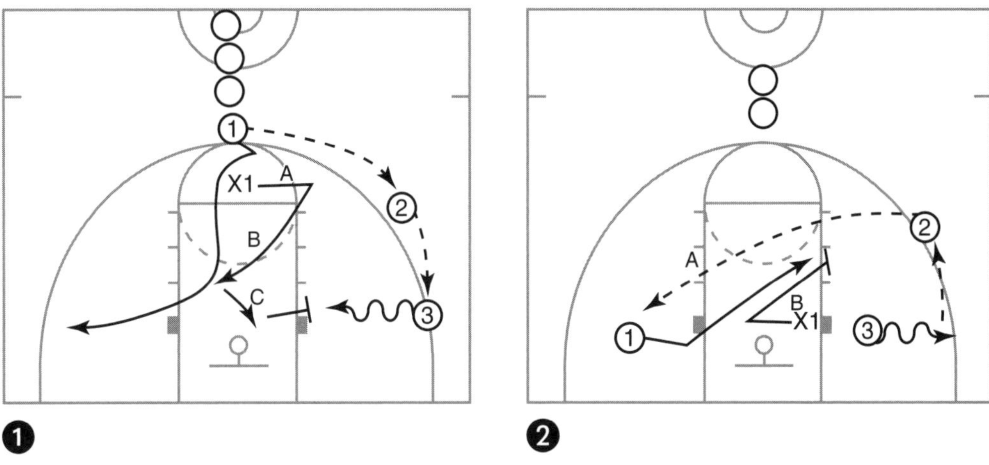

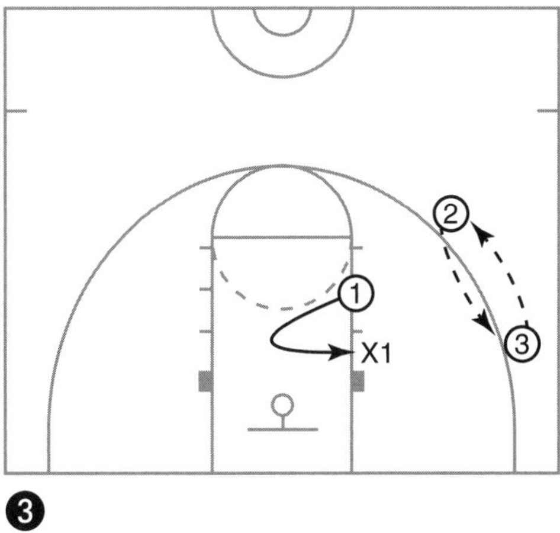

3

Related Drills *33, 79, 96, 98-101, 128-130, 137-139, 147-154*

CHAPTER

18

Team Defense

A team's defense is never stronger than the weakest individual playing it. That's why coaches spend an inordinate amount of time developing individuals. Stance is most important. All players must be adept at the fence slide (see drill 128). Without a front-foot-to-pivot-foot stance (drill 129) or a front-foot-to-free-foot stance (drill 130), defensive players can never dictate to the offense where they will allow them to go. Weak-side and interception stances must also be drilled (drill 131). Never progress to footwork until stance has been mastered.

Remind your players that there are two sides of the court: the side the ball is on (ball side) and the side away from the ball (help side). Help side was covered in drills 131 through 135. Don't ignore the help side because it is very important to overall team defense.

Attackers with the ball will be using rocker-step moves on defenders. Thus defenders need the advance step, retreat step, swing step, and slide step in their repertoire (all in drill 137). These steps should force the dribble. Defenders must also learn to overplay the dribble (drill 138) in an effort to stop the first few dribbles. Defenders want to dominate and dictate even in dribble-drive situations, so they must learn the overplay step.

Once your players have mastered proper on-the-ball defensive positioning, they are ready to help their teammates off the ball. Your off-the-ball rules:

1. Jump to the ball (see drill 146).
2. Deny the wing (drill 147).
3. Deny the flash pivot (drill 148).
4. Close out to the dribbler (drill 149)—this requires a team rotation (drill 143).
5. Close out to the pass receiver (drill 150).
6. Close the gap (drill 132).

The shell drill, drill 153, is broken into 10 parts. You can drill each part separately, or you can allow random movement by the four attackers, with defenders reacting to those choices. Then you need to drill five on five (drill 154), activating the individual techniques and tactics (the six rules previously mentioned) and the rotation drill (drill 143).

153

SHELL DRILL

Team • 10 minutes

➲ SKILL FOCUS Triple-threat position (9), rocker step (11), in and out (12, 28), crossover (13, 29), spin (14, 30), half-spin (15, 31), front pivot (35), reverse pivot (36), jump stop (37), stride stop (38), chest pass (44), bounce pass (44), interception stance (50, 131), V-cut (53), middle cut (54), backdoor cut (55), pump fake (96), pump fake crossover (96), fence slide (128), front foot to pivot foot (129), front foot to free foot (130), interception stance (131), close-the-gap stance (132), help-side defense (133-135), advance step (137), retreat step (137), swing step (137), draw the charge (141), rotation (143), jump to the ball (146), flash pivot defense (148), dribbler closeout (149), skip pass and closeout (150)

Advanced

1. Line players up in any formation: four attackers and four defenders. You should change formations from day to day—choose among 2-2, 1-3, 1-2-1, and so on. You may wish to drill against your next opponent's formation. After 2 minutes or so, rotate 1 and 2 and X1 and X2 to play 3 and 4 and X3 and X4's positions. This permits all players to play defense on guards and on wings (corners). Rotate from offense to defense after 5 minutes, or require the defense to stop the attackers two straight times before rotating.
2. You may want to stress the rotation drill (drill 143). Figure 1 illustrates the drive of the baseline, and figure 2 shows a typical drive to the inside. Both are defended using the same defensive rules: The weak-side deep defender, X4, yells "rotate" and picks up the breakaway dribbler. The weak-side outside defender, X2, drops to defend the basket. The defender on the breakaway dribbler rotates to cover the open attacker. X3 should have denied the pass to 3 in figure 1. And X2 should have closed the gap on the dribbler in figure 2. Both were defensive mistakes that occurred before the dribbler penetrated. Then both defenders on the ball did not have their players under control, dictating and dominating, before the penetrating dribble. But that is what basketball is: a series of mistakes, some compelled by excellent fakes, some by a lack of concentration. This is why the rotation tactic is so important—it allows the defense one last chance to stop the ball and correct a previous defensive mistake.
3. *Positioning:* 1, 2, 3, and 4 pass the ball around, using skip passes if they wish. Each player holds the ball 3 seconds while drilling on this phase separately. X1, X2, X3, and X4 jump to the ball while the pass is in flight. Help-side defenders always maintain ball-you-man and are in a flat triangle.
4. *Close the gap:* Players 1, 2, 3, and 4 take turns dribbling toward the basket. X1, X2, X3, and X4 must help on the drive and then recover to their own assignments. The closest defender on the drive side should step in, preventing further penetration by the dribbler. If the defender is in proper jump-to-the-ball position, this is easy to accomplish. Keep in mind defenders begin in an interception stance (drill 131) before changing to a close-the-gap-stance (drill 132).

5. *Pass penetration:* Whenever a pass is completed into a side, high, or low post, the perimeter defender nearest the pass receiver must dive into the area of the ball, forcing the pass back out to the perimeter.
6. *Flash pivot defense:* Player 1 passes to 3; 4 flash pivots. X3 should have denied the penetrating pass to 3. But now X4 must deny the flash pivot pass to 4. X2 and X1 sag to help X4 on 4. X4 and 4 play one on one until the pass comes back out to the perimeter.
7. *Cutter drill:* Whenever a pass is made, the passer cuts to another position. The defender must jump to the ball; middle cuts must never be allowed. Other attackers V-cut to maintain 15-foot (4.5-m) spacing.
8. *Screen away:* Any player who passes goes to screen away. The two players involved in the screen-away can run the screen-and-roll, screen-and-fade, or screen-and-replace. The passer must read the defense's tactics: Do they switch? Do they stay with their assignment? This tells the passer the primary target and the secondary target.
9. *Screen on ball:* Any player passing to a teammate can go screen for that teammate. They may screen-and-roll, screen-and-fade, or screen-and-replace. Defenders away from the ball should be jumping to the ball. These help-side defenders should sag even farther to help on the screening maneuvers. Defenders involved with the screen on the ball should use the jump-switching maneuvers of drill 140.
10. *Shell drill with a post:* Activate your post defense. Do you want to cover three-quarters? Do you want to front? Do you want to play behind the post? Whenever a pass goes into the post, all perimeter defenders should dive toward the ball to help the post defender.
11. *Two or more tactics:* The beauty of this drill is that you can create any combination of defensive techniques and tactics you wish to work on. For example, say you are going to work only parts 4 and 7 today. This means you are going to allow dribblers to penetrate as far as they can, and you are going to permit cutting on every pass. This use of combinations allows you to work on what gave you trouble in the last game. You can even use three parts at one time.

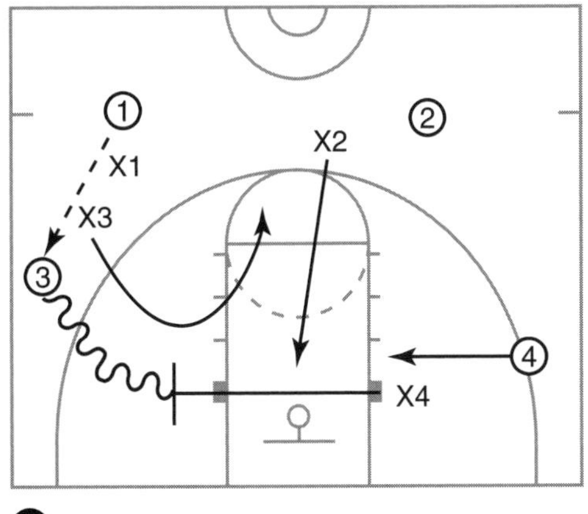

❶

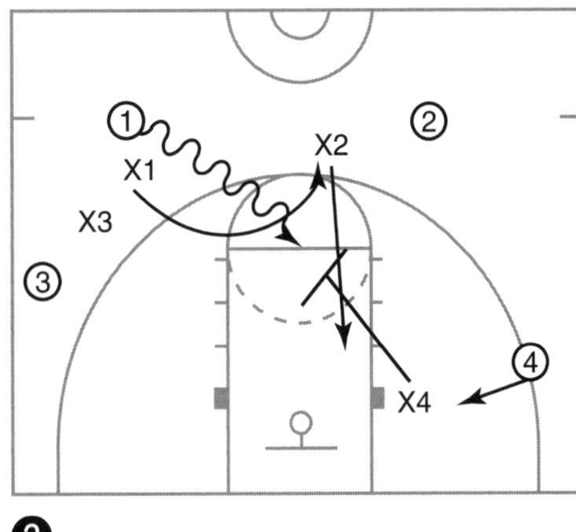

❷

Related Drills ***9, 11-15, 28-31, 35-38, 44, 53, 55, 96, 128-131, 132-135, 137-138, 140-144, 147-152, 154***

154

FIVE ON FIVE

Team • As long as needed

SKILL FOCUS Practice all learned skills; motion offense rules; defensive team rules

Beginner

1. Players line up in some type of formation. Change the formation from day to day. Review the motion offense rules and the defensive team rules. Limit the rules in accordance with your talent. If your players can handle only three offensive rules, then use only three. Same for the defensive rules.
2. Offense and defense switch roles after each score.

Options

1. Defense must stop the offense a certain number of consecutive possessions before teams switch roles.
2. Give the offense 10 possessions. Keep track of how many times they score. Now rotate and give the new offense 10 possessions. The team that scores the most wins.
3. Limit the way the offense can score. You may use several techniques and tactics, such as cutting, dribbling, and screening on the ball. But once a few techniques are designated, allow nothing else.
4. Tell the offense only a certain player can score. You will notice how hard screens are set to free that individual instead of just one-on-one play.
5. Tell the offense the only score allowed is anything shot within 5 feet (1.5 m). Notice how hard players work to pass penetrate, dribble penetrate, and rebound.

Related Drills *All*

CHAPTER 19

Team Defensive Stunts

No matter how good your team is there will be some games when you get behind and have to catch up. You will need a pressure defense to force a turnover or two so you can get back into the game.

Also, there will be those games when your opponent seems to be executing their offense at an incredible efficiency rate. You will need to change the pace of your defense to disrupt your opponent's offensive rhythm.

These two objectives are the subject of this chapter. You want to put in these defensive stunts only after your man-to-man team defense is fundamentally sound.

Drill 155 shows you how to add a two-player run-and-jump and a three-player run-and-jump into your defensive scheme. In this drill you will also add a hedge-and-recover technique to get into the mind of your opponent's point guard.

Drill 156 illustrates the run-and-trap drill. This trap is available from the two-player run-and-trap or the three-player run-and-trap. The safety trap and the all-out trap are also discussed.

Drill 157 displays the trap of the dribbler as the dribbler crosses half-court. Drill 158 reveals the trap of the first pass. Whereas the run-and-jumps may be too difficult for inexperienced players, the trap-the-dribbler and trap-the-pass are so simple even beginners can use them.

These four trapping techniques give you more than enough ammunition to force a turnover or take an efficient offensive team out of its rhythm. And all four drills are offered from two sets: the two-guard front and the one-guard front, making it easier for you to see how to teach them.

Drill 159 adds an individual channeling technique. Finally, drill 160 adds a trapper to the mix.

155

RUN AND JUMP

Individual or team • 10 minutes

SKILL FOCUS Defensive fakes (33), how to trap (50), fence slide (128), help side (133-135), slide steps (137), deny wing (147), basic team defense (153-154), two-player run-and-jump (155), three-player run-and-jump (155), hedge and recover (155)

Intermediate

1. Line players up as shown in figure 1.
2. Player 1 has the basketball and is dribbling into frontcourt. X1 keeps player 1 under control. X1 intends to hustle back in front of player 1 as 1 dribbles past the half-court line. This overplay by X1 will force 1 to change directions, hopefully with a spin-dribble. This keys X1's teammates to begin the run-and-jump.
3. X3 must deny player 3 the pass. X5 must deny player 5 the pass.
4. In figure 1, X2 runs and jumps player 1 just as 1 comes out of a spin move (or crossover dribble). X1 immediately rotates to cover 2. X4, playing proper help-side defense, using the flat triangle and ball-you-man techniques, covers both players 2 and 4. The "habit" pass is to player 2 because 2 appears open momentarily.
5. Figure 2 displays the three-player run-and-jump. X3 and X5 still deny their assignments the ball. X2 runs and jumps just as player 1 comes out of a spin move. X4 leaves at the exact moment X2 leaves. X4 shoots the gap for the steal of the "habit" pass. X1 knows the three-player run-and-jump is in effect, so X1 rotates to cover player 4.
6. In figure 3, X2 exhibits the hedge-and-recover technique. X2 begins the run-and-jump tactic just as player 1 comes out of the spin move. But this time, X2 takes only a few steps toward player 1 before going back to assignment. Frequently, player 1 will interpret this as a run-and-jump or run-and-trap (see drill 156) maneuver and will pick up the dribble, especially if player 1 has faced the run-and-jump or run-and-trap a few possessions in a row. If player 1 picks up the basketball, all defenders get in the passing lanes to their assignments, denying any pass to their assignments. This is called *dribble used.* In 5 seconds, this is a turnover.
7. As you can see, there are three defensive maneuvers in this one drill. It will leave player 1 guessing. That is the purpose. You have either forced a turnover or at least disrupted an efficient offense.
8. Change the defensive players around until all defenders have played all positions. Rotate from X1 to X2 to X3 to X4 to X5 to X1. This allows all defenders to practice the run-and-jump. Then rotate from offense to defense, and continue the drill.

Run and Jump

1. X1 must keep player 1 under control. This may require playing a half-step more off the dribbler. Just as player 1 crosses the half-court line, X1 races to

get in front of player 1. X1 can draw the charge if player 1 continues. Player 1 will change directions, hopefully by turning the back to the jumper (X2). X1 will want to time departure from player 1 to coincide with X2's arrival.

2. X2 runs directly in the passing lane between player 1 and player 2. X2 has arms up and active. X2 now must assume control of player 1.

➜ Hedge and Recover

1. X2 runs at player 1, using the run-and-jump technique. But X2 stops short of getting to player 1 and hurries back to assignment, staying in the passing lane to player 2.
2. The purpose of this hedge-and-recover is to keep player 1 guessing as to whether this is a run-and-jump, run-and-trap, or just a hedge-and-recover.

➜ TEACHING POINTS

1. Make sure all coverages on all players are fundamentally sound in man-to-man team techniques presented in earlier chapters.
2. Make sure the run-and-jump techniques are exact.

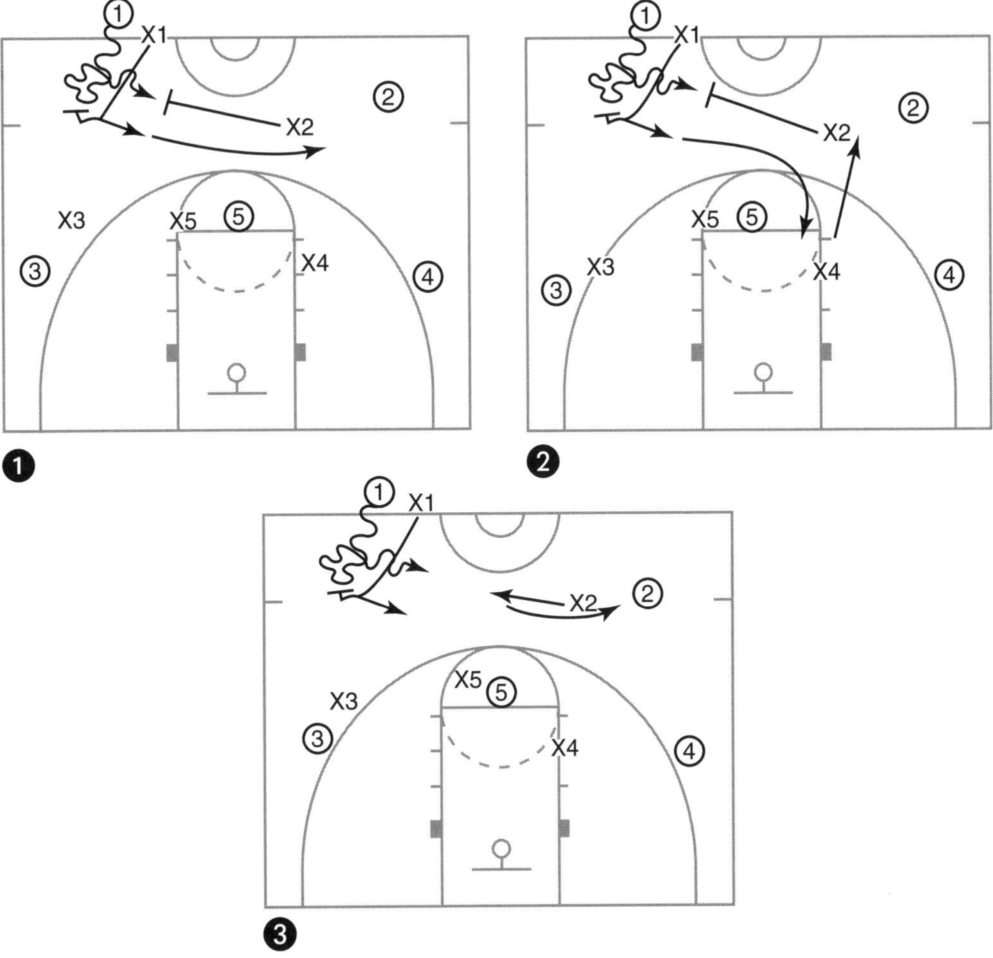

Related Drills *153-154, 156-160*

156 RUN AND TRAP

Individual or team • 7 minutes

SKILL FOCUS Defensive fakes (33), how to trap (50), fence slide (128), help-side (133-135), slide-steps (137), deny wing (147), basic team defense (153-154), two-player run-and-jump (155), three-player run-and-jump (155), hedge and recover (155), run-and-trap (156), all-out pass interception (156), safety pass interception (156)

Intermediate

1. The run-and-trap is shown from another formation in this drill (the 1-3-1 instead of the 2-1-2 used in drill 155). The reason? So you can see the run-and-jump and the run-and-trap from the two most popular formations in basketball: the even front and the odd front.
2. Make sure all defenders have played all positions before rotating from offense to defense. Defenders rotate from X1 to X2 to X3 to X4 to X5 to X1. Then continue the drill.
3. All techniques are the same in run-and-trap as in run-and-jump. The only exception is X2 stays with X1 and traps player 1. If player 1 keeps the dribble alive, X1 and X2 stay and trap as long as player 1 dribbles. The adjustments are made by the teammates who are trying to intercept.
4. Figure 1 shows the pass interception techniques of a *safety trap*. Notice player 4 is closest to the basket; thus X4 does not participate in the pass interception. X4 stays in a safety position, guarding the basket. Once the trap is set by X1 and X2, X3 moves away from playing denial and plays in the gap between players 3 and 5 for a possible interception. X3 reads player 1. Player 1's eyes will tell where the pass will go. X3 shades in that direction. At the same time, X5 plays in the gap between players 2 and 5, using the same techniques X3 used. X4 can go after any lob pass out of the trap if there is an opportunity for an interception.
5. Figure 2 displays the *all-out interception* technique. The three attackers nearest the passer are covered tightly. There should be no possible passes to those three players. The player away from the ball, player 4 in figure 2, is left alone. You are hoping player 1 cannot find player 4. In 5 seconds, you have the turnover.
6. You have to make the call: all-out interception technique or safety tactics. You can run safety tactics the entire game, but you must choose the places where you go into an all-out gamble. Time and score can help dictate which you will want to use.

Safety Trap

1. To play for the interception of the pass using the safety techniques, two defenders play between the three nearest pass receivers. These two defenders shade in the direction the passer is looking. Should the passer turn the back on one of the receivers, the two defenders who intend to intercept the pass would cover the other two receivers more tightly, leaving the receiver the passer turned the back on alone.
2. The defender nearest the basket covers the basket area, playing safety.

All-Out Interception

1. The three defenders off the trap, playing for interception of the pass, cover the three attackers nearest the ball.
2. The attacker farthest away from the ball is left open.

TEACHING POINTS

1. Make sure the trap is properly set and arms are active.
2. Make sure passing lanes are covered properly be it a safety or an all-out interception technique.

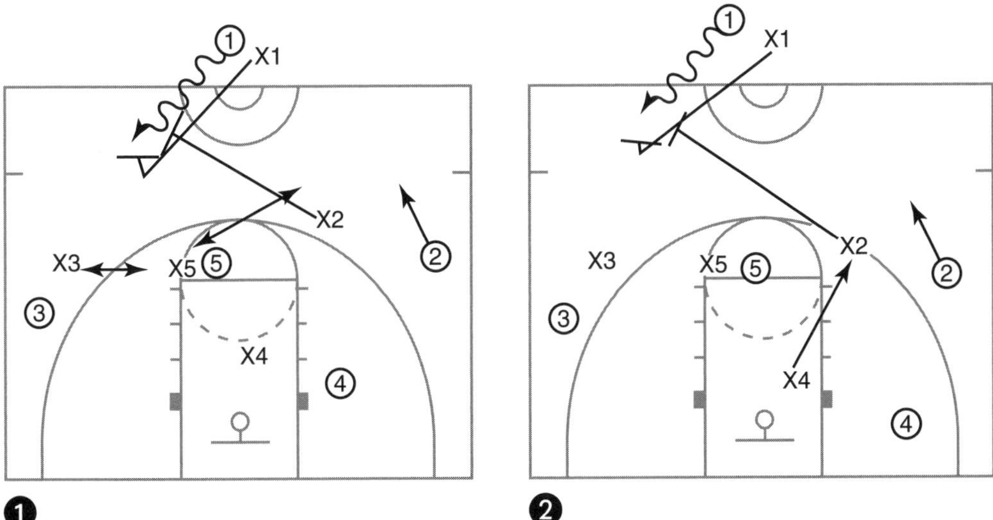

Related Drills *153-155, 157-160*

157

TRAP THE DRIBBLE

Individual or team • 5 minutes

➲ **SKILL FOCUS** Defensive fakes (33), how to trap (50), fence slide (128), help-side defense (133-135), deny wing (147), all-out interception (156), safety interception (156)

Beginner

1. Line players up as shown in the figure.
2. All defenders play each position before rotating from offense to defense. Defenders rotate from X1 to X2 to X3 to X4 to X5 to X1.
3. To trap the dribbler, X1 wants to force the dribbler toward the middle of the court before compelling the dribbler to change direction. This change of direction should occur near midcourt line. This signals the teammates to begin their slides to activate the trap-the-dribbler drill.
4. X3 must deny player 3 the ball prior to activating the trap. When X3 commences a move to set the trap, X3 still wants to stay in the passing lane between players 1 and 3. A pass to player 3 immediately breaks the trap. X5 and X2 also want to deny their assignments the ball. X4 covers 4 and watches for any careless pass by 1.
5. X3 races directly toward player 1 but stays in the passing lane to player 3. This compels player 1 to throw a lob pass or a bounce pass should 1 want to make the "habit" pass. These two passes are the slowest of all passes and so easier intercepted.
6. X3 stays with X1 and traps the dribbler as long as the dribble is alive. The adjustments are made by X2, X4, and X5. In the figure, the safety interception techniques are used against a 1-3-1 offensive formation (odd front). X2 plays in the gap between players 2 and 5. X5 plays in the gap between players 3 and 5, using interception techniques.
7. You can easily see how the same tactics are used should player 1 dribble to the other side of the court to begin the drill. X2 becomes the trapper. X5 plays between players 2 and 5. X3 plays between players 3 and 5.

➲ TEACHING POINTS

1. Make sure the trap is properly set and arms are active.
2. Make sure passing lanes are covered properly be it a safety or an all-out interception technique.

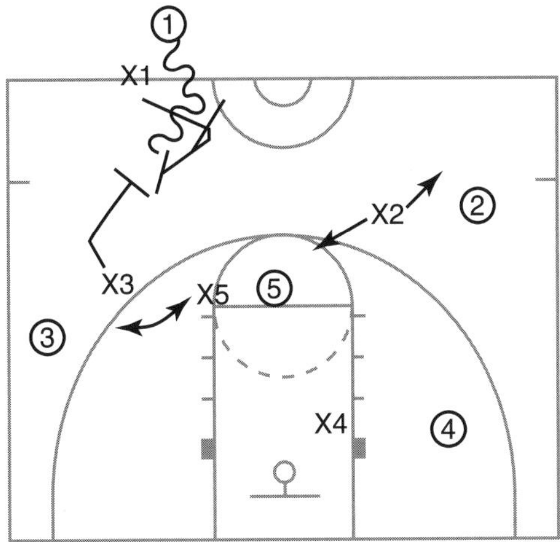

Related Drills *153-156, 158-160*

158 TRAP THE PASS

Individual or team • 7 minutes

➲ **SKILL FOCUS** Defensive fakes (33), how to trap (50), fence slide (128), help-side defense (133-135), deny wing (147), all-out interception (156), safety interception (156)

Beginner

1. Line players up as shown in the figure. Note this time the formation is 1-3-1 (odd front). The formations are changed only so you can see the effectiveness of the traps regardless of the offensive formation.
2. All defenders play all positions before rotating from offense to defense.
3. There is only one change from trap-the-dribbler. This change is X3. X3 does not want to deny the wing because X3 wants the dribbler to see a free passing lane to the wing, player 3. In fact, X3 can even hedge-and-recover from the dribbler without being in the passing lane to 3, encouraging player 1 to pass to player 3.
4. Once the pass is made, X1 and X3 trap the pass receiver. You can run either the all-out interception techniques or the safety tactics. The figure shows the safety tactics. X2 covers both players 1 and 2, playing in the gap between them, reading the passer's eyes. It would have to be a cross-court lob pass to complete the pass to player 2, easily intercepted. So X2 wants to shade harder toward player 1. X5 covers player 5 and shades to help on player 1. X4, the safety, covers player 4 and the basket.

➲ TEACHING POINTS

1. Make sure the trap is properly set and arms are active.
2. Make sure passing lanes are covered properly be it a safety or an all-out interception technique.

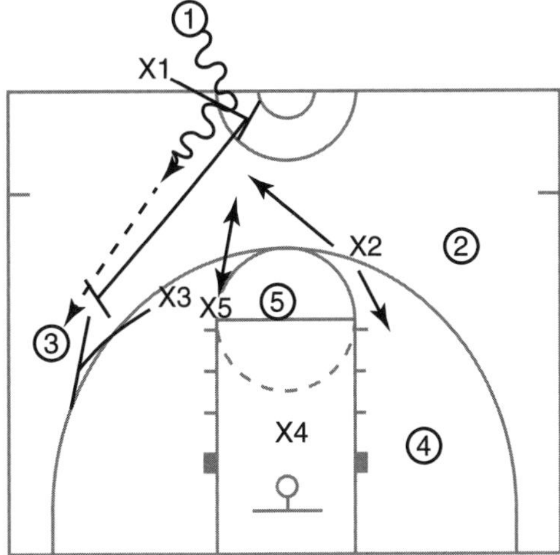

Related Drills *153-157, 159-160*

159

CHANNELING

Individual • 4 minutes

SKILL FOCUS Defensive fakes (33), slide steps (137), dribble closeout (149), channeling (159)

Intermediate

1. Line players up as shown in the figure. Rotate from player 1 to X1 to end of line.
2. Divide squad into two groups. One group works on the left side of full court, and the other group works on the right side of the court. Rotate sides of the court after two executions by each player.
3. X1 rolls the ball to player 1. Player 1 waits on the ball before beginning the dribble. A coach stands behind player 1 and signals X1 which direction to channel player 1; forcing 1 outside is called *fanning;* forcing 1 inside is called *funneling*. The defender would thus know the direction, but the dribbler would not. In the figure, the defender is fanning the dribbler. You want each defender to drill on fanning and funneling the dribbler on one side of the court before rotating to the other side of the court.
4. As the ball is rolling to player 1, X1 sprints to within a few feet (1-2 m) of player 1. X1 then comes under control. X1 wants to stay a quarter of a player's length to the side of the dribbler and slightly ahead of the dribbler. X1 wants to compel player 1 to use a speed dribble. The distance between the dribbler and the defender varies with the relative quickness of both players. But under no circumstance should X1 allow player 1 to get a vertical drive once player 1 crosses the midcourt line.
5. As player 1 dribbles across the midcourt line, X1 races to get in front of 1, compelling 1 to change directions. X1 is now funneling 1 to the inside. The defender wants to use quick shuffle-steps. This is when the run-and-jump or the trap occurs (see drills 155-158).

Advanced

1. After several days of drilling, you can allow your more advanced players to begin to use the in-and-out or crossover move to try to get by the defender.
2. After several days of drilling on these two counter moves, you can allow the advanced players to begin to use the spin or the half-spin moves to try to get by the defender.
3. When playing your basic man-to-man defense, you may want to fan or funnel the dribbler. Your help-side defenders would know the direction of the team defense and could offer even greater help.

➔ Channeling

1. *Channeling* is the term used when the defender forces the dribbler in one direction. Defenders know where the trap is to be set. It is imperative that all defenders know how to channel the attacker.
2. To compel the channeled direction, the defender must use quick shuffle-steps and stay slightly ahead of and slightly beside the dribbler. The distance depends on the relative speed and quickness of the attacker and the defender. Drilling will help determine that distance.

➔ TEACHING POINTS

1. Make sure the defender uses shuffle-steps. This keeps the defender in control of the dribbler.
2. Make sure the defender knows the distance between him- or herself and the attacker so the attacker cannot turn the corner and head in a direction other than the channeled direction.

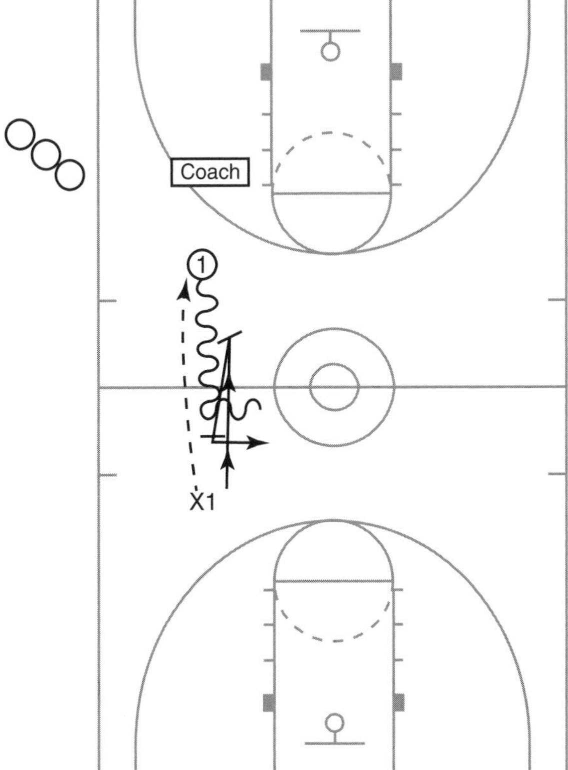

Related Drills *23-31, 155-158, 160*

160

ZIGZAG WITH A TRAPPER

Individual • 2 minutes

➲ **SKILL FOCUS** Dribbling maneuvers (23-27), dribbling moves (28-31), how to trap (50), run-and-jumps (155), run-and-trap (156), dribbling out of trap (157-158), channeling (159)

Beginner

1. Line up players as shown in the figure. Divide the squad into two groups. One group can work on one side of the court while the other group works on the other side of the court.
2. Beginners begin with the simple zigzag drill. Boundary lines are created and used for the zigzag drill. The boundary lines are the sideline and an imaginary line from the lane line to the opposite lane line. The dribbler must stay within these boundary lines.
3. In the zigzag drill, player 1 dribbles with X1 playing tight and aggressive but not allowing player 1 to drive by the defender. X1 pushes 1 over to the sideline (shown in the figure). Player 1 must change directions using either the spin dribble or the crossover dribble. X1 now pushes 1 over to the other boundary line before compelling 1 to change directions again. Forcing three changes of directions in half-court is great.
4. Player 1 goes against X1 down the court and back. The players rotate so both can play offense and defense.
5. The next two players in line begin their zigzag drill when players 1 and X1 reach the midcourt line.

Intermediate

1. Intermediate players can add a trapper (X2 in the figure).
2. Player 1 dribbles until X1 forces a change of direction.
3. When player 1 changes direction, X2 arrives to set the trap. The defenders stay with 1 until 1 is forced to pick up the dribble.
4. Once player 1 picks up the dribble, X1 goes downcourt to become the next trapper. Player 1 waits until X1 is in position, and then 1 begins to dribble against X2.
5. When X2 forces player 1 to change directions, X1 arrives to set the trap.
6. This procedure continues down the court and back before players rotate.
7. The rotation is player 1 to X1 to X2 to player 1. The drill continues until all players have played each position.

Advanced

Advanced players can be placed in the free-throw lane. This makes the boundary lines the full-court extension of the two free-throw lane lines. This is a very narrow space ideal for teaching advanced dribbling and trapping techniques.

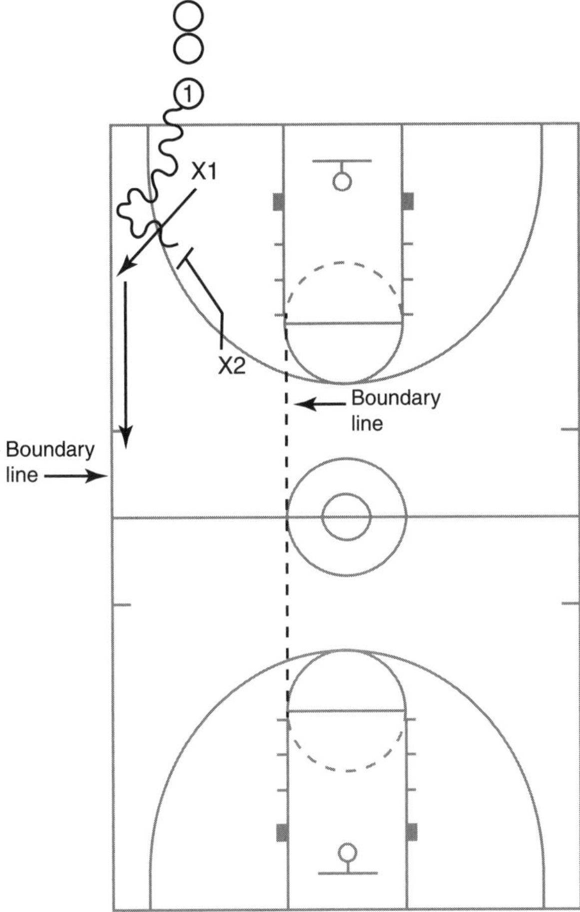

Related Drills *23-31, 155-159*

Appendix

Organizing Practice Sessions

Before you begin the season, decide which parts of the motion offense you wish to run. Your decision should be determined by your players. How old are they? How experienced are they? What type of athletes do you have? The answers to these questions should help you establish how many rules your motion offense will have. A minimum of two rules will do; this allows your players to play one on one. Then you might add the cutting maneuvers. Then, as the season progresses and your players improve, you might add the screening maneuvers.

Next you must decide how much of the man-to-man defense you want to teach. Ask the same questions. You may simply develop the one-on-one stances, footwork, and slides and leave it at that. Or you may want to add help-side defensive maneuvers. You might even get into trapping as the season progresses and your players improve.

Once these two major decisions have been made, you are ready to consider which drills you will use. You also need to establish certain rules of practice so your practice sessions will be well organized and run with zip. Kids do not like to stand around. They learn best by doing and being active.

Using the drills in this book will promote your players to learn, improve, and be active. We now conclude with a discussion of running a successful practice and organizing your drills to maximize practice time.

How to Run a Successful Practice

First, sit down before your first practice season begins and determine how much practice time you have before your first game. This will help establish which drills you can spend more time on and which will have to be relegated to smaller portions of time.

Make this your squad's first rule: Whenever you hear a whistle, stop what you are doing and meet (or stay) at a predetermined spot. We always liked for our players to stay just where they were. Several drills could be run from that spot before taking up a new sequence of drills. But if they heard two whistles—one after another—then they were to meet at a predetermined basket at the end of the court. We used this area to explain our next set of drills.

Make a second rule: Absolutely no talking for players. Only coaches can talk. You are now ready to begin practicing. It is that simple. Have a written daily practice plan. If you are a youth league coach and can get several moms or dads to help you, you will have many on-the-floor "assistant coaches." You might do all the explaining of the drills, but your assistants can help supervise. Give each member of your "coaching staff" a copy of the daily practice plan.

If you are a middle school or high school coach, you probably have paid assistant coaches. But if you know of a sandlot coach who has used this book to teach, you would be wise to add them to your staff. You can break down your numbers and get more repetitions in any drill with more coaches.

Have a method of keeping up with your weekly practices and your monthly practices by checking off each fundamental on an all-inclusive board at home. This eliminates leaving out any portion of the game. You can see immediately if something important has been omitted during the week or the month. You can then include a drill that teaches that concept in your next daily practice plan. The 19 different chapter titles in the table of contents can help you develop your list.

Now you are ready to begin drilling those eager youngsters. What's more, they will now get the maximum training from their practice time. You are organized. You are armed with knowledge (this book will give you that). And you are *enthusiastic*. Yes. You *must* be enthusiastic. Like a common cold, enthusiasm is contagious. Spread it among your players.

Keep drills short. We have limited each to no more than 10 minutes. Most are shorter. Young minds begin to wander if held to one task too long. You can change to a related drill (you might have noticed that each drill in this book lists related drills) and get the same fundamental covered without boring your players. Or you can change to an entirely different fundamental and come back to the former essential at a later time in your practice schedule.

Include as few players as possible in each drill. This allows more repetitions under supervision. The more repetitions, the more muscle memory develops, and the sooner players begin to execute the fundamental accurately and quickly. The kids will appreciate this. This is why we said earlier: Get several moms and dads to agree to be assistants.

Make drills fun and competitive. We have already done this for each drill, so you only need to follow the procedures as instructed. But keep in mind that some of the drills naturally lean toward more learning and some lean toward more fun. You can tell by the feel of your squad whether you need more learning or more fun. A good rule of thumb is to do a fun drill after every two learning drills. Then when your team starts winning (and winning and winning), you will find winning has its own form of fun, making the learning drills more enjoyable.

Explain every drill to your players in detail. Just follow the teaching points and procedures. You will want to emphasize only one or two teaching points per drill. Your players will remember a few points more readily than many points.

Demonstrate every technique that will be taught in that drill. We have held many drills to one technique. If you cannot demonstrate, get an assistant to do so while you explain the drill. There are many "older players" who would be happy to come and demonstrate at your practices.

After explaining and demonstrating, break into small groups and let the kids execute the drill. You are now ready to supervise. Keep your talking to a minimum and the drilling to a maximum. People learn best by doing.

When game time arrives, you have to deputize. Your players have to play the game. Their performance will tell you what to include in your next practice sessions. Each practice and each game should be used to further develop your players. Each practice and game should be used as an ever-expanding improvement session. That's where real success comes from.

How to Devise a Practice Schedule

Many questions need to be considered when building a practice schedule. Is it early, middle, or late season? How much practice time do you have? What are you planning on running teamwise? What did not work well in the last practice or latest game? These are just a few questions that need answers.

There are infinite components to ponder—so many that an entire book can be written just on devising a practice schedule. And to a great degree, the success of your team depends on carefully thought-out practice schedules. Sample practice schedules are presented in the following pages for 30-minute and 90-minute sessions for each of the three major phases of the season—early, middle, and late. From these samples you can get ideas of how to develop your own practice schedule. Drill numbers are listed, followed by the time it takes to run the drill, and a reason we include the drill. Use the drill finder on pages vi-xii when developing your practice schedule; each drill is listed along with the time required to run that drill.

30-Minute Practice: Early Season

Drill number	Time (minutes)	Drill activity
Drill 1	3	Fundamental foot movement and conditioning
Drill 8	3	Shooting layups
Drill 9	2	Triple-threat position
Drill 19	2	Ballhandling
Drill 23	1	Speed dribbling
Drill 28	1	Teaching a move and dribbling
Drill 29	1	Teaching another move and dribbling
Drill 30	1	Ballhandling, move, agility, conditioning
Drill 35	2	Pivoting
Drill 36	2	Pivoting
Drill 37	1	Stopping
Drill 44	3	Passing
Drill 53	3	Cutting
Drill 54	3	Cutting, triple-threat position, and moves

You can see from this practice schedule that you are planning on running your motion offense using cuts and one-on-one play.

30-Minute Practice: Midseason

Drill number	Time (minutes)	Drill activity
Drill 11	1	Rocker step
Drill 14	1	Spin dribbling move
Drill 15	1	Half-spin move
Drill 30	1	Emphasizing spin move and ballhandling
Drill 31	1	Emphasizing half-spin and ballhandling
Drill 30	1	Two-ball variation
Drill 31	1	Two-ball variation
Drill 54	5	Cutting, layups, and moves
Drill 55	3	Backdoor cuts
Drill 64	4	Team offensive tactics
Drill 90	10	Shooting

You can see from this practice schedule that you are reviewing two moves and some cutting maneuvers, working on your shots, and running your team offense.

30-Minute Practice: Late Season

Drill number	Time (minutes)	Drill activity
Drill 25	1	Ballhandling, warming up, and agility
Drill 32	2	Ballhandling, warming up, and agility
Drill 124	5	Reviewing your offense
Drill 91	6	Shooting
Drill 139	2	Reviewing your individual defense
Drill 153	10	Working on team defense
Drill 154	4	Live offense versus live defense

You can see from this practice schedule that you are reviewing your offense and defense, improving on shooting, and scrimmaging.

90-Minute Practice: Early Season

Drill number	Time (minutes)	Drill activity
Drill 1	3	Footwork, conditioning
Drill 11	1	Footwork
Drill 13	1	Another move
Drill 15	1	Another move
Drill 28	1	Stressing the chosen move, agility, ballhandling
Drill 29	1	Stressing the chosen move, agility, ballhandling
Drill 30	1	Stressing the chosen move, agility, ballhandling
Drill 31	1	Stressing the chosen move, agility, ballhandling
Drill 36	2	Pivoting
Drill 38	1	Stopping
Drill 46	2	Passing and conditioning
Drill 53	3	V-cut
Drill 54	3	Middle cut
Drill 55	3	Backdoor cut
Drill 58	3	Recognition of when to cut
Drill 71	10	Passing, cutting, and screening away
Drill 88	1	Reviewing proper shooting technique
Drill 89	10	Shooting
Drill 138	2	Reviewing individual defense
Drill 139	2	Reviewing individual defense
Drill 104	4	Live one on one
Drill 109	6	Hustle, live one on one
Drill 146	5	Reviewing phase of individual defense
Drill 148	4	Reviewing another phase of individual defense
Drill 150	6	Live one on one after reviewing closing out

You can see from this practice schedule that you have had a few prior workouts, but it is still early in the season. You are planning on your motion offense including one-on-one play, cutting, and screening. And you intend to be really good defensively because of your stress on defensive drills.

90-Minute Practice: Midseason

Drill number	Time (minutes)	Drill activity
Drill 4	1	Conditioning and defensive footwork
Drill 9	2	Offensive stance
Drill 11	1	Offensive footwork before the dribble
Drill 28	1	Conditioning, ballhandling, and footwork
Drill 29	1	Conditioning, ballhandling, and footwork
Drill 30	1	Conditioning, ballhandling, and footwork
Drill 31	1	Conditioning, ballhandling, and footwork
Drill 39	11/2	Protecting the ball
Drill 50	10	Protecting the ball and trapping
Drill 57	10	Offensive footwork
Drill 65	6	Review cutting, footwork, dribbling, and defense
Drill 151	10	Individual/team defensive fundamentals
Drill 90	10	Shooting
Drill 123	10	Review your motion offense
Drill 158	7	Trap the pass
Drill 153	10	Review your team defense
Drill 154	7	Scrimmage

You can see from this practice schedule that you had turnover trouble in your last game, so you must work to improve that. You also want to work on your fundamental offensive and defensive footwork. You want to review the traps you have added to your team defense. And at the end you want to see if that improvement was evident in scrimmage situations.

90-Minute Practice: Late Season

Drill number	Time (minutes)	Drill activity
Drill 1	3	Conditioning, agility, and footwork
Drill 16	3	All dribbling moves
Drill 28	1	Conditioning and dribble move
Drill 29	1	Conditioning and dribble move
Drill 30	1	Conditioning and dribble move
Drill 31	1	Conditioning and dribble move
Drill 41	3	Pivoting, stopping, and dribbling
Drill 64	4	Passing, cutting, and spacing: your motion offense
Drill 90	10	Shooting
Drill 91	6	Shooting
Drill 108	5	Conditioning and one-on-one play
Drill 111	6	Hustle and one-on-one play
Drill 126	9	Review your motion offense rules
Drill 145	1	Review defensive movement off the ball
Drill 151	10	Review individual defensive movement off ball
Drill 156	7	Review run-and-trap
Drill 158	7	Review trapping the pass
Drill 154	12	Scrimmage

You have had a layoff of more than a week since your last game. You need to get your team back into game condition, and you need to review your offense and your defense. The next game is still a couple of days away. So you scrimmage more as well as review different parts of your offense and defense. And your shooting was a little rusty. So you taper off the scrimmaging in your next two practice sessions and work more on fundamentals. This will improve your squad physically and make them more eager to play the game.

More games are won or lost in practices than on game day. And you can never go wrong if your players are always improving, always learning, always progressing. For them, tomorrow is much more important than today.

About the Authors

Burrall Paye has been developing young basketball players' skills for more than 30 years. He is considered one of the game's best teachers.

Coach Paye enjoyed winning seasons in 36 of the 37 years that he coached. During his career his teams won 64 championships, he was twice honored as State Coach of the Year, and he was named Outstanding Coach by the National Federation Interscholastic Coaches Association in 1985.

Retired since 1996, Coach Paye shares his expertise through his speaking and writing. He has spoken at major clinics in the United States, Canada, Mexico, and Europe. He has written 12 full-length basketball books and hundreds of articles for national basketball magazines.

Paye earned his master's degree in 1965 from the University of Tennessee. He is a member of the National High School Coaches Association and the Virginia High School Coaches Association. He lives in Roanoke, Virginia, with his wife, Nancy.

Patrick Paye is an assistant basketball coach at Elizabeth City State University, an NCAA Division II member of the CIAA. Patrick has never been part of a losing season as a player or in his 23 years of high school and collegiate coaching. He built two traditionally losing programs into playoff teams and regional champions and holds Northeastern High School's record for most wins as a coach. Patrick resides with his son, Rylan, in Grandy, North Carolina.